German-Americana:

A Bibliography

Compiled by

DON HEINRICH TOLZMANN

The Scarecrow Press, Inc.
Metuchen, N. J.   1975

Library of Congress Cataloging in Publication Data

Tolzmann, Don Heinrich, 1945-
German-Americana.

Includes index.
1. Germans in the United States--Bibliography.
2. United States--Civilization--German influences--
Bibliography.   I.   Title.
Z1361.G37T64   016.30145'131'073   74-28085
ISBN 0-8108-0784-X

To

Patricia Ann

PREFACE

My interest in German-Americana was instilled in me at an early age by my Minnesota-German father, Eckhart H. Tolzmann. His stories and discussions of life in the rural ethnic community fostered in me the desire to engage in an in-depth study of German-Americana. This desire was fulfilled in 1968 when I studied immigration and ethnic history under Dr. Rudolph Vecoli, Director of the Center for Immigration Studies at the University of Minnesota. This study enriched and broadened my perspective, and also gave me the opportunity to do a case study of the Minnesota-Germans.

Since 1968 I have received an inestimable amount of encouragement from Dr. Robert E. Ward, Editor of German-American Studies and Chairman of the Society for German-American Studies. His work has contributed greatly to the current renaissance of German-American historical and literary studies.

At the University of Kentucky College of Library Science I had the great fortune to study under and work for three outstanding scholars: Dr. Lawrence Allen, Dr. Michael Harris and Dr. Robert E. Cazden. Dr. Harris offered many helpful hints which proved useful in the compilation of this bibliography. The task was considerably facilitated by his advice. Dr. Cazden's seminars on the book trade and bibliography and my research with him on the German-American book trade have made a definite and lasting impact on me.

Several other people should be acknowledged: the late Dr. Walther Kollacks, Franz Dornstaedter and Walter Dunke of the German-American National Congress; Dr. Austin J. App of the Federation of Citizens of German Descent; Paul Kaufmann of the Milwaukee Freie Gemeinde; the Rev. John Melchert of Cologne,

Minnesota; Heinz Kloss of the Institut für deutsche Sprache in Mannheim; Erwin Single, editor of the New Yorker Staats-Zeitung; Ludwig Soellner, editor of the Milwaukee Herold; Walter Hoops, editor of the Saengerzeitung; Dr. H. A. Mayer, editor of Der Lutheraner; Werner Baroni, editor of the Amerika-Woche and Chicago Abendpost; Marie Engel, editor of the Cincinnati Kurier; Erika Metzger, editor of Lyrik und Prosa; and Dr. LaVern Rippley of St. Olaf College. Special thanks are due to a number of German-American poets: Herman Brause, Fred Karl Scheibe, Karl Theodor Marx, Mimi Grossberg, Franzi Ascher-Nash, Maria Foerster, Dora Grunewald and Anna Katarina Scheibe.

Most of all I would like to thank my Pennsylvania-German wife, Patricia Ann Himebaugh Tolzmann, for all she has done to help in the compilation of this bibliography.

Don Heinrich Tolzmann

TABLE OF CONTENTS

INTRODUCTION

Wie wär's mit eurem Staatenbunde,
Wenn nie zu euch ein Deutscher kam?

Konrad Krez

Friedrich A. Ebert, the great German bibliographer, defines bibliography as "die Wissenschaft, die sich mit der Erkenntnis der schriftstellerischen Erzeugnisse beschäftigt." In this bibliography I have compiled a selective list of books, pamphlets, records, photography albums, dissertations, government documents, newspapers and periodical articles which are relevant to the student of German-American history, literature and culture. Most of the research is recent (1941-73) and should be available in most research libraries. Library locations are listed for some of the older items and brief annotations are given when necessary. All of the major bibliographies and general histories of German-Americana are listed so that the student may gain access to earlier research in the field.

This also contains directories of present day German-American national organizations, historical and literary societies, periodicals and newspapers, book stores, printers and schools. Contact with these groups, institutions and organizations is essential for anyone engaged in research on German-Americana. The German-American press is an especially wealthy storehouse of information.

Locations of German-American journals and newspapers (entries 1032-1060, 1779-1799, 2474-2564) are listed in Arndt (2567).

I. GERMAN-AMERICAN HISTORY

Archives, Libraries & Research Centers

1 American Antiquarian Society. Salisbury St. & Park Ave., Worcester, Mass. 01609. German-American imprints and newspapers.

2 American Council for Nationalities Service: Library & Information Center. 20 W. 40th St., New York, N.Y. 10018.

3 Austrian Information Service. 31 E. 69th St., New York, N.Y.

4 Auswanderer-Archiv, Schwaben International. 7 Stuttgart 1, Charlottenplatz 6, West Germany. Suabian-Americana.

5 Baeck Institute. 129 E. 73 St., New York, N.Y. 10021. German-American Jewish sources.

6 Balch Institute. 123 S. Broad St., Philadelphia, Pa. 19109. German language newspapers on microfilm are available for research.

7 Belleville Public Library. 121 E. Washington St., Belleville, Ill. 62220. Collection established in 1883 with 8,000 volumes from the German Library of St. Clair County, Ill.

8 Bethany Theological Seminary. Oak Brook, Ill. 60523. 4,600 books and 12,000 pamphlets from the Pennsylvania German collection of Cassel.

9 Bethesda Base Hospital Library. Oak St. & Reading Rd., Cincinnati, Ohio 45206. Largest collection of German-American Methodist publications.

10 Thomas R. Brendle Memorial Library & Museum. 406 Spring Drive, Millersville, Pa. 17551. Pennsylvania German artifacts and books.

11 Bucks County Historical Society. Pine & Ashland Sts., Doylestown, Pa. 18901. 100 Pennsylvania German Fraktur.

12 Carver County Historical Society. 119 Cherry St., Waconia, Minnesota 55387. Katalog, Constitutions and 500 volumes of the Carver County German Reading Society.

1

13 Catholic Central-Verein of America. 3885 Westminster Place,
    St. Louis, Mo. 63108. Catholic German-Americana.

14 Center for Immigration Studies. 1925 Sather St., St. Paul,
    Minnesota 55113. Sources for German immigrants from Eastern
    Europe.

15 Columbus University Libraries, Special Collections. 525 W.
    114 St., New York, N. Y. Ephrata Community and Conrad
    Beissel.

16 Concordia Historical Institute. 801 DeMun Ave., St. Louis,
    Mo. 63105. Lutheran German-Americana, Nicolaus von Zinzen-
    dorf papers, diaries and journals of Hessian soldiers, letters
    and reports of German immigrants.

17 Deutsche Bibliothek, Lesesaal für Exilliteratur. 6 Frankfurt
    a. M., Zeppelinallee 8, West Germany.

18 Dickinson College, Spahr Library. Carlisle, Pa. 17013. 50
    Pennsylvania German imprints.

19 Dorsch Memorial Library. 18 E. First St., Monroe, Michigan
    48161. Papers of Eduard Dorsch, German-American poet.

20 Eastern Mennonite College. 1200 Park Ave., Harrisonburg,
    Va. 22801. Saur, Ephrata and Mennonite imprints.

21 Forschungsstelle für Nationalitäten und Sprachfragen. 355 Mar-
    burg/Lahn, Rotenberg 21, West Germany.

22 Franklin & Marshall College, Fackenthal Library. Lancaster,
    Pa. 17604. Indexes periodicals in area of Pennsylvania Ger-
    man history (160, 000 cards in index); has the Unger-Bassler-
    Pennsylvania German Society Collection, the Pennsylvania Folk-
    life Collection of genealogical material (150, 000 entries); re-
    cordings of Pennsylvania German dialect and Fraktur drawings
    1788-1842.

23 Free Library of Philadelphia, Rare Book Department. Logan
    Square, Philadelphia, Pa. 19103. 1, 800 Pennsylvania German
    imprints, 800 Fraktur items and the Ephrata Cloister Collection.

24 Freie Gemeinde Library. 2617 W. Frond Du Lac Ave., Mil-
    waukee, Wisconsin 53206. German-American poetry and free-
    thought literature.

25 German Information Center. 410 Park Ave., New York, N. Y.

26 German Society of Pennsylvania, Horner Memorial Library.
    611 Spring Garden St., Philadelphia, Pa. 19123. Saur Bibles,
    Ephrata imprints, the Library of the Carl Schurz Memorial

Foundation and much German-Americana. It is the largest collection of German-Americana in America.

27 Germantown Historical Society. 5208 Germantown Ave., Philadelphia, Pa. 19144. Pennsylvania German material.

28 Gettysburg College, Schmucker Memorial Library. Gettysburg, Pa. 17325. Pennsylvania German imprints.

29 Goethe House. 1014 Fifth St., New York, N.Y. 10028. 13,000-volume collection.

30 Goshen College, Mennonite Historical Library. 1700 S. Main St., Goshen, Indiana 46526. German-American Mennonite imprints.

31 Harvard University Library. Cambridge, Mass. 02138. Yiddish and German-American historical material.

32 Historical Society, New Ulm Public Library. 27 N. Broadway, New Ulm, Minnesota 56073. Sources for Minnesota German history.

33 Historical Society of Pennsylvania. 1300 Locust St., Philadelphia, Pa. 19107. 1,000 Pennsylvania German imprints.

34 Henry E. Huntington Library & Art Gallery. San Marino, California. 20 Ephrata imprints, 55 Germantown imprints and a 1743 Saur Bible.

35 Institut für Auslandbeziehungen. Charlottenplatz 17, 7000 Stuttgart - 1, West Germany. Largest collection in Germany of German-Americana.

36 Johns Hopkins University Libraries. Charles & 34th Sts., Baltimore, Maryland 21218. Lieber manuscripts and the Library of the Society for the History of the Germans in Maryland.

37 Juniata College. 18th & Moore, Huntington, Pa. 16652. Pennsylvania German imprints and Fraktur and the Cassel Collection.

38 Koegel Memorial Library, German-American National Congress. 4740 N. Western Ave., Chicago, Illinois 60625.

39 Lebanon Valley College. Annville, Pa. 17003. Pennsylvania German, Ephrata and Saur imprints.

40 Lehigh County Historical Society. Trout Hall, 414 Walnut St., Allentown, Pa. 18102. Pennsylvania German-Americana.

41 Los Angeles Turnverein: Bibliothekszimmer. 645 West 15th St., Los Angeles, California.

42 Lutheran School of Theology, Immigrant Archives.   820 - 38th
    St., Rock Island, Illinois.   Archives of the Lutheran Church
    in America.

43 Missouri Historical Society Library.   Jefferson Memorial Li-
    brary Building, St. Louis, Mo. 63112.   Missouri German-
    Americana.

44 Muhlenberg College, Haas Library.   Allentown, Pa. 18104.
    Manuscripts of A. C. Wuchter, German-American poet.

45 Newberry Library.   60 W. Walton St., Chicago, Illinois 60610.
    Rich source of German-American historical material.

46 New York Public Library.   Fifth Avenue & 42 St., New York,
    N. Y. 10018.   30,000 volumes of German-Americana assembled
    by Richard Helbig.

47 New York Society Library.   53 E. 79th St., New York, N. Y.
    10021.   New York City imprint collection.

48 Ohio Historical Society Library.   1982 Velma Ave., Columbus,
    Ohio 43211.   Ohio German-Americana.

49 Public Library of Cincinnati & Hamilton County.   800 Vine St.,
    Cincinnati, Ohio 45202.   Cincinnati German-Americana.

50 Research Center for Canadian Ethnic Studies, University of
    Calgary.   Calgary 44, Canada.

51 Schwenkfelder Library.   Pennsburg, Pa.   Illuminated writings
    of Christopher Dock, Fraktur, diaries of German immigrants
    and German-American imprints.

52 Society of Danube Suabians.   4219 N. Lincoln Ave., Chicago,
    Ill. 60618.   500-volume library.

53 Southern Illinois University.   Carbondale, Ill. 62901.   Contains
    the library of the St. Louis Freie Gemeinde.   The circulation
    records to this unique collection are in the Historical Society in
    St. Louis.

54 Stanford University, Hoover Institute on War, Revolution and
    Peace.   Stanford, Cal. 94305.   History and politics of emigre
    movements since 1900.

55 State Historical Society of Wisconsin.   816 State St., Madison,
    Wis. 53706.   Sources on German-American radicalism and the
    Wisconsin-Germans.

56 Stockholmer Koordinationsstelle für Erforschung der deutsch-
    sprachigen Exil-Literatur.   University of Stockholm, Stockholm,
    Sweden.   Repository of German Exile Literature.

57 Tamiment Institute Library. 7 E. 15 St., New York, N.Y. 10003. Excellent primary sources on German-American radicalism and labor history.

58 United HIAS Service, Inc. 200 Park Ave. So., New York, N.Y. 10003. Immigration history and Judaica.

59 University of Chicago Library. 1100 E. 57th St., Chicago, Ill. 60637. Illinois German-Americana.

60 University of Cincinnati Library. Cincinnati, Ohio 45221. The H. H. Fick collection of German-American literature.

61 University of Illinois, Champaign Library. Urbana, Ill. 61081. Papers and libraries of Heinrich A. Rattermann and Julius Goebel.

62 University of Kansas, Max Kade German-American Research & Document Center. 208 Strong Hall, Lawrence, Kansas 66044. Midwestern German-Americana and German-American literature.

63 University of Kentucky. Lexington, Ky. 40506. Victor Hammer's printing press and imprints.

64 University of Pennsylvania. Philadelphia, Pa. 19104. Franz Daniel Pastorius Papers.

65 University of Southern California, Feuchtwanger Memorial Library. University Park, Los Angeles, Calif. 90007.

66 University of Wisconsin Libraries. 728 State St., Madison, Wisconsin 53706. The Herman Schlueter Library of German-American labor history and radicalism.

67 Volksfest Haus Library. 301 Summit Ave., St. Paul, Minnesota 55102. Sources of Minnesota-German history.

68 Wartburg Theological Seminary, Reu Memorial Library. 333 Wartburg Place, Dubuque, Iowa 52001. Lutheran German-Americana.

69 Washington University Libraries. St. Louis, Mo. 63130. The Praetorius Memorial Collection of a St. Louis German-American editor, Emil Praetorius.

70 Yale University Library, German Seminar. 1603a Yale Station, New Haven, Conn. 06520. Excellent collection of German literature.

71 YIVO Institute for Jewish Research. 1048 Fifth Ave., New York, N.Y. 10028.

72   Youngstown State University Library. Youngstown, Ohio 44503.
     German-American literature collection assembled by Robert E.
     Ward-Leyerle.

Collection Guides

73   Albrecht, Erich and J. A. Burzle. "Bericht über die Gründung
     und Tätigkeit des Max Kade Document & Research Centers,"
     G-A Studies. 3 (1971): 4-6.

74   Alden, John E. "Out of the Ashes, A Young Phoenix. Early
     Americana in the Harvard College Library," WMQ. 3 (1946):
     487-98.

75   American Association for State and Local History. Directory
     of Historical Societies and Agencies in the U.S. and Canada.
     Columbus, 1956- .

76   American Historical Association. Committee for the Study of
     War Documents. Guide to German Records Microfilmed at
     Alexandria, Va., Washington: National Archives and Records
     Service, 1958-62. Contains guide to the Deutsches Ausland-
     Institut.

77   Appel, John. "At the Library of Congress. Accretions to
     the Carl Schurz Papers." AGR. 29, iii (1963): 33-34.

78   Ash, Lee. Subject Collections: A Guide to Special Book Col-
     lections and Subject Emphases as Reported by University, 'Col-
     lege, Public, and Special Libraries in the United States and
     Canada. 2d ed. New York: Bowker, 1961.

79   Baginsky, Paul. German Works Relating to America 1493-1800:
     A List Compiled from the Collections of the New York Public
     Library. New York: New York Public Library, 1942. Lists
     1,600 items.

80   Berlin. Staatsbibliothek. Gesamtverzeichnis der ausländischen
     Zeitschriften 1914-1924. Berlin: Staatsbibliothek, 1929.

81   Billington, Ray Allen. Guides to American History: Manu-
     script Collections in Libraries of the U.S. New York: Peter
     Smith, 1952.

82   Boston. Public Library. Judaica: A Select Reading List of
     Books in the Public Library of the City of Boston. Boston:
     The Trustees, 1934.

83   Brown University. John Carter Brown Library. Bibliotheca
     Americana: Catalog of the John Carter Brown Library in

Brown University. New York: Kraus, 1961. v.1-2. 3, 737 items.

84 Brummel, L. and E. Egger. Guide to Union Catalogues and International Loan Centers. The Hague: Nijhoff, 1961.

85 Cappel, Albert. "Auswandererakten in Pfeddersheim, " Pfalzische Familien- und Wappenkunde. 6, xi (1969): 347-53, 379.

86 Carman, H. J. and Arthur W. Thompson. A Guide to the Principal Sources for American Civilization, 1800-1900, in the City of New York: Printed Materials. New York: Columbia University Pr., 1962.

87 Carnegie Institution. Guides to Manuscript Materials for the History of the U.S. Washington: Carnegie Institution, 1906-43, 23 v.

88 Concordia Historical Institute. "Guide to Microfilm Collection of Concordia Historical Institute, " CHIQ. 31 (1958): 123-32.

89 Cunz, Dieter. "The Forty-eighter Collection at the University of Bern, " AGR. 15, i (1948): 4-5.

90 Deutrich, Mabel E. "American Church Archives: An Overview, " AA. 24 (1961): 387-402.

91 Deutsche Bibliothek von St. Clair County. Numeral-Katalog der Deutschen Bibliothek von St. Clair County, Illinois. Belleville, Illinois, 1854. This collection is now in the Belleville Public Library. DLC

92 Deutsche Gesellschaft für Amerikastudien. Americana in deutschen Sammlungen (ADS): Ein Verzeichnis von Materialen zur Geschichte der Vereinigten Staaten in Archiven und Bibliotheken der Bundesrepublik Deutschland und West Berlin. Köln: Deutsche Gesellschaft für Amerikastudien, 1967.

93 Doll, Eugene E. "The Basis for a Rare Book Collection at the Carl Schurz Memorial Foundation, " AGR. 18, i (1951): 7-10, 34.

94 Downs, Robert B. American Library Resources: A Bibliographical Guide. Chicago: ALA, 1951.

95 _____. Resources of New York City Libraries, A Survey of Facilities for Advanced Study and Research. Chicago: ALA, 1942.

96 _____. Resources of Southern Libraries, A Survey of Facilities for Research. Chicago: ALA, 1938.

97 Eastern Mennonite College. "The Menno Simons Historical

Library and Archives, " EMC Bulletin. 40, x (Oct., 1961).

98 Epstein, Fritz. German Source Materials in American Libraries. Milwaukee: Marquette University Pr., 1958.

99 _____. "The Growth of the German-Language Collections, " LCQ Journal of Current Acquisitions. 16, iii (1959): 123-30.

100 Faust, Albert. Guide to the Material for American History in Swiss and Austrian Archives. Washington: Carnegie Institution, 1916. 46 libraries and archives surveyed.

101 Fraenkel, Josef. Guide to the Jewish Libraries of the World. London: Cultural Dept. of the World Jewish Congress, 1959.

102 Frels, Wilhelm. Deutsche Dichterhandschriften von 1400 bis 1900. Leipzig: Hiersemann, 1934. Locations in German libraries.

103 Friedmann, R. "The Mennonite Historical Library of Goshen College, " AGR. 9 (1942): 12-14.

104 Gerhard, Elmer Schultz. "The Research Library and Literary Notes, " AGR. 12, iii (1946): 36. About the Carl Schurz Memorial Foundation Library.

105 "Gift of Udo Brachvogel Papers, " BNYPL. 31 (1927): 373-76.

106 Greene, E. G. and R. B. Morris. A Guide to the Principal Sources for Early American History (1600-1800) in the City of New York. 2d ed. New York: Columbia University Pr., 1953.

107 Guide to the Manuscript Collections in the Historical Society of Pennsylvania. Philadelphia: Historical Society of Pennsylvania, 1940.

108 Hale, Richard W. Guide to Photocopied Historical Materials in the United States and Canada. Ithaca: Cornell University Pr., 1961.

109 Hamer, Philip M. A Guide to the Archives and Manuscripts in the United States. New Haven: Yale University Pr., 1961.

110 Hamilton, Kenneth G. "The Moravian Archives at Bethlehem, Pennsylvania, " AA. 24, iv (1961): 415-24.

111 Hebrew Union College. Jewish Institute of Religion. American Jewish Periodical Center. Jewish Newspapers and Periodicals on Microfilm, available at the American Jewish Periodical Center. Cincinnati: Hebrew Union College, 1957.

112 Heinz, Grete and Agnes Peterson. NSDAP Hauptarchiv: Guide

to the Hoover Institution Microfilm Collection (Hoover Institution Bibliographical Series no. 17). Stanford: Hoover Institution on War, Revolution and Peace, 1964.

113 Helbig, Richard E. Deutsch-Amerikanische Forschungen: Wachstum und Benutzung der deutsch-amerikanischen Saamlung der New York Public Library während 1906-09. Chicago: Staiger Printing Co., 1909.

114 _____. Die deutsch-amerikanische Sammlung der New York Public Library. Philadelphia: International Printing Co., n.d.

115 _____. Deutsch-Amerikanisches in der New York Public Library. New York: Carl A. Stern, 1906.

116 _____. "German-American Researches: The Growth of the German-American Collection of the New York Public Library during 1906-07; Its Importance for Historical and Literary Studies," G-A Annals. 6 (1908): 257-85.

117 Hintz, Carl. "Notable Materials Added to North American Libraries, 1943-47," LQ. 19 (1949): 105-18, 186-200.

118 Hogue, Arthur R. "The Carl Schurz Memorial Foundation: The First Twenty-Five Years," IMH. 51 (1955): 335-39.

119 _____. "The Private Papers of Carl Schurz," AGR. 17, iv (1951): 4-5.

120 Holweck, F. G. "The Historical Archives of the Archdiocese of St. Louis," S. L. Cath. Hist. Rev. 1 (1918): 24-39.

121 Horsch, John. Catalogue of the Mennonite Historical Library in Scottdale, Pennsylvania. Scottdale: Mennonite Publishing House, 1929.

122 Hulbert, Archer. "The Moravian Records," Ohio Arch. & Hist. Q. 18 (1909): 199-226. Catalog of Moravian records.

123 Johnston, William and I. G. Mudge. Special Collections in the United States. Washington: GPO, 1912.

124 Jones, Elsa. "CSMF Library Development," AGR. 25, ii (1959): 40.

125 Jones, George. "A New Source of German American History," RJGAH. 32 (1966): 64-65. About the London archives of the Society for Propagating Christian Knowledge.

126 Kent, George. "Survey of German Manuscripts Pertaining to American History in the Library of Congress," JAH. 56 (1970): 868-81.

127   Kloss, Heinz. "Grenzen auslanddeutschen Schrifttums. Von
      der Sammelarbeit der Bücherei des DAI, " AD. (March 19,
      1936): 188-93.

128   _____. "Volksgruppen- und Deutschtumforschung in den
      Vereinigten Staaten 1939-1941. Versuche der Carl-Schurz-
      Gedächtnisstiftung zur zentralen Zusammenfassung der deutsch-
      amerikanischen Forschung, " VF. 5 (1942): 2-3, 193-97.

129   Kuhn, Charles. "The Busch-Reisinger Museum: Three Years
      of Collecting, " AGR. 22, vi (1956): 19-23.

130   Läugin, Theodore. "Das Schrifttum über Badener im Ausland.
      Von der Badischen Landesbibliothek, " AD. 6 (1923): 339-342.

131   Learned, M. Guide to Manuscript Materials Relating to Amer-
      ican History in German State Archives. Washington: Carnegie
      Institution, 1912. Still useful.

132   Lederer, Max. "Deutsche Bücher in der Library of Congress, "
      CQ. 22 (1949): 152-58.

133   Lenhart, John. "The Historical Library at the Central Bureau
      of the Catholic Central Verein in St. Louis, Missouri, " SJR.
      49 (1957): 348-52, 354-55, 384-87; 50 (1958): 24-27.

134   Lind, William E. "Methodist Archives in the United States of
      America, " AA. 24 (1961): 435-40.

135   "List of Books in the Library of the Historical Society of
      Schuylkill County, Pennsylvania, " Pub. Hist. Soc. of S. ' C. 4
      (1912): 93-114.

136   Loocker, Elsa. "The Germanic Libraries at the University of
      California in Los Angeles, " MLF. 25 (1941): 82-84.

137   Lutheran Historical Conference. "List of Archival Depositories
      of 23 of the 32 Synods of the Former United Luteran Church of
      America, " News Letter. 2, i (1965): 9-12.

138   M. , H. K. "Some Resources in the New York Public Library
      for the Study of Swiss in the United States, " SAHS. 1, iii
      (1965): 6.

139   Morris, John G. Catalogue of the Lutheran Historical Society's
      Collection of books, Pamphlets, Manuscripts, photographs, etc.
      Philadelphia: Lutheran Publishing House, 1890. Collection de-
      posited in the Theological Seminary at Gettysburg, Pennsylvania.

140   Mueller, B. A. Das Auslanddeutsche Schrifttum in der Staats-
      und Universitätsbibliothek in Hamburg. n. p. , n. d.   UC

141   NCSA. "A Unique Reference Source, " AGR. 28, v (1962): 28,

36. About the Union Catalog of German-Americana now located at the German Society of Pennsylvania in Philadelphia.

142 National Union Catalog: A Cumulative Author List of Works
Representing Library of Congress Printed Cards and Titles
Reported by Other American Libraries, 1953-57. Ann Arbor,
Michigan: Edwards, 1958. 28 v.

143 National Union Catalog of Manuscript Collections. Hamden,
Conn.: Shoestring, 1962-64.

144 Newberry Library. Edward E. Ayer Collection. Catalog of
the Edward E. Ayer Collection of Americana and American
Indians. Boston: Hall, 1961. 8v. Lists 90,000 items.

145 New York Public Library. Guide to the Reference Collections
of the New York Public Library. New York: New York Public Library, 1941.

146 O'Neill, James. "European Sources for American History in
the Library of Congress," QJLC. 24 (1967): 152-57.

147 Owens, M. Lilliana. "Some Catholic German Americana,"
SJR. 56 (1963): 58-60, 96-99. About St. Louis Catholic
Central-Verein Library.

148 Palmer, Philip M. "German Works on America," in: In
Honorem Lawrence Marsden Price: Contributions by his Col-
leagues and by his former Students. Berkeley: University of
California Pr., 1952, pp. 271-412. 1900 items with locations
in American and European libraries.

149 Pittsburgh. Carnegie Library. Books by Catholic Authors in
the Carnegie Library of Pittsburgh: A Classified and Annotated
List. Pittsburgh: Carnegie Library, 1911.

150 Reichmann, Felix. "The Subject Union Catalog Americana-
Germanica," School & Society. 58 (1943): 372-74.

151 Rosenberger, Homer T. "Outstanding Collections of Pennsylvania German Material," in: The Pennsylvania Germans 1891-
1965. Lancaster, Pennsylvania: Pennsylvania German Society,
1966, pp. 508-62.

152 Rosengarten, J. G. American History from German Archives
with Reference to the German Soldiers in the Revolution and
Franklin's Visit to Germany. Lancaster, Pennsylvania: New
Era Printing Co., 1904.

153 _____. "German Archives as Sources of German-American
History," GAA. 5 (1907): 357-69.

154 _____. Sources of History. A Paper Read Before the

German American Historical Society of New York and the Pio-
nier-Verein of Philadelphia.   Philadelphia: Wm. F. Fell &
Co., 1892.

155   Scherer Library.   "Scherer Collection Displayed in Showcase
at Freiberger Library," Reserve Tribune.   (November 4, 1965).
About the Scherer Collection in Western Reserve University.

156   Society for the History of the Germans in Maryland.   Catalog
of the Society.   Baltimore: Schneiderreith & Sons, 1907.

157   Special Libraries Association.   Special Library Resources.
New York: Special Libraries Association, 1941-47.   4 v.

158   Spofford, E.   "Some of the Manuscript Resources of the Historical Society of Pennsylvania," PH. 1 (1934): 88-97.

159   Staatsbibliothek der Stiftung Preussischer Kulturbesitz.   Gesamtverzeichnis ausländischer Zeitschriften und Serien 1939-1958.
Wiesbaden: Harrassowitz, 1959- .

160   Steiger Collection of German-American Newspapers and Periodicals.   Worcester, Mass.:   Karl Arndt, 1963.   Issues of
363 serials arranged by states and cities dating 1872-74.

161   Suelflow, August.   "The Buenger Collection," CHIQ. 33 (1960):
56.   Lutheran German-Americana.

162   _____.   "Microfilm and Photoduplication: A Report on the
Microfilm Activities of the Concordia Historical Institute for
1968," CHIQ. 42 (1969): 84-89.

163   Umble, John.   "Documents Relating to Bishop Jacob Schwarzendruber (1800-68)," MQR. 20 (1946): 230-39.   List of manuscripts in Schwarzendruber's library.

164   Union List of Serials in Libraries of the United States and
Canada.   3d ed., ed. by Edna B. Titus.   New York: Wilson,
1965.   5 v.

165   United States.   Library of Congress.   A Catalog of Books
Represented by Library of Congress Printed Cards.   Ann Arbor, Michigan: Edwards, 1942-46.   167 v.

166   _____.   _____.   Library of Congress Author Catalog: A
Cumulative List of Works Represented by Library of Congress
Printed Cards 1948-52.   Ann Arbor: Edwards, 1953.   24 v.

167   _____.   _____.   Card Division.   Carl Schurz: A Register of His Papers in the Library of Congress.   Washington:
GPO, 1966.

168   _____.   _____.   Division of Bibliography.   List of

References on the Pennsylvania Germans. Washington: Library of Congress, 1921.

169 _____ . _____ . _____ List of Works Relating to the Germans in the United States. Washington: GPO, 1904.

170 _____ . _____ General Reference and Bibliography Division. Union Lists of Serials: A Bibliography, compiled by Ruth S. Freitag. Washington: GPO, 1964.

171 _____ . _____ Manuscript Division. Checklist of Collections of Personal Papers in Historical Societies, Universities and Public Libraries and other Learned Institutions in the United States. Washington: GPO, 1918.

172 _____ . _____ . _____ Handbook of Manuscripts in the Library of Congress. Washington: GPO, 1918.

173 _____ . _____ . _____ Manuscripts in Public and Private Collections in the United States. Washington: GPO, 1924.

174 _____ . _____ Union Catalog Division. Newspapers on Microfilm. 5th ed., comp. under direction of G. A. Schwegmann. Washington: GPO, 1963.

175 United States. National Historical Publications Commission. Guide to Archives and Manuscripts in the U.S. ed. by P. M. Hamer. New Haven: Yale University Pr., 1961.

176 Vecoli, R. "The Immigration Studies Collection of the University of Minnesota," AA. 32 (1969): 139-45.

177 Vereinigung Schweizerischer Bibliothekare. Verzeichnis ausländischer Zeitschriften in schweizerischen Bibliotheken. 4 Aufl. Bern: Schweizerische Landesbibliothek, 1955.

178 Vielig, J. "Die Bibliothek der Emigrationsliteratur in Frankfurt a. M.," Panorama. 4, vi, xii (1960).

179 Weber, Christoph. Das Deutschtum im Ausland. Eine systematische Zusammenstellung der im Gesamtkatalog der Preussischen wissenschaftlichen Bibliotheken verzeichneten Schriften 1900-23. Berlin: Preussische Staatsbibliothek, 1925.

180 Weber, F. J. "Printed Guides to Archival Centers for American Catholic History," AA. 32 (1969): 349-56.

181 Weinberg, Gerhard. "Zu den deutschen Akten in den Vereinigten Staaten," Hist. Zeitschrift. (April 1962): 519-26.

182 Winkler, E. W. "The Vandale Collection of Texana," SwHQ. 54 (1950): 27-61. Books on the Germans in Texas.

183   Withington, Mary.   Catalog of Manuscripts in the Collection of
      Western Americana founded by William Robertson Coe, Yale
      University Library.   New Haven: Yale University Pr., 1952.

184   Wolfe, R. J.   "Early New York Naturalization Records in the
      Emmet Collection with a List of Aliens Naturalized in New
      York 1802-14, " BNYPL.   67 (1963): 211-17.

185   Yale University Library.   Catalog of the Yale Collection of
      Western Americana.   Boston: Hall, 1961.   4 v.

186   Zucker, A. E.   "The Foundation's Library--A Unique Aid to
      Scholars, " AGR.   13, ii (1946): 39-40.

German-American National Organizations

187   American Austrian Society.   1156 15th St., Washington, D. C.
      20005.

188   Amerikanischer Turnerbund.   1556 Elinton Ave. N., Rochester,
      New York 14621.

189   Austrian-American Federation, Inc.   31 E. 69th St., New York,
      N. Y. 10021.

190   Brüderschaft der Deutsch-Ungaren in Amerika.   228 E. 86th
      St., New York, N. Y.

191   Federation of American Citizens of German Descent.   460
      Chapman St., Irvington, New Jersey 07111.

192   German-American National Congress.   4740 N. Western Ave.,
      Chicago, Illinois 60625.   The largest German-American nation-
      al organization.

193   North American Swiss Alliance.   33 Public Square, Cleveland,
      Ohio 44113.   Established in 1865.

194   Steuben Society of America.   369 Lexington Ave., Suite 2003,
      New York City 10017.

195   Verband der Deutschen aus Rumänien in Amerika.   Box 119,
      College Point, New York 11356.

196   Verband der Donauschaben Amerikas.   c/o Christ N. Herr,
      1649 W. Grace, Chicago, Illinois 60631.

197   Verband der Sudetendeutschen.   Kreutzer-Halle, 228 E. 86th
      St., New York, N. Y. 10028.

Historical Societies

198 American Historical Society of the Germans from Russia. 1004A Ninth Ave., Box 1424, Greeley, Colorado.

199 North Dakota Historical Society of the Germans from Russia. Box 1671, Bismarck, North Dakota.

200 Pennsylvania German Society. R. D. 1, Box 469, Breinigsville, Pa. 18031.

201 Society for German-American Studies. 7204 Langerford Drive, Cleveland, Ohio 44129.

202 Society for the History of the Germans in Maryland. 231 St. Paul Place, Baltimore, Maryland 21202.

Bibliographical Aids

203 Alstetter, Mabel F. "Alte deutsch-amerikanische Dokumente, " DDP. 12 (1880): 143 ff., 184, 317, 341; 13 (1881): 10 ff., 142, 311, 352, 459; 14 (1882): 401 ff.; 15 (1883); 14 ff., 154.

204 America: History and Life. A Guide to Periodical Literature. Santa Barbara: Clio Press for the American Bibliographical Center, 1964- , v. 1- .

205 American Historical Association. Guide to Historical Literature. New York: Macmillan, 1961.

206 _____. Writings on American History. Washington, 1909- .

207 "Americana-Germanica, " AGR. (1942-66). This was an annual bibliography edited by A. E. Zucker, Felix Reichmann, Dieter Cunz and A. E. Schultz. From 1968 to 1970 it was published in the GQ.

208 Beers, Henry P. Bibliographies in American History: Guide to Materials for Research. New York: Wilson, 1942. Excellent bibliographies of American states.

209 Bek, William G. "Bibliography of German-Americans for the Year 1906, " GAA. 5 (1906): 124-28, 249-56, 314-20.

210 Bibliographical Index: A Cumulative Bibliography of Bibliographies. New York: Wilson, 1937- , v. 1- .

211 Bibliographie der deutschen Bibliographien: Jahresverzeichnis der selbständig erschienen und der in deutschsprachigen Büchern und Zeitschriften enthaltenen versteckten Bibliographien. Leipzig: Verlag für Buch- und Bibliothekswesen, 1954- .

212 Bibliographie des Deutschtums im Ausland. Stuttgart: Kohl-
     hammer, 1937- , v. 1- .

213 Brown, F. J. and J. Roucek. "Selected Bibliography," in:
     Our Racial and National Minorities; Their History, Contribu-
     tions and Present Problems. New York: Prentice-Hall, 1937,
     pp. 781-847.

214 Clark, Thomas D. Travels in the New South: A Bibliography.
     Norman: University of Oklahoma Pr., 1962, 2 v. German-
     Americans in the South.

215 Cole, George Watson. Catalog of Books Relating to the Dis-
     covery and Early History of North and South America. New
     York: Dodd, 1907.

216 Cunz, Dieter. "Twenty Years of German-American Studies,"
     RJGAH. 30 (1959): 9-28.

217 Dahlmann, F. and G. Waitz. Quellenkunde der deutschen
     Geschichte. 9 Aufl. Leipzig: Koehler, 1931-32, 2 v.

218 "Deutsche Amerikakundliche Veröffentlichungen," JAS. (1945-).
     An annual bibliography.

219 Dunlap, Leslie. American Historical Societies, 1790-1860.
     Madison: Privately printed, 1944.

220 Eberhardt, Fritz. Amerika-Literatur: Die wichtigsten seit
     1900 in deutscher Sprache erschienenen Werke über Amerika.
     Leipzig: Verlag von Koehler & Volckmar, 1926.

221 Eberstadt, Edward. The Annotated Eberstadt Catalogs of
     Americana, Numbers 103-38, 1935-56. New York: Argosy-
     Antiquarian Ltd., 1965, 4 v.

222 European Association for American Studies. "Current Bibli-
     ography, 1950-56," News Letter. 3 (1957): 25-36.

223 Gieselberg, Margarita. "Beiträge zum Thema 'Deutsche im
     Ausland' in der ZKA 1951-1967 ... Bibliographie," ZKA. 18
     (1968): 41-46.

224 Greene, Amy B. Handbook-Bibliography on Foreign Language
     Groups in the U.S. and Canada. New York: Council of Wo-
     men and Home Missions and Missionary Education Movement,
     1925.

225 Griffin, Appleton. Bibliography of American Historical Soci-
     eties. 2d ed., Washington: GPO, 1907.

226 Handlin, Oscar. Harvard Guide to American History. Cam-
     bridge: Belknap Press of Harvard University Pr., 1954.

227 Harrisse, Henry. Bibliotheca Americana Vestustissima: A
     Description of Works Relating to America 1492-1551. Madrid:
     Suarez, 1958, 6 v.

228 Hubach, Robert. Early Midwestern Travel Narratives: An An-
     notated Bibliography 1634-1850. Detroit: Wayne State Univer-
     sity Pr., 1961.

229 Jahresberichte der Geschichtswissenschaft. Berlin: Mittler,
     1880-1916, 36 v. Annual historical bibliography.

230 Kloss, Heinz. "Bibliographie der Veröffentlichungen von Heinz
     Kloss," VFN. 28 (1971): 51-59. 333 items, most of which
     are related to German-America.

231 _____. Bibliographisches Handbuch des Auslanddeutschtums.
     Stuttgart: Ausland & Heimat, 1932-36.

232 _____. Bücher berichten von Deutschen im Grenzland und
     Ausland. Stuttgart: DAI, 1936.

233 _____. "Deutschamerikanische Geschichtsforschung," in:
     Deutsche Heimat in Amerika. Bericht uber die erste deutsch-
     amerikanische Heimatkunde-Tagung. Berlin: Verlag Grenze
     und Ausland, 1937, pp. 46-54.

234 Knoche, W. "Dieter Cunz: A List of Published Writings,"
     RJGAH. 34 (1970): 19-22. Works of a German-American his-
     torian on German-America.

235 Koner, Wilhelm. Repertorium über die vom Jahre 1800 bis
     zum Jahre 1850 in akademischen Abhandlungen, Gesellschafts-
     schriften und wissenschaftlichen Journalen auf dem Gebiete der
     Geschichte und ihrer Hülfswissenschaften. Berlin: Nicolai,
     1852-56, 2 v. Vol. 2: 76-169 deals with America.

236 Koster, Donald. "Articles on American Studies, 1957," AQ.
     10 (1958): 225-62.

237 Larned, Josephus N. Literature of American History: A Bib-
     liographical Guide in which the Scope, Character, and Compara-
     tive Worth of Books in Selected Lists are Set Forth in Brief
     Notes by Critics of Authors. Boston: Houghton, Mifflin, 1902.

238 Mai, R. Auslanddeutsche Quellenkunde 1924-33. Berlin:
     Weidmannsche Buchhandlung, 1938.

239 Meyer, Hildegard. "Versuch einer Bibliographie in Deutsch-
     land erschienener Schriften über die Vereinigten Staaten von
     Nord-Amerika," in Nord-Amerika im Urteil des deutschen
     Schrifttums bis zur Mitte des 19. Jahrhunderts. Hamburg,
     1929, pp. 131-66.

240 Meynen, Emil. Bibliographie des Deutschtums der kolonial-
     zeitlichen Einwanderung in Nordamerika, insbesondere der
     Pennsylvanien-Deutschen und ihrer Nachkommen, 1683-1933.
     Leipzig: Harrassowitz, 1937.

241 Mönnig, Richard. Amerika und England im deutschen, öster-
     reichischen und schweizerischen Schrifttum 1945-49. Stuttgart:
     Kohlhammer, 1951.

242 _____. Deutschland und die Deutschen im englischsprachigen
     Schrifttum 1948-55: Eine Bibliographie. Göttingen: Vanden-
     hoeck & Ruprecht, 1957. Contains section on the German-
     Americans.

243 Morris, John. "List of Books Relating to the Germans in
     America, " RJGAH. 8 (1896): 53-60.

244 Nath, Dorothea. "German-American Records, Gathered from
     Niles Weekly Register, " GAA. 2 (1904): 83-105.

245 New York Public Library. Reference Department. Dictionary
     Catalog of the Americas. Boston: Hall, 1961, 28 v.

246 New Yorker Staats-Zeitung und Herold. Die Vereinswelt: Weg-
     weiser der Deutschamerikaner. New York: New Yorker
     Staats-Zeitung und Herold, 1932- . This is an excellent an-
     nual publication guide to all German-American clubs, organiza-
     tions, churches, etc.

247 Noe, Adolf von. "A Preliminary Bibliography of German
     Books on the U. S. Since 1880, " Bibliog. Soc. America. 4
     (1909): 102-19.

248 Peterson, Clarence. Consolidated Bibliography of County His-
     tories in Fifty States in 1961, Consolidated 1935-61. 2 ed.
     Baltimore: Genealogical Publishing Co., 1963.

249 Pochmann, Henry A. "Anglo-German Bibliography, " JEGP.
     (1936-41).

250 _____ and Arthur R. Schultz. Bibliography of German
     Culture in America to 1940. Madison: University of Wiscon-
     sin Pr., 1953. 12,000 items in alphabetical arrangement.

251 Sabin, Joseph. Bibliotheca Americana: Dictionary of Books
     Relating to America from its Discovery to the Present Time.
     New York: Sabin, 1868-92; Bibliographical Society of Amer-
     ica, 1928-36, 29 v. New York: Mini-Print Corp., 1966. 2v.
     Lists locations.

252 Seidensticker, Oswald. "Deutsch-amerikanische Bibliographie
     bis zum Schlusse des letzten Jahrhunderts, " DDP. 9 (1877-78):
     178-83, 241-45, 264-68, 324-28, 348-51; 10 (1878-79): 22-28,

62-66, 94-101, 133-36, 158-61, 194-99, 224-30, 264-70, 309-16, 374, 384-89, 422-29, 466-72; 12 (188081): 22-24.

253   Smith, Charles. Pacific Northwest Americana: A Check-List of Books and Pamphlets Relating to the History of the Pacific Northwest. 3d ed. Portland: Oregon Historical Society, 1950.

254   Stilwell, Margaret. "Americana: Selected Bibliographies and Bibliographical Monographs," in: Incunabula and Americana 1450 to 1800. A Key to Bibliographical Study. New York: Columbia University Pr., 1931, pp. 341-440.

255   Strassmayr, Eduard. Bibliographie zur oberösterreichischen Geschichte. Linz a. Donau: Winkler, 1929-57. 4 v.

256   United States. Library of Congress. General Reference and Bibliography Division. Guide to the Study of the United States of America: Representative Books Reflecting the Development of American Life and Thought. Washington: GPO, 1960.

257   Vail, Robert. The Voice of the Old Frontier (Rosenbach Fellowship in Bibliography, 10). Philadelphia: University of Pennsylvania Pr., 1949.

258   Verein für das Deutschtum im Ausland. Auslanddeutschtum: Ein Wegweiser durch die über das Deutschtum in Amerika erschienenen Drucksachen. Berlin: Verein für das Deutschtum im Ausland, 1917.

259   Wagner, Henry. The Plains and the Rockies: A Bibliography of Original Narratives of Travel and Adventure, 1800-65. Columbus, Ohio: Long's College Book Co., 1953.

260   Ward, Robert Elmer. "Bibliographical Notes on German-American Culture," in Symposium über deutsche Kultur in Amerika und Ohio. Cleveland: Classic Printing Co., 1973, pp. 6-8. Valuable bibliographical essay.

261   _____. "Deutschamerikanische Kulturecke: Neuere deutsch-amerikanische Publikationen," WA. (January 26, 1973).

262   _____. "Englischsprachige Literatur über Deutsche in Amerika," GAS. 3 (1971): 46-47.

263   Winther, Oscar. Classified Bibliography of the Periodical Literature of the Trans-Mississippi West 1811-1957. Bloomington: Indiana University Pr., 1961.

264   Zucker, A. E. Subject Approach to Americana-Germanica. Philadelphia: CSMF, 1943.

General Histories

265 Adams, Herbert. The Germanic Origin of New England Towns.
     Baltimore: N. Murray, 1882.

266 Alemann, Theodore. Die Zukunft des Deutschtums im Ausland.
     2 Aufl. Stuttgart: Ausland & Heimat, 1923.

267 Amerika-Institut der Universität Innsbruck. Americana-Aus-
     triaca. Beiträge zur Amerikakunde. Klaus Lanzinger, ed.
     Vienna: Braumüller, 1966-70, 2 v.

268 Arciniegas, German. Germans in the Conquering of America.
     New York: Macmillan, 1943.

269 Becker, M. J. The Germans of 1849 in America. Mt. Ver-
     non, Ohio, 1887. UC

270 Bell, Stefan and A. Braedt. "Die Gemeinschaft der Sieben-
     bürger Sachsen in den Vereinigten Staaten und Kanada,"
     Siebenbürger Sachsen Heute: Die Wegweiser. Heft 60 (1967):
     51-67.

271 Bittinger, Lucy F. The Germans in Colonial Times. Phila-
     delphia: Lippincott, 1901.

272 Boden, Emil. Deutsche Kämpfer in Amerika. Leipzig:
     Schoessmann, 1934.

273 Boelitz, Otto. Das Grenz- und Auslanddeutschtum: Seine
     Geschichte und Seine Bedeutung. 2 Aufl. Munich: Oldenburg
     Verlag, 1930.

274 Bokum, Hermann. "The American Germans, " Eck. (Feb. 9,
     16, 1963). An 1836 description.

275 Bruncken, Ernest. "Germans in America, " AHAAR. (1898):
     345-53.

276 Bund der Auslanddeutschen. Ausland und Heimat: Die Tagung
     des Auslanddeutschtums in der Heimat, Berlin, Aug. /Sept.
     1925 ... Gehaltene Ansprachen und erstattete Berichte. Ber-
     lin: Zentralverlag, 1926.

277 Chicago. German-American National Alliance. Die Deutschen
     in Amerika: Festschrift zum deutschen Tag in Chicago, ge-
     feiert am Sonntag, den 4 Okt. 1908, im Auditorium, von Zweig-
     Verband. Chicago: H. Eosicke Printing Co., 1908.

278 Cronau, Rudolf. Drei Jahrhunderte deutschen Lebens in Amer-
     ika: Ruhmesblätter der Deutschen in den Vereinigten Staaten.
     Berlin: D. Reimer A-G, 1926. An important history. ICJ
     IU MH MPL NB NcD NN NPV OCIW

279 Cronberg, Allen T. The Volksbund für das Deutschtum im Ausland: Völkisch Ideology and German Foreign Policy, 1881-1939. Dissertation: Stanford University, 1970.

280 Cunz, Dieter. "Die Deutsch-Amerikaner: Zu dem Buch von John Hawgood 'The Tragedy of German-America', " MFD. 33 (1941): 343-48.

281 _____. "The German-Americans, " in: F. Brown and J. Roucek, One America. New York: Prentice-Hall, 1952, pp. 104-20.

282 _____. "The German Americans: Immigration and Integration, " RJGAH. 28 (1953): 29-43.

283 _____. "Les Germano-Americains, " Documents, Revue Mensuelle des Questions Allemandes. 10 (1955): 457-74.

284 Davis-Dubois, Rachel and E. Schueppe. The Germans in America. New York: Nelson, 1936.

285 Deubel, Stefan. Der Deutsch-Amerikaner von Heute: Deutschamerikanisches Adressbuch für die USA und Westdeutschland. Cleveland: Wächter und Anzeiger, 1963.

286 Douai, Adolf. Land und Leute in der Union. Berlin: O. Janke, 1864. DLC

287 Faust, Albert. The German Element in America. New York: Steuben Society of America, 1927. Extensive bibliography, pp. 480-562.

288 _____. Striking Facts about the Germans in the U.S. Hoboken, 1926.

289 Fick, H. H. German Contributions to American Progress. Boston, 1902. UC

290 Fritsch, W. A. Deutschamerikaner, Deutsche Sprache und Deutsches Streben in Amerika. New York, 1907. UC

291 Fürstenwärter, Mor. Freih. von. Die Deutschen in Amerika. Stuttgart: J. G. Cotta, 1818.

292 Fulda, Ludwig. Amerikanische Eindrücke. Berlin: J. G. Cotta, 1906.

293 Gay, Kathlyn. Germans Helped Build America (Ethnic Heritage Series). New York: Messner, 1971.

294 Gehring, Albert. German-American Achievements. Cleveland, n.d. UC

295   German-American National Alliance.   The German Element in
      the U.S.   n.p.,   n.d.   UC

296   Gilhoff, Johannes.   Deutsche Bauern in Amerika.   5 Aufl.
      Frankfurt: Diesterweg, 1942.

297   Goebel, Julius.   Das Deutschtum in den Vereinigten Staaten von
      Nordamerika (Der Kampf ums deutsche Wesen, Heft 16).
      Munich, 1904.

298   _____.   "Geschichte des Auslanddeutschtum.   Vereinigte
      Staaten von Nordamerika," JFDG. 3 (1927): 732-35; 5 (1929):
      706-13; 8 (1932): 700-13.

299   _____.   Der Kampf um deutsch Kultur in Amerika: Auf-
      sätze und Vorträge zur deutsch-amerikanischen Bewegung.
      Leipzig: Dürr, 1914.   UC

300   _____.   "The Place of the German Element in America,"
      AHAAR.   (1909):   181-89.

301   Götz, Karl.   Brüder über dem Meer.   Stuttgart: J. Engel-
      horns, 1942.   UK UM

302   Grebner, Constantin.   Die Deutschen, Mit einem Anhang: Die
      Deutsch-Amerikaner.   Milwaukee, 1902.   UC

303   Grueninger, J. P.   The Swiss in the U.S.   Madison, 1940.

304   Hanghans, Paul.   Deutsche Erde: Beiträge zur Kenntnis
      deutschen Volkstums allerorten und allerzeit.   Gotha: Paul
      Langhans, 1902-14, 13 v.

305   Hassel, Georg v.   Die Auslanddeutschen.   Berlin, 1926.   UC

306   Hawgood, John.   The Tragedy of German-America.   New York
      Putnam, 1940.

307   Heinrici, Max.   Das Buch der Deutschen in Amerika.   Phila-
      delphia: German-American National Alliance, 1909.

308   Heinzen, Karl.   "Die Deutschen und die Amerikaner (1860),"
      DAG. 15 (1915): 145-80.

309   Hemmerle, Rudolf.   "Sudeten Germans in America," Sudeten
      Bulletin. 5, ii (1957): 18-20.

310   Holland, Ruth.   The German Immigrants in America.   New
      York: Grosset & Dunlap, 1970.

311   Huebener, Theodore.   The Germans in America.   Philadelphia
      Chilton, 1962.

312 Institut für Auslandbeziehungen. "Chronik des deutschen Kul-
turlebens im Ausland. Vereinigte Staaten von Amerika, Kan-
ada, " MIA. 11 (1961): 57-59, 218-20, 284-86; 12 (1962): 69-
71; ZKA. 12 (1962): 266, 268-71, 362-63; 13 (1963): 49-52,
143-47, 254-58, 332-33; 16 (1966): 63-65, 192-94, 278-82; 19
(1969): 54, 213, 275, 340-42.

313 Johnson, P. L. "Germans in the United States, " New Catholic
Encyclopedia. Washington, 1967, 6:425-28.

314 Kapp, Friedrich. Aus und über Amerika. Thatsachen und
Erlebnisse. Berlin: J. Spring, 1876.

315 "Ein Kartenwerk über die Volksgruppen in den USA, " Mitteilungen des Instituts für Auslandsbeziehungen. 4 (1954): 191-
92.

316 Kloss, Heinz. "Deutschamerikanische- Panamerikaner, " Neue
Zeit. 12, xviii (1930): 5-7.

317 _____. "Gegenwart und Zukunft des Deutschtums der
Vereinigten Staaten, " Deutschtum im Ausland. (August 21,
1938): 486-96.

318 _____. Statistisches Handbuch der Volksdeutschen im Über-
see. Stuttgart: Publikationsstelle, 1943.

319 _____, "Überlegungen zum zweiten deutsch-amerikanischen
Kongress in Philadelphia am 6. Okt. 1933, " Volk & Reich. 1
(1934): 67-70.

320 _____. "Das Überseedeutschtum, " Zeitwende. (August 5,
1929): 168-73.

321 _____. "Übersehenes Deutschtum in Amerika, " Jungnation-
ale Stimmen. 2 (1929): 29-53.

322 _____. Um die Einigung des Deutschamerikanertums. Die
Geschichte einer unvollendeten Volksgruppe. Berlin: Volk
und Reich, 1937.

323 Klotz, Johann. "Americanisch Historie, " Eck. (May 17, 24,
31, June 7, 14, 21, 28, 1958).

324 Knortz, Karl. Aus der transatlantischen Gesellschaft. Nord-
amerikanische Kulturbilder. Leipzig: B. Schlicke, 1882.
DLC

325 _____. Deutsche in Amerika. Leipzig: C. L. Hirschen-
feld, 1906. DLC

326 _____. Das Deutschtum der Vereinigten Staaten. Hamburg,
1898.

327   Koerner, Gustav. Das deutsche Element in den Vereinigten
      Staaten von Nordamerika, 1818-48. Cincinnati: A. E. Wilde,
      1880. DLC UC UM MPL

328   Kunz, Virginia. The Germans in America. Minneapolis:
      Lerner Publications, 1967.

329   Landsmannschaft der Deutschen aus Russland. Heimatbuch
      der Deutschen aus Russland. Stuttgart: Landsmannschaft der
      Deutschen aus Russland, 1963.

330   Löher, Franz von. Geschichte und Zustände der Deutschen in
      Amerika. Cincinnati: Eggers & Wulkop, 1847. DLC UC UM

331   Lohr, Otto. First Germans in North America and the German
      Element of New Netherland. New York: Stechert & Co.,
      1912.

332   Maisel, Albert Q. "The Germans among Us, " Reader's Di-
      gest. (March, 1955): 97-101.

333   March, Hans. Memorandum by American Friends of Demo-
      cratic Sudetens. New York: Democratic Sudetens Committee,
      1953.

334   Marx, Karl Theodore. "Die Deutschen in Amerika, " Die Re-
      portage. 5 (1970). Marx is a German-American poet.

335   Mencken, H. L. "Die Deutsch-Amerikaner, " Neue Rundschau.
      39 (1928): 489-95.

336   Meyer, Georg. The German-Americans. Milwaukee, 1890.
      UC

337   Münsterberg, Hugo. Aus Deutsch-Amerika. Berlin: Ernst
      Siegfried Mittler & Sohn, 1909.

338   Nock, Samuel. America's German Pioneers: Two Centuries
      of German Achievements in the U.S. 2 Aufl. Leipzig: Teub-
      ner-Verlag, 1955.

339   O'Conner, Richard. The German-Americans: An Informal
      History. Boston: Little, Brown & Co., 1968.

340   Peterson, Carl and Otto Scheel. Handwörterbuch des Grenz-
      und Auslanddeutschtums. Breslau: Ferdinand Hirt, 1933, 3 v.

341   Rattermann, Heinrich A. "Das deutsche Element in den Ver-
      einigten Staaten vor 1848, " DDP. 12 (July, 1880).

342   _____. Ein Leitfaden der deutsch-amerikanischen Geschichte
      Cincinnati, 1883. UC

343   Rauner, Friedrich.   Die Vereinigten Staaten von Nordamerika.
      Philadelphia, 1846.   UC

344   Rie, Robert.   "Austrians in the United States, " AGR.   29, i
      (1962): 30-31.

345   Sallet, Richard.   "Russlanddeutsche Siedlungen in den Vereinig-
      ten Staaten, " DAG.   (1931): 1-49.

346   _____.   "Germans in American Life 100 Years Ago, " AGR.
      9 (1942): 27-28, 38.

347   Schrader, Frederick.   The Germans in the Making of America.
      New York: Stratford, 1924.

348   Schreiber, Georg.   Deutschtum und Ausland: Studien zum Aus-
      landdeutschtum und zur Auslandkultur.   Münster: Aschendorf-
      fische Verlagsbuchhandlung, 1926.

349   Senn, Alfred.   The Swiss Record: Yearbook of the Swiss-
      American Historical Society.   Madison, Wisconsin: Swiss-
      American Historical Society, 1949-50, 2 v.

350   Smith, Rufus B.   The Influence of the Germans of the U.S. on
      its Life and Institutions.   n.p., n.d.   UC

351   Spaulding, E. Wilder.   The Quiet Invaders: Story of the Aus-
      trian Impact upon America.   Vienna: Oesterreichischer Bun-
      desverlag für Unterricht, Wissenschaft und Kunst, 1968.

352   Spier, H. O.   Man and Events in German-American History.
      New York: Stuyvesant Pr., 1940.

353   Spohr, Wilhelm.   Deutsche Arbeit in den Vereinigten Staaten.
      Berlin: Braun, 1931.

354   Statling, Gerhard.   Das goldene Buch der Deutschen in Amer-
      ika.   n.p., n.d.   UC

355   Stein, Herbert.   "Deutschland in Amerika--Vom Germany Val-
      ley, Germany Creek, Germanya und anderen deutschen Namen, "
      in Deutsch-Amerika Almanach.   New York: Verlag Plattdütsche
      Post, Inc., 1957.

356   Steinach, Adelrich.   Geschichte und Leben der Schweizer
      Kolonien in den Vereinigten Staaten von Nord-Amerika, New
      York, 1889.

357   Stumpp, Karl.   The German Russians.   New York: Atlantic
      Forum, 1967.

358   Swift, Lucius B.   The Germans in America.   Indianapolis,
      1916.   UC

359   Von Bosse, Georg. Das deutsche Element in den Vereinigten
      Staaten unter besonderer Berücksichtigung seines politischen,
      ethischen, sozialen und erzieherischen Einflusses. New York:
      1908. An important historical study. MPL UC UM

360   Von Hagen, Victor. Der Ruf der Neuen Welt. Deutsche bauen
      Amerika. Munich: Droemer, Knaur, 1970.

361   Von Loesch, Karl. Deutsche Züge im Antlitz der Erde:
      Deutsches Siedeln, Deutsche Leistung. Munich: Verlag F.
      Bruckmann, 1935.

362   Von Skal, Georg. Das amerikanische Volk. Berlin, 1908.
      UC

363   Walter, Hilde. "Die Deutschamerikaner, " Der Monat. 4 (1952):
      478-85.

364   Ward, Robert Elmer. Made in Germany--Some Reflections on
      Germany, America and German-America. Youngstown, Ohio,
      1969. A speech by the Chairman of the Society for German-
      American Studies.

365   Weaver, Glenn. "German Settlements in British North Amer-
      ica before the French and Indian War, " Social Studies. 44
      (1954): 283-90.

366   Wilk, Gerhard. "Mit Mozart in die Wildnis. Die deutschen
      Staatengründer in den Vereinigten Staaten, " NYSZH. Sonder-
      beilage (Dec. 28, 1969): 3, 12, 14, 16, 18.

367   Wittke, Carl. The Germans in America: Students Guide to
      Localized History. New York: Teachers College Pr., 1967.

368   _____. We Who Built America: The Saga of the Immi-
      grant. Rev. ed. Cleveland: Press of Western Reserve Uni-
      versity, 1964, pp. 67-100, 186-256.

369   Wust, Klaus. "Deutschamerikanische Geschichte auf Brief-
      marken, " DZf Briefmarkenkunde. 30 (1955): 868-69.

370   Zucker, A. E. "Natural Selection and the German-Americans, "
      RJGAH. 25 (1942): 7-12.

State Histories

ALABAMA

371   Thompson, Lawrence S. "Foreigners in Alabama, " AR. 5
      (1952): 282-89.

ARIZONA AND THE SOUTHWEST

372 Anderson, Lillie G. "A New Mexico Pioneer of the 1880's,"
     NMHR. 29 (1954): 245-58.

373 Bandelier, Adolf F. The Southwestern Journals of Adolf F.
     Bandelier, 1880-82. Ed. by C. H. Lange and C. Riley. Al-
     buquerque: University of New Mexico Pr., 1965.

374 Barnard, B. and C. F. Higham. True Story of Jacob Walzer.
     Apache, Arizona: Ranco Del Superstition, 1953. About Ari-
     zona-German prospectors.

375 Fierman, Floyd S. "Ernest Angerstein: Soldier, Merchant,
     Accused Secessionist and Post Trader," Password. (April,
     1962): 42-62.

376 _____. The Spiegelbergs of New Mexico, Merchants and
     Bankers 1844-1893 (Southwestern Studies, I). El Paso: Texas
     Western College Pr., 1964.

377 _____. "The Triangle and the Tetragrammaton," MNHR.
     37 (1962): 310-21.

378 Schroeder, Albert. "Documentary Evidence to the Early His-
     toric Period of South Arizona," NMHR. 27 (1952): 137-67.

379 Stein, Herbert. "Ein Deutscher findet Gold in Arizona," in:
     Der Deutsch-Amerikaner: Kalender für 1959. Staten Island:
     Verlag Stein, 1958.

ARKANSAS

380 Evans, Clarence. "A Cultural Link Between 19th Century
     Germany and the Arkansas Ozarks," MLJ. 35 (1951): 523-30.

381 _____. "Friedrich Gerstaecker: Social Chronicler of the
     Arkansas Frontier," AHQ. 6 (1948): 440-49.

382 _____. "Memoirs, Letters and Diary Entries of German
     Settlers in Northwest Arkansas, 1853-1863," AHQ. 6 (1947):
     225-49.

383 _____ and L. Albrecht. "Friedrich Gerstaecker in Arkan-
     sas. Selections from His Streif- und Jagdzüge durch die
     Vereinigten Staaten Nordamerikas," AHQ. 5 (1946): 39-57.

384 Geisler, Samuel W. "Heinrich Carl Beyrich in Arkansas
     Territory, 1834," Field & Lab. (June, 1956).

385 Gerbich, Otto. "More about the Reverend Adam Buerkle,
     Founder of Stuttgart, Arkansas," Grand Prairie HSB. 12 (Jan-
     uary, 1969): 3-6.

386 Hollyday, Guy. "Albert von Halfern's Der Squire: A Novel about Life in Early Arkansas," AHQ. 37 (1968): 226-45.

387 Kiech, V. C. "The Kiech Family and Nettleton," Craighood CHQ. 8 (1970): 2-14.

388 Mitchell, John B. "An Analysis of Arkansas' Population by Race, Nativity and Residence," AHQ. 8 (1949): 115-32.

389 Rothrock, Thomas. "David Bridenthal," AHQ. 17 (1958): 73-78.

390 Thompson, Lawrence. "Foreign Travel Books on Arkansas, 1900-1950," AHQ. 11 (1952): 176-83.

391 Westermeier, Therese. "Die Grand Prairie von Arkansas," AHQ. 15 (1956): 76-84.

392 Wolf, J. "Journal of Charles Heinrich, 1849-1856," AHQ. 24 (1965): 241-83.

393 Wolfe, Jonathan. "Background of German Immigration to Arkansas," AHQ. 25 (1966): 151-82, 248-78, 354-85.

CALIFORNIA

394 Baegert, John. Observations in Lower California. Trans. by M. Brandenburg and C. Baumann. Berkeley: University' of California Pr., 1951.

395 Broadbent, Thomas. "The Schiller Centennial in Columbia: California Germans in a Gold-Rush Town," AGR. 24, vi (1963): 7-13.

396 Dillon, Richard. Fool's Gold: The Decline and Fall of Captain John Sutter of California. New York: Coward-McCann, 1967.

397 Dyck, Cornelius. "In the California Gold Rush," ML. 11 (1956): 25-28, 80-81.

398 Dyck, Mrs. Wilhelm. "Drei Monate im goldenen Staat Kalifornien," M. Rundschau. (Oct. 7, 17, 24, 1973).

399 Francl, Joseph. The Overland Journey of Joseph Francl: The First Bohemian to Cross the Plains to the California Gold Fields. San Francisco: Wreden, 1968.

400 Geiger, V. Trail to California: The Overland Journey of Vincent Geiger and Wakeman Bryarly. Rev. ed. by D. Potter. New Haven: Yale University Pr., 1962.

401 Gerstäcker, Friedrich. Scenes of Life in California. Trans. by G. Cosgrave. San Francisco: Grabhorn, 1942.

402 Goethe Bicentennial, San Francisco, 1749-1949. San Francisco: German-American Societies of San Francisco, 1949.

403 Gudde, Erwin. "The Goethe Festival in San Francisco, " AGR. 16, iii (1950): 20-21.

404 _____. "The Two Sequoias, " NA. 1 (1953): 118-27.

405 Hauschild-Thiessen, Renate. Die ersten Hamburger im Goldland Kalifornien. (Vorträge und Aufsätze hrsg. vom Verein für Hamburgische Geschichte, 17). Hamburg: Hans Christian, 1969.

406 Lenhart, John. "Fr. Weninger's Trip from Oregon to San Francisco in 1869, " SJR. 36 (1954): 43-44, 129-131.

407 Lewis, Oscar. Sutter's Fort: Gateway to the Gold Fields. Englewood Cliffs: Prentice-Hall, 1966.

408 Lienhard, Heinrich. From St. Louis to Sutter's Fort, 1846. Ed. & trans. by Erwin and E. Gudde. Norman: University of Oklahoma Pr., 1961.

409 Och, Joseph. Missionary in Sonora: The Travel Reports of Joseph Och, S. J., 1775-67. Ed. by T. Treutlein. San Francisco: California Historical Society, 1965.

410 Pfefferkorn, Ignaz. Sonora: A Description of the Province. Ed. by T. Treutlein. Albuquerque: University of New Mexico Pr., 1949.

411 Raup, H. F. "Anaheim: A German Community of Frontier California, " AGR. 12 (1945): 7-11.

412 _____. German Colonization of Anaheim, California. Berkeley, 1932.

413 Rocq, Margaret. California Local History: A Bibliography and Union List of Library Holdings. 2d ed. Stanford: Stanford University Pr., 1970.

414 Rosenberger, F. The Robinson-Rosenberger Journey to the Gold Fields of California 1849-50: The Diary of Zirkle D. Robinson. Iowa City, Iowa: Prairie Pr., 1966.

415 Stewart, George. The Opening of the California Trail. Berkeley: University of California Pr., 1953.

416 Studer, Jack. "Julius Kellersberger: A Swiss as Surveyer and City Planner in California, 1851-1857, " CHSQ. 47 (1968): 3-14.

CAROLINAS

417   Alfonte, James.   "New Crop for Winston-Salem, " Opera News.
       33 (1969): 6 ff.

418   Boehme, Anton.   Das verlangte, nicht erlangte Canaan bei den
       Lustgräbern: Oder ausführliche Beschreibung von der unglück-
       lichen Reise derer jüngsthin aus Teutschland nach den Engel-
       ländischen in Amerika gelegenen Carolina... Frankfurt: An-
       drea, MDCCXL NN

419   Bolzius, Johann.   "Journal of a Trip from Georgia to South
       Carolina, " Luth Q. 16 (1964): 164 ff.

420   Chyet, Stanley.   "Ludwig Lewisohn in Charleston 1892-1903, "
       AJHQ. 59 (1965): 296-322.

421   Coenen, F.   "German Settlements of Ridgeway, North Carolina, "
       AGR. 17, i (1950): 15-16.

422   Dill, A. T.   "Eighteenth Century New Bern: A History of the
       Town and Craven County, 1700-1800, " NCHR. 22 (1945): 1-21.

423   Godcharles, F.   "New Bern, " NCHS 13 (1943): 119-25.

424   Graeff, Arthur.   "In Dixieland, " Eck. (Feb. 7, 14, 21, 1953).

425   Hammer, Carl.   Rhinelanders on the Yadkin: The Story of
       the Pennsylvania Germans in Rowan and Caburrus.   Salisbury,
       North Carolina: Rowan Printing Co., 1943.

426   Keller, Hans.   "Christoph von Graffenried und die Gründung
       von Neu-Bern in Nord-Carolina, " Archiv des Hist. Vereins
       des Kantons Bern. (1953): 249-90.

427   Lawson, John.   A Voyage to Carolina.   Chapel Hill: Univer-
       sity of North Carolina Pr., 1969.

428   Lefler, H. T.   Guide to the Study and Reading of North Caro-
       lina History.   3d ed.   Chapel Hill: University of North Caro-
       lina Pr., 1969.

429   Nixon, Joseph.   German Settlers in Lincoln County and West-
       ern North Carolina.   Chapel Hill: University of North Carolina
       Pr., 1912.

430   Patton, James.   "Letters from North Carolina Emigrants in
       the Old Northwest, 1830-34, " MVHR. 47 (1960): 227-63.

431   Quattlebaum, Paul.   "Quattlebaum: A Palatine Family in
       South Carolina, " SCHGM. 48 (1947): 1-11; 49 (1948): 41-56,
       104-18, 170-86, 231-45.

432   Ramsey, Robert. Carolina Cradle: Settlement of the North-
      west Carolina Frontier, 1747-62. Chapel Hill: University of
      North Carolina Pr., 1964.

433   Schirmer, Jacob. "The Schirmer Diary," SCHM. 67 (1966):
      167-71, 229-33; 68 (1967): 37-41.

434   Thompson, Lawrence S. "Foreigners in North Carolina,"
      NCHR. 31 (1954): 34-40.

435   Tobler, John. "John Tobler's Description of South Carolina,"
      SCHM. 71 (1970): 141-61, 257-65.

436   Turnbull, R. J. Bibliography of South Carolina 1563-1950.
      Charlottsville: University of Virginia Pr., 1956.

437   Urlsperger, Samuel. Der ausführliche Nachrichter von der
      Königlich-Gross-Britanischen Colonie Saltzburgischer Emigranten
      in Amerika. Halle: In Verlegung des Waysenhauses, 1735-52.
      NN

438   Van de Luyster, Nelson. "The German Friendly Society of
      Charleston," AGR. 26, iv (1960): 20-23, 36.

439   Velthusen, Johann. Nordcarolinische Kirchennachrichten. Leip-
      zig, 1790. NN

440   Voigt, Gilbert. "Cultural Contributions of German Settlers to
      South Carolina," SCHGM. 53 (1952): 183-89.

441   Weeks, Stephen. Bibliography of the Historical Literature of
      North Carolina. Cambridge: Harvard University, 1895.

442   Wust, Klaus. "The Pennsylvania Germans in North Carolina:
      A Challenge to Future Historians," Eck. (July 18, 1964).

                          COLORADO

443   Goodykoontz, Colin. "The People of Colorado," CM. 23 (1946):
      241-55.

444   Henel, Heinrich. "The Goethe Bicentennial Convocation at
      Aspen," MO. 41 (1949): 295-302.

445   MacArthur, Mildred. Germans in Colorado. Repr.: San
      Francisco: R & E Associates, 1972.

446   Spieler, G. "The Germans of Colorado," AGR. 10 (1944): 20-
      23.

447   Westermeier, Therese. "Colorado Festivals," CM. 28 (1951):
      172-83.

448   Wilcox, Virginia. Colorado: A Selected Bibliography of its
      Literature 1858-1952. Denver: Sage Books, 1954.

                              DAKOTAS

449   Brost, Carl. "Dakota Mission," AGR. 27, v (1961): 26-27.

450   Janssen, Hans. "Bishop Martin Marty in the Dakotas," AGR.
      27, v (1961): 24-26.

451   _____. "The Wetzlaff Family: Cultivated Pioneers in
      Dakota Territory," AGR. 27, vi (1961): 29-31.

•452 Jennewein, J. Leonard and J. Boorman. Dakota Panorama.
      Mitchell, South Dakota: Dakota Territorial Centennial Com-
      mission, 1961.

453   Miller, Tarrel. The Dakotans. Menno, South Dakota, 1964.

454   Mutschelknaus, Friedrich. "Migration of the First Russian
      Germans to Dakota," NH. 49 (1968): 383-92.

455   "North Dakota Historical Society of Germans from Russia, Inc.:
      100-jähriges Jubiläum der Deutschen von Russland vom 8. bis
      zum 10. Juni 1973 in Bismarck, North Dakota," DMH. (June
      7, 1973).

456   Rolfsrud, Erling. "Wrong Side Up," NDG. 18 (1951): 41-44.

457   Schell, Herbert. "The German Heritage in South Dakota,"
      AGR. 27, v (1961): 5-9.

458   Schnell, Kempes. "John F. Funk's Land Inspection Trips as
      Recorded in His Diaries 1872 and 1873," MQR. 24 (1950): 295-
      311.

459   Stevens, O. A. "Maximilian in North Dakota: 1833-34,"
      NDH. 28 (1962): 163-69.

460   Zimmerman, Joseph. "The Letters of Fr. Joseph A. Zim-
      merman, S. J.," SJR. 54 (1962): 311-14, 348-52, 387-89; 55
      (1963): 273-79.

                              DELAWARE

461   Abeles, Julius. The German Element in Wilmington from 1850
      to 1914. Dissertation: University of Delaware, 1949.

462   Hesselius, Andreas. "Journal, 1711-1724 edited by Amandus
      Johnson," Del. H. 2 (1947): 69-118.

GEORGIA

463   Bolzius, Johnann. "August, 1748 in Georgia, from the Diary
       of John Martin Bolzius, " GaHQ. 47 (1963): 204-16.

464   _____. "Johann Martin Bolzius Answers a Questionnaire
       on Carolina and Georgia, " WMQ. 14 (1957): 218-61; 15 (1958):
       228-52.

465   _____. "John Martin Bolzius Reports on Georgia, " GaHQ.
       47 (1963): 216-19.

466   _____. "Pastor Bolzius Letter of June, 1737 to a Friend
       in Berlin, " G. Rev. 18 (1964): 457-62.

467   _____. "The Secret Diary of Pastor Johann Martin Bolt-
       zius, " GaHQ. 53 (1969): 78-110.

468   _____. "September, 1748 in Georgia, from the Diary of
       John Martin Bolzius, " GaHQ. 47 (1963): 320-32.

469   Callaway, James. The Early Settlement of Georgia. Athens:
       University of Georgia Pr., 1948.

470   Coulter, E. M. List of Early Settlers of Georgia. Athens:
       University of Georgia Pr., 1948.

471   DeBaillou, Clemens. "The Diaries of the Moravian Brother-
       hood at the Cherokee Mission in Spring Place, Georgia, for
       the Years 1800-1804, " GaHQ. 54 (1970): 125-39.

472   Huth, Hans. "Salzburgers in Georgia, " AGR. 9 (1943): 17-20.

473   Jones, G. Fenwick. "Collection of Georgia Historical Society,
       Other Documents and Notes: The Secret Diary of Pastor Jo-
       hann Martin Boltzius, " GaHQ. 49 (1965): 78-110.

474   _____. Detailed Report on the Salzburger Emigrants Who
       Settled in America.... Ed. by Samuel Ursperger. Athens:
       University of Georgia Pr., 1968.

475   _____. "The German Element in Colonial Georgia, "
       RJGAH. 31 (1963): 71-82.

476   _____. "In Memoriam: John Martin Boltzius, 1703-65, "
       Luth. Q. 17 (1965): 151-66.

477   _____. "Von Reck's Second Report from Georgia, " Will.
       & Mary Q. 22 (1966): 319-33.

478   Kramer, Johann. Neueste und richtigste Nachrichten von der
       Landschaft Georgia in dem Engelländischen Amerika. Göttin-
       gen: Universitätsbuchdruckerei, 1746. NN

479 Lewis, Andrew. Collections of the Georgia Historical Society,
     Other Documents and Notes: Henry Muhlenberg's Georgia Cor-
     respondence, " GaHQ. 49 (1965): 424-54.

480 Newman, Henry. Henry Newman's Salzburger Letterbooks.
     Ed. by G. F. Jones. (Wormsloe Foundation Publ., 8). Ath-
     ens: University of Georgia Pr., 1966.

481 Rowland, Arthur. Bibliography of the Writings on Georgia His-
     tory. Hamden, Conn.: Shoe String Pr., 1966.

482 Rubincam, Milton. "Historical Background of the Salzburger
     Emigration to Georgia, " GaHQ. 35 (1951): 99-115.

483 Strobel, P. A. The Salzburgers and Their Descendents.
     Athens: University of Georgia Pr., 1953.

484 Tresp, Lothar. "Pastor Bolzius Reports Life in Georgia
     among the Salzburgers, " AGR. 29, iv (1963): 20-23, 39.

485 Urlsperger, Samuel. Amerikanisches Ackerwerk Gottes: Oder
     zuverlässige Nachrichten ... von salzburgischen Emigranten
     erbauten Pflanzstad Ebenezer in Georgien. Augsburg, 1754-
     67. 5 v. NN

486 _____. Ausführliche Nachrichten von den saltzburgischen
     Emigranten ... wie auch eine Beschreibung von Georgien.
     Halle: In Verlegung des Waysenhauses, 1774. NN

487 _____. Detailed Reports on the Salzburger Emigrants Who
     Settled in America. Ed. by G. F. Jones. Athens: University
     of Georgia Pr., 1969.

488 Von Reck, Philipp. "Commissary von Reck's Report on Geor-
     gia, " GaHQ. 47 (1963): 95-110.

489 _____. "Journal of Travel in Colonial America, May-July
     1734, " RJGAH. 31 (1963): 95-110.

490 Weaver, Herbert. "Foreigners in Ante-Bellum Savannah, "
     GaHQ. 37 (1953): 1-17.

                               ILLINOIS

491 Angle, Paul. "A German Family in Chicago, 1856, " Chic. H.
     4 (1957): 309-17.

492 Baroni, Werner. "Zur 8. Steubenparade das Verdienstkreuz, "
     A-W. (Sept. 9, 1973).

493 Baus, John. An alle Deutschen zum deutschen Tag. Chicago,
     1893. UC

494 Becker, Sabine. "Sixty Years Chicago Columbia Club, " AGR.
     20, i (1953): 18-19.

495 Bettis, Norman. The Swiss Community of Highland, Illinois:
     A Study in Historical Geography. Macomb: Western Illinois
     University Pr., 1968.

496 Cavanagh, Helen. Seed, Soil and Science: The Story of Eu-
     gene Funk. Chicago: Lakeside Pr., 1959.

497 "Dr. Ludwig A. Fritsch beging seinen 80. Geburtstag, " DDA.
     (Sept., 1973).

498 Dundore, M. Walter. "Pennsylvania German Transplants in
     Illinois, " Eck. (April 23, 30, 1960).

499 Gustorf, Frederick. "Frontier Perils Told by an Early Illinois
     Visitor, " JIHS. 55, ii (1962): 136-56.

500 Klett, Ada. "Belleville Germans Look at America, " JIHS. 40,
     i (1947): 23-37.

501 "Leonard Enders, " A-W. (August 26, 1973). About a national-
     ly known Illinois-German.

502 Liedloff, Helmut. "German Climate in Illinois, " AGR. 31
     (1964): 33-36.

503 Ochs, Debbie. "Germans in Illinois: Belleville was First, "!
     Illinois H. 23 (1970): 127.

504 Sanders, Walter. "Settlers in Montgomery County, Illinois
     Previous to 1840, " NGSQ. 39, ii (1952): 72-75.

505 Short, Karen. "Germans in Illinois: The Freeport Way, "
     Illinois H. 23 (1970): 128.

506 Tonsor, Stephen. "I am My Own Boss: A German Immigrant
     Writes from Illinois, " SHS. 54 (1961): 392-404.

                          INDIANA

507 Andressohn, John. "The Kothe Letters, " IMH. 43 (1947): 171-
     80. Letters of an 1850 emigrant.

508 Barba, Preston. "The Story of Tell City, " AGR. 8 (1942):
     28-31.

509 Borntreger, Hans. Zum Andenken von Joseph Borntreger.
     Shipshewana, Indiana: R. S. Borntreger, 1952.

510 Frederick, Robert. Colonel Richard Lieber: Conservationist

and Park Builder: The Indiana Years. Dissertation: Indiana
University, 1960.

511   Gudde, Erwin. "Robinson Crusoe in the Sierra Nevada: The
      Story of Moses Schallenberger at Donner Lake in 1844-45,"
      Sierra Club B. 36 (1951): 19-28. About an Indiana-German.

512   Land, Elfrieda. "An Analysis of Northern Indiana's Popula-
      tion in 1850," IMH. 49 (1953): 17-60.

513   _____. "Conditions of Travel by German Immigrants to
      Dubois County, Indiana," IMH. 41 (1945): 327-44.

514   _____. "German Immigration to Dubois County, Indiana
      During the 19th Century," IMH. 41 (1945): 131-51.

515   _____. "German Influence in the Churches and Schools of
      Dubois County, Indiana," IMH. 42 (1946): 151-72.

516   _____. "The Settlement of Dubois County," IMH. 41 (1945):
      245-64.

517   _____. "Some Characteristics of German Immigrants in
      Dubois County, Indiana," IMH. 42 (1946): 29-46.

518   Lilly, Eli. Schliemann in Indianapolis. Indianapolis: Indiana
      Historical Society, 1961.

519   Yoder, Marie. "The Balk Dutch Settlements near Goshen, In-
      diana," MQR. 30 (1956): 32-43.

                                    IOWA

520   Binder-Johnson, Hildegard. "The Claus Groth Guild of Daven-
      port, Iowa," AGR. 11 (1944): 26-29.

521   Calkin, Homer. "The Coming of the Foreigners," Palimpsest.
      43 (1962): 153-60.

522   "Diamond Jubilee: German Russian Colonists, 1876-1951,"
      KHQ. 20 (1952): 72.

523   "Iowa's Notable Dead," AI. 33 (1956): 468-69. About Alfred
      Steiner.

524   Peterson, William. "The Switzerland of Iowa: Then and Now:
      The Land of Enchantment," Palimpsest. 47 (1966): 385-90.

525   Schreiber, Augusta. "The Pioneer Boyhood of Charles August
      Ficke," AGR. 12, iv (1946): 12-13.

526   "Source Material of Iowa History," IJH. 70 (1954): 150-51.

527 "Wilhelm Schneider, " Des Moines Sunday Reg. (August 21,
     1949).

KANSAS

528 Beyer, George. "Pennsylvania Germans Move to Kansas, " PH.
     32 (1965): 25-48.

529 Carman, J. N. Foreign-Language Units of Kansas: Historical
     Atlas and Statistics. Lawrence: University of Kansas, 1962.

530 _____. "German Settlements along the Atchison, Topeka
     and Santa Fe Railway, " KHQ. 38 (1962): 310-16.

531 _____. "Germans in Kansas, " AGR. 27, iv (1961): 4-8.

532 Dyck, A. J. "Hoffnungsau in Kansas, " ML. 4, iv (1949): 18-
     19.

533 Johannes, Mary. Study of the Russian-German Elements in
     Ellis County, Kansas. (Studies in Sociology, 14). Washington:
     Catholic University of America, 1946.

534 Möllhausen, H. B. "Over the Santa Fe Trail through Kansas
     in 1858, " KHQ. 16 (1948): 337-80.

535 Mueller, Amelia. There Have to be Six: A True Story of
     Pioneering in the Midwest. Scottdale, Pa.: Herald Pr., 1966.

536 Pekari, Matthew. "German-Russian Settlements in Ellis County,
     Kansas, " Ellis County News. (October 11, 18, 1951).

KENTUCKY

537 Bier, Justus. "Carl C. Brenner: A German American Land-
     scapist, " AGR. 17, iv (1951): 20-25, 33.

538 Jillson, Willard. Kentucky History: A Check and Finding List
     of the Principal Published and Manuscript Sources of the Gen-
     eral, Regional and County History of the Commonwealth 1729-
     1936. Louisville: Standard Printing, 1936.

539 Jordan, Terry. "Between the Forest and the Prairie, " AH.
     38 (1964): 205-16.

540 Koester, Leonard. "A Checklist: The German I. O. O. F. in
     Kentucky, " FCHQ. 39 (1965): 249-57.

541 _____. "The First Turner Society in America, " in 100th
     Anniversary, Louisville Turners. Louisville: Louisville
     Turners, 1950, pp. 5-11.

542   Noe, Sam v. "The Louisville Public Schools: Their Names
      and Their History," FCHQ. 38 (1964): 242-60.

543   Robertson, John.   "Paducah: Origins to Second Class," KHS.
      66 (1968): 108-36.

544   Rowell, Elsie.   The Social and Cultural Contributions of the
      Germans in Louisville from 1848 to 1855.   Dissertation: Uni-
      versity of Kentucky, 1941.

545   Schmidt, Albert.   "A European Commentary on Kentucky and
      Kentuckians, circa 1825," KHS. 57 (1959): 243-56.

546   Stein, Louis E.   "Das Deutschtum in Kentucky," DAG. 8 (Jan-
      uary, 1908).

547   Stierlin, Ludwig.   Der Staat Kentucky und die Stadt Louisville
      mit besonderer Berücksichtigung des deutschen Elementes.
      Louisville: Anzeiger, 1873.   UC UK

548   Tolzmann, Don Heinrich.   "Deutsch-Amerikanisches aus Ken-
      tucky," DMH. (Oct. 18, 1973).

549   Weisert, John.   "Germans and the Southern Labor Shortage,
      1865-66," AGR. 30 (1964): 29-31.

                              LOUISIANA

550   Blume, Helmut.   "Deutsche Kolonisten im Mississippidelta,"
      JAS. (1955): 177-83.

551   Deiler, J. H.   The Settlement of the German Coast of Louisi-
      ana.   Repr.:   Baltimore: Genealogical Pub., 1972.

552   Fossier, A. E.   "Dr. Otto Lerch, 1855-1948," LHQ. 33
      (1952): 343-48.

553   Goessl, Alfred.   "Die ersten deutschen Ansiedler am Unterlauf
      des Mississippi," in The 43d National Saengerfest of the North
      American Singer's Union.   New Orleans: Deutsches Haus,
      1958, pp. 41-45.

554   Nau, John F.   The German People of New Orleans.   Leiden,
      Netherlands: Brill, 1958.

555   Oppel, Jorst.   "Die deutsche Siedlung in Louisiana im Spiegel
      des Amerika-Romanes der Goethezeit," in Studies in German
      Literature (Louisiana State University Studies, Humanities
      Series, 13).   Baton, 1963.

556   Reinders, Robert.   A Social History of New Orleans 1850-60.
      Dissertation: University of Texas, 1958.

557 Schlegel, Hans. "Deutsches Haus of New Orleans and the
     German Settlers," in: The 43d National Saengerfest of the
     North American Singer's Union. New Orleans: Deutsches
     Haus, 1958, pp. 47-51.

558 Thompson, Lawrence S. "Books in Foreign Languages about
     Louisiana, 1900-50," LHQ. 34 (1953): 35-57.

MAINE

559 Riley, Thomas. "Maine," AGR. 31, vi (1965): 25-26.

560 Stahl, Jasper. History of Old Broad Bay and Waldoboro.
     Portland, Maine: Bond Wheelwright Co., 1956.

MARYLAND

561 Adler, Betty and John Wilhelm. H. L. M.: The Mencken Bib-
     liography. Baltimore: Johns Hopkins Pr., 1961.

562 Ankrum, Freeman. Maryland and Pennsylvania Historical
     Sketches. West Newton, Pa.: Author, 1947.

563 Beadenkopf, Anne. "The Baltimore Public Baths and Their
     Founder Rev. Thomas M. Beadenkopf," MdHM. 45 (1950): 201-
     14.

564 Beirne, Francis. The Amiable Baltimoreans. New York:
     Dutton, 1951.

565 Brooks, Van Wyck. "Mencken in Baltimore," ASch. 20 (1951):
     409-21.

566 Caspari, Fritz. "The Baltimore Riots of 1861," Newberry Lib.
     B. (May, 1952). About Wilhelm Rapp.

567 Century of Health 1849-1949, American Turners, Baltimore.
     Baltimore: American Turners, 1949.

568 Cunz, Dieter. "The Baltimore Germans in the Year 1848,"
     AGR. 10 (1943): 30-33.

569 _____. "Contributions of the German Element to the Growth
     of the University of Maryland," RJGAH. 26 (1945): 7-15.

570 _____. "DeKalb and Maryland," RJGAH. 25 (1942): 18-22.

571 _____. "The German-Americans in Cumberland, Md.,"
     AGR. 13, ii (1946): 15-16, 35.

572 _____. "German Settlers in Early Colonial Maryland,"
     MdHM. 42 (1947): 101-08.

573   . "The Germans in Maryland: A Story of Useful
Citizens," RJGAH. 31 (1963): 11-18.

574   . "The Goethe Societies of Maryland and the District
of Columbia, 1948-51," MO. 43 (1951): 414-15.

575   . The Maryland Germans: A History. Princeton:
Princeton University Pr., 1948.

576   . "Die Marylander Goethe Gesellschaft," MO. 38
(1946): 367-70.

577   . "The Otterbein Church Incident in Baltimore, "
AGR. 14, i (1947): 15-17.

578   . "The Rise and Fall of the German Americans in
Baltimore," CG. 7, iii (1947): 61-71.

579   . "Wiesenthal's Pioneer Medical Work," AGR. 9
(1942): 13-14, 37.

580   Davis, Arthur. "German Settlements on the Eastern Shore of
Maryland, " RJGAH. 25 (1942): 23-26.

581   Foster, Augustus. "Sir Augustus J. Foster in Maryland.
Edited by Margaret K. Latimer," MdHM. 47 (1952): 283-96.

582   Franke, Otto. "One Hundred Years of the General German
Orphan Home in Baltimore, 1863-1963, " RJGAH. 31 (1963):
47-58.

583   Gleis, Paul. "Eighteenth Century Maryland through the Eyes
of German Travellers, " RJGAH. 28 (1953): 44-53.

584   Hart, Archibald. Calvert and Hillyer, 1897-1947. Baltimore:
Waverly Pr., 1947.

585   Klein, Frederic. "Union Mills: The Shriver Homestead, "
MHM. 52 (1957): 290-306.

586   Land, Aubrey. "A Land Speculator in the Opening of Western
Maryland, " MHM. 48 (1953): 191-203.

587   Mish, Mary. "Jonathan Hager of Hagerstown, " AGR. 15, .iii
(1949): 20-23.

588   Prahl, Augustus J. "American Goethe Society, " MO. 51 (1959):
248.

589   . "The Goethe Societies of Baltimore and Washington, "
RJGAH. 29 (1956): 58-63.

590   . "History of the German Gymnastic Movement in

Baltimore, " RJGAH. 26 (1945): 16-29.

591 Quynn, William. "The Diary of Jacob Engelbrecht: Chronicle
of Life in Frederick, Maryland from 1819 Until 1878, " RJGAH.
31 (1963): 63-65.

592 Schwartz, Ernest. "Jacob Engelbrecht's Diary, " AGR. 28
(1962): 8-9.

593 Semmes, Raphael. Baltimore, As Seen by Visitors 1783-1860.
Baltimore: Maryland Historical Society, 1953.

594 Snyder, William. "Charles Frederick Wiesenthal (1726-89):
An Appraisal of the Medical Pioneer of Baltimore, " RJGAH.
32 (1966): 47-58.

595 Steiner, Carl. "Die Goethe Gesellschaft von Washington, "
MFDU. 60 (1968): 394-97.

596 Thompson, Lawrence S. "Foreign Travellers in Maryland:
1900-50, " MHM. 48 (1953): 337-43.

597 Werbow, Stanley. "Goethe Celebrations in Maryland 1949, "
RJGAH. 27 (1950): 71-73.

598 Wust, Klaus. "Beiträge zur Geschichte der Deutschen im
Distrikt von Columbia, " WJ. (Sept. 2; Oct. 4, 11, 17, 25;
Nov. 8, 15, 22, 29; Dec. 6, 1957; Jan. 3, 10, 17, 24; Feb.
14, 21, 28; March 7; April 4, 11, 18; Oct. 10, 17, 1958).
First historical study on the Germans in the District of Colum-
bia.

599 _____. Pioneers in Service: The German Society of
Maryland, 1783-1958. Baltimore: The German Society, 1958.

600 _____. "A Proud Record of Service: The German Society
of Maryland, 1783-1958, " AGR. 24, iii (1958): 29-30, 39.

601 _____. "A Silesian Village in Maryland: Silesia, Founded
in 1892, " RJGAH. 31 (1963): 91.

602 Zucker, A. E. "A Mencken Reminiscence, " RJGAH. 29 (1956):
68-69.

MICHIGAN

603 Braun, Frank and Robert Brown. "Karl Neidhard's Reise nach
Michigan, " MichH. 35 (1951): 32-84.

604 Florer, W. W. Early Michigan Settlements. Ann Arbor:
The Author, 1941-52, 2 v.

605   Frank, Louis. Pionierjahre der deutsch-amerikanischen Fami-
      lien Frank-Kerber in Wisconsin-Michigan 1849-64. Milwaukee,
      1911. UC

606   Germania: Fünfzig Jahre deutschen Strebens. Saginaw, Michi-
      gan, 1906. UC

607   Groos, Joseph and H. Vanderberghe. Trail of the Pioneers.
      Escanaba, Mich.: Mead, 1960.

608   Jenks, William. "Michigan Immigration, " MHM. 28 (1944):
      67-100.

609   Nelson, June. "Port Crescent: Saginaw Bay Ghost Town to
      Life Again, " MichH. 46 (1962): 303-10.

610   Perejda, Andrew. "Sources and Dispersal of Michigan's Popu-
      lation, " MHR. 32 (1948): 355-66.

611   Schultz, Gerard. A History of Michigan's Thumb. Elkton:
      G. Schultz, 1964.

612   Vander Hill, C. Warren. Settling the Great Lakes Frontier:
      Immigration to Michigan, 1847-1924. Lansing: Michigan His-
      torical Commission, 1970.

                                MINNESOTA

613   Blegen, Theodore and T. Nydahl. Minnesota History: A Guide
      to Reading and Study. Minneapolis: University of Minnesota
      Pr., 1960.

614   "Deutsche Tagfeier am 9. Juni, " OVZT. (June 7, 1968).

615   Flanagan, John T. "Thirty Years of Minnesota Fiction, " MH.
      31 (1950): 129-47.

616   Gilman, Rhoda. "Zeppelin in Minnesota: A Study in Fact and
      Fable, " MH. 39 (1965): 278-85.

617   Heilbron, Bertha. "Some Sources for Northwest History,
      Pennsylvania German Baptismal Certificates in Minnesota, "
      MH. 27 (1946): 29-32.

618   Hilger, Frederick. "Die Reise nach Amerika: Aus einem
      alten Tagebuch, " ZKA. 20, (1970): 33-36.

619   Hoeffler, Adolf and J. F. Francis. "Minnesota 100 Years
      Ago, " MH. 33 (1952): 112-25.

620   Iverson, Noel. Germania, U. S. A.: Social Change in New
      Ulm, Minnesota. Minneapolis: University of Minnesota Pr.,
      1966.

621   James, Jean. "Minnesota: A Blend of New and Old Worlds, "
      Minn. Trib. Centennial Edition. (August 28, 1949).

622   Johnson, Hildegard B. "The Distribution of the German Pio-
      neer Population in Minnesota, " Rural Soc. 6 (1941).

623   _____. "Eduard Pelz and German Emigration, " MH. 31
      (1950): 222-30.

624   _____. "The Founding of New Ulm, Minnesota, " AGR. 12,
      vi (1946): 8-12.

625   _____. "Intermarriages Between German Pioneers and
      Other Nationalities in Minnesota in 1860 and 1870, " AJS. 51
      (1946): 299-304.

626   _____. "The Volksfest Association of Minnesota, " AGR.
      25, iv (1959): 31-32.

627   Kingston, C. S. "The Northern Overland Route in 1867, "
      PNQ. 61 (1950): 234-53.

628   Krahn, Cornelius. "Some Letters of Bernhard Warkentin Per-
      taining to the Migration of 1873-75, " MQR. 24 (1950): 248-62.

629   Lewis, Henry. The Valley of the Mississippi Illustrated. Ed.
      by B. Heilbron and trans. by H. Poatgieter. St. Paul: Min-
      nesota Historical Society, 1968.

630   Minnesota German Radio Committee: 1973 Schedule: German
      Radio Services on WCAL. Northfield, Minnesota: Minnesota
      German Radio Committee, 1972. Lists German-speaking min-
      isters.

631   Nix, Jacob. Der Ausbruch der Sioux-Indianer in Minnesota
      im August 1862. New Ulm, 1887. UC

632   Qualey, Carlton. "Some National Groups in Minnesota, " MH.
      31 (1950): 18-32.

633   Rippley, LaVern. "Clearing Timberland was Big Job for Pio-
      neers, " GN. (July 26, 1972).

634   _____. "Minnesota Worked Hard to Attract German Immi-
      grants, " GN. (Nov. 17, 1971).

635   Robison, Charles. "Minnie Eysenbach, 1840-1927, " Allen Cty.
      Reporter. (1968): pp. 55 ff. About a New Ulm German.

636   Rothfuss, Hermann E. "Deutsche Geselligkeit an der Indianer-
      grenze, " NYSZH. (Oct. 7, 14, 21, 28; Nov. 4, 11, 1951).

637   _____. "German Witnesses of the Sioux Campaigns, " NDH.
      25 (1958): 123-33.

638   "Stimmungsvolle Weihnachtsfeier des deutschsprachigen Rund-
       funksenders KUXL, " OVZT. (Dec. 12, 1969).

639   Tolzmann, Don Heinrich. "New Ulm, Minnesota, " DMH.
       (July 5, 1973).

640   Tyler, Alice. "William Pfaender and the Founding of New
       Ulm, " MH. 30 (1949): 24-35.

MISSISSIPPI

641   Futrell, Robert. "Efforts of Mississippians to Encourage Im-
       migration, 1865-1880, " JMH. 20 (1958): 59-75.

642   Smith, Claude. "Official Efforts by the State of Mississippi
       to Encourage Immigration, 1868-86, " JMH. 32 (1970): 327-40.

643   Thompson, Lawrence S. "Bibliography of Foreign Language
       Books about Mississippi, " JMH. 14 (1952): 202-07.

644   Weaver, Herbert. "Foreigners in Ante-Bellum Mississippi, "
       JMH. 16 (1954): 151-63.

MISSOURI

645   [Bek.]   "William G. Bek, " MHR. 43 (1948): 186.

646   Bek, William G. "Nicholas Hesse: German Visitor to Mis-
       souri, 1835-37, " MHR. 41 (1946): 19-44, 164-83, 285-304,
       373-90; 42 (1947): 34-49, 140-52, 241-48.

647   Blum, Virgil. The German Element in St. Louis, 1859-61.
       Dissertation: St. Louis University, 1945.

648   Bowen, Elbert. "Amusements and Entertainments in Early
       Missouri, " MHR. 47 (1952): 310-11.

649   _____. "The Circus in Early Rural Missouri, " MHR. 47
       (1952): 1-7.

650   Christopher, Adrienne. "Franz Hahn: The Village Black-
       smith, " Westport HQ. 5 (March, 1970).

651   Crockett, Norman. "A Study of Confusion: Missouri's Mi-
       gration Program, 1865-1916, " MHR. 57 (1962): 248-60.

651A   Espenschied, Lloyd. "Conrad Weber and His Family: Set-
       tlers on an Historica Carondelet Site, " MHSB. 21 (1965): 100-
       08.

652   _____. "Louis Espenschied and His Family, " MHSB. 18
       (1962): 87-103.

653 Finckh, Alice. "Gottfried Duden: An Altruist, " AGR. 14, i
(1947): 9-10, 30.

654 _____. "Gottfried Duden Views Missouri, 1824-27, " MHR.
43 (1948): 334-43; 44 (1949): 21-30.

655 Gammon, William. "A Belated Census of Earliest Settlers of
Cape Girardeau County, Missouri, " NGSQ. 44 (1956): 56-59,
87-91.

656 Gempp, Elizabeth. "Henry Gempp- Pioneer Doctor, " MHSB.
18 (1962): 260-64.

657 Hazzard, Florence. "Pioneer Women of Washtenaw County, "
MHR. 42 (1947): 181-201.

658 Henlein, Paul. "Journal of F. and W. Renick on an Exploring
Tour to the Mississippi and Missouri Rivers in the Year 1819, "
AgH. 30 (1956): 174-85.

659 Hesse, Anna. "This is Our Heritage, " AGR. 27, iv (1961): 28-
31. About Hermann, Missouri.

660 Hoops, Walther. "Alle Vereine in guter Stimmung, " D. Wochenschrift. (June 8, 1972).

661 House, Roy. "St. Louis Germans, anno 1851, " AGR. 9 (1943):
4-6.

662 Kirschten, Ernest. Catfish and Crystal. New York: Doubleday, 1960. Social history of St. Louis.

663 Lenhart, John. "Early German Settlements in America, " SJR.
52 (1960): 510-13, 348-52.

664 Ramsay, R. "The Secrets of Franklin County Place Names:
The German Heritage, " Wash. Missourian. (Aug. 30, 1951).

665 Sasse, Alvin. "A German Pioneer Homestead, " AGR. 27, vi
(1961): 32-33.

666 Schillerverin von St. Louis. Bericht. St. Louis, 1908. UC

667 Schneider, Carl. "The Establishment of the First Prussian
Consulate in the West, " MVHR. 30 (1944): 507-20.

668 Shoemaker, Floyd. "Herman: A Bit of the Old World in the
Heart of the New, " MHR. 51 (1957): 235-44.

669 _____. "This Week in Missouri History, " MHR. 49 (1955):
363-67. Carl Schurz and Gottfried Duden.

670 Streufert, Waldemar. "Clementine Buenger Neumueller,

Saxon Immigrant, " CHIQ. 26 (1953): 132-35.

671   Wellenkamp, Henry. "The Autobiography of Henry Wellenkamp,
      MHSB. 19 (1963): 311-27.

                          NEBRASKA

672   Friesen, J. "Remaking a Community: Henderson, Nebraska, "
      ML. 5 (1950): 10-12.

673   Griess, Peter. "The First Settlement of Russian Germans in
      Nebraska, " NH. 49 (1968): 393-99.

674   Luebke, Frederick. "German Immigrants and the Churches in
      Nebraska, 1889-1915, " M-A. 50 (1968): 116-30.

675   Miller, D. "Peter Jansen: A Nebraska Pioneer, " NH. 35
      (1954): 223-30.

676   _____. "The Story of Jansen, Nebraska, " ML. 9 (1954):
      173-75.

                         NEW JERSEY

677   Chambers, T. Early Germans in New Jersey: Their History,
      Church and Genealogies. Repr.: Baltimore: Genealogical
      Pub., 1969.

678   Cunz, Dieter. "Egg Harbor City, New Germany in New Jer-
      sey, " NJHS. 73 (1955): 89-123.

679   _____. "Egg Harbor City: New Germany in New Jersey, "
      RJGAH. 29 (1956): 9-30.

680   _____. "German Street Names in Egg Harbor, " AGR. 22,
      iii (1956): 27-29.

681   Federation of American Citizens of German Descent Inc. 20th
      German American Day, Schuetzenpark, New Jersey June 4,
      1972. n.p., 1972. Much material on the New Jersey German

682   Hoffman, Robert. "New Jersey in the Revolutionary Scene, "
      AmIll. 36 (1942): 27-66.

683   Schmidt, Hubert. "The Germans in Colonial New Jersey, "
      NJ Genesis. (Oct., 1956): 103-09; (Jan., 1957): 127-33, 139-
      43.

684   _____. "Germans in Colonial New Jersey, " AGR. 24, v
      (1958): 4-9.

685   Theurer, Louise. "The German Language House, New Jersey
      College for Women, 1929-54," AGR. 21 (1954): 13-15.

NEW YORK

686   "Austrian Institute," AGR. 29, iv (1963): 26-27.

687   Carter, John. "The Palatine Migration, Schoharie to Tulpe-
      hocken," NCoHSP. 20 (1954): 1-15.

688   Ernst, Robert. Immigrant Life in New York City, 1825-63.
      New York: Columbia University Pr., 1949.

689   Espenschied, Lloyd. "Early Wayne County Settlers and Their
      Rhineland Origins," Lyons Republican. (Nov. 13, 20, 27; Dec.
      4, 11, 18, 25, 1962).

690   _____. "Erstansiedler aus dem Rheinland in Wayne County,
      New York, USA," Pfälz, FWK. 8 (1959): 185-92.

691   Flacke, Lieselotte. "Literary Society Inc. New York, ZKA.
      12 (1962): 332.

692   Frankhouser, Earle. "The Bib Spring Farm," HRBC. 31
      (1966): 48, 50, 62-63.

693   Franz, Eleanor. "Gemütlichkeit," NY Folkl. Q. 25 (1969): 137-
      58.

694   Kapp, Friedrich. Geschichte der Deutschen im Staate New
      York bis zum Anfange des 19. Jahrhunderts. New York:
      Steiger, 1869. UC UM

695   Karnbach, William. "Long Islandiana, The Old Dutchman:
      Martin Kalbfleisch of Brooklyn," JLIH. 9 (1969).

696   Kierschner, A. "New York Turn-Verein: 100th Anniversary,"
      AGR. 16, vi (1950): 7-13.

697   King, Rolf. German Influence in Rochester's Cultural History,
      1830-70. Dissertation: Murray State College, Kentucky, 1951.

698   Klath, M. "Pomeranian Homesteads in New York State," AGR.
      11, vi (1945): 4-5, 22.

699   Klemm, Frederick. "Story of the Schoharie Germans," AGR.
      17 (1951): 14-16.

700   Koenig, Karl. "Sherburne's Community Forest," AGR. 19,
      iii (1953): 15, 37.

701   Leach, Richard. "The Impact of Immigration Upon New York

1840-60, " NYH. 31 (1950): 15-30.

702   Leder, Lawrence. "Jacob Leisler and the New York Rebellion
of 1689-1691," Typescript in the New York Historical Society,
1954.

703   _____. "Politics of Upheaval in New York 1689-1709,"
NYHSQ. 44 (1960): 413-27.

704   _____. "Records of the Trials of Jacob Leisler and His
Associates," NYHSQ. 36 (1954): 431-57.

705   Lichtenhaeler, Frank. "The Schoharie-Tulpehocken Rieths,"
Eck. (November 4, 11, 1950).

706   _____. "Storm Blown Seed of Schoharie," PGFS. 9 (1946):
3-105.

707   Lohr, Otto. "Deutschamerikanische Jubiläen," MIA. 10 (1960):
141-42.

708   _____. "Deutsche Beteiligungen an der Kolonie Neu-Sch-
weden in Nordamerika," MIA. 10 (1960): 3-5.

709   McKelvey, Blacke. "The Germans of Rochester, Their Traditions and Contributions," RH. 20 (1958): 1-28.

710   _____. "The Lure of the City: Rochester in the 1890's,"
RH. 28 (1966): 1-24.

711   _____. "Rochester's Ethnic Transformation," RH. 25 (1963)
1-24.

712   Mason, B. "Aspects of the New York Revolt of 1689," NYH.
30 (1949): 165-80.

713   Meier, Henry. "Fifty Years of Literarischer Verein," AGR.
22, iii (1956): 13-14.

714   Nestler, Harold. Bibliography of New York State Communities:
Counties, Towns, Villages. Port Washington, New York: I. J
Friedman, 1968.

715   New York Turn-Verein. Historical Journal: A Souvenir of the
Centennial Celebration of the New York Turn-Verein, 1850-
1950. New York: Turn-Verein, 1950. UK

716   "New Yorker Turnverein leistet Entwicklungshilfe, " DMH. (Aug.
      30, 1973).

717   Prahl, Augustus.   "The Goethe Club of the City of New York
      1873-78, " MO. 44 (1952): 291-302.

718   Ramm, H.   "Ostfriesen unter den Gründern von Neu-Niederland,
      dem Vorläufer von New York, " Quellen & Forsch. zur Ostfr.
      FWK. 3 (1969).

719   Reich, Jerome.   Jacob Leisler's Rebellion: A Study of Democ-
      racy in New York 1664-1720. Chicago: University of Chicago
      Pr., 1953.

720   "Steubenparade 1973, " NYSZH. Sektion B (Sept. 15-16, 1973):
      1-28. Extensive information on the New York Germans.

721   Ulke, Titus.   "Aboard the Bark, Charlotte--from Bremer-
      haven to New York, 1852, " AGR. 12, iv (1946): 21-24, 35.

722   Vrooman, John.   "Conrad Weiser and the New York Colony, "
      HRBC. 25, iii (1960): 76-79, 97-99.

723   Wallace, Paul.   "Conrad Weiser and His New York Contacts, "
      NYH. 28 (1947): 170-79.

724   Wilk, Gerard.   "Pfaffs Romantischer Keller, " AGR. 32, v
      (1966): 27-28.

725   _____.   "Yorkville: Twenty Years After, " Commentary.
      17, i (1954): 41-48.

726   Zollinger, James.   The Swiss Benevolent Society of New York:
      A Brief History of its First One Hundred Years 1846-1946.
      New York: The Society, 1947.

727   "22. September: Steubenparade in New York, " Aufbau. (Sep-
      tember 14, 1973).

                                OHIO

728   Barnett, James.   "The Vilification of August Willich, " BCHS.
      24 (1966): 29-40.

729   Bartha, Stephen.   "The German Element in Toledo, " NW Ohio
      Q. 18 (1946): 25-38.

730   Berges, Ruth.   "Lenau's Quest in America, " AGR. 28, iv
      (1963): 14-17.

731   Blanchard, Homer.   "Lenau's Ohio Venture, " OH. 78 (1969):
      237-51.

732 Brause, Herman. "1. Deutsch-amerikanisches Symposium für deutsche Kultur in Amerika, " DW. (October 31, 1973).

733 Busch, Moritz. "The Cincinnati Germans, Anno 1850, " AGR. 9 (1942): 28, 30.

734 Cleveland. German-American National Congress. Symposium über deutsche Kultur in Amerika und Ohio. Cleveland: Classic Printing, 1973. Contains bibliographical essay.

735 "The Deaconess and Her Heritage, " ML. 3 (1948): 3-037. About a Cincinnati hospital.

736 Dickore, Marie. "Der Deutsche Pionier Verein von Cincinnati Membership, " HPSO. 21 (1963): 217-19, 278-82.

737 Dobbert, G. A. "The Cincinnati Germans, 1870-1920: Disintegration of an Immigrant Community, " BCHS. 23 (October, 1965).

738 _____. "The Zinzinnati in Cincinnati, " BCHS. 22 (1964): 209-220.

739 Downes, Randolph. "Background History and Development of Toledo, " NWO. 30 (1958): 211-21.

740 Finckh, Alice. "Medieval Knights in Cleveland, " AGR. 14, iii (1948): 8-11.

741 Fleischhauer, Wolfgang. "German Communities in Northwestern Ohio, " RJGAH. 34 (1970): 23-34.

742 _____. "Westphalian in Ohio, " AGR. 30, i (1963): 26-30.

743 Gebhard, Bruno. "From the Dresden Hygiene Museum to the Cleveland Health Museum, " Ohio State Med. J. 64 (1968): 3-8.

744 Gorbach, August. Das Hilfswerk und Cincinnatis Deutsche Vereine. Cincinnati, 1917. UC

745 Grätz, Delbert. "Swiss Mennonites Come to Putnam County, Ohio, " ML. 15 (1960): 165-67.

746 Gutmann, Joseph. "Watchman on an American Rhine: New Light on Isaac M. Wise, " AJA. 10 (1958): 135-44.

747 Harlow, Alvin. The Serene Cincinnatians. New York: Dutton, 1950.

748 Havighurst, Walter. Wilderness for Sale. New York: Hastings House, 1956.

749 Heuck, Robert. "More about Over-the-Rhine, " HPSO. 20 (1962): 245-54.

750 Jones, Wilbur. "Some Cincinnati German Societies a Century
     Ago, " AGR. 18, i (1951): 22-24; also in HPSO. (1962): 38-43.

751 Klauprecht, E. Deutsche Chronik in der Geschichte des Ohio-
     Thales und seiner Hauptstadt Cincinnati ins Besondere. Cin-
     cinnati: Druck und Verlag von G. Hof und M. A. Jacobi,
     1864.

752 Koester, Leonard. "Early Cincinnati and the Turners, from
     Mrs. Karl Tafel's Autobiography, " Hist. & Phil. Soc. B. 7
     (1949): 18-22.

753 Lowitt, Richard. "The Ohio Boyhood of George W. Norris, "
     NWO. 30 (1958): 70-81.

754 McMurtry, R. "Lincoln Visited by a German Delegation of
     Workingmen in Cincinnati, Ohio, February 12, 1861, " Lincoln
     Lore. No. 1575 (May, 1969): 1-3.

755 Mahr, August. "A Chapter of Early Ohio Natural History, "
     OJS. 49 (1949): 45-69.

756 _____. "Down the Rhine to the Ohio: The Travel Diary
     of Christoph Jacob Munk, April 21-August 17, 1832, " OSAHQ.
     57 (1948): 266-310.

757 Matthews, Stanley. "Aftermath of a Golden Jubilee, " HPSO.
     16 (1958): 143-50. About the Cincinnati 1899 Sängerfest.

758 Nicolai, Edna. "Groesbeck, Ohio, " HPSO. 16 (1958): 179-86.

759 Raid, Howard. "Schwietzer Tag--Swiss Day, " ML. 11 (1956):
     56-57, 72.

760 Rattermann, Heinrich. "Deutsche Bilder aus der Stadt Cincin-
     nati, " DDP. 9 (1877-78): 16-17, 62-73, 389-98, 422-34, 459-
     68; 10 (1878-79); 3-12, 43-56, 106-13, 234-48, 317-23, 429-
     35, 474-87.

761 Rippley, LaVern J. "The Columbus Germans, " RJGAH. 33
     (1968): 1-45.

762 Roseboom, Eugene and F. P. Weisenburger. A History of
     Ohio. Columbus: Ohio State Archeological and Historical
     Society, 1953.

763 Schoolfield, George. "The Great Cincinnati Novel, " HPSO.
     20 (1962): 44-59.

764 Schreiber, William. "Pennsylvania German Pioneers in Ohio, "
     Eck. (Nov. 9, 16, 23, 1957).

765 Schroeder, Armin. "The Rev. J. Strieter Comes to Elyria,
     Ohio, " CHIQ. 19 (1946): 51-57.

766   Schulenberg, Ernst von. Sandusky Then and Now. Cleveland:
      Western Reserve Hist. Soc., 1960.

767   Smith, Dwight. "Nine Letters of Nathaniel Dike on the West-
      ern Country, 1816-1818, " OHQ. 67 (1958): 189-220.

768   Thomas, Bill. "Touch of Old Germany in the Middle of Ohio, "
      NY Times. (April 21, 1968).

769   Thomson, Peter G. A Bibliography of the State of Ohio:
      Being a Catalog of the Books and Pamphlets Relating to the
      History of the State. Cincinnati: Thomson, 1880.

770   Titus, Leo. "Swiss Emigrants Seek Home in America: Diary
      Describes their Impressions of Ohio in 1831, " Hist. & Phil.
      Soc. B. 14 (1957): 167-85.

771   Tolzmann, Don Heinrich. "Dr. Robert Ward-Leyerle und das
      Deutsch-Amerikanertum, " DMH. (November 1, 1973).

772   Wittke, Carl. "The Germans of Cincinnati, " HPSO. 20 (1962):
      3-14.

773   _____. "Ohio's Germans 1840-1875, " OHQ. 66 (1957): 339-
      54.

774   Yoder, Don. "From the Palatinate to Frontier Ohio: The
      Risen Letters (1932-33), " MQR. 30 (1956): 44-64.

                              OKLAHOMA

775   Hefley, Maurice. "A Pioneer at the Land Openings in Okla-
      homa, " COO. 40 (1962): 150-58.

776   Willibrand, W. "German in Okarche, 1892-1902, " COO. 28
      (1950): 284-91.

                              OREGON

777   Douglas, Jesse. "Origins of the Population of Oregon in 1850, "
      PNQ. 61 (1950): 95-108.

778   Johannsen, R. "John Burkhart and the Oregon Territory, "
      OHQ. 53 (1952): 196-203.

779   Merk, Fredrick. Albert Gallatin and the Oregon Problem.
      Cambridge: Harvard University Press, 1950.

780   Meyer, Nathaniel. "Journey into Southern Oregon: Diary of
      a Pennsylvania Dutchman, " OHQ. 59 (1958): 375-407.

PENNSYLVANIA

781 Alderfer, E. The Montgomery County Story. Norristown, Pa.:
Pennsylvania German Society, 1951.

782 _____. "Pastorius and the Origins of the Pennsylvania German Culture, " AGR. 17 (1951): 8-11.

783 Aurand, Ammon Monroe. Catalog of Pennsylvania: A Bibliography of the Keystone State. Harrisburg, Pa.: Aurand
Press, 1928. Lists 1, 000 items.

784 _____. The Germans in Pennsylvania: A Bibliography;
Pennsylvania German Library; or the Pleasure of "Riding" a
Hobby. Harrisburg, Pa.: Aurand Press, 1930.

785 _____. Where to Dine in the Pennsylvania Dutch Region:
A Guide to Travel Information, Historic Places, Points of Interest, Antique Dealers, Card and Gift Shops, Rare Book Dealers. Rev. ed. Harrisburg, Pa.: Aurand Press, 1946.

786 Barba, Preston A. "The Autograph Album of Annie Trexler, "
Eck. (Feb. 18, 25, 1956).

787 _____. "Gottlieb Mittelberger's Journey to Pennsylvania in
the Year 1750, " Eck. (Sept. 3, 10, 17, 24; Oct. 1, 8, 15,
22, 29; Nov. 5, 12, 19, 26, 1960).

788 _____. "The Pennsylvania German in Fiction, 1935-55, "
PD. 7 (1956): 22-27.

789 _____. They Came to Emmaus. Emmaus, Pa.: Borough
of Emmaus, 1959.

790 Bausman, Lottie. A Bibliography of Lancaster County, Pa.
1745-1912. Philadelphia: Pennsylvania Federation of Historical Societies, 1912.

791 Beers, Henry. "Pennsylvania Bibliographies, " PH. 2 (1934):
104-08, 178-82.

792 Bergey, Nelson. "Some Accounts of the Early German Settlements of Bradford County, " Eck. (Jan. 12, 26; Feb. 2,
1946).

793 Bergfeld, Annabelle. "The Pennsylvania Dutch, " SAQ. 49
(1950): 324-31.

794 Berky, Andrew. "Yesteryear in Dutchland, " PD. 8 (1956):
10-15.

795 Bining, A. C. Writings on Pennsylvania History: A Bibliography. Harrisburg, Pa.: Historical and Museum Commission,
1946.

796   Bokum, Hermann.   "A German Emigrant's View of the Pennsyl-
      vania Dutch--1836, " PD. (January 15, 1951).

797   Brackhill, Martin.   "The Eisenhowers in Pennsylvania, " PH.
      20 (1953): 79-89.

798   Braugh, Fritz and Friedrich Krebs.   "Pennsylvania Dutch Pio-
      neers from South Palatine Parishes, " PD. 8 (1957): 39-42.

799   Brendle, Thomas.   "The Pennsylvania German Society, " PH.
      23 (1956): 340-45.

800   Breneman, Mae.   "Pennsylvania Farm Museum, Landis Val-
      ley, " AGR. 20, vi (1954): 10-13.

801   Brenner, Scott.   Pennsylvania Dutch: The Plain and the Fancy.
      Harrisburg, Pa.:   Stackpole, 1957.

802   Bressler, Leo.   "Agriculture Among the Germans in Pennsyl-
      vania During the Eighteenth Century, " PH. 22 (1955): 103-33.

803   [Brumbaugh.]   "Dr. Gaius M. Brumbaugh, Deceased, " NGSQ.
      40 (1952): 108.   Member of important German family in
      Pennsylvania.

804   Bucher, Robert.   "The Cultural Backgrounds of Our Pennsyl-
      vania Homesteads, " HSMC. 15 (1966): 22-26.

805   Buchwalter, Grace.   "Naturalization of German Settlers in
      Pennsylvania, " AGR. 17, vi (1951): 22-23.

806   Buffington, Albert.   "Seller Nixnutz, " Eck. (May 22, 29; June
      5; July 31; August 14, 1948).

807   Carter, E. A.   "A Symposium on Pennsylvania German Studies
      AGR. 8 (1942): 28-29.

808   "A Communication on the Relation of Franconia and Lancaster
      Mennonites in Colonial Pennsylvania, " MQR. (April, 1952):
      161-63.

809   Cummings, Hobertis.   "John Augustus Roebling and the Public
      Works of Pennsylvania, " International Affairs, Commonwealth
      of Pa. (May-Sept., 1960).

810   DeChant, Alliene.   Down Oley Way.   Kutztown, Pa.:   Kutz-
      town Publishing Co., 1953.

811   _____.   Of the Dutch I Sing.   Kutztown, Pa.:   Kutztown
      Publishing Co., 1951.

812   Doll, Eugene.   The Pennsylvania Magazine of History and Bi-
      ography Index, Volumes 1-75 (1877-1951).   Philadelphia:

Historical Society of Pennsylvania, 1954.

813 _____ . "Research in Pennsylvania German Areas: Taking Stock," AGR. 25, i (1958): 31-32.

814 _____ . Twenty-Five Years of Service 1930-55. Philadelphia: Carl Schurz Memorial Foundation, 1955.

815 Dundore, M. "A Population Study of the Pennsylvania Germans in Berks and Neighboring Counties," HRBC. 28 (1963): 113-17.

816 Dunkelberger, George. The Story of Snyder County from its Earliest Times to the Present Day. Selingsgrove, Pa.: Snyder County Historical Society, 1948.

817 Elkinton, Howard. "Francis Daniel Pastorius," AGR. 17 (1951): 3.

818 Faust, Albert. Franz Daniel Pastorius and the 250th Anniversary of the Founding of Germantown. Philadelphia: Carl Schurz Memorial Foundation, 1934.

819 Fisher, Elwood. "Briefe vum Solwell Files," Eck. (Jan. 27-Feb. 17, 1968).

820 Fletcher, S. W. "The Expansion of the Agricultural Frontier," PH. 18 (1951): 119-29.

821 _____ . Pennsylvania Agriculture and Country Life, 1640-1840. Harrisburg, Pa.: Historical and Museum Commission, 1950.

822 _____ . Pennsylvania Agriculture and Country Life, 1840-1940. Harrisburg, Pa.: Historical and Museum Commission, 1955.

823 Gagliardo, John. "Germans and Agriculture in Colonial Pennsylvania," PMHB. 83 (1960): 192-218.

824 Gerberich, Albert. "A Journey to America Two Centuries Ago," NGSQ. 45 (1957): 31-32.

825 Gerhard, Elmer Schultz. "Lorenz Ibach, the Stargazing Blacksmith," HRBC. 14 (1949): 45-47.

826 _____ . "Seeing Ourselves as Others Saw Us in Pennsylvania a Hundred Years Ago," BHSM. 7 (1950): 40-62.

827 "A Germantown Chronology," AGR. 25, i (1958): 13-16.

828 Gilbert, Russell. A Picture of the Pennsylvania Germans. 3d ed. Gettysburg, Pa.: Pennsylvania Historical Association, 1962.

829   Graber, Ellis. "Germantown Commemorates 275th Anniversary," <u>ML.</u> 13 (1958): 167-68.

830   Grace, Alonzo. "The Aaronsburg Story," <u>AGR.</u> 19 (1953): 3, 40.

831   Graeff, Arthur. "As Shadows Lengthen, 1930-50," <u>AGR.</u> 16, v (1950): 4-6, 33.

832   _____. "Conrad Weiser," <u>Eck.</u> (Jan. 10-Dec. 19, 1942).

833   _____. <u>Conrad Weiser: Pennsylvania Peacemaker.</u> Philadelphia: University of Pennsylvania, 1945.

834   _____. "Echoes From the Past," <u>Eck.</u> (May 31, June 21, 1947).

835   _____. "Es Schneckeharn Verzaehlt," <u>Eck.</u> (April 10, 17, 24; May 1, 1948).

836   _____. "The First Half-Century of the Pennsylvania German Society: 1890-1940," <u>HRBC.</u> 31, ii (1966): 59-60, 65-66.

837   _____. <u>History of Pennsylvania.</u> Philadelphia: J. C. Winston, 1944.

838   _____. <u>It Happened in Pennsylvania.</u> Philadelphia: J. C. Winston, 1947.

839   _____. <u>The Keystone State: Its Geography, History and Government.</u> Philadelphia: John C. Winston, 1953.

840   _____. "1942 in Pennsylvania German History," <u>PGFS.</u> 7 (1942): 163-70. This review of Pennsylvania German history continued through volume 14 (1950).

841   _____. "On the Trail of the Pennsylvania Germans," <u>Eck.</u> (May 16, 23, 30; June 6, 13, 1953).

842   _____. "Outstanding Events in 1945," <u>Eck.</u> (March 2, 1946

843   _____. "Pennsylvania Dutchmen Contributed to Growth of Leading Steel State," <u>Eck.</u> (July 6, 1946).

844   _____. <u>The Pennsylvania Germans: A Study in Stability.</u> Allentown, 1945.

845   _____. "Renascence of History," <u>PD.</u> 6, v (1955): 36-38.

846   Gramm, Hans. <u>The Oberlaender Trust: 1931-53.</u> Philadelphia: Carl Schurz Memorial Foundation, 1956.

847   Groshens, David. "Men of Montgomery County Who Aided

Ratification of our Federal Constitution by the Commonwealth of Pennsylvania, " BHSM. 5 (1946): 125-34.

848   Hark, Ann. The Story of the Pennsylvania Dutch. New York: Harper, 1957.

849   Harper, John and Martha B. "The Palatine Migration--1723-- from Schoharie to Tulpehocken, " HRBC. 25 (1960): 80-82.

850   Harter, Thomas. "The Pennsylvania Germans, " Eck. (Jan. 16, 1960; Aug. 24, 31, 1968).

851   Heckler, James. History of Franconia Township. Harleysville, Pa.: Carroll D. Hendricks, 1966.

852   _____. History of Harleysville and Lower Salford Township. Schwenksville, Pa.: Robert C. Bucher, 1958.

853   Heckman, O. "Pennsylvania Bibliography, " PH. 11 (1944): 63-65.

854   Herr, Fred. "Herr's Island, " Western Pa. Hist. Mag. 53 (1970): 211-26.

855   Hirsch, Helen. "Philadelphus Philadelphia: Scientist and Magician, " AGR. 24, vi (1958): 34-36.

856   Hoch, Daniel. "Journey to Weiser Park, " HRBC. 15 (1950): 238-41.

857   Hollenbach, Raymond. "Gibs un Glee, " Eck. (June 25; July 2 1949).

858   _____. "The Pennsylvania Germans and Grape Culture, " Eck. (Feb. 3, 10, 17, 1951).

859   _____. "Public Sale of Personal Property of the Deceased Adam Scheurer: Whitehall Township, Lehigh County, May 17, 1805, " Eck. (Feb. 16, 1946).

860   Hollenbeck, R. "Solomon Fisler, der Wagner, " Eck. (March 22, 1947).

861   Hoover, Margaret. "The Trappe Neighbors of Henry Melchior Muhlenberg as Mentioned in His Journals, Vol. 1777-1787, " Bulletin of the Hist. Soc. of Montgomery Co. 16 (1968): 139-60.

862   Hostetler, John. "Revived Interest in Pennsylvania German Culture, " ML. 11 (1956): 65-72.

863   Hubben, William. "Pilgrims from Krefeld, " AGR. 25, i (1958): 8-11.

864   Jantz, Harold.   "Pastorius: Intangible Values, " AGR.   25, i
      (1958): 4-7.

865   Kemp, A. F.   "The Pennsylvania German Versammlinge, "
      PGFS. 9 (1946): 189-218.

866   Keyser, N. H.   "Fiction Dealing with Pennsylvania Germans, "
      PG. 7 (1906): p. 272 ff.

867   Klees, Frederic.   The Pennsylvania Dutch.   New York: Mac-
      millan, 1950.

868   Klein, Frederic and Charles Carlson.   Old Lancaster: From
      its Beginnings to 1865.   Lancaster, 1964.

869   Kloss, Heinz.   "Ein unbekannter Stamm: Die Pennsylvania-
      deutschen, " AD. 11 (1928): 96-99.

870   Krebs, Friedrich.   "Emigrants from Baden-Durlach to Pennsyl-
      vania 1749-55, " NGSQ. 45 (1957): 30-31.

871   _____.   "Pennsylvania Dutch Pioneers, " PD. 7, iii (1955):
      38-39, 8, i (1956): 57-59.

872   _____.   "Pennsylvania Pioneers from the Neckar Valley, "
      PD. 5 (1953): 13.

873   Kuhns, Oscar.   The German and Swiss Settlements of Colonial
      Pennsylvania.   Harrisburg, Pa.:   Aurand Pr., 1946.

874   Lemon, James.   "The Agricultural Practices of National
      Groups in Eighteenth Century Southeastern Pennsylvania, "
      GeoR. 56 (1966): 467-96.

875   Long, Harriet.   "A Select Bibliography of the Pennsylvania
      Germans, " PG. 11 (1910): 400-76.

876   Mendels, Judy.   "Schweizer Reminiszenzen im Lande der
      Pennsylvania Dutch, " Echo. 36, 12, 15-17 (1956).

877   Messerschmidt, H.   "Ein anderer Ananias, " AGR. 13, v-vi
      (1947): 24-25.

878   Miller, Lester.   The Pennsylvania Dutch.   Reading, Pa.:   L.
      Miller, 1958.

879   Mittelberger, Gottlieb.   Journey to Pennsylvania.   Cambridge,
      1960.

880   Mook, Maurice.   "The Changing Pattern of Pennsylvania Ger-
      man Culture 1855-1955, " PH. 23 (1956): 311-39.

881   Neuberger, Otto.   "Francis Daniel Pastorius, " Friends Intelli-
      gencer. (Oct. 6, 1951).

882 "The Pastorius Tercentenary, " AGR. 18, i (1951): 40.

882A Pflueger, Luther. "Pennsylvania, " Eck. (Aug. 16, 23, 30;
Sept. 6, 13, 20, 27; Oct. 4, 11, 18, 1958).

883 Pfund, Harry. A History of the German Society of Pennsylvania: Bicentenary Edition 1764-1964. 2d rev. ed. Philadelphia: German Society of Pennsylvania, 1964.

884 Prahl, Augustus. "The Goethean Literary Society of Franklin
and Marshall College, " AGR. 16, i (1949): 29-30.

885 Rice, William. "Some Pennsylvania Landmarks Revisited, "
AGR. 13, v-vi (1947): 17-19.

886 Roach, Hannah. "Hans Georg Hertzel: Pioneer of Northampton County and His Family, " PGM. 24 (19): 151-84.

887 Robacker, Earl. "Dream in Dutchland, " NYFQ. 12 (1956):
287-90.

888 Rosenberger, Homer. "Migrations of the Pennsylvania Germans
to Western Pennsylvania, " Western Pa. Hist. Mag. 53 (1970):
319-35.

889 _____. "On a Montgomery County Heritage, " Der Reggeboge. (Dec., 1969): p. 14.

890 Rothermund, Dietmar. "The German Problem of Colonial
Pennsylvania, " PMHB. 84 (1960): 3-21.

891 Sachse, Julius. "Title-pages of Books and Pamphlets that In-
fluenced German Emigration to Pennsylvania, " PG. 5 (1897):
199-256.

892 [Seuren.] "Willy Seuren, " AGR. 22, ii (1955): 31. About a
Philadelphia German radio announcer.

893 Singmaster, Elsie. I Heard of a River: A Story of the Pennsylvania German. Philadelphia: John C. Winston, 1948.

894 _____. Pennsylvania's Susquehanna. Harrisburg, Pa.,
1950.

895 Smith, Edward. Traditionally Pennsylvania Dutch. New York:
Hastings House, 1947.

896 Stoudt, John. The Pennsylvania Dutch: An Introduction to
their Life and Culture. Allentown: Schlechters, 1950.

897 Tinkom, H. M. and M. B. and Grant Simon. Historic Germantown. Philadelphia: American Philosophical Society, 1955.

898 Trexler, Ben. Skizzen aus dem Lecha-Thale. Allentown:
    Trezler & Hartzell, 1880-86. Retold in English by David Kauf-
    mann, Eck. (March 6, 13; April 25; May 9; June 6, 20, 27;
    July 11; Oct. 17, 1964; June 12, 19; Sept. 11, 18; Dec. 4,
    1965).

898A Troutman, Carrie. "Pioneer Days in Mahantango Valley,"
    Eck. (Oct. 2, 9, 16, 1948).

899 Von Reck, Georg. "Diary from the Hallesche Nachrichten ex-
    cerpted as 'Early Descriptions of Philadelphia and German-
    town'," Eck. (March 26, 1966).

900 Wallace, Paul. Conrad Weiser 1696-1776: Friend of Colony
    and Mohawk. Philadelphia: University of Pennsylvania Pr.,
    1945.

901 _____. The Muhlenbergs of Pennsylvania. Philadelphia:
    University of Pennsylvania Pr., 1950.

902 Watson, John. "Excerpts from Annals of Philadelphia and
    Pennsylvania," Eck. (Jan. 6; May 4; June 8; July 13-27, 1968).

903 Weaver, Samuel. Autobiography of a Pennsylvania Dutchman.
    New York, 1953.

904 Weimann, H. "Germantown and Lübeck," AGR. 24, iv (1958):
    15-16.

905 Weiser, Frederick. "Conrad Weiser: Peacemaker of Colonial
    Pennsylvania," HRBC. 25 (1960): 83-97.

906 Wenger, J. C. Hans Herr. Lancaster, Pa.: Hans Herr
    House Restoration Committee, 1970.

907 Werner, William. "The First Novel About the Pennsylvania
    Germans," Eck. (Nov. 2, 1957).

908 Wilkinson, Norma. Bibliography of Pennsylvania History. 2d
    ed. Harrisburg: Pennsylvania Historical and Museum Com-
    mission, 1957.

909 _____. "Current Writings on Pennsylvania," PH. 16 (1949):
    326-30.

910 William, David. "The Lower Jordan Valley Pennsylvania Ger-
    man Settlement," Proc. Lehigh Co. Histy. Soc. 18 (1951):
    181 pp.

911 Wirt, George. "Joseph Trimble Rothrock--Father of Forestry
    in Pennsylvania," Eck. (Sept. 24, 1955).

912 Wollenweber, L. A. Gemälde aus dem Pennsylvanischen Volks-
    leben. Philadelphia, 1869. UC

913 _____. "Zwei treue Kameraden: Die beiden ersten deutschen Ansiedler in Pennsylvania," Eck. (Oct. 5, 12, 19, 26; Nov. 2, 9, 16, 1963).

914 Wood, Jerome. Conestoga Crossroads: The Rise of Lancaster, Pennsylvania 1730-89. Brown University: Dissertation, 1968.

915 Wood, Ralph. The Pennsylvania Germans. Princeton: Princeton University Pr., 1942. Wood is a fifth-generation Pennsylvania German author.

916 _____. "The Pennsylvania Germans," WPHM. 40 (1957): 109-14.

917 Wust, Klaus. "Jacob Funk, Jr.," Eck. (Dec. 10, 1966).

918 Yates, W. Ross. Bethlehem of Pennsylvania: The First One Hundred Years 1741-1841. Bethlehem: Bethlehem Chamber of Commerce, 1968.

919 Yoder, Don. "Notes and Documents: Eighteenth Century Letters from Germany," PF. 19 (1970): 30-33.

920 _____. "Pennsylvania German Pioneers from the County of Wertheim," PGFS. 12 (1949): 147-289.

921 _____. "Pennsylvania German Pioneers from Wertheim," AGR. 17, vi (1951): 6-8.

922 _____. "Plain Dutch and Gay Dutch," PD. 8 (1956): 34-55.

TENNESSEE

923 Belissary, C. G. "Tennessee and Immigration, 1865-1880," THQ. 7 (1948): 229-48.

924 Cooper, Hobbart S. "German and Swiss Colonization in Morgan County, Tennessee. University of Tennessee: Dissertation, 1958.

925 [No entry.]

926 Thompson, Lawrence. "Foreign Books About Tennessee, 1900-50," THQ. 11 (1952): 274-81.

927 Wust, Klaus. "Wartburg: Dream and Reality of the New Germany in Tennessee," RJGAH. 31 (1963): 21-45.

62   German-Americana

TEXAS

928   Altgelt, Emma. Sketches of Life in Texas. Trans. and ed.
      by H. Dielmann. AGR. 26, v (1960): 40.

929   Bierschwale, Margaret. "Mason County, Texas: 1845-80,"
      SwHQ. 52 (1949): 379-97.

930   Biesele, Rudolph. "Dr. Ferdinant Roemer's Account of the
      Llano-San Saba Country," SwHQ. 62 (1958): 71-74.

931   _____. "Early Times in New Braunfels and Comal County,"
      SwHQ. 50 (1949): 75-92.

932   Blumburg, Carl. "The True Effectiveness of the Mainz So-
      ciety for Emigration to Texas as Described in a Letter of No-
      vember 3, 1846," Texana. (Winter 1969): 295-312.

933   Bopp, Marie-Joseph. "Die elsässische Auswanderung nach
      Texas," Der Elsass Kalender. 7 (1952): 147-53.

934   Carroll, H. "A Texas Volksfest," SwHQ. 60 (1957): 412.

935   Darst, Maury. "Six Weeks to Texas," Texana. 6 (1968): 140-
      52.

936   Erhard, Cayton. "Cayton Erhard's Reminiscences of the Texan
      Santa Fe Expedition, 1841," SwHQ. 66 (1963): 424-79.

937   Etzler, Herbert. "Zur deutschen Einwanderung in Texas,"
      ZKA. 19 (1969): 20-24.

938   Fierman, Floyd. "Samuel J. Freudenthal, El Paso Merchant
      and Civic Leader: From the 1880's through the Mexican Revo-
      lution," Southwestern Studies. 3, iii (1965): 44 pp.

939   Flach, Vera. A Yankee in German-America: Texas Hill
      Country. San Antonio: Naylor Co., 1973.

940   Fornell, Earl. "The German Pioneers of Galveston Island,"
      AGR. 22, iii (1956): 15-17.

941   Freud, Max. Gustav Dresel's Houston Journal: Adventures
      in North America and Texas, 1837-1841. Austin: University
      of Texas Pr., 1954.

942   Geiser, Samuel. "William H. von Streeruwitz (1833-1916),"
      Field and Laboratory. (Jan., 1957). A geologist.

943   Geue, Ethel. New Homes in a New Land: German Immigra-
      tion to Texas 1847-61. Waco: Texian Pr., 1970.

944   Gustorf, Fred. The Uncorrupted Heart: Journals and Letters

of Frederick Julius Gustorf, 1800-45.   Columbia: University
of Missouri Pr., 1969.

945   Jenkens, John.   Cracker Barrel Chronicle: A Bibliography of
Texas Town and County Histories.   Austin: Pemberton Pr.,
1965.

946   Jordan, Gilbert.   Southwest Goethe Festival.   Dallas, 1949.
Author is a German-American poet.

947   Jordan, Terry.   A Geographical Appraisal of the Significance
of German Settlement in Nineteenth Century Texas Agriculture.
University of Wisconsin: Dissertation, 1965.

948   _____.   The German Element of Gillespie County, Texas.
University of Texas: Dissertation, 1961.

949   _____.   German Seed in Texas Soil: Immigrant Farmers in
Nineteenth Century Texas.   Austin: University of Texas Pr.,
1966.

950   _____.   "The German Settlement of Texas after 1865, "
SwHQ.   73 (1969):   193-212.

951   _____.   "Letters of a German Pioneer in Texas, " SwHQ.
69 (1966):   193-212.

952   _____.   "The Pattern of Origins of the Adelsverein German
Colonists, " Texana.   6 (1968):   245-57.

953   _____.   "Population Origins in Texas, 1850, " Geogr. Rev.
59 (1969):   83-102.

954   Koeltzow, Otto.   "From the Brazos to the North Fork; The
Autobiography of Otto Koeltzow, " COO.   40 (1962):   100-49.

955   Kossok, Manfred.   "Prussia, Bremen and the Texas Question
1835 to 1845, " Texana.   (Fall 1965):   227-69.

956   Kowert, Art.   "LBJ's Boyhood: Among the German-Americans
in Texas, " AGR.   34 (1968):   2-6.

957   Lathrop, Barnes.   "Migration into East Texas, 1835-60, "
SwHQ.   52 (1948):   184-208.

958   Love, K.   "German Winter Festivals in Fredericksburg, Texas, "
AGR.   16, i (1949):   17-20.

959   McKay, S.   Texas Politics, 1906-44:   With Special Reference
to German Counties.   Lubbock: Texas Technical Pr., 1952.

960   Mullins, Marion.   The First Census of Texas, 1829-1836, to
Which are Added Texas Citizenship Lists, 1821-45, and Other

64   German-Americana

Early Records of the Republic of Texas. Washington, D. C.,
1959.

961   "The 100th Anniversary of the Founding of Fredericksburg,
      Texas (1846-1946), " AGR. 12, vi (1946): 41.

962   "The 100th Anniversary of the Founding of New Braunfels,
      Texas (1846-1946), " AGR. 12, vi (1946): 40.

963   Roper, Laura. "Frederick Law Olmsted and the Western
      Texas Free Soil Movement, " AHR. 56 (1950): 58-64.

964   Streeter, Thomas. Bibliography of Texas, 1795-1845. Cam-
      bridge: Harvard University Pr., 1955-60, 5 volumes.

965   Thompson, Lawrence. "Travel Books on Texas Published in
      Foreign Countries, 1900-50, " SwHQ. 57 (1953): 202-21.

966   Tiling, Moritz. History of the German Element in Texas from
      1820-50, And Historical Sketches of the German Singer's League
      and the Houston Turnverein from 1853-1913. Houston: M.
      Tiling, 1913.

967   Wilhelm, Hubert. Organized German Settlement and its Effects
      on the Frontier of South Central Texas. Louisiana State Agri-
      cultural and Mechanical College: Dissertation, 1968.

968   Wooster, Ralph. "Foreigners in the Principal Towns of Ante-
      Bellum Texas, " SwHQ. 66 (1962): 208-20.

                    VIRGINIA AND WEST VIRGINIA

969   "Addenda to Virginia Bibliography, " RJGAH. 34 (1970): 48-49.

970   Ambler, Charles. "West Virginia Forty-Niners, " WVah. 3
      (1941): 59-75.

971   Brown, William. History of Nicolas County, West Virginia.
      Richmond: Dietz, 1954.

972   Cometti, Elizabeth. "Swiss Immigration to West Virginia,
      1864-84, " MVHR. 47 (1960): 66-87.

973   Germanna Record. Harrisonburg, Va.: Memorial Foundation
      of the Germanna Colonies, 1961.

974   Henkel, Abbie. "Rev. Henkel's Diaries of 1790 Missions, "
      Daily News Record. (Sept. 7, 1950).

975   Holtzelaw, B. C. The Second Germanna Colony of 1717, Oth-
      er Germanna Pioneers, The So-called Third Germanna Colony
      of 1719, and Later Comers to the Hebron Church Community.

Harrisonburg, Va.: Memorial Foundation of the Germanna
Colonies, 1965.

976   Huffman, Charles.   The Germanna Foundation: Story of the
      First Decade 1956-66. Harrisonburg, Va.: Memorial Founda-
      tion of the Germanna Colonies, 1966.

977   _____. The Story of Germanna Descendents in Reunion at
      Siegen Forest, Virginia 1958. Harrisonburg, Va.: Memorial
      Foundation of the Germanna Colonies, 1959.

978   Hummel, Ray. A List of Places Included in 19th Century Vir-
      ginia Directories. Richmond: Virginia State Library, 1960.

979   Lück, Alfred. Eisen, Erz und Abenteuer. Siegen: Hütten-
      werke Siegerland, 1955. About 18th century settlers in Ger-
      manna and Germantown, Pa.

980   Miller, Mildred. "Bibliography of Books by Natives and Resi-
      dents of Harrisonburg and Rockingham County, Va.," Rocking-
      ham Recorder. 2 (1961): 270-80.

981   Rights, Douglas and W. Cumming. The Discoveries of John
      Lederer, with Unpublished Letters by and about Lederer to
      Governor John Winthrop, Jr. and an Essay on the Indians of
      Lederer's Discoveries. Charlottesville: University of Virginia
      Pr., 1958.

982   Smith, E. L. The Pennsylvania Germans of the Shenandoah
      Valley. Allentown: Pennsylvania German Folklore Society,
      1964.

983   Stoner, Robert. A Seed-Bed of the Republic--Early Botetourt:
      A Study of the Upper Valley of Virginia. Roanoke: Roanoke
      Historical Society, 1962.

984   Virginia German Bibliography. Edinburg, Va.: Shenandoah
      History, 1970.

985   Wayland, John. The German Element of the Shenandoah Val-
      ley of Virginia. Bridgewater, Va.: Carter, 1964.

986   _____. Germanna: Outpost of Adventure 1714-1956. Har-
      risonburg, Va.: Memorial Foundation of the Germanna Colo-
      nies, 1956.

987   Wust, Klaus. "Auf den Spuren deutscher Pionier im Shenan-
      doahtal," Washington Journal. (April 17, 1959).

988   _____. "Dr. John Peter Ahl (1748-1827), Medical Pioneer
      of Keezletown, Virginia," Rockingham Recorder. 2 (1959):
      138-44.

989   "Elder John Kline: A Life of Pacifism Ended in Martyrdom, "
       Va. Cavalcade. 14 (1964): 24-32.

990   _____. "German Influences in the Settlement of Alexan-
       dria, Va., " Alexandria Gaz. (March 5, 1954).

991   _____. "German Settlement and Immigrants in Virginia:
       A Bibliography, " RJGAH. 33 (1968): 47-59.

992   _____. "The Saxons Who Never Came to Virginia, " RJGAH
       35 (1972): 52-56.

993   _____. The Virginia Germans.   Charlottesville: Univer-
       sity of Virginia Pr., 1969.

994   _____. "Virginische Blätter: Beiträge zur Geschichte,
       Volkskunde und Sprache der deutschen Einwanderung, " Washing-
       ton Journal. (Jan. 21-Nov. 25, 1966).

995   _____. "The Wythe County Germans, " Eck. (Feb. 6,
       1969).

WASHINGTON

996   Bancroft, H.   "Henry Yesler and the Founding of Seattle, "
       PNQ. 40 (1951): 271-76.

997   Sauerlander, Annemarie.   "Henry L. Yesler in Early Seattle, '
       AGR. 26, iii (1960): 7-12.

WISCONSIN

998   "Alte Kamderaden besuchen die Heimat der Vorfahren, " DMH.
       (Oct. 11, 1973).   Wisconsin Germans visit Germany.

999   BeBeau, Wilfred.   "A German Immigrant Farmer Pioneer in
       Northern Wisconsin, " WMH. 38 (1955): 239-44.

1000   Brush, John.   "A Swiss Colony in Wisconsin: New Glarus, "
       GeoR. 46 (1956): 568-69.

1001   Bubolz, Gordon.   Land of the Fox: Saga of Outagamie Coun-
       ty.   Appleton: Outagamie County Centennial Committee, 1949.

1002   Dundore, M. Walter.   "The Saga of the Pennsylvania Germans
       in Wisconsin, " PGFS. 19 (1955): 33-166.

1003   Dunn, James.   "The Plaster Doctor of Somerset, " WMH. 39
       (1956): 245-50.

1004   Easum, Chester.   "Carl Schurz in Watertown, " AGR. 14, v
       (1948): 34-35.

1005   Eichoff, Juergen. "Wisconsin's German-Americans: From Ethnic Identity to Assimilation, " GAS. 2, ii (1970): 44-54.

1006   Eiselmeier, John. "St. Nazianz: A German Settlement in Wisconsin, " AGR. 8 (1942): 22-24.

1007   Fellwock, J. Friedrich. "Memoirs of J. Friedrich Fellwock, 1831-1919, " CHIQ. 23 (1950): 75-86.

1008   Fuess, Claude. "The Making of an American Family, " CG. 3 (1943): 24-29.

1009   Hense-Jensen, Wilhelm. Wisconsins Deutsch-Amerikaner. Milwaukee: Im Verlag der Deutschen Gesellschaft, Druck der Germania, 1900-02. UC UM

1010   Hofmeister, Burkhard. "Wisconsin--eine kulturgeographische Skizze, " JA. 4 (1959): 249-83.

1011   Homes, Fred. Old World Wisconsin: Around Europe in the Badger State. Eau Claire: E. M. Hale, 1944.

1012   _____. Side Roads: Excursions into Wisconsin's Past. Madison: State Historical Society of Wisconsin, 1949.

1013   Jordan, Gilbert and Terry Jordan. "Wisconsin, " AGR. 31, vi (1965): 27-28.

1014   "Karl Schurz Memorial Park Association, " DMH. (Sept. 27, 1973).

1015   Koss, Rudolph. Milwaukee. Milwaukee, 1871. UC

1016   Kubly, Herbert. "An American Finds America, " CG. 3 (1943): 49-56.

1017   Millard, William. The Sale of Culture. University of Minnesota: Dissertation, 1969. About New Glarus.

1018   Mueller, Theodore. "Milwaukee's Heritage: Das Deutsch-Athen am Michigan-See, " HM. 24 (1968): 84-95.

1019   Neuse, Eloise. "The Watertown of Carl Schurz, " AGR. 21, i (1954): 22-25.

1020   Owen, R. D. "The Hour-glass of Migration, " AGR. 11 (1945): 18-20.

1021   Patek, Rose. "50 Jahre Deutscher Sportverein, " DMH. (Aug. 30; Sept. 5, 1973).

1022   Plumb, Ralph. "Highlights of Manitowac, " WMH. 31 (1948): 412-17.

1023   Raney, William. "Appleton, " WMH. 33 (1949): 135-51.

1024   Sanford, Albert and H. Hirshheimer. A History of La Crosse,
        Wisconsin, 1841-1900. La Crosse: La Crosse County His-
        torical Society, 1951.

1025   Schelbert, Leo. New Glarus 1845-1970: The Making of a
        Swiss American Town. Glarus: Verlag Tschudi, 1970. Con-
        tains bibliography of Swiss-Americana.

1026   Schlicher, I. I. "History of St. Nazianz, " WMH. 31 (1947):
        84-91.

1027   Soellner, Ludwig. "Schlaraffia Milwaukia, " DMH. (Aug. 30,
        1973).

1028   _____. "Schön war die deutsche Tagfeier, " DMH. (Aug.
        23, 1973).

1029   _____. "Vom Goethe Haus, " DMH. (Sept. 13, 1973).

1030   Still, Bayrd. Milwaukee: The History of a City. Madison:
        State Historical Society of Wisconsin, 1948.

1031   Wells, Robert. This is Milwaukee. Garden City, N. Y.:
        Doubleday, 1970.

Journals of German-American History

1032   American-German Review. Philadelphia: Carl Schurz Mem-
        orial Foundation, 1934-70.

1033   American Historical Society of Germans from Russia: Work-
        ing Papers. Greeley, Colorado: American Historical Society
        of Germans from Russia, 1968- .

1034   Columbia Informations- und Nachschlagewerk-Kalender: All-
        gemeines Jahrbuch für Deutsche in Amerika. Erie, Pa.:
        Erie Printing, 1908.

1035   Deutsch-Amerikanische Geschichtsblätter. Chicago, Illinois:
        German-American Historical Society of Illinois, 1901-37.

1036   Deutsch-Amerikanisches Vereins-Adressbuch. Milwaukee:
        German-American Directory Publishing Co., 1911. An exten-
        sive list of German-American organizations, authors and
        journalists.

1037   Deutsche Geschichtsforschung für Missouri. Sedalia, Mo.:
        State Branch of the German-American National Alliance, 1913-?.

1038 Der Deutsche Pionier. Cincinnati: Der Deutsche Pionier-
      Verein, 1869-87. The best nineteenth century journal of
      German-American history.

1039 German-American Annals. Philadelphia: University of Penn-
      sylvania, 1897-1919.

1040 German-American Studies. Cleveland: Society for German-
      American Studies, 1969- . Currently, the leading journal of
      German-American history.

1041 Geschichtsblätter. New York: E. Steiger, 1884-86.

1042 Der Geschichtsfreund. Savannah, Georgia, 1882-84.

1043 Historic Schaefferstown Record. Millersville, Pa.: Historic
      Schaefferstown, Inc., 1967- .

1044 Jahrbuch der Deutschen in Amerika. New York: E. Steiger,
      1873-1917.

1045 Jahrbuch der Deutschen in Chicago. Chicago: German Year-
      book Publishing Co., 1915-18.

1046 Jahrbuch der Neu-Braunfelser Zeitung. New Braunfels, Texas:
      Neu-Braunfelser Zeitung, 1905-54.

1047 Jahresberichte der Deutschen Gesellschaft von Milwaukee.
      Milwaukee: Germania, Auerbach, Hake-Stern Co., 1880-1917.

1048 Jahresberichte des Vorstandes des Deutschen Pionier-Vereins
      von Cincinnati. Cincinnati: Pionier-Verein, 1868-1931.

1049 Leo Baeck Institute Yearbook. New York: Leo Baeck Insti-
      tute, 1956- .

1050 Mitteilungen des Deutsch-Amerikanischen National-Bundes der
      Vereinigten Staaten von Amerika. Philadelphia: German-
      American National Alliance, 1909-18.

1051 Neuer Deutsch-Amerikanischer Vereinskalender. New York:
      Scherl-sche Almanach Gesellschaft, 1907-14. Index to Ger-
      man-American organizations.

1052 Newsletter of the Society for German-American Studies.
      Youngstown/Cleveland, Ohio: Society for German-American
      Studies, 1968- .

1053 Penn Germania. Lebanon, Pa.: P. C. Croll, H. Schules,
      H. Kriebel, 1900-14.

1054 Der Pennsylvaanisch Deitsch Eileschpiggel. Bethlehem: Le-
      high University, 1943-46.

1055   Pennsylvania Dutchman.   Lancaster, Pa.:   Pennsylvania
        Dutch Folklore Center, Inc., 1949-   .

1056   Pennsylvania German Folklore Society.   Allentown: Pennsyl-
        vania German Folklore Society, 1936-65.

1057   Pennsylvania German Society: Proceedings and Addresses.
        Breinigsville, Pa.:   Pennsylvania German Society, 1895-   .

1058   Der Reggeboge.   Breinigsville, Pa.:   Pennsylvania German
        Society, 1967-   .

1059   Report: Journal of German-American Studies.   Baltimore:
        Society for the History of the Germans in Maryland, 1887-   .

1060   Schütze's Jahrbuch für Deutsch-Texaner.   San Antonio: A.
        Schütze, 1882-1940.

Emigration and Immigration

1061   Alander, Ursel.   "Die Auswanderung von der Insel Föhr in
        den Jahren 1850-75, " JNI.   7 (1961): 244, 262.

1062   Ander, O. F.   In the Trek of the Immigrants: Essays Pre-
        sented to Carl Wittke.   Rock Island, Illinois: Augustana His-
        torical Society, 1964.   Contains bibliography of Wittke's work.

1063   Anti-Defamation League.   Immigration and Citizenship: A
        Selected Bibliography.   New York, 1956.

1064   "The Arrival of Volga Germans in the USA, " American Hist.
        Soc. of Germans from Russia, Working Paper. 3 (1970): 39-41.

1065   Baden, Anna.   Immigration and Its Restriction in the U. S.:
        A List of Recent Writings.   Washington Library of Congress,
        1930.

1066   Baeumer, Otto.   "A Siegerland Emigrant List of 1938, " PF.
        19 (1970): 46.

1067   Barba, Preston.   "An Old Letter, " Eck. (March 19, 1955).
        Describes emigration.

1068   Bennet, Marion T.   American Immigration Policies: A His-
        tory.   Washington: Public Affairs Pr., 1964.

1069   Bennion, Lowell.   German Migration and Colonization: In-
        ventory and Prologue to Geographic Study.   Syracuse Univer-
        sity: Dissertation, 1963.

1070   Bergel, Egon.   "Die Eigenart der österreichischen Einwanderung nach Amerika, " Americana-Austriaca. 2, No. 10 (1970).

1071 Bernard, William and others. American Immigration Policy:
A Reappraisal. New York: Harper, 1950.

1072 Beutlin, Ludwig. Bremen und Amerika. Bremen: Schüne-
mann Verlag, 1953.

1073 Blendinger, Friedrich. "Die Auswanderung nach Nordamerika
aus dem Regierungsbezirk Oberbayern in den Jahren 1846-
52, " Z. für bayer. Landesges. 27 (1964).

1074 Bogen, Frederick. The German in America, or Advice and
Instruction for the German Immigrants in the U. S. of America.
2d ed. Boston: Greene, 1851. An immigrant handbook.

1075 Boston. Public Library. Americanization: A Selective List
of Books in the Public Library of the City of Boston. Boston:
Trustees, 1919.

1076 Bowers, D. Foreign Influences in American Life: Essays
and Critical Bibliography. Princeton: Princeton University
Pr. , 1944.

1077 Braun, Fritz. "Amerikaauswanderer aus Odernheim am
Glan, " NPfG. 40 (1960): 438-39.

1078 _____. "Auswanderer aus der Umgebung von Ludwigshfaen
a. Rh. auf dem Schiff Thistle of Glasglow, " Pfälz. Familien-
und Wappenkunde. 8 (1959): 253-72.

1079 _____. Auswanderer aus Steinweiler in drei Jahrhunderten.
(Schriften zur Wanderungsgesch. d. Pfälzer, no. 27). Kaiserslautern, 1968.

1080 _____. "The Eighteenth Century Emigration from the Palatinate: New Documentation, " PFI. 15 (1966): 40-48.

1081 _____. "German Emigrants from Palatinate Parishes, "
PGM. 25 (1968): 246-62.

1082 _____ and F. Krebs. Amerika-Auswanderer des 18.
Jahrhunderts aus südpfälzischen Gemeinden. Ludwigshafen
am Rh.: Louis, 1956.

1083 Bremner, R. H. "The United States and Bremen, " AGR.
16, vi (1950): 26-30.

1084 Bridgers, Frank. "Passenger Arrival Records in the National Archives, " NGSQ. 50 (1962): 140-45.

1085 Buffalo, Public Library. Our Immigrants of Foreign Tongues
in Their Old Homes and in America: A Selected Reading List.
Buffalo: Public Library, 1920.

1086   Cole, D. B. Immigrant City: Lawrence, Massachusetts,
        1945-1921. Chapel Hill: University of North Carolina Pr.,
        1963.

1087   Commager, Henry S. Immigration and American History:
        Essays in Honor of Theodore C. Blegen. Minneapolis: Uni-
        versity of Minnesota Pr., 1961.

1088   Converse, C. L. German Immigrant. Boston: Humphries,
        1953.

1089   Cook, Katherine and F. Reynolds. The Education of Native
        and Minority Groups: A Bibliography. Washington: Office
        of Education, 1935.

1090   Crawford, Rex. The Cultural Migration. Philadelphia: Uni-
        versity of Pennsylvania Pr., 1953.

1091   Cunz, Dieter. "Einwanderung und Einordnung der Deutsch-
        amerikaner," Deutsche Rundschau. 81 (1955): 132-43.

1092   Curti, Merle and K. Birr. "The Immigrant and the Ameri-
        can Image," MVHR. 37 (1950): 203-30.

1093   Davie, Maurice. Refugees in America. New York: Harper,
        1947.

1094   Divine, Robert. American Immigration Policy, 1924-52.
        New Haven: Yale University Pr., 1957.

1095   Duffy, John. "The Passage to the Colonies," MVHR. 37
        (1951): 21-38.

1096   Eckerson, Helen. "Immigration and National Origins," APSS.
        367 (1966): 4-14.

1097   Edwards, R. H. Immigration Studies in American Social
        Conditions. Madison, 1909.

1098   Engelsing, Rolf. Bremen als Auswanderungshafen 1683-1880
        (Veröffentlichungen aus d. Staatsarchiv d. Freien Hansestadt
        Bremen, Heft 29). Bremen: Schünemann Verlag, 1961.

1099   _____. "Deutschland und die Vereinigten Staaten im 19.
        Jahrhundert," Die Welt als Gesch. 18 (1958): 138-56.

1100   Fenske, C. "German Immigration in the City of Oswego,"
        Pub. Oswego Co. Hist. Soc. 28 (1966-67): 54-61.

1101   Finke, Günter. "Norddeutsche in aller Welt: Auswanderer
        aus der Probstei Ostholstein," Norddeutsche Familienkunde.
        18 (1969): 223-26, 252-54.

Emigration and Immigration 73

1102   Franzen, Max. "The Door of Immigration, " AGR. 14, ii
        (1947): 12-14.

1103   Frey, Julius. "Auswanderungen nach Nordamerika aus der
        Landschaft zwischen Vogelsberg und Speisart im 18. Jahrhun-
        dert, " Heimat-Jahrbuch des Kreises Gelnhausen. (1962): 56-
        57.

1104   Fröbel, Julius. Aus Amerika: Erfahrungen, Reisen und
        Studien. Leipzig: Weber, 1857-58. DLC

1105   _____. Die deutsche Auswanderung und ihre culturhistor-
        ische Bedeutung: Fünfzehn Briefe an den Herausgeber der
        Allgemeinen Auswanderer-Zeitung. Leipzig: Wagner, 1858.
        DLC

1106   Froehlich, Hugo. "Pioneers from Stauderheim, " PD. 8 (1957):
        43-46.

1107   Glazer, Nathan. "The Immigrant Groups and American Cul-
        ture, " Yale Review. 48 (1959): 382-97.

1108   Graafen, R. Die Aus- und Abwanderung aus der Eifel in den
        Jahren 1815 bis 1955. (Forschungen zur D. Landeskunde,
        127). Berlin, 1961.

1109   Grant, Madison. List of Authoritative Works on Immigration.
        Washington: GPO, 1928.

1110   Griffin, A. P. C. A List of Books on Immigration. Washing-
        ton: GPO, 1907.

1111   Hacker, Werner. Auswanderungen aus dem früheren Hochstift
        Speyer nach Südosteuropa und Übersee im 18. Jahrhundert:
        Eine Dokumentation in Regestenform nach Unterlagen des
        Badischen Generallandesarchivs Karlsruhe. (Schriften zur
        Wanderungsgesch. d. Pfälzer, no. 28). Kaiserslautern, 1969.

1112   Handlin, Oscar. A Pictorial History of Immigration. New
        York: Crown, 1972.

1113   _____. The Positive Contribution by Immigrants. Paris:
        UNESCO, 1955.

1114   _____. This was America. Cambridge: Harvard Univer-
        sity Pr., 1949.

1115   _____. The Uprooted: The Epic Story of the Great Mi-
        gration that Made the American People. Boston: Little
        Brown, 1951.

1116   Hansen, Marcus L. Atlantic Migration 1607-1860. Repr.:
        Gloucester, Mass.: Peter Smith, 1972.

1117 _____. Die Einwanderer in der Geschichte Amerikas.
Stuttgart: Franz Mittelbach Verlag, 1948.

1118 Hilsenrad, Helen. Brown Was the Danube. New York:
Thomas Yoseloff, 1966. Story of an Austrian immigrant.

1119 Hinrichsen, H. C. "Beiträge zur Auswanderung von Föhr
und Amrum nach Amerika, " JNI. 7 (1961): 225-43.

1120 Hölzhuber, Franz. "Sketches from Northwestern America and
Canada--Skizzen aus dem Nordwesten von Amerika u. Canada
aufgenommen in den Jahren 1856 bis 1860 von Franz Hölzhuber, " AH. 16 (1965): 49-64.

1121 Huber, Armin. "Dokumente zur pfälzischen Auswanderung
des 18. Jahrhunderts nach Amerika, " Die Schaumbirg-Lippische Heimat. 13 (1962): 22-33.

1122 _____. "Dokumente zur pfälzischen Auswanderung des 18.
Jahrunderts nach Amerika, " Pfälzer Heimat. 13 (1962): 54-
55.

1123 Hutchinson, E. P. Immigrants and Their Children, 1850-
1950. New York: Wiley, 1956.

1124 Immigrant Groups in the U.S. New York: Russel Sage Foundation, 1932.

1125 Immigration. Washington: GPO, 1916.

1126 Johnson, Hildegard Binder. "The Location of German Immigrants in the Middle West, " AAG. 41 (1951): 1-41.

1127 Jones, Maldwyn. American Immigration. Chicago: University of Chicago Pr., 1960.

1128 Kapp, Friedrich. Geschichte der deutschen Einwanderung in
Amerika. New York: Steiger, 1867.

1129 Keller, Hansheinz. "Auswanderung: Das grosse Abenteuer
in alten Briefen, " ZKA. 13 (1963): 306-16.

1130 Kennedy, John F. A Nation of Immigrants. New York:
Harper & Row, 1964.

1131 Klebaner, Benjamin. "State and Local Immigration Regulatio
in the U.S. Before 1882, " Int. Rev. Soc. Hist. 3 (1958): 269
95.

1132 Krauss, Michael. The Atlantic Civilization: Eighteenth Century Origins. Ithaca: Cornell University Pr., 1949.

1133 _____. Immigration: The American Mosaic, from Pilgrims to Modern Refugees. Princeton: Van Nostrand, 1966.

1134   Krebs, Friedrich. "Amerika-Auswanderer des 18. Jahrhunderts aus dem Gebiet der Pfalz und dem ehemaligen pfälzischen Unterelsass, " Genealogie. 19 (1970): 175 ff.

1135   . "Amerikaauswanderer des 18. Jahrhunderts aus
der Nordpfalz, " NPfG. 41 (1961): 556-57.

1136   . "Auswanderer nach Amerika im 18. Jahrhundert
aus dem ehemaligen Herzogtum Zweibrücken und dem Kur-
pfälzischen Oberamt Germersheim, " Mitteil. z. Wanderungsgesch. d. Pfälzer. No. 3 (1967).

1137   . "Beiträge zur Amerikaauswanderung des 18. Jahrhunderts aus Altwürttemberg, " Südwestdeutsche Blätter f. F.
u. W. 12 (1961): 186-89.

1138   . "18th Century Emigrants from Edenkoben, " PD.
4 (1953): 9.

1139   . "Eighteenth Century Emigrants to America from
the Duchy of Zweibrücken and the Germersheim District, "
PFI. 18 (1969): 44-48.

1140   . "Ein Aufruf zur Auswanderung nach dem amerikanischen Staat Massachusetts aus dem Jahre 1751, " Hess.
Familienkunde. 5 (1961): 435-37.

1141   . "Einige Amerika-Auswanderer des 18. Jahrhunderts
aus Otterberg, " NPfG. 38 (1958): 236.

1142   . "Emigrants to America from the Duchy of Zweibrücken: Excerpts from the Records of the Protestant Church
of Zweibrücken, " PGM. 23 (1964): 255-56.

1143   . "New Materials on the 18th Century Emigration
from the Speyer State Archives, " PFI. 16 (1966): 40-41.

1144   . "New Materials on the 18th Century Emigration
from Württemberg, " PFI. 16 (1966): 22-23.

1145   and Milton Rubincam. Emigrants from the Palatine
to the American Colonies in the Eighteenth Century. Norristown, Pa.: Pennsylvania German Society, 1953.

1146   and Don Yoder. "Lists of German Immigrants to
the American Colonies from Zweibrücken in the Palatinate,
1750-71, " PGFS. 16 (1953): 171-83.

1147   Laistner, M. "The Palatine Emigration of 1709, " NY Hist.
23 (1942): 460-64.

1148   Lancour, Harold. A Bibliography of Ship Passenger Lists
        1538-1825: Being a Guide to Published Lists of Early Immi-
        grants to North America. 3d ed. Baltimore: Genealogical
        Book Co., 1963.

1149   Lawrence, Elwood. The Immigrant in American Fiction.
        Western Reserve University: Dissertation, 1944.

1150   Lederle, M. "Aus Lippstadt nach Amerika, " Heimatblätter:
        Organ f. d. Belange des Heimatbundes L. 44 (1963): 95.

1151   Lenhart, John. "Address of Peter Cahensely on the Care of
        Emigrants Delivered at the General Meeting of the German
        Societies in Trier, Sept. 11, 1865, " SJR. 52 (1959): 22-27.

1152   _____. "The Central Verein and Immigrant Care, " SJR.
        52 (1959): 96-97.

1153   _____. "King Ludwig 1 of Bavaria and the Missions of
        the Germans in the United States, " SJR. 59 (1966): 218-22.

1154   Leonard, Henry. The Open Gates: The Protest Against the
        Movement to Restrict European Immigration, 1896-1924.
        Northwestern University: Dissertation, 1967.

1155   Lewis, Ward. "The New World and the Yankee: Emigration
        as a Theme in the Works of Johannes Schlaf, " GAS. 6 (1973):
        3-20.

1156   MacGeorge, A. E. "Restriction of Immigration, 1920-25: A
        Selected Bibliography, " Monthly Labor Rev. 22 (1926): 510-
        26.

1157   Mahrenholtz, Hans. "Auswanderungen aus den Aemtern Cat-
        lenburg-Lindau, Duderstadt und Gieboldehausen 1831-63 bezw.
        1839-66, " Norddeutsche Familienkunde. 10 (1961): 245-49.

1158   Maisel, Albert. They All Chose America. New York:
        Thomas Nelson, 1957.

1159   Matthias, Erich. Sozial-Demokratie und Nation: Zur Ideen-
        geschichte der Sozialdemokratischen Emigration 1933-38.
        Stuttgart: Deutsche Verlagsanstalt, 1952.

1160   Mayfield, George. "The Diary of a German Immigrant, "
        THQ. 10 (1951): 249-81.

1161   Meier, Heinz. The U. S. and Switzerland in the Nineteenth
        Century. (Studies in American History, Vol. 1). The
        Hague: Mouton and Co., 1963.

1162   Meinart, Hermann. "Kassel und Washington, Hessen und
        Amerika, " in Hessen, Kultur und Wirtschaft. Wiesbaden:
        Max Krause, 1952, pp. 53-56.

1163   Mergen, Josef.   "Die Auswanderung aus dem Moselland nach
        Nordamerika im 19. Jahrhundert, " Kurtrierisches Jahrbuch.
        4 (1964).

1164   Meyer, Luciana.   German-American Migration and the Ban-
        croft Naturalization Treaties, 1868-1910.   University of New
        York: Dissertation, 1970.

1165   Mundel, Hedwig.   "A List of Wittgenstein Emigrants, " Penn.
        Gen. Mag.   26 (1970):   133-43.

1166   Norwood, Frederick.   Strangers and Exiles.   Nashville:
        Abingdom, 1969.

1167   Pabst, Frederick.   "Our Ancestors in Their Native Rhineland:
        Their Way of Life, 1650-1850, " Eck.   (July 31, 1954).

1168   Panunzio, C.   The Immigrant Portrayed in Biography and
        Story: A Selected List with Notes.   New York: Foreign
        Language Information Service, 1925.

1169   Pittsburgh, Carnegie Library.   Foreign Born Americans:
        Their Contributions to American Life and Culture: A Select
        List.   Pittsburgh: Carnegie Library, 1920.

1170   Postma, Johan.   Das niederländische Erbe der Preussisch-
        Russländischen in Europa, Asien und America.   Emmen,
        Netherlands: The Author, 1959.

1171   Radkau, Joachim.   Die deutsche Emigration in den USA: Ihr
        Einfluss auf die amerikanische Europapolitik.   Düsseldorf:
        Bertelsmann Universitätsverlag, 1971.

1172   Ray, Mary.   The Immigration Problem: A Bibliography.
        Madison: Wisconsin Free Library Commission, 1909.

1173   Rein, Gustav.   Europa und Uebersee: Gesammelte Aufsätze.
        Göttingen: Musterschmidt, 1961.

1174   A Report on World Population Migrations as Related to the
        United States of America: An Exploratory Survey of Past
        Studies.   St. Louis: Washington University, 1956.

1175   Rimpau, Hans.   "Passagier-Listen von Einwanderer-Schiffen
        nach den USA, " Geneologie.   13 (1964):   280-84.

1176   Robbins, Walter.   "Swiss and German Emigrants to America
        in Rotterdam, 1736:   Excerpts from the Travel Diary of
        Hieronymus Annoni, SAHS.   1 (1965):   16-18.

1177   Roggenbauer, Josef.   "Ueber die schweren Anfänge einer
        deutschen Siedlung in Neu-England aus der Mitte des 18. Jahr-
        hunderts, " ZKA.   19 (1969):   297-302.

1178 Roucek, Joseph. The Immigrant in Fiction and Biography. New York: Bureau for Intercultural Education, 1945.

1179 Ruhe, R. "Die Auswanderung aus der Oberherrschaft des ehemaligen Fürstentums Schwarzburg-Rudolstadt im 19. Jahrhundert und ihre Beweggründe, " R. Heimathefte. 6 (1960): 301-16.

1180 _____. "Die deutsche Auswanderung im 19. Jahrhundert im Spiegel der Gesetzgebung des ehemaligen Fürstentums Schwarzburg-Rudolstadt, " R. Heimathefte. 7 (1961): 278-84.

1181 Rushmore, E. Immigrant Backgrounds. New York: Russel Sage Foundation, n. d.

1182 Saveth, Edward. American Historians and European Immigrants 1875-1925. New York: Columbia University Pr., 1948.

1183 Schechtman, Joseph. The Refugee in the World: Displacement and Integration. New York: A. S. Barnes, T. Yoseloff, 1964.

1184 Schlag, Wilhelm. "A Survey of Austrian Emigration to the United States, " Hietsch. (1962): 139-96.

1185 Schmidt, Martin. Wort Gottes und Fremdlingsschaft: Die Kirche vor dem Auswanderungsproblem des 19. Jahrhunderts. Rothenburg: Luther, 1955.

1186 Schock, Adolph. In Quest of Free Land. San Jose: The Author, 1965.

1187 Schomaker, Karl. "Die Auswanderung aus Mecklenburg, speziell im 19. Jahrhundert, " Archiv f. Sippenforschung u. a. verwandten Geb. 28 (1962): 260-66.

1188 Schreiber, Edward. Landed on New Shores. New York: Pageant Pr., 1957.

1189 Schuchmann, Heinz. "Sibylla Charlotta Winchenbach, Die Ehefrau Josua Kocherthals, " Mitteilungen z. Wanderungsgesch. d. Pfälzer. (1970): 25-28.

1190 _____. "Der 1708 nach Amerika ausgewanderte Pfarrer Josua Kocherthal hiess ursprünglich Josua Harrsh, " Mitteilungen z. Wanderungsgesch. d. Pfälzer. (1967): Heft 4.

1191 Schünzel, Eva. Die deutsche Auswanderung nach Nordamerika im 17. und 18. Jahrhundert. Würzburg University: Dissertation, 1959.

1192 Die Schweiz und die Vereinigten Staaten von Amerika: Bezie-

hungen der Schweiz zu den Vereinigten Staaten: Die schweizerische Auswanderung. Bern: Bibliographische Auskunftsstelle
der Landesbibliothek, 1964. Bibliography of 550 articles and
books.

1193   Seidel, Friedrick. Die neue Einwanderung: Geschichte und
        Problematik der Ueberseewanderung nach den Vereinigten
        Staaten zwischen 1880 und 1930. Köln: Dissertation, 1958.

1194   Seidensticker, Oswald. Die erste deutsche Einwanderung in
        Amerika. Philadelphia: Globe Printing House, 1883. UC

1195   Siefarth, Günter. "Return Migration, " AGR. 31, iii (1965):
        17-18, 26.

1196   Siegl, Walter. "Auswanderung im 18. Jahrhundert aus dem
        Kirchspiel Thaleischweiler, " PFH. 8 (1960): 55.

1197   Smith, Abbot. "Some Facts About Eighteenth Century Ger-
        man Immigration, " PH. 10 (1943): 105-17.

1198   Solomons, Barbara. Ancestors and Immigrants: A Changing
        New England Tradition. Cambridge: Harvard, 1956.

1199   Spencer, Frank. "An Eighteenth Century Account of German
        Emigration to the American Colonies, " J. Mod. Hist. 28
        (1956): 55-59.

1200   Stange, Douglas. "Lutheran Involvement in the American
        Colonization Society, " M-A. 49 (1967): 140-60.

1201   Steinemann, Ernst and Don Yoder. "A List of Eighteenth
        Century Emigration from the Canton of Schaffhausen to the
        American Colonies, 1734-52, " PGFS. 16 (1953): 185-96.

1202   Stoessingers, John. The Refugee and the World Community.
        Minneapolis: University of Minnesota, 1957.

1203   Stoetzner, Fridel. The Transplanted. New York: McGraw-
        Hill, 1966.

1204   Stourzh, Gerald. "Bibliographie der deutschsprachigen Emi-
        gration in den Vereinigten Staaten, 1933-63: Geschichte und
        Politische Wissenschaft, " JAS. 10 (1965): 232-66; 11 (1966):

1205   _____. "Die deutschsprachige Emigration in den Vereinig-
        ten Staaten: Geschichtswissenschaft und Politische Wissen-
        schaft, " JAS. 10 (1965): 59-77.

1206   Struck, Wolf-Heino. Die Auswanderung aus dem Herzogtum
        Nassau 1806-66: Ein Kapitel der modernen politischen und
        sozialen Entwicklung. (Geschichtliche Landeskunde, 4). Wies-
        baden: F. Steiner, 1966.

1207   Sturmberger, Hans. "Die Amerika-Auswanderung aus Ober-
        österreich zur Zeit des Neo-Absolutismus, " Mitteilungen d.
        oberöst. Landesarchives. 7 (1970).

1208   Tyler, Poyntz. Immigration and the U.S. New York: H. W.
        Wilson Co. , 1956.

1209   Ulbrich, Harald. "Auswanderer aus Sachsen nach USA, "
        Archiv f. Sippenforschung u. a. verwandten Geb. 28 (1962):
        394-95.

1210   United States. Library of Congress. Brief List of Recent
        References on Immigration and the Labor Supply. Washing-
        ton: GPO, 1920.

1211   _____ . _____ . Brief List of Recent References on Im-
        migration and the Refugee in the U.S. Washington: GPO,
        1941.

1212   _____ . _____ . Brief List of References on Immigra-
        tion. Washington: GPO, 1920.

1213   _____ . _____ . Brief List of References on Recent
        Immigration Legislation in the U.S. Washington: GPO, 1923.

1214   _____ . _____ . Brief List of References on the Immi-
        grants on our Shores. Washington: GPO, 1922.

1215   _____ . _____ . Citizenship: A List of Books. Wash-
        ington: GPO, 1933.

1216   _____ . _____ . Deportation of Aliens: A Bibliograph-
        ical List. Washington: GPO, 1931.

1217   _____ . _____ . List of Books on Immigration. Wash-
        ington: GPO, 1907.

1218   _____ . _____ . List of Recent References on Immigra-
        tion in the U.S., With Special Reference to the Immigration
        Act, 1924. Washington: GPO, 1924.

1219   _____ . _____ . List of References on American Immi
        gration, including Americanization, Effect of War, etc. Was
        ington: GPO, 1918.

1220   _____ . _____ . List of References on the National Ori
        gins Provision of the Immigration Act of 1924. Washington:
        GPO, 1924.

1221   _____ . _____ . Select List of References on Immigra-
        tion Restriction by Educational Test. Washington: GPO, 19

1222   Vagts, A. Deutsch-Amerikanische Rückwanderung. Heidelbe
        1962.

1223   Von Hofe, Harold. "August Wilhelm Schlegel's American Emi-
       gration Plans: Biographical-Literary Notes, " Wert und Wort:
       Festschrift für Else M Fleissner. Aurora, New York: Wells
       College, 1965.

1224   Walker, Mack. Germany and the Emigration 1816-1885.
       (Harvard Historical Monographs, no. 56). Cambridge: Har-
       vard University Pr., 1964.

1225   Weaver, Herbert. "Foreigners in Antebellum Towns of the
       Lower South, " JSH. 13 (1947): 62-73.

1226   Weil, Louise. Aus dem schwäbischen Pfarrhaus nach Ameri-
       ka: Reiseskizzen. Stuttgart, 1860. UC

1227   Weitz, Wilhelm. "Beiträge zur Auswanderung aus Ostfries-
       land im 19. Jahrhundert, " Fries. Jahrbuch. (1958): 110-35.

1228   Wellek, Albert. "Der Einfluss der deutschen Emigration auf
       die Entwicklung der nordamerikanischen Psychologie, " JAS.
       10 (1965): 34-58.

1229   _____. "The Impact of the German Immigration on the De-
       velopment of American Psychology, " J. Hist. Beh. Sci. 4
       (1968): 207-229.

1230   Wellhausen, Marianne. Ueber deutsche Auswanderung nach
       den Vereinigten Staaten im 19. Jahrhundert, unter besonderer
       Berücksichtigung Mittelfrankens. University of Erlangen:
       Dissertation, 1949.

1231   Wendte, Charles W. Deutschland und Amerika. Boston,
       1910. UC

1232   Wenzlaff, Theodore. "The Russian Germans Come to the
       U.S., " NH. 49 (1968): 379-82.

1233   Wittke, Carl. "The Immigrant Theme on the American
       Stage, " MVHR. 39 (1952): 211-32.

1234   _____. "Immigration Policy Prior to World War I, " APSS.
       262 (1949): 5-14.

1235   Wuerfell, Stella. "Women of the Saxon Immigration, " CHIQ.
       34 (1961): 61 ff.; 35 (1962): 14 ff.

1236   Wyman, David. Paper Walls: America and the Refugee
       Crisis, 1938-41. Amherst: University of Massachusetts
       Pr., 1968.

1237   Zoff, Otto. Tagebücher aus der Emigration 1939-41. Heidel-
       berg: Schneider, 1968.

1238   Zwingmann, A. C. and M. Pfister-Ammende. Uprooting and
       After. New York: Springer-Verlag New York Inc., 1973.

Ethnicity and Acculturation

1239   Anderson, Charles. White Protestant Americans: From Na-
       tional Origins to Religious Groups. Englewood Cliffs: Pren-
       tice-Hall, 1970.

1240   Angoff, Charles. "Mencken as a German American," Chic.
       Jewish Forum. 25 (1967): 143-46.

1241   App, Austin. "May Lawbreakers Smear German-Americans
       as Nazis," DDA. (Sept. 1973): 2

1242   Baughlin, William. "The Development of Nativism in Cin-
       cinnati," Bul. C. Hist. Soc. 22 (1961): 240-55.

1243   Bayor, Ronald. Ethnic Conflict in New York City, 1929-41.
       University of Pennsylvania: Dissertation, 1970.

1244   Beals, Carleton. Brass-Knuckle Crusade: The Great Know-
       Nothing Conspiracy: 1820-60. New York: Hastings House,
       1960.

1245   Bode, Carl. "Henry Louis Mencken," RJGAH. 29 (1956): 70-
       73.

1246   Borach, Leona. "Settlement of St. Ansgar: A Miniature Melt-
       ing Pot," IJHP. 46 (1948): 296-315.

1247   Cray, Edward. "More Ethnic and Place Names as Derisive
       Adjectives," WF. 24 (1965): 197-98.

1248   Cunz, Dieter. "H. L. Mencken," NYSZH. (Feb. 12, 1955).

1249   Davie, Maurice and Samuel Koenig. "Adjustment of Refugees
       to American Life," APSS. 262 (1949): 159-65.

1250   Deusner, Charles. "The Know Nothing Riots in Louisville,"
       KHSR. 61 (1963): 122-47.

1251   Dietz, Paul. "The Transition from German to English in the
       Missouri Synod from 1910 to 1947," CHIQ. 22 (1949): 97-127.

1252   Dinnerstein, Leonard and F. Jaher. A History of Ethnic
       Minorities in America. New York: Appleton-Century-Crofts,
       1970.

1253   Drachsler, Julius. Democracy and Assimilation: The Blend-
       ing of Immigration Heritages in America. Repr.: Westport,
       Conn.: Negro University Pr., 1972.

1254 "Foreign Language Press Discusses Prejudice: Results in Prize Contest," CG. 8 (1948): 77-83.

1255 Glazer, N. and D. Moynihan. Beyond the Melting Pot. Boston: MIT Pr., 1963.

1256 Gleason, P. "The Melting Pot: Symbol of Fusion or Confusion?" AQ. 16 (1964): 20-46.

1257 Goebel, Julius. Ueber die Zukunft unseres Volkes in Amerika. New York, 1884. UC

1258 Gordon, Milton. "Assimilation in America: Theory and Reality," Daedalus. 90 (1961): 263-85.

1259 _____. Assimilation in American Life: The Role of Race, Religion and National Origin. New York: Oxford University Pr., 1964.

1260 Graebner, Alan. The Acculturation of an Immigration Lutheran Church: The Lutheran Church-Missouri Synod, 1917-29. Columbia University: Dissertation, 1965.

1261 Greeley, A. M. Why Can't They Be Like Us? New York: Dutton, 1971.

1262 Hagedorn, Hermann. The Hyphenated Family: An American Saga. New York: Macmillan, 1960. History of a German-American family.

1263 Handlin, Oscar. Boston's Immigrants: 1790-1880, A Study in Acculturation. Cambridge: Belknap Pr., 1959.

1264 _____. Children of the Uprooted. New York: Braziller, 1966.

1265 _____. "Historical Perspectives on the American Ethnic Group," Daedalus. 90 (1961): 220-32.

1266 _____. Immigration as a Factor in American History. New York: Prentice-Hall, 1961.

1267 _____. Race and Nationality in American Life. New York: Little, 1957.

1268 Hartmann, Edward. The Movement to Americanize the Immigrant. New York: Columbia University Pr., 1948.

1269 Herr, Christ. "Sturmgeläute: Rettet das Deutschamerikanertum," DDA. (July, 1973). An important essay on German-American ethnicity.

1270 Higham, John. Strangers in the Land: Patterns of American

Nativism 1860-1925. New York: Atheneum Pr., 1963.

1271 Hilbig, Frederick. Anglicized German Surnames in America.
       University of Utah: Dissertation, 1955.

1272 Jockers, Ernst. Gedenke, dass Du ein Deutscher bist. Bar-
       celona: C. Seither, 1915. DLC D&Y NN

1273 Johnson, Dale. "Lutheran Dissension and Schism at Gettys-
       burg Seminary, 1864," PH. 33 (1966): 13-29. On use of
       German in the church and seminary.

1274 Juhnke, James. "The Political Acculturation of the Kansas
       Mennonites, 1870-1940," MQR. 43 (1969): 247 ff.

1275 Kaufman, David. "English and German," Eck. (Jan. 4, 11,
       1964). German- and Anglo-American relations in Pennsyl-
       vania.

1276 Kennedy, Philip. "The Know-Nothing Movement in Kentucky:
       Role of M. J. Spalding, Catholic Bishop of Louisville," Filson
       CHQ. 38 (1964): 17-35.

1277 Kleppner, Paul. The Cross of Culture: A Social Analysis of
       Midwestern Politics, 1850-1900. New York: The Free Pr.,
       1970.

1278 Kloss, Heinz. "Assimilationsfragen des Pennsylvaniadeutsch-
       tums," Pfälzer Heimat. 3 (1952): 83-87.

1279 _____. Das Nationalitätenrecht der Vereinigten Staaten von
       Amerika. (Ethnos, I). Wien: Braumüller, 1963.

1280 _____. Volksgruppenrecht in den Vereinigten Staaten.
       Essen: Essener Verlagsanstalt, 1940.

1281 Knill, William. "The Hutterites: Cultural Transmission in
       a Closed Society," Alberta Hist. Rev. 16 (1968): 1-10.

1282 Knortz, Karl. Die Deutschfeindlichkeit Amerikas. Leipzig:
       T. Gerstenberg, n. d. DLC

1283 Kollacks, Walter. "Bericht des Hauptvorstandes," DDA. (Oct.
       1973): 1. About the German-American National Congress.

1284 _____. "Hier spricht der Präsident," DDA. (1962-73).
       Monthly column by the President of the German-American
       National Congress.

1285 Kreider, Henry. "The English Language Schism in the Lu-
       theran Church in New York, 1794-1810," CHIQ. 21 (1948): 50-
       60.

1286   Krodel, Gerhard. "CBS TV and the Germans, " AGR_ 34
       (1968):

1287   Kurokawa, M. "Psycho-Social Roles of Mennonite Children in
       a Changing Society, " Canadian Rev. of Soc. & Anthrop. 6
       (1969): 15-35.

1288   Lantz, Marian. "Who Are Our Neighbors?" AGR_ 13, iv
       (1947): 22-23o

1289   Lieberson, Stanley. Ethnic Patterns in American Cities.
       New York: Free Press of Glencoe, 1963.

1290   Leonard, P. "The Beginnings of Nativism in California, "
       PHR。 30 (1961): 23-38.

1291   Luebke, Frederick. Ethnic Voters and the Election of Lincoln.
       Lincoln: University of Nebraska Pr., 1971.

1292   Mann, Georg. "Furor Teutonicus: Upper Mississippi Abeit-
       lung, " Yale Rev. 60 (1970): 306-20.   Excellent essay on Ger-
       man-American life.

1293   Marx, Karl T. "Second-Class Citizens, " Steuben News. (May,
       1973).

1294   Mockler, W. E.   "Surnames of Trans-Alleghany Virginia,
       1750-1800, " NA. 4 (1956): 96-118.   About Anglicized names.

1295   Motsch, Markus.   "H. L. Mencken and German Kultur, " GAS.
       6 (1973): 21-42.

1296   Novak, Michael.   "The New Ethnicity, " The Humanist. 33
       (1973): 18-21.

1297   O'Brien, Kenneth.   "Education, Americanization and the Su-
       preme Court: The 1920's, " AQ. 13 (1961): 161-74.   About
       anti-German hysteria.

1298   Olson, Audrey. St. Louis Germans, 1850-1920: The Nature
       of an Immigrant Community and its Relation to the Assimila-
       tion Process.   University of Kansas: Dissertation, 1970.

1299   Peachey, Paul。 "Identity Crisis Among American Mennonites, "
       MQR. 42 (1968): 243-59。

1300   Peters, Otto. H. L. Mencken's Attitude Towards Germany.
       University of Berlin: Dissertation, 1956.

1301   Rapp, Wilhelm. Erinnerungen eines Deutsch-Amerikaners an
       das alte Vaterland: In Reden und Briefen.   Chicago: Druck
       der Franz Gendeler Printing Co., 1890. DLC

1302   Riley, Marvin. Farmers' Attitudes Toward the Hutterite
        Brethren: A Study in Intergroup Relations. University of
        Missouri: Dissertation, 1968.

1303   Rodgers, Jack. "The Foreign Language Issue in Nebraska,
        1918-23, " NH. 39 (1958): 1-22. About the suppression of
        the German language.

1304   Schneider, Carl. "Americanization of Karl August Rauschen-
        busch, 1816-99, " ChH. 24 (1955): 3-14.

1305   Singer, Louis. "Now an American: The Autobiography of
        Louis E. Singer, " Am. Jewish Archives. 22 (April, 1970).

1306   Smith, Elmer. A Study of Acculturation in an Amish Com-
        munity. Syracuse University: Dissertation, 1956.

1307   Sommer, Martin. "How English Preaching Began in St.
        Louis, " CHIQ. 23 (1950): 21-24.

1308   Soule, Leon. The Know-Nothing Party in New Orleans.
        Baton Rouge: Louisiana State University Pr., 1962.

1309   Struble, George. "The French Element Among the Pennsyl-
        vania Germans, " PH. 22 (1955): 267-76.

1310   Sweet, William. "Cultural Pluralism in the American Tradi-
        tion, " Christendom. 1 (1947): 316-26, 501-08.

1311   Tolzmann, Don Heinrich. "A History of Anti-Germanism in
        America, " DDA. (July, 1973).

1312   _____ . "Was ist des Deutschamerikaners Vaterland?" DMH.
        (Nov. 29, 1973).

1313   "U. S. -Deutsche sind keine Wurstzipfel-Faschisten, " DW.
        (March 14, 1973).

1314   Vagts, Alfred. "The Germans and the Red Man, " AGR. 24,
        i (1957): 13-17.

1315   Weaver, Glenn. "Benjamin Franklin and the Pennsylvania
        Germans, " WMQ. 14 (1958): 536-59.

1316   Weiss, James. "The Problem of Language Transition among
        Lutherans in Ohio, 1836-58, " CHIQ. 39 (1966): 19.

1317   White, W. Bruce. The Military and the Melting Pot: The
        American Army and Minority Groups, 1865-1924. University
        of Wisconsin: Dissertation, 1968.

1318   Wittke, Carl. "Fissures in the Melting Pot, " in The Immi-
        gration of Ideas: Studies in the North Atlantic Community.

Rock Island: Augustana Historical Society, 1968.

1319 _____. "National Unity and Cultural Diversity, " AGR. 11
(1945): 31-32, 36.

1320 Wrede, Franz-Otto. Schmelztiegel Amerika. Berlin, 1941.

1321 Wust, Klaus. "German Immigrants and Nativism in Virginia
1840-60, " RJGAH. 29 (1956): 31-50.

German-Americans in American Politics and Wars

1322 Allen, Oliver. "The Lewis Albums, " American Heritage. 14,
i (1962): 65-80. About a Hessian soldier.

1323 Allman, C. B. Lewis Wetzel, Indian Fighter: The Life and
Times of a Frontier Hero. New York: Devin-Adair, 1961.

1324 App, Austin. "Die Deutschen der USA: Ihre einstige Macht
und ihr Niedergang, " OVZT. (March 15-April 5, 1968).

1325 _____. "German-Americans and Wilson's Peace Making, "
SJR. 56 (1963): 93-96, 107, 126-30, 166-71.

1326 Barnett, James. "August Willich, Soldier Extraordinary, "
HPSO. 20 (1962): 60-74.

1327 Beard, Eva. "Doctor-Naturalist on Tour, 1783-84, " AGR.
25, i (1958): 27-29. About a Revolutionary surgeon.

1328 Becker, Carl. "The Death of John Frederick Bollmeyer:
Murder Most Foul?" Bul. C. Hist. Soc. 24 (1966): 249-69.
About an anti-war spokesman murdered in 1862.

1329 Bell, Leland. Anatomy of a Hate Movement: The German
American Bund, 1936-41. University of West Virginia: Dissertation, 1968.

1330 _____. "The Failure of Nazism in America: The German
American Bund, 1936-41, " Pol. Sci. Q. 85 (1970): 585-99.

1331 Berlin, Ira. "A Wisconite in World War I: Reminiscences
of Edmund P. Arpin, Jr. , " WMH. (1967-68): 124-38, 218-
37.

1332 Bischoff, Ralph. Nazi Conquest Through German Culture.
Cambridge: Harvard University Pr. , 1942.

1333 Boeck, George. "A Historical Note on the Uses of Census
Returns, " MA. 44 (1962): 46-50. The foreign-born vote in
the Northwest.

1334   Bonadio, Felice.   "The Failure of German Propaganda in the
        United States, 1914-17," MA. 41 (1959): 40-57.

1335   Boxerman, Burton.   Reaction of the St. Louis Jewish Com-
        munity to Anti-Semitism: 1933-45.   St. Louis University:
        Dissertation, 1967.

1336   Brock, Peter.   Pacifism in the United States from the Colon-
        ial Era to the First World War.   Princeton: Princeton Uni-
        versity Pr., 1968.

1337   Burlingham, Charles and others.   The Germans Reich and
        Americans of German Origin.   New York: Oxford University
        Pr., 1938.

1338   Butler, Loula.   "A Hessian Soldier in Cambridge," Vermont
        Hist. 24 (1956): 178.

1339   Callahan, E. W.   List of Officers of the Navy of the U. S.
        and of the Marine Corps from 1775 to 1900; Compiled from
        the Official Records.   New York: Hamersly, 1901.

1340   Cary, Lorin.   "The Wisconsin Loyalty Legion, 1917-1918,"
        WMH. 53 (1969): 33-50.

1341   Child, Clifton.   The German-Americans in Politics 1914-17.
        Madison: University of Wisconsin Pr., 1939.

1342   Chyet, Stanley.   "Ohio Valley Jewry During the Civil War,"
        HPSO. 21 (1963): 179-87.

1343   Claussen, W. E.   "The Revolutionary War in Lower Berks,"
        HRBC. 34 (1969): 70-73.

1344   Closen, Ludwig von.   The Revolutionary Journal of Baron Lud-
        wig von Closen 1780-83.   Acomb, Chapel Hill: University of
        North Carolina Pr., 1958.

1345   Cöster, G. C.   Hessian Soldiers in the American Revolution:
        Records of Their Marriages, and Baptisms of Their Children
        in America, Performed by the Rev. G. C. Cöster, 1776-81,
        Chaplain of Two Hessian Regiments.   Cincinnati, 1959.

1346   Conners, Michael.   "Development of Germanphobia," SJR.
        53 (1961): 328-31, 371-74.

1347   Cronau, Rudolph.   Our Hyphenated Citizens, Are They Right
        or Wrong?   Should They Be Allowed to Stay, or Should They
        Be Deported, Or Confined in Detention Camps?   New York:
        Cronau, 1915.   DLC

1348   Cuddy, Edward.   "Pro-Germanism and American Catholicism,
        1914-17," CathHR. 54 (1968): 427-54.

1349 Cunz, Dieter. "The Baltimore Germans and the Oath of Allegiance in 1778, " RJGAH. 25 (1942): 31-33.

1350 _____. "Civil War Letters of a German Immigrant, Ferdinand Cunz, " AGR. 11 (1944): 30-33.

1351 Davidson, Robert. War Comes to Quaker Pennsylvania 1682-1756. Philadelphia: Temple University Publications, 1957.

1352 Davis, Gerlad. The History of the German-American Bund. Vanderbilt University: Dissertation, 1955.

1353 DeBaillou, Clemens. "Baron Friedrich von Riedesel, 1738-1800, " MO. 44 (1952): 212-16.

1354 Dickore, Marie. "A Hessian Soldier in Lexington, Kentucky, " Filson CHQ. 36 (1962): 181-85.

1355 Dobbert, G. A. "The Ordeal of Gotthard Deutsch, " AJA. 20 (1968): 129-55. About anti-German hysteria.

1356 Döhla, J. C. "The Doehla Journal, " WMCQ. 22 (1942): 229-74.

1357 Dornbusch, Charles. Regimental Publications and Personal Narratives of the Civil War: A Check-List. New York: New York Public Library, 1961-62.

1358 Dorpalen, Andreas. "The German Element and the Issues of the Civil War, " MVHR. 29 (1942): 55-76.

1359 Douglass, Elisha. "German Intellectuals and the American Revolution, " WMQ. 17 (1960): 200-18.

1360 Dybvig, Paul. "Lutheran Participation in the Civil War, " LuQ. 14 (1962): 294 ff.

1361 Ehrenberg, Hermann. With Milam and Fannin: Adventures of a German Boy in Texas' Revolution. Austin: Pemberton Pr., 1968.

1362 Esslinger, Dean. "American-German and Irish Attitudes Toward Neutrality, 1914-17: A Study of Catholic Minorities, " CathHR. 53 (1968): 194-216.

1363 Ewen, David. "German Music in America and the First World War, " Decision. 3 (1942): 47-53.

1364 Foerster, Friedrich and T. H. Teters. Open Letter to the Loyal Americans of German Descent. New York, 1943.

1365 Frese, Hans. "A Soldier's Diary, " AGR. 28 (1961): 17-19.

1366 _____. "Ein vergessener deutscher Soldat im amerikanischen Bürgerkrieg, " MIA. 11 (1961): 22-28.

1367 Frye, Alton. Nazi Germany and the American Hemisphere 1933-41. New Haven: Yale University Pr., 1967.

1368 Gibson, James. "Bodo Otto, Jr., " NJHS. 66 (1948): 171-83. The doctor at Valley Forge.

1369 _____. "John Augustus Otto, " Berks Co. Hist Soc. 13 (1947): 14-18.

1370 Goldstein, Franklin. "The People Yes--Berks County in World War I, " HRBC. 22 (1957): 42-47, 59-66.

1371 Gottlieb, Moshe. "The First of April Boycott and the Reaction of the American Jewish Community, " AJHQ. 57 (1968): 516-56.

1372 Gould, James. "Did an Iowan Start a War in the Indies?" AI. 34 (1957): 81-91.

1373 Graebner, Alan. "World War I and Lutheran Union: Documents from the Army and Navy Board, 1917 and 1918, " CHIQ. 40 (1968): 51-64.

1374 Graeff, Arthur. Conrad Weiser: Pennsylvania Peacemaker. Fogelsville: Pennsylvania German Folklore Society, 1945.

1375 _____. "Regina, the Indian Captive, " Eck. (Jan. 24, 1959

1376 Grebner, Constantin. Die Neuner (9 Regiment Ohio Vol. Infanterie). Cincinnati, 1897. UC

1377 Green, F. M. "A People at War: Hagerstown, Maryland, 1863, " MdHM. 40 (1945): 251-60.

1378 Harter, F. A. Erinnerungen aus dem amerikanischen Bürger krieg. Chicago, 1895. UC

1379 Heitman, Francis. Historical Register and Dictionary of the U. S. Army from its Organization, September 29, 1789 to March 2, 1903. Washington: GPO, 1903.

1380 _____. Historical Register of Officers of the Continental Army During the War of the Revolution, April, 1775 to December, 1783. New Rev. Ed. Washington: Rare Book Publishing Co., 1914.

1381 Hendrickson, Kenneth. "The Socialists of Reading, Pennsylvania and World War I: A Question of Loyalty, " PH. 36 (1969): 430-50.

1382   Hershberger, Guy. The Mennonite Church in the Second
       World War. Scottdale, Pa.: Mennonite Publishing House,
       1951.

1383   _____. "Mennonites in the Civil War," MQR. 18 (1944):
       131-44.

1384   "Hessian's Diary is Unusual Find, " NY Times. (Nov. 26, 1961):
       37. About a 540-page manuscript.

1385   Hirst, David. German Propaganda in the United States, 1914-
       17. Northwestern University: Dissertation, 1962.

1386   Horner, Harlan. "Lincoln Scolds a General, " WMH. 36 (1953):
       90-96, 143-46. About Carl Schurz.

1387   Huling, Polly. "Missourians at Vicksburg, " MHR. 50 (1955):
       1-15.

1388   Jacobsen, Edna. "The Herkimer Family and Battle of Oris-
       kany Portfolio, " NYH. 29 (1948): 342-48.

1389   Johnson, Niel. George Sylvester Viereck: German-American
       Propagandist. Urbana: University of Illinois, 1972.

1390   _____. "The Patriotism and Anti-Prussianism of the Lu-
       theran Church-Missouri Synod, 1914-18, " CHIQ. 39 (1966):
       99-118.

1391   Johnson, Roy. "Jacob Horner of the 7th Cavalry, " NDH. 16
       (1949): 75-100.

1392   Jung, Charles. Aus meinem Marineleben. Pittsburgh, n. d.
       UC

1393   Kaufmann, Wilhelm. Die Deutschen in amerikanischen Bür-
       gerkriege. Munich, 1911. UC

1394   Kavasch, Paul. "The Lutheran Church-Missouri Synod During
       the Early Years of the Civil War, " CHIQ. 31 (1958): 65-78.

1395   Keller, Phyllis. German-America and the First World War.
       University of Pennsylvania: Dissertation, 1969.

1396   Kerr, Thomas. "German-Americans and Neutrality in the
       1916 Election, " MA. 43 (1961): 95-105.

1397   Kieffer, Elizabeth. "George Schaffner: An American Revo-
       lutionist Who Died in the French Royalist Cause, " LCHP. 50
       (1946): 1-27.

1398   Kuehl, Michael. "Die exilierte deutsche demokratische Linke
       in USA, " Z. f. Politik. 4 (1957): 273-89.

1399   Larter, Harry. "German Troops with Burgoyne, 1776-77,"
       Bul. of the Fort Ticonderoga Museum. 9 (1952): 13-24.

1400   Lenel, Edith. "Zwei Briefe von Carl Schurz," AGR. 13, v-
       vi (1947): 13-16.

1401   Lohr, Otto. "Das Deutschamerikanertum vor hundert Jahren
       und der Krieg von 1812-1818," DAGB. 14 (1914): 392-450.

1402   Lonn, Ella. Foreigners in the Union Army and Navy. Baton
       Rouge: Louisiana State University Pr., 1951.

1403   Losch, Philipp. "Bibliographie des Subsidienwesens, insbe-
       sondere des hessischen mit besonderer Berücksichtigung der
       Hessen in Amerika," in: Soldatenhandel. Kassel, 1933,
       pp. 61-110.

1404   Luebke, Frederick. "The German-American Alliance in Ne-
       braska, 1910-17," NH. 49 (1968): 165-86.

1405   _____. "Superpatriotism in World War I: The Experience
       of a Lutheran Pastor," CHIQ. 41 (1968): 3-11.

1405A Luecke, Martin. Der Bürgerkrieg der Vereinigten Staaten,
       1861-65. St. Louis, 1892. UC

1406   Luecker, Erwin. "The Stance of Missouri in 1917," CHIQ.
       40 (1967): 119-26.

1407   McKelvey, Blake. "The Mayors of Rochester's Mid-Years:
       1860-1900," RH. 28 (1966): 1-24.

1408   Manley, R. "Language Loyalty and Liberty: The Nebraska
       State Council of Defense and the Lutheran Churches, 1917-
       18," CHIQ. 37 (64): 1 ff.

1409   May, Ernest. "Nazi Germany and the United States: A Re-
       view Essay," JMH. 41 (1969): 207-14.

1410   Müller, Wilhelm. Die Deutschamerikaner und der Krieg.
       Wiesbaden, 1921. UC

1411   Müller-Borbach, Heinrich. Johann Gottfried Seume. East
       Berlin: Rütten & Loening, 1957. History of a poet in the
       Revolution.

1412   Munden, K. W. and H. P. Beers. Guide to Federal Archive
       Relating to the Civil War. Washington: National Archives,
       1962.

1413   Niven, Alexander. "The Role of German Volunteers in St.
       Louis, 1861," AGR. 28, iii (1962): 29-30.

1414   Nohl, Frederick. "The Lutheran Church-Missouri Synod Re-
        acts to United States Anti-Germanism During World War I, "
        CHIQ. 35 (1962): 49 ff.

1415   Ohlinger, Gustave. Their True Faith and Allegiance. New
        York: Macmillan, 1916. An attack on the patriotism of
        German-Americans.

1416   Padover, Saul. "Abraham Lincoln's Young Man, " AGR. 31,
        iv (1965): 2-3. About Schurz.

1417   Parish, Arlyn. Kansas Mennonites During World War I.
        Hays: Fort Hays Kansas State College, 1968.

1418   Pfeffer, Anton. Treudeutsch unterm Sternenbanner. Rothen-
        burg a. Neckar, 1924. UC

1419   Powell, William. List of Officers of the Army of the U.S.
        From 1779-1900, Embracing a Register of All Appointments.
        New York: Hamersly, 1900.

1420   Pritchett, M. H. and E. von Zemensky. "The Three Wills
        of Baron von Steuben, " RJGAH. 35 (1972): 19-20.

1421   Ralphelson, Alfred. "Alexander Schimmelpfennig: A German-
        American Campaigner in the Civil War, " PMHB. 57 (1963):
        156-81.

1422   _____. "The Unheroic General, " AGR. 29, i (1962): 26-
        29.

1423   Remak, Joachim. "Friends of the New Germany: The Bund
        and German-American Relations, " JMH. 29 (1957): 38-41.

1424   Riedesel, Frederika. Baroness von Riedesel and the Ameri-
        can Revolution. Chapel Hill: University of North Carolina
        Pr., 1964.

1425   Rodgers, Harrell. Community Conflict, Public Opinion and
        the Law: The Amish Dispute in Iowa. Columbus: Charles
        E. Merrill, 1969.

1426   Rogge, O. John. The Official German Report. New York:
        Yoseloff, 1961.

1427   Rosengarten, Joseph. The German Soldier in the Wars in the
        United States. 2d ed. Philadelphia: Lippincott, 1890.

1428   Ruff, Joseph. "Civil War Experiences of a German Emigrant,
        as Told by the Late J. R. of Albion, " MHM. 27 (1943): 271-
        301, 442-62.

1429   Scheidt, David. "Some Effects of World War I on the General

Synod and General Council, " CHIQ. 43 (1970).

1430   Schlesinger, Sigmund. "The Beecher Island Battlefield-Diary
        of Sigmund Schlesinger, " CM. 29 (1952): 161-69.

1431   Schmidt, H. D. "The Hessian Mercenaries: The Career of
        a Political Cliche, " History. 43 (1958): 207-12.

1432   Scott, Kenneth. "Jacob Leisler's Fifty Militismen, " NY Gen.
        & Biog. Record. 94 (1963): 65-72.

1433   Seume, J. G. "Memoirs of a Hessian Conscript: J. G.
        Seume's Reluctant Voyage to America, " WMQ. 5 (1948): 553-
        70.

1434   Slagle, Robert. The Von Lossberg Regiment: A Chronicle
        of Hessian Participation in the American Revolution. Ameri-
        can University: Dissertation, 1959.

1435   Smith, Arthur. The Deutschtum of Nazi Germany and the
        United States. (International Scholars Forum, 15). The
        Hague: Nijhoff, 1965.

1436   _____. "The Kamderadschaft USA, " JMH. 34 (1962): 398-
        408.

1436A   Smith, Thomas. "A Letter from Cedar Falls, " IJH. 55
        (1957): 275-78.

1437   Soderberg, Mrs. Gertrude. "Captain John Soder's Company,
        1776, " NGSQ. 53 (1965): 35.

1438   Stolz, Paul. "Dr. Bodo Otto, Senior Surgeon of the Valley
        Forge Encampment, " HRBC. 27 (1961): 6-12.

1439   Stortz, John. "Experiences of a Prisoner During the Civil
        War In and Out of the Hands of the Rebels, " Annals of Iowa.
        37 (1965): 167-94.

1440   Stuber, Johann. Mein Tagebuch über die Erlebnisse im Revo-
        lutionskrieg, 1861-65. Cincinnati, 1896.

1441   [Taussig.] "Joseph Kieffer Taussig, " MHR. 42 (1948): 196-
        97. A German-American Naval officer.

1442   Tharp, Louise. The Baroness and the General. Boston:
        Little, Brown, 1962.

1443   Thrapp, Dan. Al Sieber: Chief of Scouts. Norman: Univer-
        sity of Oklahoma Pr., 1964.

1444   Throne, Mildred. "Iowa Troops in Dakota Territory, 1861-
        64, " IJH. 57 (1959): 97-190.

1445   Trillin, Calvin. "The War in Kansas, " New Yorker. 43 (1968):
        51-145.

1446   Uhlendorf, Bernhard. Revolution in America: Confidential
        Letters and Journals 1776-84 of Adjutant General Baurmeister
        of the Hessian Forces. New Brunswick: Rutgers University
        Pr., 1957.

1447   Unruh, John. "The Hutterites During World War I, " ML. 29
        (1969): 130-37.

1448   Walker, Mack. "The Mercenaries, " New Eng. Q. 39 (1966):
        390-98.

1449   Wallace, Andrew. Soldier of the Southwest: The Career of
        General A. V. Kautz, 1869-86. University of Arizona: Dis-
        sertation, 1968.

1450   Weaver, Glenn. "The German Reformed Church during the
        French and Indian War, " JPHS. 35 (1957): 265-77.

1451   _____. "The Germans of British North America during
        the French and Indian War, " Social Studies. 48 (1957): 227-
        35.

1452   _____. "The Lutheran Church during the French and In-
        dian War, " LQ. 6 (1954): 248-56.

1453   _____. "The Moravians during the French and Indian War, "
        ChH. 24 (1955): 239-56.

1454   Wehner, Alfred. From Hitler Youth to U.S. Citizen. New
        York: Carlton, 1972.

1455   Weisenburger, Francis. "Lincoln and His Ohio Friends, "
        OHQ. 68 (1959): 223-56.

1456   Wentz, F. "American Catholic Periodicals React to Nazism, "
        CH. 31 (1962): 400-20.

1457   _____. "American Protestant Journals and the Nazi Re-
        ligious Assault, " CH. 23 (1954): 321-38.

1458   Wildermuth, Larry. "The Hessians and the Citizens of Read-
        ing, " HRBC. 35 (1970): 46-49, 66-68, 70-75.

1459   Wilkins, Robert. "Referendum on War? The General Elec-
        tion of 1916 in North Dakota, " NDH. 36 (1969): 296-335.

1460   Wittke, Carl. "American Germans in Two World Wars, "
        WMH. 27 (1943): 6-16.

1461   _____. German-Americans in the World War. Columbus:

Ohio State Archaeological and Historical Society, 1936. Best history of the subject.

1462   Wollenweber, Ludwig. "General Peter Muhlenberg and his German Soldiers in the American War for Independence," Eck. (May 12-August 18, 1951).

1463   Work, John. "The First World War," WMH. 41 (1957): 42-44.

1464   Zucker, Adolf Eduard. General DeKalb: Lafayette's Mentor. Chapel Hill: University of North Carolina Pr., 1966.

1465   _____. "An Interesting Baron de Kalb Letter," RJGAH. 31 (1963): 59-62.

Political Activities

1466   Alexander, James. A Brief Narrative of the Case and Trial of John Peter Zenger: Printer of the New York Weekly Journal. Cambridge: Belknap Pr., 1963.

1467   Allen, Howard and D. Homer. "Studies of Political Loyalties of Two Nationality Groups: Isolation and German-Americans, the Rockford Swedish Community," J. Ill. State Hist. Soc. 57 (1964): 143-55.

1468   Altgeld, John Peter. The Mind and Spirit of John Peter Altgeld: Selected Writings and Addresses. Ed. by Heinz Christman. Urbana: University of Illinois Pr., 1960.

1469   Armstrong, William. "The Godkin-Schurz Feud, 1881-83: Over Policy Control of the New York Evening Post," NY HSQ. 48 (1964): 5-19.

1470   Atkinson, Henry. Theodore Marburg: The Man and His Work New York: Littmann, 1952. A Baltimore German.

1471   Barba, Preston. "Negro Slavery and the Pennsylvania Germans," Eck. (Mar. 14, 1959).

1472   Bek, William. "The Civil War Diary of John T. Buegel, Union Soldier," MHR. 40 (1946): 307-29.

1473   Blum, Virgil. "The Political and Military Activities of the German Element in St. Louis, 1859-61," MHR. 42 (1948): 103-29.

1474   Bowman, Rufus. "The Church of the Brethren and the State, Brethren Life and Thought. 1 (1956): 42-68.

1475 [Brant.] "David Brant's Iowa Political Sketches," Iowa City
      Repub. (Jan. 10, 1918). Repr.: IJH. 53 (1955): 341-66.

1476 Brown, Bernard. American Conservatives: The Political
      Thought of Francis Lieber and John W. Burgess. New York:
      Columbia University Pr., 1951.

1477 Buranelli, Vincent. The Trial of Peter Zenger. New York:
      New York University Pr., 1957.

1478 Burlingame, Michael. Carl Schurz: The Roots of His Per-
      sonality and Career. John Hopkins University: Dissertation,
      1967.

1479 Byrne, Frank. "Maine Law Versus Lager Beer: A Dilemma
      of Wisconsin's Young Republican Party," WMH. 42 (1959): 115-
      20.

1480 Cohen, Norman. "The Philadelphia Election Riot of 1742,"
      PMHB. 92 (1969): 306-19.

1481 Conrad, Frederick. "Muhlenberg: Speaker of the First Con-
      gress," Eck. (May 30, 1942).

1482 Cozzens, Arthur. "Conservatism in German Settlements in
      the Ozarks," Geog. Rev. 33 (1943): 286 ff.

1483 Crisler, Robert. "Republican Areas in Missouri," MHR. 42
      (1948): 299-309.

1484 Cross, Jasper. "The Forty-Eighters and the Election of
      1860," Hist. Bul. 27 (1951): 79-80, 87-89.

1485 Cunningham, John. "John H. Klippart, Secretary of the Ohio
      State Board of Agriculture, 1856-78," OSAHQ. 61 (1952): 51-
      65.

1486 Daniels, George. "Immigrant Vote in the 1860 Election:
      The Case of Iowa," MA. 44 (1962): 146-62.

1487 Dante, Harris. "Western Activities and Reconstruction Poli-
      tics in Illinois 1865-72," ISHS. 49 (1956): 149-62.

1488 Dorpalen, Andreas. "The German Element in Early Pennsyl-
      vania Politics 1789-1800: A Study in Americanization," PH.
      9 (1942): 176-90.

1489 Dues, Michael. "The Bizarre Mayoralty of Philip Tomppert,
      1865-67," Filson CHQ. 42 (1968): 243-52. About a Louis-
      ville German.

1490 Dunson, A. A. "Notes on the Missouri Germans on Slavery,"
      MHR. 59 (1965): 355-66.

1491   Elkinton, Howard. "Carl Schurz Through the Lens of Time,"
        AGR. 17, iv (1951): 3.

1492   "Erinnerungen an Carl Schurz," AGR. 12, iv (1946): 25-26.

1493   Fast, Howard. The American: A Middle Western Legend.
        New York: Duell, Sloan and Pearce, 1946.

1494   Faust, Albert. "Francis J. Grund and Carl Schurz: A Con-
        trast," AGR. 9 (1943): 12-14.

1495   Freidel, Frank. Francis Lieber: Nineteenth Century Liberal.
        Baton Rouge: Louisiana State University Pr., 1947.

1496   Fretz, J. Herbert. "The Germantown Antislavery Petition of
        1688," MQR. 33 (1959): 42-59.

1497   _____. "Germantown Anti-Slavery Protest," ML. 13
        (1958): 183-86.

1498   Gerson, Louis. The Hyphenate in Recent American Politics
        and Diplomacy. Lawrence: University of Kansas Pr., 1964.

1499   Gerstein, Irving. Carl Schurz: Editorial Monitor of the
        American Conscience. Washington University: Dissertation,
        1951.

1500   Gordon, Gerald. "From European Romantic Liberalism to
        American Democratic Idealism: The Evolution of the Political
        Thought and Action of Carl Schurz, 1848-1906," Susquehanna
        Univ. Stud. 7 (1963): 83-101.

1501   "Hard Times Faces Fruitful Hutterites," Life. 45 (1958): 33-
        38. Conflict with state authorities.

1502   Henle, Hans. Dwight D. Eisenhower. Frankfurt: Europäische
        Verlagsanstalt, 1952. First German study of Eisenhower.

1503   Höwing, Hans. Carl Schurz: Rebell, Kämpfer, Staatsmann.
        Wiesbaden: Limes-Verlag, 1948.

1504   Hogue, Arthur. "Civil Service Reform 1869," AGR. 18, v
        (1952): 5-8, 39.

1505   Huthmacher, J. "Senator Robert F. Wagner and the Rise of
        Urban Liberalism," AJHQ. 58 (1969): 330-46.

1506   James, H. P. "Political Pageantry in the Campaign of 1860
        in Illinois," ALQ. 4 (1947): 313-55.

1507   Johnson, Hildegard B. "Carl Schurz and Conservation," AGR.
        23, iii (1957): 4-8.

1508 _____. "The Election of 1860 and the Germans in Minnesota," MH. 28, i (1947): 20-36.

1509 Katz, Irving. August Belmont: A Political Biography. New York: Columbia University Pr., 1968. Belmont was Democratic Party National Chairman.

1510 Keller, Morton. The Art and Politics of Thomas Nast. New York: Oxford University Pr., 1968.

1511 Kelso, Thomas. The German-American Vote in the Election of 1860: The Case of Indiana with Supporting Data from Ohio. Ball State University: Dissertation, 1967.

1512 Kinzer, Donald. "The Political Uses of Anti-Catholicism: Michigan and Wisconsin 1890-94," MichH. 39 (1955): 312-26.

1513 "Kissinger-Ehrungen bei der Steubenparade," Aufbau. (Sept. 28, 1973).

1514 Kleppner, Paul. "Lincoln and the Immigrant Vote: A Case of Religious Polarization," Mid-America: An Hist. Rev. 48 (1966): 176-95.

1515 Kluke, Paul. "Zwei unbekannte Briefe von Carl Schurz," Hist. Z. 171 (1951): 79-87.

1516 Kretzmann, Karl. "Henry Wisner: Patriot and Congressman, 1776," AGR. 14, iii (1948): 12-13.

1517 Lindeman, Jack. The Relationship of Carl Schurz with Rutherford B. Hayes Prior to March 2, 1877. University of Mississippi: Dissertation, 1950.

1518 Luckey, Henry. Eighty-Five American Years. New York: Exposition Pr., 1955.

1519 Luebke, Frederick. Immigrants and Politics: The Germans of Nebraska, 1880-1900. Lincoln: University of Nebraska Pr., 1969.

1520 Luecking, F. Dean. "Roots of the Radical Right," LuQ. 18 (1966): 197-204.

1521 Lourdes, Joan. "Elections in Colonial Pennsylvania," WMQ. 11 (1954): 385-401.

1522 Luthin, Reinhold. "Lincoln Appeals to German American Voters," AGR. 25, v (1959): 4-6, 15.

1523 Maass, Joachim. "Carl Schurz stürzt sich in die Politik," AGR. 17, iv (1951): 11-12.

1524 _____. Der unermüdliche Rebell: Leben, Taten und Vermächtnis des Carl Schurz. Hamburg: Classen & Goverts, 1949.

1525 McClung, Quantrille. "The Governors of Colorado," CM. 23 (1946): 97-105.

1526 McLendon, James. "John A. Quitman: Fire-Eating Governor," JMH. 15 (1953): 73-89.

1527 Mahaffey, Joseph. "Carl Schurz's Letter from Alabama, August 15-16, 1865," AR. 3 (1951): 134-45.

1528 _____. "Carl Schurz's Letters from the South," GaHQ. 35 (1951): 222-57.

1529 Marx, Henry. "Gedenken an Carl Schurz," MH. (June 7, 1973).

1530 Miller, Elizabeth. From the Fiery Stakes of Europe to the Federal Courts of America. New York: Vantage Pr., 1963. About the Amish.

1531 Millsap, Kenneth. "The Election of 1860 in Iowa," IJHP. 48 (1950): 97-120.

1532 Müller, Wilhelm. Carl Schurz: Aus der Jugend des grössten Deutschamerikaners. Leipzig, n. d. UC

1533 [Nast.] Thomas Nast: Freiheitskämpfer mit dem Zeichenstift. Frankfurt: U. S. Information Service, 1957.

1534 Padover, Saul. "Altgeld of Illinois: Eagle Forgotten," AGR. 32, v (1966): 5-8.

1535 Parks, Edd. "Zollikoffer: Southern Whig," THQ. 11 (1952): 346-55.

1536 Plumb, Ralph. "The Schurz-Hobart Joint Debate: 1859," WMH. 39 (1955): 40-43.

1537 Rader, B. J. and K. Barbara. "Carl Schurz: Patriarch of the Anti-Imperialist Movement," MHS Bul. 22 (1964): 295-306.

1538 Rauchle, Bob. "The Political Life of the Germans in Memphis, 1848-80," THQ. 27 (1968): 165-75.

1539 Reed, John. "The Papers of Jenry Juncken, Tory and His Wife, of Springfield Township," HSMC. 14, iv (1965): 315-30.

1540 Reynolds, Robert. "A Man of Conscience in an Era when Political Morality Had Sunk Low, An Immigrant, Carl Schurz,

Helped Rally the Republic to Its Ancient Ideals, " AH. 14
(1963): 20-23, 82-91.

1541   Rosenberg, Morton.   "The Election of 1859 in Iowa, " IJH.
57 (1959): 1-22.

1542   Rothermund, Dietmar.   The Layman's Progress: Religion
and Political Experience in Colonial Pennsylvania 1740-70.
Philadelphia: University of Pennsylvania Pr. , 1961.

1543   Sallet, Richard.   "On Francis Lieber and His Contribution to
the Law of Nations Today, " in Recht im Dienste der Menschen-
würde: Festschrift für Herbert Kraus.   Würzburg: Holzner,
1964, 547 ff.

1544   Schmidt, Frederick.   He Chose.   The Other Was a Tread-
mill Thing.   Santa Fe, New Mexico: Frederick Schmidt,
1968.   About Ernst Schmidt, a Chicago political leader.

1545   Schottenhamel, George.   "How Big Bill Thompson Won Control of Chicago, " JILLHS. 45 (1952): 30-50.

1546   Schurz, Carl.   The Autobiography of Carl Schurz.   New York:
Scribners, 1961.

1547   _____.   Lebenserinnerungen.   Zürich: Manesse, 1948.

1548   [Schurz.]   "Carl Schurz Centennial Observances, " AGR. 18,
iv (1952): 3-5.

1549   [Schurz.]   "Carl Schurz Commemoration Issue, " AGR. 18, vi
(1952): 2-32.

1550   Spael, Wilhelm.   Karl Schurz: Ein rheinischer Jüngling.
Essen: Fredebeul & Koenen, 1948.

1551   Sparks, David.   "The Birth of the Republican Party in Iowa
1854-56, " IJH. 54 (1956): 1-34.

1552   _____.   "The Decline of the Democratic Party in Iowa
1850-60, " IJH. 53 (1955): 1-30.

1553   Stange, Douglas.   "A Compassionate Mother to Her Poor
Negro Slaves: The Lutheran Church and Negro Slavery in
Early America, " Phylon. 29 (1968): 272-81.

1554   Steinitz, Hans.   "Henry Kissinger im Amt: Ein historisches
Ereignis, " Aufbau. (Sept. 28, 1973).

1555   _____.   "Nobelpreis für Kissinger, " Aufbau. (Oct. 19,
1973).

1556   Straetz, Ralph.   PR Politics in Cincinnati: Thirty-Two Years of City Government through Proportional Representation.   New York: New York University Pr., 1958.

1557   Strauss, Lewis.   "Oscar Strauss: An Appreciation, " PAJHS. 40 (1950): 1-16.   German-American diplomat.

1558   Thiessen, Peter.   The Mennonites and Participation in Politics.   University of Manitoba: Dissertation, 1963.

1558A   Throne, Mildred.   "The Liberal Republican Party in Iowa 1872, " IJH. 53 (1955): 121-52.

1559   Tutt, Clara.   Carl Schurz: Patriot.   Madison: State Historical Society of Wisconsin, 1960.

1560   U. S. Congress.   Biographical Directory of the American Congress, 1774-1961.   Washington: GPO, 1961.

1561   .   Official Congressional Directory for the Use of the U. S. Congress.   Washington: GPO, 1809- .

1562   U. S. Department of State.   Biographical Register.   Washington: GPO, 1870- .

1563   Vinson, J. C.   "Thomas Nast and the American Political Scene, " AQ. 9 (1957): 337-44.

1564   Weaver, Glenn.   "The German Reformed Church and the Civil Government 1787-1855, " PH. 16 (1949): 303-25.

1565   Weibull, Jürgen.   "The Wisconsin Progressives 1900-14, " MA. 47 (1965): 191-221.

1566   Wittke, Carl.   "Carl Schurz and Rutherford B. Hayes, " OHQ. 65 (1956): 337-55.

1567   Wryman, Roger.   "Wisconsin Ethnic Groups and the Election of 1890, " WMH. 51 (1968): 269-93.

1568   Younger, Edward.   "The Rise of John A. Karson in Iowa Politics 1857-59, " IJHP. 50 (1952): 289-314.

II. GERMAN-AMERICAN LANGUAGE AND LITERATURE

The German Language in America

1569 Albrecht, Erich. "Deutsche Sprache, Deutsche Literatur und Deutscher Unterricht in New Orleans, Louisiana," GAS. 3 (1971): 18-21.

1570 Arndt, Karl. "Sealsfield's Command of the English Language," MLN. 67 (1952): 310-13.

1571 Ashcom, B. B. "Notes on the Language of the Bedford, Pennsylvania Subarea," AS. 28 (1953): 241-55.

1572 Barba, Preston. "Alle Sadde Wadde," Eck. (Feb. 22, 1964-Dec. 4, 1965). Word studies.

1573 _____. "Alle Sorte Worte," Eck. (Mar. 22; May 10; July 12, 1947).

1574 Beam, C. R. "Alle Sadde Wadde," Eck. (Apr. 20; May 25; June 29; Aug. 24, 1968).

1575 _____. "A Guide for the Co-Workers of the Pennsylvania German Dictionary," Eck. (July 2, 9, 1966).

1576 _____. "Pennsylvania German Riddles," Eck. (Aug. 20, 27, 1966).

1577 Benson, Evelyn. "The Earliest Use of the Term 'Conestoga Wagon'," PD. 4 (1953): 6-8.

1578 Buffington, Albert. "Dutchified German," Eck. (June 1, 1946).

1579 _____. "The Influence of the Pennsylvania German Dialect on the English Spoken in the Pennsylvania German Area," in Helen Adolf Festschrift. New York: Ungar, 1968, pp. 30-41.

1580 _____. "Linguistic Variants in the Pennsylvania German Dialect," PGFS. 13 (1949): 217-52.

1581 _____. "Ninety-one Ways to Spell a Word," Eck. (Apr. 12, 1952).

103

1582 _____. "The Origins, Peculiar Phonological Features, and Curious Connotations of Certain Pennsylvania German Words," Eck. (July 11, Oct. 24, Nov. 28, 1953; Mar. 10, Apr. 7, 1956).

1583 _____. "Pennsylvania German as a Foundation for the Study of Standard German," GQ. 24 (1951): 76-83.

1584 _____. "The Perennial Problems of Our Pennsylvania German Orthography," Eck. (Sept. 4, 11, 1948).

1585 _____. "Similarities and Dissimilarities Between Pennsylvania German and the Rhenish Palatinate Dialects," Publications, PGS. 3 (1970): 91-116.

1586 _____ and Preston Barba. A Pennsylvania German Grammar. Allentown: Schlecters, 1954.

1587 _____ and _____. "Pennsylvania German Sounds and Their Representation," PGFS. 16 (1953): 150-55.

1588 Carman, J. Neale. Foreign-Language Units of Kansas. Lawrence: University of Kansas Pr., 1962.

1589 Cohn, Bernhard. "Early German Preaching in America," HJ. 15 (1953): 86-134.

1590 Danner, E. R. Pennsylvania Dutch Dictionary and Handbook. Spring Grove, Pa.: The Author, 1951. Emphasis on the York County, Pa. dialect.

1591 Dehning, Gustav. "Plattdeutsch in Neu-York," Mut. 76 (1966) 261-63.

1592 Donnelly, Dale. The Low German Dialect of Sauk County, Wisconsin: Phonology and Morphology. University of Wisconsin: Dissertation, 1969.

1593 Doroshkin, Milton. Yiddish in America: Social and Cultural Foundations. Rutherford: Fairleigh Dickinson University Pr. 1969.

1594 Dunkelberger, George. The Story of Snyder County. Selinsgrove, Pa.: Snyder County Historical Society, 1948. Pp. 249-71 deal with the Pennsylvania German dialect.

1595 Eikel, Fred. "New Braunfels German," AS. 41 (1966): 5-16.

1596 _____. The New Braunfels German Dialect: Phonology and Morphology. John Hopkins University: Dissertation, 195

1597 _____. "The Use of Cases in New Braunfels German," AS. 24 (1949): 278-81.

1598   Ellingsworth, Huber. "John Peter Altgeld as a Public Speaker, " JILLHS. 46 (1953): 171-77.

1599   Feinsilver, Lilian. "Like Influences from Yiddish and Pennsylvania German, " AS. 33 (1958): 231-32.

1600   Fleischhauer, Wolfgang. A Study of the Low German Dialect in Auglaize County, Ohio. Ohio State University: Dissertation, 1960.

1601   Foster, Brian. "Foreign Influences, " in The Changing English Language. London: Macmillan, 1968. Pp. 81-106 discuss German-Americans.

1602   "Foster-Mother Tongue: A Symposium, " BA. 23 (1949): 237-42.

1603   Frey, William. "A Comparison of Pennsylvania German with the Amana Dialect of Iowa, " Eck. (Aug. 29, Sept. 5, 1942).

1604   _____. "Familiar Letters to Those Who Speak Pennsylvania Dutch, " PD. 3 (1952): 1-7.

1605   _____. "Notes on the Diphthong 'oi' in Pennsylvania Dutch, " AS. 18 (1943): 112-16.

1606   _____. "Pennsylvania Dutch, " PFL. 12 (1962): 12-13.

1607   _____. "The Phonemics of English Loan Words in Eastern York County Pennsylvania Dutch, " AS. 17 (1942): 94-101.

1608   _____. "The Present Status of Research in the Pennsylvania Dutch Dialect, " SAB. 8 (1943): 7.

1609   _____. A Simple Grammar of Pennsylvania Dutch. Clinton, South Carolina: The Author, 1942.

1610   _____. "This Question of Pennsylvania German Orthography, " Eck. (Nov. 14, 1942).

1611   Friesen, J. J. "Sprechen die Mennoniten in den Vereinigten Staaten noch deutsch?" Mitteilungen I. f. Auslandsbeziehungen. 2 (1952): 14.

1612   Gehman, Ernest. "En Iwwerbligg uff die Pennsylveenje-Deitsch Schbrooch, " AGR. 34, iii (1968): 30-32.

1613   _____. Lautlehre der Pennsylvania-Deutschen Mundart von Balley, Pennsylvania. Heidelberg University: Dissertation, 1949.

1614   _____. "Pennsylvania German in the Shenandoah Valley, " Eck. (Mar. 16, 23, 30, 1963).

1615   Gerhard, Elmer. "Pennsylvania German: The Picturesque-
        ness and Directness of the Dialect, " HRBC. 21 (1956): 123-
        28.

1616   Gilbert, Glenn. "Dative vs. Accusative in the German Dia-
        lects of Central Texas, " Z. f. Mundartforschung. 32 (1965):
        288-96.

1617   _____. "English Loanwords in the German of Fredericks-
        burg, Texas, " AS. 40 (1965): 102-112.

1618   _____. "The German Dialect of Kendall and Gillespie
        Counties, Texas, " Z. f. Mundartforschung. 31 (1964): 138-72.

1619   _____. The German Language in America: A Symposium.
        Austin: University of Texas Pr., 1971. Contains an ex-
        cellent bibliography.

1620   _____. Linguistic Atlas of Texas. Austin: University of
        Texas Pr., 1970.

1621   _____. Texas Studies in Bilingualism: Spanish, French,
        German, Czech, Polish, Serbian and Norwegian in the South-
        west. (Studia Linguistica Germanica, 3). Berlin: De Gruy-
        ter, 1970. Contains three articles on the Texas-German dia-
        lect.

1622   Gilbert, Russell. "The Oratory of the Pennsylvania Germans
        at the Versammlinge, " Susquehanna Univ. Stud. 4 (1951): 187-
        213.

1623   _____. "Progress and Problems in Pennsylvania German
        Research, " Susquehanna Univ. Stud. 5 (1955): 137-62.

1624   _____. "Religious Services in Pennsylvania German, "
        Susquehanna Univ. Studies. 5 (1955): 277-89.

1625   _____. "Worship in the Pennsylvania German Dialect Con-
        tinues, " Susquehanna Univ. Stud. 6 (1959): 411-21.

1626   Green, Archie. "Dutchman: An On-The-Job Etymology, "
        AS. 35 (1960): 270-74.

1627   _____. "John Neuhaus: Wobbly Folklorist, " JAF. 73
        (1960): 189-217. Study of Neuhaus' language.

1628   Grunewald, Dora. "Von der Sprache, " DMH. (Sept. 13, 1973).

1629   Gumpertz, John. The Swabian Dialect of Washtenaw County,
        Michigan. University of Michigan: Dissertation, 1954.

1630   Haile, H. G. "Thomas Mann und der Anglizismus, " MO.
        51 (1959): 263-69.

1631   Harris, Jesse. "German Language Influences in St. Clair
       County, Illinois, " AS. 23 (1948): 106-110.

1632   Haugen, Einar. "Bilingualism in the Americas: A Bibliogra-
       phy and Research Guide, " Pubs. Am. Dialect Soc. No. 26
       (1956).

1633   Hays, H. M. On the German Dialect Spoken in the Valley
       of Virginia. n.p., n.d. UC

1634   Heard, Betty. A Phonological Analysis of the Speech of Hays
       County, Texas. Louisiana State University and Agric. &
       Mech. College: Dissertation, 1969.

1635   Hofmann, Margaret. "Can the Mother Tongue Be Retained
       for Children of German Immigrants?" AGR. 23, vi (1957):
       15-17.

1636   Hollenbach, Raymond. "Ungeziffer, " Eck. (July 25, 1953).
       Dialect terms for vermin and insects.

1637   Kehlenbeck, Alfred. "An Iowa Low German Dialect, " Pubs.
       Am. Dialect Soc. No. 10 (1948).

1638   Kelz, Heinrich. Phonologische Analyse des Pennsylvania-
       deutschen. University of Bonn: Dissertation, 1969.

1639   _____. "The R-Sound in Pennsylvania German: A Phono-
       logical Problem, " Eck. (Mar. 1, 8, 1969).

1640   Kliewer, Warren. "Low German Children's Rimes, " ML.
       14 (1959): 141-42. About the Minnesota German dialect.

1641   Klingberg, Frank. "Foreign Language Groups in America, "
       PH. 23 (1956): 408-10.

1642   Kloss, Heinz. "Deutsch als Gottesdienstsprache in den
       Vereinigten Staaten von Amerika, " AD. 14 (1931): 630-34,
       689-92, 715-21.

1643   _____. "Drei Grundwerke zur auslanddeutschen Mundart-
       forschung, " Volk & Reich. 5 (1929): 134-37.

1644   _____. Die Entwicklung neuer germanischer Kulturspra-
       chen von 1800 bis 1950. München: Pohl, 1952.

1645   _____. "Etwas von der pennsylvaniadeutschen Sprache, "
       Hamburg-Amerika-Post. (Sept. 2-Oct., 1930): 286-94.

1646   _____. "The Father-tongue of Mr. President, " Eck. (Nov.
       21, 1953). About the Pennsylvania German background of
       President Eisenhower.

1647   _____. "German-American Language Maintenance Efforts, "
in Language Loyalty in the United States. The Hague: Mouton, 1966, pp. 206-52.

1648   _____. "German as an Immigrant, Indigenous, Foreign
and Second Language in the U. S., " in The German Language
in America: A Symposium.   Austin: University of Texas
Pr., 1970.

1649   _____. "Die Muttersprachenzählung von 1940 und die
Zukunft der nichtenglischen Sprachen in den USA, " Erdkunde.
7 (1953): 220-25.

1650   _____. "Proben aus dem pennsylvaniadeutschen Schrifttum, "
Neue Zeit. 11 (1929): 6-8, 9-10.

1651   _____. "Die Sprache der Pennsylvaniadeutschen und die
Gegenwart, " Muttersprache. 62 (1952): 337-40.

1652   _____. "Über die mittelbare kartographische Erfassung
der jüngeren deutschen Volksinseln in den U. S., " Deutsches
Archiv f. Landes & Volksf. 3 (1939): 457-74.

1653   _____. "Varianten der pennsylvaniadeutschen Sprache, "
Monatshefte. (1929): 1-6.

1654   _____. "What's in a Name?" Eck. (Oct. 2, 1954).

1655   _____. "Who are the Shapers of New Cultural Tongues?"
Eck. (Jan. 10, 1953).

1656   _____. "Wo in Ost-Pennsylvanien spricht man deutsche
Mundart?" DIA. 26 (1934): 2-9.

1657   Krahn, Cornelius. "Mennonite Plattdeutsch, " MQR. 33 (1959):
256-59.

1658   Kratz, Henry and H. Milnes. "Kitchener German: A Pennsylvania German Dialect, " MLQ. 14 (1953): 274-83.

1659   Kreider, Mary. "Dutchfied English: Some Lebanon Valley
Examples, " PFL. 12 (1962): 40-43.

1660   Krumpelmann, J. T.   "Charles Sealsfield's American, " AS.
19 (1944): 196-99.

1661   Kulp, Clarence. "A Study of the Dialect Terminology of the
Plain Sects of Montgomery County, Pa., " PFL. 12 (1961): 41-
47.

1662   Kurath, Hans.   A Word Geography of the Eastern United
States.   Ann Arbor: University of Michigan, 1949.

1663 Larson, Robert. The English Language of Carl Schurz: A Study in Germanic Background. University of Bonn: Dissertation, 1956.

1664 Leopold, Werner. "American Children Can Learn Their German Mother Tongue, " AGR. 24, ii (1957): 4-6.

1665 _____. Speech Development of a Bilingual Child. Evanston: Northwestern University Pr., 1939-48, 4 vols.

1666 Lewis, B. A. The Phonology of the Glarus Dialect in Green County, Wisconsin. University of Wisconsin: Dissertation, 1968.

1667 Lohmann, F. H. Die deutsche Sprache: Was können wir beitragen zu ihrer Erhaltung in diesem Lande. Chicago, 1904. UC

1668 McDavid, R. "Two Decades of the Linguistic Atlas, " JEGP. 50 (1951): 101-10.

1669 Oswald, Victor. The Phones of a Lehigh County Dialect of Pennsylvania. Columbia University: Dissertation, 1949.

1670 Palmer, Francis. "Several Mennonite Americanisms, " AS. 22 (1947): 72-73.

1671 Politzer, Heinz. "America in the Later Writings of Thomas Mann, " MLF. 37 (1952): 91-100. Linguistic influence of American on Mann.

1672 Proechel, Glen. Minnesota Liturgical German. Mankato State College: Dissertation, 1973. An excellent linguistic analysis of the German-American clergy in Minnesota.

1673 Rahn, C. R. A Pennsylvania Dutch Dictionary. 2d ed. Quakertown, Pa.: Meredith, 1948.

1674 Reed, Carroll E. "The Adaptation of English to Pennsylvania German Morphology, " AS. 23 (1949): 239-44.

1675 _____. "Double Dialect Geography, " Orbis. 10 (1961): 308-19. On Pennsylvania German.

1676 _____. "The Gender of English Loan Words in Pennsylvania German, " AS. 17 (1942): 25-29.

1677 _____. "Pennsylvania German, " Le Maitre Phonetique. No. 106 (1957): 37-38.

1678 _____. The Pennsylvania German Dialect Spoken in the Counties of Lehigh and Berks: Phonology and Morphology. Seattle: University of Washington Pr., 1949. See also MLQ. 9 (1948): 448-66.

1679 _____. "A Survey of Pennsylvania German Morphology, "
MLQ. 9 (1948): 322-42.

1680 _____ and Lester Seifert. A Linguistic Atlas of Pennsylvania German. Marburg: Becker, 1954.

1681 _____ and Herbert Wiese. "Amana German, " AS. 32
(1957): 243-56.

1682 Reichmann, Felix. "Francis Lieber, Pennsylvania German
Dialect, Edited from a Manuscript in the Henry E. Huntington
Library, " AGR. 11 (1945): 24-27.

1683 Rettig, Lawrence. Grammatical Structure in Amana German.
University of Iowa: Dissertation, 1970.

1684 Rockwell, Leo. "Older German Loan-Words in American
English, " AS. 20 (1946): 247-57.

1685 Rosten, Leo. The Joys of Yiddish: A Relaxed Lexicon of
Yiddish, Hebrew and Yinglish Words Often Encountered in
English. London, 1970.

1686 _____. "Yiddish and English: Towards a New Lexicon, "
Encounter. 31 (1968): 21-32.

1687 Rothenberg, Julius. "The English of Aufbau, " AS. 19 (1944):
92-102.

1688 Rupp, William. "Pennsylvania German Bird Names, " Eck.
(Apr. 9, 1949).

1689 Sachs, Emmy. "The Gender of English Loan Words in the
German of Recent Immigrants, " AS. 28 (1953): 256-70.

1690 Sacket, S. J. "Folk Speech in Schoenchen, Kansas, " WF.
19 (1960): 277.

1691 Schach, Paul. "Comments on Some Pennsylvania German
Words in the Dictionary of Americanisms, " AS. 29 (1955): 45-
54.

1692 _____. "The Formation of Hybrid Derivation in Pennsylvania German, " SY. 3 (1949): 114-29.

1693 _____. "Hybrid Compounds in Pennsylvania German, " AS.
33 (1948): 121-34.

1694 _____. "Die Lehnprägung der pennsylvania-deutschen
Mundart, " Z. f. Mundartforschung. 22 (1955): 215-22.

1695 _____. "The Pennsylvania-German Contribution to the
American Vocabulary, " HRBC. 19 (1953): 2-7; Eck. (June 2,
19, 1954).

1696 _____. "Semantic Borrowing in Pennsylvania German, "
AS. 26 (1952): 257-67.

1697 _____. "Types of Loan Translations in Pennsylvania German, " MLQ. 13 (1952): 268-76.

1698 Schurz, Carl. "Die deutsche Sprache in Amerika, " ZKA. 12
(1962): 331-32. Reprint of a speech given before the German Liederkranz of New York in 1897.

1699 Seifert, Lester. "Causes of Dialect Differences Between and
Within Western Berks and Western Lehigh Counties, Pennsylvania, " Eck. (Aug. 2, 1942).

1700 _____. "A Contrastive Description of Pennsylvania German and Standard German Stops and Fricatives, " in Approaches
in Linguistic Methodology. Madison, 1967.

1701 _____. "The Diminutives of Pennsylvania German, " MO.
39 (1947): 285-93.

1702 _____. "Lexical Differences Between Four Pennsylvania
German Regions, " PGFS. 11 (1948): 155-69.

1703 _____. "Methods and Aims of a Survey of the German
Spoken in Wisconsin, " Trans. Wisc. Acad. Sci., Arts & Letters. 40 (1951): 201-10.

1704 _____. "The Problem of Speech-Mixture in the German
Spoken in Northwestern Dane County, Wisconsin, " Trans.
Wisc. Acad. Sci., Arts & Letters. 39 (1949): 127-39.

1705 _____. "Stress Accent in Dane County Kölsch, " Monatshefte. 55 (1963): 195-202.

1706 Shenker, Israel. "From Nudnik to Peacenik: It's All Yiddish, " NY Times. (Jan. 25, 1969): p. 18.

1707 Shoemaker, Alfred. "Moshey and Bellyguts, " PD. 8 (1956):
16-17, 59.

1708 Snader, H. B. Glossary of 6167 English Words and Expressions and Their Berks County Pennsylvania Dutch Equivalent.
Temple, Pa.: The Author, 1948.

1709 Spitzer, Leo. "Confusion Schmooshun, " JEGP. 51 (1952):
226-33.

1710 Springer, Otto. "Pennsylvania German Och dem 'Atem' and
the Problem of Hypercorrect Forms, " Monatshefte. 35 (1943):
138-50.

1711 _____. A Working Bibliography for the Study of the

Pennsylvania German Language and its Sources.   Philadelphia:
University of Pennsylvania Pr., 1941.

1712   Spuler, Linus. "Deutsch in den Vereinigten Staaten," Sprach-
        spiegel. 12 (1956): 67-71.

1713   Stewart, John and Elmer Smith. "The Survival of German
        Dialects and Customs in the Shenandoah Valley," RJGAH. 31
        (1963): 66-70.

1714   Suderman, Elmer. "Arnold Dyck Explains the Origin of Low
        German," ML. 24 (1969): 5-7.

1715   "Symposium," PFI. 17 (1958): 8-47.   The issue is devoted to
        the Pennsylvania German dialect.

1716   Thierfelder, Franz. Die deutsche Sprache im Ausland. Ham-
        burg: Decker, 1956.

1717   Thiessen, John. "Das Niederdeutsche der Mennoniten," ZKA.
        15 (1965): 165-67.

1718   Toepper, Robert. "Rationale for Preservation of the German
        Language in the Missouri Synod of the Nineteenth Century,"
        CHIQ. 41 (1969): 156-67.

1719   Tolzmann, Don Heinrich. "Deutsch in den Kirchen," A-W.
        (Sept. 9, 1973).

1720   _____. "Deutsche Gottesdienste in Nordamerika," Der
        Lutheraner. (March-April, 1973): 15-16.

1721   _____. "Deutschsprachige Gottesdienste in Minnesota,"
        DMH. (July 5, 1973).

1722   _____. "German Language Services in Thirty-Fourth Sea-
        son," Luth. Standard. (May 1, 1973).

1723   Travis, D. C. "Texas Symposium: The German Language
        in America," Die Unterrichtspraxis. 2 (1969): 104-12.

1724   Veith, Werner. "Pennsylvaniadeutsch: Ein Beitrag zur
        Entstehung von Siedlungsmundarten," Z. f. Mundartforschung.
        35 (1968): 254-83.

1725   Viereck, Wolfgang. "German Dialects Spoken in the United
        States and Canada and Problems of German-English Lan-
        guage Contact, Especially in North America: A Bibliography,"
        Orbis. 17 (1968): 532-35.

1726   _____. "Wortmischung im Englischen und Deutschen,"
        LeS. 10 (1965): 162-63.

1727 Voss, Carl. "Auch in Nebraska spricht man Plattdütsch,"
DMH. (Dec. 6, 1973).

1728 Wacker, Helga. Die Besonderheiten der deutschen Schrift-
sprache in Amerika. (Duden-Beiträge, Sonderreihe). Mannheim: Bibliographisches Institut, 1964.

1729 Ward, Robert Elmer. "Brigandedeutsch in Amerika," Viertel-
jahrschrift f. d. kult. Leben in Stadt u. Land. 3 (1968): 24-
27.

1730 Wellemeyer, John. "Foreign Language Needs of Municipal
Employees in Ten Metropolitan Areas," MLA: Report. (1961):
245-52.

1731 Wenger, Marion. A Swiss-German Dialect Study: Three
Linguistic Islands in Midwestern USA. Ohio State University: Dissertation, 1969.

1732 Whyte, John. American Words and Ways: Especially for
German-Americans. New York: Viking Pr., 1943.

1733 Willibrand, W. A. "English Loan Words in the Low German
Dialect of Westphalia, Missouri," Pubs. Am. Dialect Soc.
27 (1958): 16-21.

1734 Wilson, Arthur. "English Spoken by Pennsylvania Germans
in Snyder County, Pennsylvania," AS. 23 (1949): 236-38.

1735 Wilson, Joseph. "The Texas German of Lee and Fayette
Counties," Rice Inst. Pamphlet. 47 (1960): 83-98.

1736 Wood, Ralph. "Die deutsche Volkssprache in Nordamerika,"
Wirkendes Wort. 11 (1961): 202-09.

1737 _____. "Pennsilfaanisch: Eine neudeutsche Sprache Nordamerikas," in Deutsche Philologie im Aufriss. Berlin:
Erich Schmidt Verlag, 1952, pp. 786-807.

1738 _____. "Pennsylvania High German," GR. 20 (1945): 299-
314.

1739 _____. "Die pennsylvanische Schärfung," Z. f. deutsche
Phil. 78 (1959): 225-38.

1740 Yoder, Donald Herbert. "Dutchified Surnames," Eck. (Sept.
21, 1946).

1741 Yudel, Mark. "The Yiddish Language: Its Cultural Impact,"
AJHQ. 59 (1970): 210.

Bio-Bibliographies of German-American Literature

1742   Albrecht, Erich.   "Nordamerika," in Grundriss der deutschen
       Dichtung aus den Quellen von Karl Goedeke.   Zweite ganz
       neubearbeitete Auflage.   Berlin: Akademie-Verlag, 1966, vol.
       15: 516-661.

1743   Albrecht, Günter.   Lexikon deutscher Schriftsteller von den
       Anfängen bis zur Gegenwart.   Leipzig: Bibliographisches
       Institut, 1967.

1744   Berthold, Werner.   Exil-Literatur 1933-45:   Eine Ausstellung
       aus Beständen der Deutschen Bibliothek.   Zweite Auflage.
       Frankfurt a. M., 1966.

1745   Bornemann, Felix.   Sealsfield-Bibliographie, 1945-65.   Stutt-
       gart: Verlag der Charles Sealsfield-Gesellschaft, 1966.

1746   Brümmer, Franz.   Lexikon der deutschen Dichter und Prosai-
       sten vom Beginn des 19. Jahrhunderts bis zur Gegenwart.   6
       Aufl.   Leipzig, 1913,   8 vols.

1747   Fick, H. H.   Bibliographie der deutschamerikanischen Schön-
       literatur.   (Manuscript).   UC

1748   Geissler, Max.   Führer durch die deutsche Literatur des 20.
       Jahrhunderts.   Weimar: Alex. Duncker Verlag, 1913.

1749   Grossberg, Mimi.   Austrian Writers in the U. S.,   1938-68.
       New York: Austrian Institute & Austrian Forum, Inc., 1968.

1750   _____.   Österreichische Autoren in Amerika: Geschick
       und Leistung der österreichischen literarischen Emigration ab
       1938 in den Vereinigten Staaten.   Wien: Im Auftrage des
       Bundesministeriums für Unterricht, 1970.

1751   _____.   Österreichische Emigration in den Vereinigten
       Staaten 1938.   Wien: Europa Verlag, 1970.

1752   Jahresberichte für deutsche Sprache und Literatur.   Bear-
       beitet unter Leitung von Gerhard Marx.   Berlin: Akademia-
       Verlag, 1960- .

1753   Köster, Kurt.   Exil-Literatur 1933-45:   Ausstellung der
       Deutschen Bibliothek, Frankfurt am Main, Mai bis August
       1965.   (Sonderveröffentlichung der Deutschen Bibliothek).
       Frankfurt: Deutsche Bibliothek, 1965.

1754   Kosch, Wilhelm.   Deutsches Literatur-Lexikon: Biograph-
       isches und bibliographisches Handbuch.   2 Aufl.   Bern:
       Francke, 1947-58,   4 vols.

1755   Kürschners deutscher Literatur-Kalender.   Berlin: De

Gruyter, 1879- .   Useful biographical record.

1756   Kürschners Nekrolog, 1901-35.   Berlin: De Gruyter, 1936.

1757   Kutzbach, Karl August.   Autorenlexikon der Gegenwart.   Bonn:
       Bouvier, 1950- .

1758   Legler, H. E.   "A Wisconsin Group of German Poets, with
       a Bibliography, " Wisc. Acad. Sci., Arts & Letters.   14 (1914):
       471-84.

1759   Lexikon sozialistischer deutscher Literatur, von den Anfängen
       bis 1945:   Monographisch-biographische Darstellung.   Halle:
       Verlag Sprache und Literatur, 1963.

1760   Rattermann, Heinrich A.   "Deutsch-Amerikanische Schrift-
       steller- und Künstler-Pseudonyme, " D-A Mag.   1 (1886-87):
       143-56.

1761   _____.   Deutsch-Amerikanisches Biographikon und Dich-
       teralbum der ersten Hälfte des 19. Jahrhunderts.   Cincinnati:
       Selvstverlag, 1911, 3 vols.

1762   Reichard, Harry Hess.   Pennsylvania German Dialect Writings
       and Their Writers.   Lancaster, Pa.:   New Era Printing Co.,
       1918.

1763   Schneider, Max.   Deutsches Titelbuch: Ein Hilfsmittel zum
       Nachweis von Verfassern deutscher Literaturwerke.   2 Aufl.
       Berlin: Poschke, 1927.

1764   Schroeder, Adolph.   "A Century of Sealsfield Scholarship, "
       RJGAH.   32 (1966):   13-23.

1765   Schweitzer, Christoph.   "Deutsche Dichterhandschriften in
       der Historical Society of Pennsylvania, " Jahrbuch d. d.
       Schillergesellschaft.   8 (1966):   344-81.

1766   Soffke, Günther.   Deutsches Schrifttum in Exil (1933-50):
       Ein Bestandsverzeichnis.   (Bonner Beiträge zur bibliograph-
       iscnen Bückerkunde, 11).   Bonn: Bouvier, 1965.

1767   Spiller, R. E. and W. Thorp.   "German and Pennsylvania
       German Literature, " GAS.   3, i (1971):   24-28.

1768   _____.   Literary History of the U.S.   New York: Mac-
       millan, 1948, pp. 286-91.

1769   Sternfeld, Wilhelm and Eva Tiedemann.   Deutsche Exil-Lit-
       eratur, 1933-45:   Eine Bio-bibliographie.   Heidelberg: Lam-
       bert Schneider, 1962.

1770   Tergit, Gabriele.   Autobiographien und Bibliographien.

London: P. E. N. Zentrum deutschsprachiger Autoren im Ausland, 1957.

1771   Ward, Robert Elmer. "Auswahlbibliographie, " in Deutsche Lyrik aus Amerika. N.Y.: Literary Society, Inc., 1969, pp. 94-6.

1772   _____. "A Bibliography of Works on German-American Literature. " (Manuscript) P. 28. 1970.

1773   _____. "Bio-Bibliographien, " in Deutsche Lyrik aus Amerika. New York: Literary Society, Inc., 1969, pp. 97-109.

1774   _____. Handbook of German-American Creative Literature (In Press). Contains bio-bibliographical information on 3, 000 German-American authors. Library locations are listed for each work. It is a most valuable work.

Literary Societies

1775   Die literarische Gesellschaft von Chicago. 4725 N. Washtena Chicago, Illinois 60625.

1776   Literarischer Verein, Inc. 6th E. 87th St., New York, N. Y.

1777   Literary Society Foundation, Inc. Box 373, Gracie Station, 229 E. 85th St., New York, N. Y. 10028.

1778   Society for German-American Studies. 7204 Langerford Drive, Cleveland, Ohio 44129.

1778A Verband deutschsprachiger Autoren in Amerika. 2545 Harrison Ave., Cincinnati, Ohio 45211.

Literary Journals: A Chronological List

1779   Readinger Magazin für Freunde der deutschen Literatur in Amerika. Reading, Pa.: Johann Carl Gossler, 1824-25.

1780   Die Fackel. Baltimore, New York, St. Paul and Cincinnati: Samuel Ludvigh, 1843-67. Contains Ludvigh's articles on the German-Americans in various parts of the country.

1781   Atlantis. Detroit, Milwaukee, Cleveland, Buffalo and New York: C. Esselen, 1853-58. One of the highest quality German-American journals.

1782   Deutsche Monatshefte. New York: H. J. Meyer, A. Kolatschek, P. Bernhard, 1853-56. Was edited by Rudolph Lexov German-American author.

1783   Prairie Blume. La Grange, Texas: Texas German Literary
        Society, 1857-61.

1784   Novellen-Schatz: Journal für gute deutsche und deutsch-
        amerikanische Novellen. New York: S. Zickel & J. Wei-
        mann, 1860-1903.

1785   Deutsch-Amerikanische Monatshefte für Politik, Wissenschaft
        und Literatur. Chicago: Caspar Butz, 1861-5.

1786   Steigers literarischer Monatsbericht. N.Y.: E. Steiger, 1869-71.

1787   Vierteljährliches Magazin der Modernen Literatur. New York:
        Herald Co., 1876-1901.

1788   New York Figaro: Belletristische Wochenschrift für Theater,
        Musik, Kunst, Literatur und Unterhaltung. New York: A.
        Rothmüller, Figaro Pub. Co., Leon von Raven, 1879-1900.

1789   Der arme Teufel. Detroit: Robert Reitzel, 1884-1900. Reit-
        zel was a leading German-American poet.

1790   Deutsch-Amerikanisches Magazin. Cincinnati: Heinrich A.
        Rattermann, 1886-87. An excellent publication.

1791   Deutsch-Amerikanische Dichtung. N. Y.: Konrad Nies, 1888-?.

1792   Deutsch-Texanische Monatshefte. San Antonio: L. F. La-
        frentz, R. Penninger, 1895-1910.

1793   Kritik der Kritik: Zeitschrift für Künstler und Kunstfreunde.
        New York, 1905-08.

1794   Rundschau zweier Welten. New York: Louis & Georg S.
        Viereck, 1907-12. Georg S. Viereck was a leading spokesman
        of German-Americans until 1940.

1795   Der Deutsche Kulturträger. Chicago: 1913-14.

1796   Jahrbuch des Literarischen Vereins. New York: Literari-
        scher Verein, 1926-37.

1797   Deutsches Dichten in Amerika. Chicago: University of Chi-
        cago, 1936-39.

1798   German-American Studies. Cleveland: Society for German-
        American Studies, 1969- .

1799   Lyrik und Prosa. Buffalo, New York: Erika Metzger, 1973- .

1799A   Mitteilungsblatt. Cincinnati: Association of German Lan-
        guage Authors in America, 1974.

118   German-Americana

Histories of German-American Literature

1800   Akselrod, Rose-Marie. "Deutsche Literatur an der Indianer-
        grenze, " KFLQ. 4 (1957): 113-18.

1801   Albrecht, Erich. "Ein deutschamerikanisches Regenlied, "
        GAS. 1 (1969): 1-2.

1802   Bender, Elizabeth. "Three Amish Novels, " MQR. 19 (1945):
        273-84.

1803   Betz, Gottlieb Augustus. Die deutschamerikanisches patrio-
        tische Lyrik der Achtundvierziger und ihre historische Grund-
        lage. University of Pennsylvania: Dissertation, 1913.

1804   Cazden, Robert E. German Exile Literature in America,
        1933-50: A History of the Free German Press and Book
        Trade. Chicago: ALA, 1970.

1805   Condoyannis, George E. German-American Prose Fiction
        from 1850-1918. Columbia University: Dissertation, 1953.

1806   _____. "German-American Prose Fiction: Synopses of
        38 Works, " GAS. 4 (1972): 1-126.

1807   Davis, Richard. "Three Poems from Colonial North Carolina
        NCHR. 46 (1969): 33-41.

1808   "Deutschamerikanische Dichtung, " DMH. (Aug. 2, 1973).

1809   Dickson, Paul. Das Amerikabild in der deutschen Emigrante
        literatur seit 1933. University of Munich: Dissertation, 195

1810   Durzak, M. Die deutsche Exilliteratur, 1933-45. Stuttgart:
        Reclam, 1973. Bio-bibliographical data on 400 authors.

1811   Exile Literature 1933-45. Bad Godesberg: Inter Nationes;
        Köln: Verlagsgesellschaft Rudolf Müller, 1968. Report of
        a symposium.

1812   Fahnenbruck, Heinz. "Die Frühzeit der deutsch-amerikani-
        schen Literatur Ohios, " Cin. K. (Feb. 17, 1967).

1813   Falbisaner, Adolf. Das deutsche Lied in der deutsch-ameri-
        kanischen Literatur. Chicago, 1902.

1814   Faust, Albert. "German-American Literature, " in Cam-
        bridge History of American Literature. New York: Putnam,
        1921, vol. 4: 572-90.

1815   Frick, W. K. "Notes on the Pennsylvania-German Litera-
        ture, " Mühlenberg Monthly. 4-5 (June, 1887-June, 1888).

1816   Friedmann, Robert.   Mennonite Piety Through the Centuries:
        Its Genius and Its Literature.   Goshen: Mennonite Historical
        Society, 1949.

1817   Funk, Ralph.   "Collecting and Editing Dialect Poetry, " PFL.
        10 (1959): 24-27.

1818   Görlich, Ernst.   "Oesterreichische Dichter in angelsächsicher
        Emigration: Mit unveröffentlichen Briefen Theodor Kramers
        an den Verfasser, " Hietsch. (1962): 197-206.

1819   Gong, A.   "Capital of Our Time: Foreign Writers Experi-
        ence New York: A Literary Montage, " AGR. 30 (1964): 6-14.

1820   Heintz, Georg.   "Deutsche Exilliteratur: Bericht über eine
        Tagung, " Muttersprache. 80 (1970): 171-79.

1821   Hofacker, Erich.   German Literature as Reflected in the Ger-
        man Language Press of St. Louis Prior to 1898. St. Louis:
        Washington University Pr. , 1946.

1822   Jockers, Ernst.   "Deutsch-Amerikanische Dichtung, " AD. 12
        (1929): 321-26.

1823   Kamman, William F.   Socialism in German-American Litera-
        ture.   Philadelphia: Americana-Germanica Pr. , 1917.

1824   Kesten, Hermann.   Deutsche Literatur im Exil: Briefe euro-
        päischer Autoren 1933-49.   München: Verlag Kurt Desch,
        1964.

1825   Kindermann, Heinz.   Rufe über Grenzen: Antlitz und Lebens-
        raum der Grenz- und Auslandsdeutschen in ihrer Dichtung.
        Berlin: Junge Geneatin Verlag, 1938.

1826   Klein, Karl Kurt.   "Literaturgeschichte des Deutschtums im
        Ausland, " in Schrifttum und Geistesleben der deutschen Volks-
        gruppen im Ausland vom Mittelalter bis zur Gegenwart.   Leip-
        zig, 1939.

1827   Kloss, Heinz.   "Deutsch-Amerikanisches Schrifttum in USA, "
        Dichtung und Volkstum. 35 (1934): 399-403.

1828   _____ .   "Die pennsylvaniadeutsche Literatur, " MDA. 7
        (1931): 230-72.

1829   _____ .   "Pennsylvania German Dialect Writings, North and
        West, " Eck. (Jan. 28, Feb. 4, 11, 1950).

1830   _____ .   "A Plea for an Anthology of Pennsylvania German
        Prose, " Eck. (Oct. 30, Nov. 6, 1954).

1831   _____ .   "Three Pennsylvania German Versions of the

Parable of the Prodigal Son, " Eck. (Aug. 27, 1949).

1832   Knortz, Karl. "Die plattdeutsche Literatur Nordamerikas, "
        AG. 1 (1897): 76-83.

1833   Krahn, Cornelius. "Literary Efforts Among the Mennonites
        of Russian Background, " ML. 24 (1969): 166-68. About Ger-
        man-Russians.

1834   Kunisch, Herman. Handbuch der deutschen Gegenwartslitera-
        tur. München: Nymphenburger Verlagshandlung, 1965.

1835   Learned, M. D. "The German-American Turner Lyric, "
        RJGAH. 10 (1896).

1836   Leser, L. L. "Deutsche Dichtkunst in den Vereinigten
        Staaten, " in Das Buch der Deutschen in Amerika. Philadel-
        phia: German American National Alliance, 1909.

1837   Mann, Golo. "Deutsche Literatur im Exil, " Neue Rundschau.
        79 (1968): 38-49.

1838   Meier, Henry. "Forty Years of the Literarischer Verein, "
        AGR. 12, v (1946): 20-21, 37.

1839   Metzenthin-Raunick, Selma Marie. Deutsche Schriften in
        Texas. San Antonio, 1935-36.

1840   Moll, Lloyd. "Am Schwarze Baer, " PGFS. 12 (1949): 11-
        146. Twenty-five dialect sketches.

1841   Pfeiler, William. German Literature in Exile: The Concern
        of the Poets. Lincoln: University of Nebraska Pr., 1957.

1842   Reichard, Henry. "The Christmas Poetry of the Pennsylvania
        Dutch, " PGFS. 6 (1941).

1843   _____. "Pennsylvania German Dialect Writing and Writers
        PGS: Proc. & Addresses. 26 (1918).

1844   _____. "Pennsylvania German Literature, " in The Penn-
        sylvania Germans. Princeton: Princeton University Pr.,
        1942, pp. 165-224.

1845   Robacker, Earl. Pennsylvania German Literature: Changing
        Trends from 1683 to 1942. Philadelphia: University of
        Pennsylvania Pr., 1943.

1846   Rothensteiner, Johannes. Die literarische Wirksamkeit der
        deutsch-amerikanischen Katholiken. St. Louis, 1922. GSP

1847   Schaumann, Hermann. Grundzüge deutscher Lyrik in Ameri-
        ka. Cornell University: Dissertation, 1934.

1848   Schneider, Wilhelm. Die auslandsdeutsche Dichtung unserer
        Zeit. Berlin: Weidmann, 1936. GSP

1849   Seifert, L. "Pennsylvania German Dialect Literature," AGR.
        8 (1942): 26-27, 36.

1850   Shenk, Stanley. "American Mennonite Fiction," ML. 23
        (1968): 119 ff.

1851   Spuler, Linus. Deutsches Schrifttum in den Vereinigten
        Staaten von Amerika: Beiträge von Amerika-Schweizern.
        (Beilage zum Jahresberichte der kantonalen höheren Lehren-
        stalten Luzern). Luzern, 1959-60.

1852   _____. "Von deutsch-amerikanischer Dichtung," GAS. 1,
        i (1969): 8-16.

1853   Stoeffler, E. E. "Mysticism in the German Devotional Lit-
        erature of Colonial Pennsylvania," PGFS. 14 (1950): 1-173.

1854   Stoudt, John. "Pennsylvania German Poetry Until 1816: A
        Survey," GL&L. 13 (1960): 145-53.

1855   Tolzmann, Don Heinrich. "Deutschamerikanische Dichtung:
        1675-1973," DMH. (Aug. 2, 1973). A brief survey.

1856   Uhlendorff, Bernhard. "Die politische Lyrik der Deutschen
        in Amerika," Der deutsche Gedanke. 3 (1926): 115-24.

1857   Vom Ende, Amalia. "German-American Literature," Poet
        Lore. 17 (1906): 108-17.

1858   Walter, Hans-Albert. "Zur Situation der deutschen Exilver-
        lage, 1933-45," Frank. Hefte. 20 (Feb., 1965).

1859   Willibrand, W. A. "Occasional German Verse at Westphalia,
        Missouri in the 1880's," Studies in G. L. (1964): 39-39, 155-
        56.

1860   Wittich, Benjamin. Unsere Literatur: Vortrag. Cincinnati,
        1898. UC

1861   Wittke, Carl. "Melting-Pot Literature," EJ. 7 (1946): 189-
        97.

1862   Wood, Ralph. "German-American Poetry," AGR. 23, iv
        (1957): 3.

1863   Yoder, Donald Herbert. "Hegins Valley in Song and Poetry,"
        Eck. (Jan. 11, 18, 25, 1957).

1864   Zimmermann, G. A. Handbuch der deutschen Literatur
        Europas und Amerikas. Chicago, 1876. Contains a 112-
        page appendix, "Deutsch-Amerikanische Dichter."

Anthologies of German-American Literature
(Chronologically arranged)

1865 Marxhausen, Conrad. Deutsch-Amerikanischer Dichterwald:
      Eine Sammlung von Original-Gedichten deutsch-amerikanischer
      Verfasser. Detroit: Verlag von August & Conrad Marx-
      hausen, 1856. The first anthology of German-American po-
      etry. DLC, GSP, UC

1866 Muskenklänge aus dem Süden: Eine Sammlung von Original-
      Gedichten von Hugo Weidemann, Christian F. Vogler, Georg
      Hoffmann und Franz Melchers. Charleston, 1858.

1867 Bruhin, Thomas Acquinas. Blumenlese deutsch-amerikanischer
      Gedichte. Zürich: F. Schul, 1869. MH, MiD, PU, IU,
      PPULC

1868 Steiger, Ernst. Heimathgrüsse aus Amerika. New York:
      E. Steiger, 1870.

1869 _____. Dornrosen: Erstlingsblüthen deutscher Lyrik in
      Amerika. New York: E. Steiger, 1871. GSP, UC

1870 Arbeiter Liederbuch: Gedichte und Lieder freisinniger Ten-
      denz. Chicago: G. A. Lönnecker, 1873. DLC, GSP, PPG,
      PPULC

1871 Warns, P. F. L. Blüten und Perlen: Sammlung neuerer
      und älterer Gedichte ausländischer und einheimischer Dichtung.
      Milwaukee, 1886. GSP, UC

1872 Zimmerman, G. A. Deutsch in Amerika: Beiträge zur
      Geschichte der deutsch-amerikanischen Literatur. Chicago:
      Eyller, 1894. DLC, GSP, UM

1873 Haussmann, William A. "German-American Hymnology, 1683-
      1800, " AG. 2 (1898-99): 1-61.

1874 Miller, Daniel. Pennsylvania German: A Collection of Penn-
      sylvania German Productions in Poetry and Prose. Reading,
      Pa.: D. Miller, 1903-11, 2 vols.

1875 Neef, Gotthold. Vom Lande des Sternenbanners: Eine Blu-
      menlese deutscher Dichtungen aus Amerika. Ellenville, New
      York: Neef's German Authors Agency, 1905. DLC, GSP,
      UC, UM

1876 "Deutsch-Amerikanische Dichtungen: Anthologie, " in Das Buch
      der Deutschen in Amerika. Philadelphia: German-American
      National Alliance, 1909, pp. 399-419.

1877 Jahrbuch des Verbandes deutscher Schriftsteller in Amerika.
      New York: Verband deutscher Schriftsteller in Amerika, 1911.
      GSP, UM

1878   Rattermann, Heinrich A.   Deutsch-Amerikanische Dichter und
       Dichtungen des 17. und 18. Jahrhunderts: Eine Anthologie.
       Chicago: German-American Historical Society of Illinois, 1914.
       DLC, GSP, UC, UM

1879   Sanders, Irving T.   Aus ruhmreicher Zeit: Deutsch-Ameri-
       kanische Dichtungen aus dem ersten Jahre des Weltkrieges.
       New York: Stechert, 1915.   DLC, GSP

1880   Uhlendorff, Bernhard.   "German-American Poetry: A Con-
       tribution to Colonial Literature, " DAG.   22-23 (1922-23): 109-
       295.

1881   Gemeinschaft für Kultur.   Anthologie deutsch-amerikanischer
       Dichtung.   New York: Gemeinschaft für Kultur, 1925.   UC

1882   Jockers, Ernst.   Deutsch-Amerikanischer Musenalmanach.
       New York: Heiss, 1925.   GSP, InU, NIC, TXU, OCU, LU,
       NRU, MH, NN, MdU, ICN, NjP, UC, UM

1883   Kloss, Heinz.   Lewendiche Schtimme aus Pennsilveni:
       Schreiwes vun Charles R. Roberts, Astor C. Wuchter un
       Charles C. More.   Stuttgart: Ausland und Heimat; New York:
       Westermann, 1929.

1884   . Ich schwetz in der Muttersproch: Pennsylvania-
       deutsche Texte.   Wiesbaden: Verlag Deutsche Volksbücher,
       1936.

1885   Reichard, Harry Hess.   Pennsylvania German Verse: An An-
       thology of Representative Selections in the Dialect Popularly
       Known as Pennsylvania Dutch.   Norristown, Pa.:   Pennsyl-
       vania German Society, 1940.

1886   Arndt, Karl.   Early German-American Narratives.   New
       York: American Book Co., 1941.

1887   Aurand, Ammon Monroe.   Wit and Humor of the Pennsylvania
       Germans: A Collection of Anecdotes, Stories and Witticisms
       --Some Old, Some New.   Harrisburg, Pa.:   Aurand, 1946.
       NN, IEN, NcD, ICarbS, OR

1888   Stoudt, John J.   Pennsylvania German Poetry, 1685-1830.
       Allentown, Pa.:   Schlechter, 1955.

1889   Schlösser, Manfred.   An den Wind geschrieben.   Darmstadt:
       Agora Verlag, 1960.   UK

1890   Gong, Alfred.   Interview mit Amerika: 50 deutschsprachige
       Autoren in der neuen Welt.   München: Nymphenburger Ver-
       lagshandlung, 1962.   NN, IU, UM

1891   The Reichard Collection of Early Pennsylvania German Dialogues and Plays. (Pennsylvania German Society, 61). Lancaster, Pa.: Fackenthal Library, Franklin and Marshall College, 1962.

1892   Wood, Ralph and Fritz Braun. Pennsilfaanisch-deitsch: Erzählungen und Gedichte der Pennsylvaniadeutschen. (Pfälzer in der weiten Welt, 6). Kaiserslautern, 1966.

1893   Pratschke, Gottfried. Alle Wunder dieser Welt. Wien: Europäischer Verlag, 1968.

1894   Grossberg, Mimi. Kleinkunst aus Amerika. Wien: Europäischer Verlag, 1969.

1895   Pratschke, Gottfried. Aber den Feind sollten wir nicht lieben. Wien: Europäischer Verlag, 1969.

1896   Ward, Robert Elmer. Deutsche Lyrik aus Amerika. New York: Literary Society Foundation, Inc., 1969. Contains biobibliographical data. GSP, DLC, UM

German-American Authors

1897   Allen, George. "Two Pennsylvania-Dutch Poets: Henry Harbaugh and Henry Lee Fisher," AGR. 8 (1942): 10-12, 34; 9 (1942): 10-12, 37.

1898   Apsler, Alfred. "Writers from across the Sea," EJ. 9, i (19): 19-24.

1899   Arndt, Karl. "Charles Sealsfield and the Courier des Etats-Unis," PMLA. 68 (1953): 170-88.

1900   _____. "The Litigious Mr. Sealsfield," MLN. 78 (1963): 527-32.

1901   _____. "New Light on Sealsfield's Cajütenbuch and Gesammelte Werke," JEGP. 41 (1942): 210-22.

1902   _____. "Plagiarism: Sealsfield or Simms?" MLN. 69 (1954): 577-81.

1903   _____. "Recent Sealsfield Discoveries," JEGP. 52 (1954): 160-71.

1904   _____. "Sealsfield and Strubberg at Vera Cruz," MO. 44 (1952): 225-28.

1905   _____. "Sealsfield's Claim to Realism," Monatshefte. 35 (1943): 271-85.

1906 _____. "Sealsfield's Early Reception in England and America, " GR. 18 (1943): 176-95.

1907 Aufderheide, Elfriede. Das Amerikaerlebnis in den Romanen von Charles Sealsfield. University of Göttingen: Dissertation, 1945.

1908 Barba, Preston. Balduin Moellhausen: The German Cooper. Philadelphia: University of Pennsylvania, 1914.

1909 _____. "Edward Hermany, a Pennsylvania German Poet, " Lehigh CHS. 12 (1959): 37-76.

1910 _____. "Edward Hermany: A Pennsylvania German Poet (1832-1896), " Eck. (July 20, Aug. 31, 1963).

1911 _____. "John Birmelin: Distinguished Pennsylvania German Dialect Poet, " HRBC. 16, iii (1951): 79-80, 95-96.

1912 _____. The Life and Works of Friedrich Armand Strubberg. Philadelphia: University of Pennsylvania, 1913.

1913 _____. "A Literary Discovery, " Eck. (Feb. 15, 1947). On Henry Harbaugh.

1914 _____. "Ludwig A. Wollenweber, " HRBC. 7 (1941-42): 74-77.

1915 _____. "Rachel Bahn: Pennsylvania German Poetess, " PGS, Pubs. 3 (1970): 55-90.

1916 _____. "Der Sim Schmalzgsicht vum Leder Eck Poshta, " Eck. (Nov. 3, 1956). On Charles W. Weiser.

1917 _____. "Who was Tobias Witmer?" Eck. (July 3, 1948).

1918 [Baum.] "Curt Baum, " AGR. 28, iv (1962): 36.

1919 Berger, David. "A Conversation with Johannes Urzidil, " AGR. 32, i (1965): 23-24.

1920 Bergholz, Harry. "Julius Bab, " BA. 25, i (19): 26-27.

1921 Boyer, Walter. "Solly Hulsbuck, the People's Poet, " PD. 4, v (1952): 1-2, 14-15. About Harvey M. Miller, a prolific German-American poet.

1922 Brause, Herman. "Handbuch eines Deutschamerikaners, " DW. (Mar. 28, 1973).

1923 Breuer, Robert. "Hermann Broch: Poet and Philosopher, " AGR. 23, iii (1957): 12-14. Broch's life in America.

1924   Briner, Andres. "Conrad Beissel and Thomas Mann, " AGR.
        26, ii (1959): 24-25, 38.

1925   Broadbent, T. L. "Hans Besenstiel: Immigrant Satirist, "
        Western Hum. Rev. 12 (1958): 151-57.

1926   Buffington, Albert F. "Henry Meyer: An Early Pennsylvania
        German Poet, " PGFS. 19 (1955): 1-32.

1927   _____. "Lyman Baker: The Bard of Bannerville, " Eck.
        (July 10, 17, 1954).

1928   Castle, Eduard. Der grosse Unbekannte: Das Leben von
        Charles Sealsfield. Wien: Karl Werner, 1955.

1929   [Croll.] "Philip C. Croll: Antiquarian, Author and Man of
        God, " HRBC. 18 (1952): 8-11.

1930   Cunz, Dieter. "Carl Heinrich Schnauffers literarische Ver-
        suche, " PMLA. 59 (1944): 524-39.

1931   Downs, L. "Albert Wolff, " MHist. 27 (1946): 327-29.

1932   Durnbaugh, Donald. "Johann Adam Gruber: Pennsylvania
        German Prophet and Poet, " PMHB. 83 (1959): 382-408.

1933   Ehrhardt, Jacob. "Einführung in das lyrische Werk von Rose
        Ausländer, " GAS. 2, ii (1970): 55-62.

1934   _____. "Ernst Waldinger in Memoriam, " GAS. 2, i
        (1970): 1.

1935   Evans, Clarence. "Gerstäcker and the Konwells of White
        River Valley, " AHQ. 10 (1951): 1-36.

1936   Fick, H. H. Meine deutschamerikanischen Poetenbekannt-
        schaften. UC

1937   Flanagan, John. "Conrad Richter: Romancer of the South-
        west, " SWRev. 43 (1958): 189-96.

1938   Freidel, Frank. "Francis Lieber: Transmitter of European
        Ideas to America, " Bul. J. Rylands L. 38 (1956): 342-59.

1939   Frenz, Horst. "Karl Knortz: Interpreter of American Lit-
        erature and Culture, " AGR. 13, ii (1946): 27-30.

1940   _____. "Walt Whitman's Letters to Karl Knortz, " AL. 20
        (1948): 155-63.

1941   Funk, Ralph. "Pen Names, " PD. 5 (1954): 7. On Pennsyl-
        vania German poets.

1942   Grant, Jesse. "A Forgotten Poet, " MHSB. 19 (1963): 356-58.

1943   Gross, Elizabeth. "Poet William Gross, " PD. 4 (1953): 12.
       Includes a checklist of his work.

1944   "Grossveranstaltung am 6. Okt. 1973 in der Eagle Halle, "
       DMH. (Oct. 18, 1973). About Dora Grunewald.

1945   Gudde, Erwin. "Friedrich Gerstaecker: World Traveler and
       Author, 1816-72, " J. West. 7 (1968): 345-50.

1946   Guyot, Wilma. "A Biographical Note on William Mueller
       1845-1931, " HPSO. 20 (1962): 88-91.

1947   _____. "William Mueller, " AGR. 28, iii (1962): 14-15.

1948   Hagemann, E. R. "A Checklist of the Work of B. Traven
       and the Critical Estimates and Biographical Essays on Him:
       together with a Brief Biography, " PBSA. 53 (1959): 37-67.

1949   Hartmann, Horst. George Catlin und Balduin Möllhausen:
       Zwei Interpreten der Indianer und des alten Westens. Ber-
       lin: Reimer, 1963.

1950   "Herr Don Heinrich Tolzmann, " DMH. (July 19, 1973).

1951   Hess, Mary. "Elsie Singmaster, " Eck. (June 16-Aug. 25,
       1956).

1952   House, Roy T. "Gustav Mueller and the Schüttelreim: A
       Swiss-American's Contribution to a Unique German Verse
       Form, " AGR. 14, iii (1948): 21-23.

1953   Jannach, Hubert. "B. Traven: An American or German
       Author?" CQ. 36 (1963): 459-68.

1954   _____. "The B. Traven Mystery, " Books Abroad. 35
       (1961): 28-29.

1955   _____. "A Literary Curiosity, " CQ. 38 (1965): 404-06.

1956   Jantz, Harold. "Charles Sealsfield's Letter to Joel R. Poin-
       sett, " GR. 27 (1952): 155-64.

1957   Johnson, Hildegard B. "Caspar Butz of Chicago: Politician
       and Poet, " AGR. 12, vi (1946): 4-7; 13, i (1946): 9-11.

1958   Jordan, E. L. America, Glorious and Chaotic Land: Charles
       Sealsfield Discovers the Young United States. Englewood
       Cliffs: Prentice-Hall, 1969.

1959   Kauf, Robert. "Ernst Waldinger: An Austro-American
       Poet, " AGR. 27, vi (1961): 11-13.

1960   Keller, Eli. "The Life and Works of Eli Keller, Pennsylvania German Poet, 1825-1919, " Eck. (Aug. 15-Dec. 12, 1964).

1961   Kennedy, Thomas. "Francis Lieber (1798-1982): German-American Poet and Transmitter of German Culture to America, " GAS. 5 (1972): 28-50.

1962   Kieffer, Elizabeth. "Henry Harbaugh in Lancaster, " LCHP. 46 (1942): 57-83.

1963   _____. "Henry Harbaugh, Pennsylvania Dutchman, 1817-67, " PGSP. 51 (1945): 365 pp.

1964   Kisch, Guido. "Two American Jewish Pioneers of New Haven, " HJUD. 4 (1942): 16-37. On poetry of Sigmund Wassermann.

1965   Klein, H. M. "Diaries and Private Papers of Dr. Henry Harbaugh, " NCHS. 12 (1942): 179-203.

1966   Kloss, Heinz. "Columnist-Advertiser Early Radio Author: Being the Dialect Record of George W. Kunsman, " Eck. (Apr. 19, 1952).

1967   _____. "Edmund Daniel Leisenring: Pennsylvania German Dialect Writer, " Eck. (Apr. 24, May 1, 1954).

1968   _____. "Edward Montgomery Eberman or Danny Kratzer: Popular German Columnist, " Eck. (Dec. 12, 19, 1953).

1969   _____. "En Bissel Wollenweberisch, " Eck. (Oct. 19, 1957). About Ludwig August Wollenweber.

1970   _____. "George K. Hoffman: Columnist, Antiquarian, Chronicler of Olden Days, " Eck. (Jan. 28, 1956).

1971   _____. "Hiram Hollerheck: Teller of Tales Once Widely Read, " Eck. (Mar. 28, Apr. 4, 1953). About Oscar Knauss.

1972   _____. "John Wesley von Nieda: Pennsylvania German Novelist, " Eck. (July 23, 1949).

1973   _____. "Sim Schmalzgsicht: Once Locally Famous Allentown Humorist, " Eck. (Oct. 20, 1956).

1974   _____. "Snyder County's Edwin Charles, " Eck. (Feb. 19, 1955).

1975   _____. "Tobias Winter, " Eck. (Nov. 6, 1948).

1976   _____. "Uncle Mike: Unknown Saga from the Saucony, " Eck. (Sept. 22, 1956).

1977 _____. "William H. Erb, Columnist," Eck. (Nov. 7, 1953).

1978 _____. "Zur Erinnerung and en pennsylvaniadeutschen Mundarterzähler Charles C. Moore," Deutsche Kultur im Leben d. Völker. (1941): 433-40.

1979 _____. "Zwei pennsylvaniadeutsche Lyriker," Muttersprache. (1955): 28-29. About Charles Ziegler and John Birmelin.

1980 [Knecht.] "Dr. George Knecht: Dentist, Astronomer, Poet," Eck. (Apr. 2, 9, 16, 1966).

1981 Knief, Frederick. "Johann Jakob Meyer," AGR. 17, iv (1951): 8-9.

1982 Knoche, Carl H. "Alexander Conze: An Early Milwaukee German-American Poet," GAS. 5 (1972): 148-62.

1983 Koenig, Karl. "Henry (Vater) Mirbach: Volksdichter," AGR. 16, v (1950): 25-27.

1984 Krumpelmann, John. "Sealsfield and Sources," MO. 43 (1951): 324-26.

1985 _____. "Sealsfield's Observations Concerning the Blooming of Magnolias in Louisiana," MLN. 84 (1969): 796-98.

1986 Landa, B. The American Scene in Friedrich Gerstäcker's Works of Fiction. University of Minnesota: Dissertation, 1953.

1987 Leidy, Rosanne. "Thomas J. B. Rhoads, Poet and Physician of Boyertown," HRBC. 26 (1961): 50-51.

1988 Metzenthin-Raunick, Selma. "Johannes Christlieb Nathanael Romberg, German Poet of Texas," AGR. 12, iii (1946): 32-35.

1989 Miller, Charles. "B. Traven, Continued," NYTBR. (Nov. 20, 1966): p. 84.

1990 Moder, Donald. "Charles Siegel, Dialect Poet," Eck. (June 12, 1948).

1991 Nettl, Paul. "Hermann Broch," AGR. 17, vi (1951): 35.

1992 Neuburger, Hans. "Lyrik eines Deutschamerikaners," AGR. 26, iv (1960): 30.

1993 Patterson, Jerry. "Brantz Mayer, Man of Letters," MHM. 52 (1957): 275-89.

1994   Peters, Elisabeth. "A Tribute to Arnold Dyck, " ML. 24
       (1969): 3-5.

1995   Picard, Jacob. "Ernst Waldinger at Sixty, " BA. 31 (1957):
       28-29.

1996   Posselt, Erich. "The Story of an American Poet, " AGR. 17,
       i (1950): 25-26. On Hugo Karl Tippmann (1875-1942).

1997   Prahl, Augustus. "America in the Works of Gerstäcker, "
       MLQ. 4 (1943): 213-24.

1998   _____. "Friedrich Gerstäcker: The Frontier Novelist, "
       AHQ. 14 (1955): 43-50.

1999   Recknagel, Rolf. B. Traven: Beiträge zur Biographie.
       (Reclam Universal-Bibliothek, 269). Leipzig: Reclam, 1965.

2000   Reichart, W. "Thomas Mann: An American Bibliography, "
       Monatshefte. 37 (1945): 309-408.

2001   Ritter, Erwin F. "Robert Reitzel, A. T.   (1849-98), " GAS.
       5 (1972): 12-26.

2002   Roemer, Hans. "Konrad Krez, Poet Between Continents, "
       GAS. 3 (1971): 12-17.

2003   Ruppius, Otto. "A Career in America, " AGR. 9 (1943): 28-
       33.

2004   Scheibe, Fred Karl. "Heinrich A. Rattermann: German-
       American Poet, 1832-1923, " GAS. 1, i (1969): 3-7.

2005   Schroeder, Adolf. Charles Sealsfield in the Red River Val-
       ley. Louisiana State University: Dissertation, 1947.

2006   _____. "New Sources of Charles Sealsfield, " JEGP. 46
       (1947): 70-74.

2007   Schultz, H. "Friedrich Gerstäcker's Image of the German
       Immigrant in America, " GAS. 5 (1972): 98-116.

2008   Schurz, Carl. "Carl Schurz Letters, " AGR. 22, iv (1956):
       6, 40. Correspondence with Edward F. Leyh, a Maryland
       poet.

2009   Shoemaker, Alfred. "George Keller DeLong: The Blind
       Dutch Poet, " PD. 3 (1952): 1-2.

2010   _____. "Johann Valentin Schuller: Fractur Artist and
       Author, " PD. (Oct. 15, 19).

2011   Spanheimer, M. E.   Heinrich Arnim Rattermann: German-

American Author, Poet and Historian, 1832-1923.   Washington, 1937.

2012   Spuler, Linus.   "New Yorker Gedichte: Zur Grossstadtdich-
       tung des Schweizer-Amerikaners Oskar Kollbrunner, " Euphor-
       ion. 47 (1953): 341-50.

2013   _____. Oskar Kollbrunner: Leben, Werk und literar-
       historistorische Stellung eines Schweizer Dichters in der neuen
       Welt. Huber: Frauenfeld, 1953.

2014   _____. "Oskar Kollbrunner: Swiss-American Poet, 1895-
       1932, " AGR. 21 (1955): 9-11.

2015   Stahl, Albert.   "Novelist J. Fred Bachman, " PD. 4 (1953):
       9, 15.

2016   Stoll, Karl-Heinz.   "The Literary Activity of Georg Edward, "
       GAS. I, i (1969): 17-32.

2017   Tappert, Theodore.   "Muhlenberg as Author, " CHIQ. 34
       (1962): 82 ff.

2018   Thiessen, Jack.   "Arnold Dyck: The Mennonite Artist, " ML.
       24 (1969): 77-83.

2019   Tolzmann, Don Heinrich.   "Ein deutscher Dichter in Wiscon-
       sin, " DMH. (Aug. 23, 1973).   About Konrad Krez.

2020   _____. "Handbuch eines Deutschamerikaners, " DDA.
       (March, 1973).

2021   _____. "Herman Brause: Auf fernen Wegen, " DMH. (Aug.
       23, 1973).   About an American-born poet.

2022   Van de Luyster, Nelson.   "Gerstäcker's Novels about Emi-
       grants to America, " AGR. 20, v (1954): 22-23, 36.

2023   Vines, Mary Jo.   "A Pioneer Poet of Texas, " AGR. 14, v
       (1948): 28-30.   About Marie Weisselberg (1835-1911).

2024   Voigt, Frieda.   "Kurt Baum: German Poet in Milwaukee, "
       HM. 24 (1968): 71-78.

2025   _____. "Letters and Postcards to My Husband from Oskar
       Maria Graf and Julius Bab, " GAS. 3, ii (1971): 24-45.

2026   _____. "Martin Drescher: A German-American Poet, "
       Can. Mod. Lang. Rev. (Winter, 1966).

2027   Von der Heydt, Alfred.   "Oskar Maria Graf, " GQ. 41 (1968):
       401-12.

2028   Von Ende, Amalie. "Deutsch-Amerikanische Dichter, " Das litterarische Echo. 1 (1899): 997-1003.

2029   Ward, Robert Elmer. "Dr. Egon Frey in Memoriam, " GAS. 6 (1973): 1.

2030   _____. "Dr. J. H. Stepler: Cleveland's German-American Pastor Poet, " GAS. 5 (1972): 69-96.

2031   _____. "Edward Dorsch and Otto Roeser: German-American Poets in Michigan, " MIch. Heritage. 11 (1969): 61-69.

2032   _____. "Ernst Anton Zuendt: Profile of a German Writer in the Midwest, " G. P. Hist Bul. 14, i (1971): 1-6.

2033   _____. "German Poems by Lutheran Pastors in America, " CHIQ. 44 (1971): 114-21.

2034   _____. "Konrad Nies: German-American Literary Knight, ' GAS. 3 (1971): 7-11.

2035   _____. "Lutherische Pastoren, die zur deutschamerikanischen Literatur beigetragen haben, " GAS. 6 (1973): 68-71.

2036   Ward-Leyerle, Robert Elmer. "Clevelands deutschamerikanische Dichter," W&A. (June 21, 1968).

2037   _____. "Deutsch-amerikanische Dichter: Ihr Leben und Schaffen," W&A. (Feb. 7, 1969-). A continuous series.

2038   Weisert, John. "Lewis N. Dembitz and Onkel Toms Hütte, " AGR. 19, iii (1953): 7-8.

2039   Wiley, Norman. "Sealsfield's Unrealistic Mexico, " MO. 48 (1956): 127-36.

2040   Wittke, Carl. "Karl Heinzen's Literary Ambition, " Monatshefte. 37 (1945): 88-98.

2041   Woodson, Leroy. American Negro Slavery in the Works of Strubberg, Gerstaecker and Ruppius. Washington: Catholic University of America Pr., 1949.

2042   Yoder, Don. "Bad Luck Farm: The Story of Harry Hower," PD. (Dec. 1, 1951).

2043   Zucker, A. E. "A Monument to Robert Reitzel: Der Arme Teufel, Berlin, " GR. 20 (1945): 141-52.

German-American Literature: 1700-1974
(Arranged chronologically)

2044 Pastorius, Franz Daniel. Umständige geographische beschreibung der zu allerletzt erfundenen provintz Pennsylvania. Frankfurt: Zu finden bey Andreas Otto, 1700. DLC

2045 Göttliche Liebes- und Lobesthöne. Philadelphia: Benjamin Franklin, 1730. Contains 31 hymns by Conrad Beissel. HSP

2046 Vorspiel der neuen Welt. Welches sich in der letzten Abendröthe als ein paradisischer Lichtesglanz unter den Kindern Gottes hervor gethan. Philadelphia: Benjamin Franklin, 1732. HSP

2047 Jacobs Kampff- und Ritter-Platz, Allwo der nach seinem ursprung sich sehnende geist der in Sophiam verliebten seele mit Gott um den neuen namen gesungen, um den Sieg davon getragen. Philadelphia: Benjamin Franklin, 1736. Mystical poetry. HSP

2048 Gruber, Johann. Einfältige Warnungs- und Wächter-Stimme an die gerufene Seelen dieser Zeit. Germantown: Saur, 1741. HSP

2049 _____. Ein Zeignis eines Betrübten, der seine Klage ausschüttet über die unzeitige, eigenmächtige, übereilte Zusammen-Berufung und Sammlung verschiedener Partheyen und erweckten Seelen, so unter dem Namen Immanuels vorgegeben wird. Germantown: Saur, 1742. HSP

2050 Zinzendorf, Nicolaus Ludwig. Hirten-Lieder von Bethlehem. Germantown, 1742. AAS

2051 Funck, Heinrich. Ein Spiegel der Tauffe mit Geist, mit Wasser und mit Blut. Germantown: Saur, 1744. HSP

2052 Beissel, Conrad. Urstaendliche und Erfahrungsvolle Hohe Zeugnisse wie man zum Geistlichen Leben und dessen Vollkommenheit gelangen moege. Ephrata: Brüderschaft, 1745. AAS

2053 Güldene Aepfel in Silbern Schalen, Oder: Schöne und nützliche Worte und Wahrheiten zur Gottseligkeit. Ephrata: Brüderschaft, 1745. AAS, LCP

2054 Das Gesang der einsamen und verlassenen Turtel-Taube, Nemlich der Christlichen Kirche. Oder geistliche u. u. Erfahrungsvolle Leidens-Gethöne. Ephrata: Brüderschaft, 1747. HSP

2055 Hildebrand, Joh. Ein ruffende Wächterstimme an alle Seelen die nach Gott und seinem Reich hungernd sind. Germantown: Saur, 1747. HSP

2056   Göttliche Liebes-Andacht mit einer Anweisung und Unterricht,
        wie man die Liebes-Andacht in der Stille und Ruhe des Ge-
        müths üben soll vor Gott.   Germantown: Saur, 1750.   NYPL

2057   Muehlenberg, Heinrich.   Unpartheyische Gedanken in Reimen
        bey Einweihung einer Evangelischen Kirche in Germantown.
        Germantown: Saur, 1752.   HSP

2058   Ein angenehmer Geruch der Rosen und Lilien, die im Thal
        der Demuth unter Dornen hervor gewachsen.   Alles aus der
        herrlichen Gesellschaft in Bethania.   Ephrata: Brüderschaft,
        1756.   LCP

2059   Ein Spiegel der Eheleute.   Nebst schönen Erinnerungen vor
        ledige Personen, welche willens sind, sich in den Stand der
        Ehe zu begeben.   Vorgestellt in einem Gespräch zwischen
        einem Jüngling und Meister.   Germantown: Saur, 1758.   HSP

2060   Die Erzählungen von Maria le Roy und Barbara Leininger,
        welche viertehalb Jahre unter den Indianern gefangen gewesen
        und am 6ten May in dieser Stadt glücklich angekommen.   Aus
        ihrem Munde niedergeschrieven und zum Druck befördert.
        Philadelphia: Teutsche Buchdruckerey, 1759.   HSP

2061   Mack, Alexander.   Eine Anmuthige Erinnerung zu einer
        Christlichen Betrachtung von der wunderbaren Allgegenwart
        des Allwissenden Gottes.   Germantown: Saur, 1760.   HSP

2062   Abgeforderte Relation oder Erscheinung eines entleibten Geists,
        dem Publico zur Nachricht getreulich aus dem Munde derer,
        die von Anfang bis ans Ende interessiret aufgeschrieben.
        Ephrata: Brüderschaft, 1761.   Mystical visions.   HSP

2063   Geistlicher Irrgarten mit vier Gnadensbrunnen.   Philadelphia:
        Miller, 1762.   HSP

2064   Lampe, Friedrich.   Erste Wahrheits-Milch für Säuglinge am
        Altar und Verstand.   Oder kurzgefasste Grund-Regeln des Re-
        formirten Christentums.   Philadelphia: Armbruester, 1762.
        HSP

2065   Neu-vermehrte Gesänge der einsamen Turtel-Taube.   Zur ge-
        meinsamen Erbauung gesammelt und ans Licht gegeben.   Eph-
        rata: Brüderschaft, 1762.   Hymns by Beissel and others.
        AAS

2066   Paradisisches Wunder-Spiel.   Ephrata: Typis et Consensu
        Societatis, 1766.   Contains 441 hymns by Beissel.   AAS,
        HSP

2067   Ein schön Lied von dem Schweizerischen Erz-Freyheitssohn
        Wilhelm Tellen, dem Urheber der löbl. Eydgenossenschaft.
        Samt einem andern Liede von dem Ursprung und Herkommen

der Schweizer. Philadelphia: Miller, 1768. HSP

2068 Frantzen, M. Einfältige Lehr-Betrachtungen und kurtz-
gefasstes Glaubersbekenntnis des gottseligen Lehrers Michael
Frantzen. Germantown: Saur, 1770. HSP

2069 Lutz, Samuel. Die Paradisische Alve der jungfräulichen
Keuschheit, welche Gott giebt allen, die da sind aus dem
Glauben an den Herrn Jesum. Germantown: Saur, 1770.
AAS

2070 Erzehlung derer durch Samuel Brand verübten gantz unmensch-
lichen Thaten un siner darauf erfolgten Hinrichtung. Lancaster, Pa.: Franz Bailey, 1774. LCP

2071 Inwendige Glaubens- und Liebes-Uebung einer Seele gegen
Gott und dessen Gegenwart. Ephrata: Brüderschaft, 1775.
HSP

2072 Kunze, Johann Christoph. Einige Gedichte und Lieder. Philadelphia: Sowers, 1778. AAAS

2073 Helmuth, Justus. Empfindungen des Herzens in einigen Liedern. Philadelphia: Steiner, 1781. AAS

2074 Kunze, Johann Christoph. Etwas vom rechten Lebenswege.
Philadelphia: Steiner, 1781. LOC

2075 Helmut, Justus. Die frohe Weihnachtsfreude, 1784. Und
Neujahrs-Andacht, 1785. Philadelphia: Steiner, 1784. PPLT

2076 _____. Charfreytags-Gesänge, und Osterlieder. Philadelphia: Steiner, 1785. PPLT

2077 Kunze, Johann Christoph. Elisas betränter Nachruf. Philadelphia: Steiner, 1787. HC

2078 Göttliche Wunderschrift, darinnen entdecket wird, wie aus
dem ewigen Guten hat koennen ein Böses urständen. Ephrata:
Brüderschaft, 1789. HSP

2079 Schroeder, Johann Georg. Merkwürdige Geschichte von
einem Menschen, der mit dem Teufel in einen Bund getreten
auf 18 Jahr und wieder durch Christum erlöset worden ist.
Ephrata, 1790. HEH

2080 Dell, Wilhelm. Prüfung der Geister sowohl in den Lehrern
als in den zuhöhoerern. Philadelphia: Carl Cist, 1792. UOP

2081 Zimmermann, Johann Georg, Ritter von. Von der Einsam-
keit. Philadelphia: Steiner & Kämmerer, 1793. AAS

2082 Kunckler, Sebastian. Poesien und Anecdoten zum Zeitver-

treib: Geschichten von einem das Land-Leben Liebenden.
Germantown: Leibert, 1795. JC

2083 Helmuth, Justus. Lieder gesungen in der Zions-Kirche den
27sten November 1796. Philadelphia: Steiner & Kämmerer,
1796. PPLT

2084 Das merkwürdige Leben ... von einem ehrlichen Deutschen.
Lancaster, Pa.: Albrecht, 1798. LCP

2085 Washingtons Ankunft im Elysium: Eine dialogisirte Skizze
nebst Gedichten von einem bewunderer des erblassten Helden.
Lancaster, Pa.: Huetter, 1800. LOC

2086 Helmuth, Justus. Am Feste d. Heil. Dreyeinigkeit 1801 in
der Deutsch-Evangelischen Lutherischen Zions-Kirche. Philadelphia: Helmbold & Geyer, 1801. LTS-Gettysburg

2087 _____. Empfindungen am Heiligen Todes und Auferstehungs-
Tage des Herrn Jesu. Philadelphia: Geyer, 1805. PPLT

2088 Langennecker, Christian. Eine Vertheidigung der Wahrheit
u. s. w. Ephrata, 1806. CSmH, MWA, MiU-C, PHi

2089 Helmuth, Justus. Auf das heilige Pfingstfest. Philadelphia:
Zentler, 1807. PPLT

2090 Jung, Johann Heinrich. Der christliche Menschenfreund in
Erzählungen für Bürger und Bauern. Hägerstown: Gruber,
1807. DLC, CSmH, MWA, MdHi, NN, PPLT

2091 Helmuth, Justus. Auf das Fest der Geburt und Menschwerdung
Jesu Christi, 1808, und auf das Neue Jahr, 1809. Philadelphia Zentler, 1808. PPLT

2092 Kurzer Zeitvertreib, bestehend in einigen Liedern, dienlich
zur Sittenlehre. New Market, Va.: Henkel, 1810. ViU

2093 Helmuth, Justus. Auf den Tod einer liebenswürdigen jungen
Freundin. Philadelphia: Zentler, 1811. PPLT

2094 Das kleine Je länger je lieber. Ist ein kurzer Anhang zur
aufgehenden Lilie. Lancaster: Ehrenfried, 1816. MWA,
PHi

2095 Leben und Thaten des berüchtigten Räubers Johannes Bückler,
genannt Schinderhannes. n. p., 1818. MWA, P, PAtM, PHi

2096 Kaufmann, Peter. Betrachtung über den Menschen. Philadelphia: Zentler, 1823. PPL

2097 Helmuth, Justus. Gesänge bey der Confirmation am Palmsonn-
tage, 1824. Philadelphia: Zentler, 1824. PPLT

2098 Kleine Liedersammlung, oder Auszug aus dem Psalterspiel
der Kinder Zions, zum Dienst inniger heilsuchender Seelen,
insonderheit aber der Brüderschaft der Täufer. Hagerstown:
Gruber & May, 1826. DLC, MdBE, PHi, PPCS

2099 Hertz, Daniel. Poetischer Himmelsweg. Lancaster, Pa.:
Villee, 1828. CtHT-W, DLC, PHi, PPL

2100 Sealsfield, Charles. Das Cajütenbuch. Elberfeld, 1841. UC

2101 Harring, Harro. Werke. New York, 1844-46. GSP, UC

2102 Heinzen, Karl. Mehr als zwanzig Bogen. Darmstadt, 1845.
GSP

2103 Glaeser, A. M. and others. Geheimnisse von Philadelphia:
Tendenznovelle. Philadelphia, 1850. GSP

2104 Archert, Joseph. Die Zauberschuerze oder Weiberlist geht
ueber Teufelslist. New York: Associations-Buchdruckerei,
1851. GSP

2105 Boernstein, Heinrich. Die Geheimnisse von St. Louis: Roman. Cassel, 1851. UC

2106 Henkel, Ambrose. Kurzer Zeitvertreib. Dayton, Ohio, 1851.
GSP

2107 Kirsten, A. Skizzen aus den Vereinigten Staaten von Nordamerika. Leipzig, 1851. UC

2108 Schnauffer, Carl Heinrich. Todten-Kränze. 4 Aufl. Baltimore: Baltimore Herold, 1851. MdHi, MdBP, PPG

2109 Hassaurek, Friedrich. Hierarchie und Aristokratie: Roman.
Cincinnati, 1852. UC

2110 Ludvigh, Samuel. Kossuth, oder der Fall Ungarn: Historisches Drama in fünf Acten. Baltimore: Ludvigh, 1853.
DLC, MdHi, WHi

2111 Klauprecht, Emil. Cincinnati, oder Geheimnisse des Westens.
Cincinnati, 1854. UC

2112 Schnauffer, Carl Heinrich. König Carl I, oder Cromwell und
die englische Revolution: Trauerspiel in 5. Acten. Baltimore: Baltimore Wecker, 1854. CtY, MdHi, WU

2113 Schuenemann-Pott, Friedrich. Lieder und Gedichte zum Ge-
brauch für Versammlung, Schule und Haus freier Gemeinden.
Philadelphia: Selbstverlag, 1855. GSP

2114 Mölling, Peter. Golfblumen in Arabesken gewunden um einige
Säulen im Heiligthum. Cincinnati, 1855. UC

2115   Lilienthal, M.   Freiheit, Frühling und Liebe, Gedichte.   Cin-
        cinnati, 1857.   UC

2116   Roathenheim, W.   Rabbi Bela, Episches Gedicht.   Cincinnati,
        1858.   UC

2117   Straubenmueller, Johann.   Pocahantas, oder: Die Gründung
        von Virginien: Poetische Erzählung.   Baltimore: Schmidt,
        1858.   DLC, IaDaP, MdBG, PPCS, UC

2118   Bruekmann, Arthur.   Ein Siegel auf die Lippen.   Baltimore:
        Kroh, 1858.   GSP

2119   Douai, Adolph.   Fata Morgana.   St. Louis, 1858.   UC

2120   Griesinger, Theodor.   Emigrantengeschichten: Erzählungen
        aus dem amerikanischen Leben.   Tuttlinge, 1858.   GSP

2121   _____.   Lebende Bilder aus Amerika.   Stuttgart, 1858.
        GSP

2122   Schiller-Album zur hunderjährigen Feier der Geburt des Dich-
        ters.   Philadelphia: Schaefer & Konradi, 1859.   GSP

2123   Heinzen, Karl.   Lustspiele.   New York, 1859.   GSP

2124   Wichtige historische Enthüllungen über die Fleisches-Religion
        der Freien Männer.   3. Aufl.   Baltimore: Jünglings-Verein,
        1859.   GSP

2125   Frommel, Emil.   Der Heinerle von Lindelbronn.   Reading,
        Pa.:   Pilger-Buchhandlung, 1859.   GSP

2126   Arming, W.   Ein deutscher Baron.   Preis Roman.   St. Louis,
        1860.   This novel won a prize as the best German-American
        novel for 1860.   UC

2127   Zirndorf, Heinrich.   Gedichte.   Leipzig, 1860.   UC

2128   Stolle, Ferdinand.   1813:   Historischer Roman.   Philadelphia:
        Thomas, 1860.   GSP

2129   Beharrell, T. G.   Die Brüderschaft: Sonderbare Brüder.
        Cincinnati, 1861.   UC

2130   Egenter, F. J.   Amerikanische Spätrosen: Junge Liebe in
        alten Tagen: Gedichte.   Stuttgart, 1861.   GSP

2131   W. D. R.   Juan, der weisse Sklave, oder: Die Tochter des
        Rebell Pflanzers.   Philadelphia: Reichner, 1861.   GSP

2132   Ruppius, Otto.   Genre-Bilder aus dem deutsch-amerikanische
        Leben, Erzählungen.   Berlin, 1861.   UC, GSP

2133 Kempe, Henriette. Laienblüthen. New York, 1862. UC

2134 Solger, Reinhold. Anton in Amerika, Roman. Bromberg, 1862. UC

2135 Strodtmann, Adolf. Lieder und Balladenbuch amerikanischer und englischer Dichter. Hamburg, 1862. UC

2136 Bungeroth, Julius August. Larenblüthen. New York: Ludwig, 1862. GSP

2137 Hering, Constantin. Drei Novelletten. Sonderhausen, 1863. GSP

2138 Fox, Gustav and W. Winckler. Schleswig-Holstein Album. Cincinnati, 1864. GSP

2139 Anneke, Mathilde. Das Geisterhaus in New York: Roman. Jena, 1864. UC

2140 Schramm, Karl. Rückblicke ins Burschenleben: Gedichte. New York: Westermann, 1865. GSP

2141 Vom See, Henricus. Gedichte. Milwaukee, 1866. UC

2142 Pfefferkörner in Poesie und Prosa. Chicago, 1866. UC

2143 Zapf, Philipp. Hiob: Ein dramatisch-didaktisches Bild aus dem Morgenlande mit einem Anhang von Sonetten. Brooklyn: Rose, 1866. GSP

2144 Mueller, Niclas. Neuere Lieder und Gedichte. New York, 1867. UC

2145 Rapp, Wilhelm. Dichterische Versuche. n. p., 1867. UC

2146 Lange, Heinrich. Gedichte. New Albany, 1867. UC

2147 Heinzen, Karl. Gedichte. 3. Aufl. Boston, 1867. UC

2148 Wolff, Albert. Gedichte vermischten Inhalts. St. Paul: Minnesota Staatszeitung, 1867. GSP

2149 Meierhofer, A. Die sieben Schwaben oder die Hasenjagd. New York: Selbstverlag, 1867. GSP

2150 Moelling, Karl. Johanna von Aragon: Ein Trauerspiel in fünf Aufzügen. Philadelphia, 1867. GSP

2151 Stühler, Josef. Freischärlers Wanderschaften. Brooklyn: Leser, 1868. UC

2152 Staerkel, W. Napoleans des Dritten Riesenplan oder: Die

drei grossartigen Leichenbegängnisse der Jahre 1868 bis 1880:
In Prosa und Poesie. Allentown, Pa.: Trexler, 1868. GSP

2153   Zwei Mueller, Geschichten. Allentown, Pa.: Trexler, 1869.
GSP

2154   Winckler, Willibald. Lieder eines Wandervogels. Chicago:
Staats-Zeitung, 1869. GSP

2155   Kuehnbold, Marianne. Harmonien. New York: Schmidt,
1869. GSP

2156   Hieronymus, Jacobus. Dr. Erasmus Puff und Magister Peter
Simpel: Ein Heldengedicht. Hudson City: McGregor &
Goetze, 1869. GSP

2157   Horn, W. O. Die Spelunke. Allentown, Pa.: Trexler, 1869.
GSP

2158   Rattermann, Heinrich A. Die Vehme im Froschreiche: Fast-
nachtsschwank. Cincinnati, 1869. UC

2159   Hess, George. Die Macht der Kunst: Allegorisches Spiel.
New York, 1870. GSP

2160   Scheifele, Johann Georg. Gedichte in schwäbischer Mundart.
New York: Steiger, 1870. GSP

2161   Weiterhausen, Carl. Gedichte. Allegheny City, Pa.: Selbstverlag, 1870. GSP

2162   Giorg, Kara. Poesien des Urwalds. New York: Benzinger
Bros., 1871. GSP, UC

2163   Hinterleitner, G. A. Eine ernsthafte Kriegsgeschichte in
Versen. Pottsville, Pa.: Hender, 1871. GSP

2164   Kruegel, Hugo. Frankreichs Maul und Deutschlands Faust:
Kriegslied für 1870-71. Philadelphia: Thomas, 1871. GSP

2165   Kutschke, August. Sämmtliche Napolium-Lieder, Anecdoten
u. s. w. aus dem letzten deutsch-französischen Kriege. New
York: Gerhard, 1971. GSP

2166   Lange, Heinrich. Gedichte. Philadelphia: Selbstverlag,
1871. GSP

2167   Redwitz, Oscar von. Das Lied vom neuen deutschen Reich.
Philadelphia: Schaefer & Konradi, 1871. GSP

2168   Dilthey, Karl. Novellen und Erzählungen. New York: Steiger, 1872. UC, GSP

2169 Heinzen, Karl. Der teutsche Editoren-Kongress zu Cincinnati oder das gebrochene Herz. Boston: Selbstverlag, 1872. GSP

2170 _____. Ein neues Wintermärchen. Boston: Selbstverlag, 1872. GSP

2171 Jörger, M. J. Waldveilchen, Gedichte. Baltimore, 1872. UC

2172 Lexow, Friedrich. Gedichte. New York, 1872. UC

2173 _____. Novellistisches. New York, 1872. UC

2174 Lexow, Rudolph. Romane und Novellen. New York, 1872.

2174A Lohmann, Ferdinand. Texas-Blüthen. Utica: American Authors Agency, 1872. GSP

2175 Solger, Reinhold. Anton in Amerika: Novelle aus dem deutsch-amerikanischen Leben. New York: Steiger, 1872. GSP

2175A Strodtmann, Adolf. Rohanna, Episches Gedicht. Berlin, 1872. UC

2176 Freimund, Elias. Extrasitzung des Herrn Diabolus mit seinen Gesellen und Lehrlingen, gehalten im 19 Jahrhundert in seiner Hauptstadt Teuflingen. Allentown, Pa.: Selbstverlag, 1873. GSP

2177 Griesinger, Theodor. New York vor zwanzig Jahren: Oder die alte Brauerei: Criminal-Roman. New York: Zickel, 1873. GSP

2178 Klingner, Heinrich. Die Jonathanier Gallerie interessanter Charakterbilder aus der Neuen Welt. Hartford, Conn.: Selbstverlag, 1873. GSP

2179 Thomann, Rudolf. Leben und Thaten von Hannis Schaute, alias John Shoddy oder Von Buxtehude nach San Francisco: Ein Gedicht. San Francisco: California Democrat, 1873. GSP

2180 Asmus, Georg. Amerikanisches Skizzebüchelche: Eine Epistel in Versen. 2 Aufl. New York: Willmer & Rogers, 1874. GSP

2181 Frick, Louis. Die Weltgeschichte in 100 Versen. Baltimore: Juenger & Mueller, 1874. GSP

2182 Harbaugh, Heinrich. Harbaughs Harfe. Philadelphia, 1874. UC

2183   Querner, Emil.   Wilde Blumen: Gedichte.   2 Aufl.   Phila-
       delphia, 1874.   GSP

2184   Arnemann, Alfred.   Fierabend, Plattdeutsche Gedichte und
       Erzählungen.   Davenport, 1875.   UC

2185   Hering, Margarethe.   Gedichte.   Leipzig: Palz, 1875.   GSP

2186   Hundt, Ferdinand.   Elegie an der Bahre Sr. Excellenz Ga-
       briel Garzie Moreno's. Präsident der Republik Ecuador.
       Cincinnati: Pustet, 1875.   GSP

2187   Krez, Konrad.   Aus Wiskonsin, Gedichte.   New York, 1875.
       UC

2188   Wollenweber, L. A.   Aus Berk County's schwerer Zeit.
       Reading, Pa.: Rosenthal, 1875.   GSP

2189   Bruck, Julius.   Ahasver, alter Sage neue Dichtung.   New
       York: Willmer & Rogers, 1876.   GSP, UC

2190   Von Ende, Herman.   Mississippi und Rhein, Gedichte.   Mil-
       waukee, 1876.   UC

2191   Eyser, J.   Farrago, Gedichte.   St. Louis, 1876.   UC

2192   Hopp, E. O.   Transatlantisches Skizzenbuch.   Berlin: Janke
       1876.   GSP

2193   Knortz, Karl.   Amerikanische Skizzen.   Halle, 1876.   UC

2194   Strobel, Wilhelm.   Heimatklänge.   St. Louis: Wiebusch,
       1876.   GSP

2195   Berger, Heinrich.   Aus späten Tagen, Geschichtliche Dichtur
       New York, 1877.   UC

2196   Hassaurek, Friedrich.   Gedichte.   Cincinnati: Burgheim,
       1877.   GSP

2197   Jocundas, Frater (Wilhelm Mueller).   Schabiade, Leben und
       Thaten des Fritz Schaebig, Eine erbauliche Historie in lusti-
       gen Reimen.   Milwaukee: Doerflinger, 1877.   GSP

2198   Kleeberg, Minna.   Gedichte.   2 Aufl.   Louisville: Knoefel,
       1877.   GSP, UC

2199   Knortz, Karl.   Humoristische Gedichte.   Baltimore: Ross-
       mässler & Morf, 1877.   DLC

2200   Maerklin, Edmund.   Familien-Bilder.   Milwaukee: Doerflin
       er, 1877.   GSP, ·UC

2201 Zur Windmuehlen, Friedrich. Heimath und Fremde. Balti-
      more: Kroh, 1877. DLC

2202 Ruhland, H. Aehrenlese, Gedichte. Milwaukee, 1878. UC

2203 Luebkert, Louis. Durch das Weltall, Ein Märchen von Heut-
      zutage. Baltimore: Mühsam, 1878. DLC

2204 Muenter, Carl. Nu suend wi in Amerika, En plattdeutsch
      Riemels. Cincinnati: Bloch, 1878. GSP, UC

2205 Schmidt, Paul. Gedichte. Cincinnati: Mecklenborg & Rosen-
      thal, 1878. GSP, UC

2206 Soubron, Otto. Souvenir, Gedichte. Milwaukee, 1878. UC

2207 Wahlde, Hermann von. Gedichte. Louisville: Deuser, 1878.
      GSP

2208 Butz, Caspar. Gedichte eines Deutsch-Amerikaners. New
      York: Steiger, 1879. GSP, UC

2209 Giorg, Kara. Die Heldin des Amazon. Cincinnati: Mecklen-
      borg & Rosenthal, 1879. GSP, UC

2210 Loebel, Paul. Gedichte. Chicago, 1879. UC

2211 Puchner, Rudolf. Klänge aus dem Westen. Milwaukee:
      Doerflinger, 1879. GSP

2212 Schnauffer, Carl Heinrich. Lieder und Gedichte aus dem
      Nachlass. Baltimore: Baltimore Wecker, 1879. CoDB, DLC,
      IU, MdHi, NN, WU, GSP, UC

2213 Schumacher, Herman. Petrus Martyr, der Geschichtsschrei-
      ber des Weltmeeres. New York, 1879. UC

2214 Sutro-Schuecking, K. Umsonst, Novelle. Baltimore: Ross-
      mässler & Morf, 1879. DLC

2215 Zuendt, Ernst Anton. Dramatische und lyrische Dichtungen.
      St. Louis: Roeslein, 1879. GSP, UC

2216 Berghold, Alexander. Prairie-Rosen, Gedichte und Prosa.
      St. Paul: Volkszeitung, 1880. GSP

2217 Bloomfield, H. Heins Gedichte. Marburg, 1880. UC

2218 Bruck, Julius. Bunte Blüthen, Scherz und Ernst in Versen.
      2. Aufl. New York: Zickel, 1880. GSP, UC

2219 Keilmann, Wilhelm. Herzensblüthen. Evansville, 1880. UC

2220   Doerflinger, Carl.   Onkel Karl.   Milwaukee: Doerflinger,
       1881.   UC

2221   Lafrentz, Ferdinand.   Nordische Klänge.   Chicago, 1881.   UC

2222   Lampe, F.   Gedichte.   Altoona, Pa.:   Lamade & Gamber,
       1881.   GSP

2223   Moras, Ferdinand.   Gedichte und Randzeichnungen.   Philadel-
       phia, 1882.   GSP, UC

2224   Schuricht, H.   Mythus, Sagen und Geschichten Alt-Amerikas.
       Milwaukee, 1882.   UC

2225   Castelhun, Friedrich.   Gedichte.   Milwaukee, 1883.   UC, UK

2226   Giorg, Kara.   Charlotte, eine Episode aus der Colonial-
       Geschichte Louisiana's.   Cincinnati: Mecklenborg, 1883.
       GSP, UC

2227   Schlag, Hugo.   Thomas Münzer, Trauerspiel.   New York,
       1883.   UC

2228   Dorsch, Eduard.   Aus der Alten und Neuen Welt, Gedichte.
       New York: International News Co., 1884.   GSP, UC

2229   Grzybowski, Paul.   Künstlerliebe, Erzählungen.   Cincinnati,
       1884.   UC

2230   Knortz, Karl.   Neue Gedichte.   Glarus: Vogel, 1884.   GSP

2231   _____.   Neue Epigramme.   Zürich, 1884.   UC

2232   Rattermann, Heinrich A.   Nord-amerikanische Vögel in Lie-
       dern.   Cincinnati: Selbstverlag, 1884.   GSP

2233   Rittig, Johann.   Federzeichnungen aus dem deutsch-ameri-
       kanischen Stadtleben.   New York: Steiger, 1884.   GSP, UC

2234   Steinlein, A.   Bunte Blüthen, Gedichte.   La Crosse, Wiscons
       1884.   UC

2235   Asmus, Georg.   Amerikanisches Skizzebuechelche.   Cologne,
       1885.   UC

2236   Haering, T.   Gedichte.   Cincinnati, 1885.   UC

2237   Maerklin, Edmund.   Im Strome der Zeit, Gedichte.   Milwau
       kee: Selbstverlage, 1885.   GSP, UC

2238   Michaelson, F.   Gedichte.   Milwaukee, 1885.   UC

2239   Nagler, F.   Immanuel oder Bilder aus der Höhe.   Cincinna
       1885.   UC

2240   Rösch, Friedrich.   Biedermanniade, Gedichte.   Chicago,
        1885.   UC

2241   Seeger, Eugen.   Der Leiermann.   Chicago, 1885.   UC

2242   Sigel, Albert.   Gedichte.   St. Louis, 1885.   UC

2243   Werkmeister, Maria.   Vergebnis, Roman.   Chicago: Gindele,
        1885.   GSP

2244   Bruck, Julius.   Von Hüben und Drüben, Scherz und Ernst in
        Versen.   3. Aufl.   Kepzig: Reissnen, 1886.   GSP

2245   Carus, Paul.   Ein Leben in Liedern, Gedichte eines Heimath-
        losen.   Milwaukee, 1886.   UC

2246   Butz, Caspar.   Grossvaterlieder.   Chicago, 1887.   UC

2247   Puchner, Rudolf.   Aglaja.   Milwaukee, 1887.   UC

2248   Sutro, Emil.   Gedichte.   n. p. , 1887.   GSP

2249   Wahlde, Hermann von.   Natur und Heimath.   Cincinnati, 1887.
        UC

2250   Deitz, Johann.   Herbstblätter, Gedichte.   Chicago, 1888.   UC

2251   Heintz, Jacob.   Aus Musestunden, Gedichte und Lieder.   New
        York: Lauter, 1888.   GSP, UC

2252   Hering, Alma.   Festgedichte zu lebenden Bildern am 50
        jährigen Stiftungsfeste des Heringschen Gesangvereins.   n. p. ,
        1888.   GSP

2253   Müller, Wilhelm.   Am Wege gepflückt.   Glarus, 1888.   UC

2254   Richard, Ernst.   Alte Geschichten aus dem Mohawkthal.   New
        York: Herkemer, 1888.   GSP, UC

2255   Bielfeld, Heinrich.   Gedichte.   Milwaukee: Freidenker Pub-
        lishing Co. , 1889.   GSP, UC

2256   Hachtmann, Adolph.   Lieder eines Deutsch-Amerikaners, in
        hoch- und plattdeutsch.   New York, 1889.   UC

2257   Neuer, Minna.   Am Wege gepflückt, Gedichte.   Washington,
        D. C. :   Waldecker, 1889.   GSP

2258   Pacquet, L.   Nach Westen, Ein Bild aus dem Wanderleben
        des deutsch-amerikanischen Farmers, und kleinere Gedichte.
        Milwaukee: Caspar, 1889.   GSP, UC

2259   Straubenmueller, Johann.   Herbstrosen, Gesammelte Gedichte.
        New York: Steiger, 1889.   GSP

2260   Stürenburg, C.   Klein-Deutschland, Skizzen.   3. Aufl.   New
York, 1889.   UC

2261   Friedlaender, Victor.   Von Hüben und Drüben, Gedichte.
New York, 1890.   UC

2262   Fritzsche, F.   Blutrosen, Gedichte.   Baltimore, 1890.   UC

2263   Hammer, Bonaventura.   Herz Jesu Grüsse, Gedichte.   Cincinnati, 1890.   UC

2264   Kirchhoff, Theodor.   Eine Reise nach Hawaii.   Altona, 1890.
UC

2265   Thormählen, Anton.   Lenzblüthen und Herbstblätter, Gedichte.
Milwaukee, 1890.   UC

2266   Berghold, Alexander.   Land und Leute, Skizzen.   St. Paul:
Der Wanderer, 1891.   UC

2267   Gerok, Karl.   Blumen und Sterne.   Philadelphia: Kohler,
1891.   GSP

2268   Herrig, Hans.   Martin Luther.   Ein kirchliches Festspiel.
Philadelphia: Kohler, 1891.   GSP

2269   Weil-Zehnder, Louise.   Geläuterte Freuden und Leiden eines
Schwabenmädchens in Amerika.   Stuttgart, 1891.   UC

2270   Eberhard, J.   Abendglocken.   St. Louis, 1892.   UC

2271   Creutz, Maria.   Volksgedichte.   Chicago, 1892.   UC

2272   Grill, Friedrich.   Amerika, Gedichte.   Philadelphia: Kohler,
1892.   GSP, UC

2273   Heerbrandt, Gustav.   Gedichte in schwäbischer Mundart.   New
York: Selbstverlag, 1892.   GSP

2274   Ilgen, Pedro.   Welt- und Gottesreichs-Klänge, Gedichte.
Highlands, Illinois, 1892.   UC

2275   Steinlein, A.   Bunte Blüthen, Gedichte.   Winona, Minnesota,
1892.   UC

2276   Gieseler, Ernst.   Gedichte.   New York: Lauter, 1893.   GSP,
UC

2277   Neuer, Minna.   Gedichte.   New York, 1893.   UC

2278   Rübesamen, Friedrich.   Grenzesleben, Skizzen.   Chicago,
1894.   UC

2279   Bauer, Karl. Gedichte. Chicago, 1894. UC

2280   Stechhan, Otto. Lieben und Leben, Gedichte. Chicago: Kenkel, 1894. GSP, UC

2281   Sutro-Schücking, K. Doctor Zernowitz, Villa Montrose. Chicago, 1894. UC

2282   Wireman, Henry. Rimed Verses, English and German Poems. Philadelphia: Lane & Scott, 1894. GSP

2283   Woerner, J. G. and Charles Gildehaus. Die Rebellin, Amerikanisches Schauspiel in fünf Aufzügen. St. Louis, 1894. GSP

2284   Wolff, Albert. Poesie und Prosa aus dem literarischen Nachlass von Albert Wolff. St. Paul: Volkszeitung, 1894. MHS

2285   Zuendt, Ernst Anton. Ebbe und Fluth, Gesammelte lyrische Dichtungen und Jugurtha. Milwaukee: Freidenker Publishing Co., 1894. GSP, UC

2286   Binder, H. Liederklänge aus vier Jahrzehnten, Gedichte. New York, 1895. UC

2287   Boettcher, Dorothea. Deutsche Klänge in Amerika, Gedichte. Chicago: Koelling & Klappenbach, 1895.

2288   Moeller, Hugo. Aus Deutsch-Amerika, Novellen und Erzählungen. Galveston, Texas: Selbstverlag, 1895. GSP

2289   Haacke, Heinrich. Gedichte. Cincinnati, 1896. UC

2290   Haun, Ewald. Wie Kandidat Daniel Amerika liebgewann. Basil, 1896. UC

2291   Keck, Karl. Wie die Lerche singt, Gedichte. Cincinnati, 1896. UC

2292   Runck, C. L. Primrosen, Saamlung von Dornrosen und dramatischen Scenen. Newport, 1896. UC

2293   Semich, Franz. Irrlichter: Schauspiel. Milwaukee, 1896. UC

2294   Voigt, Anna. Vergissmeinnicht, Gedichte. Chicago, 1896. UC

2295   Glauch, Hermann. Gedichte. Oakland, California, 1897. GSP, UC

2296   Gramm, William. Phantasie und Leben, Erzählungen. New York, 1897. UC

2297 Krüger, F. Was ich ersonnen, was ich erlebt, Gedichte.
New York, 1897. UC

2298 Partz, August. Der Weltgeist und die Pfaffen, erbauliche
Dichtungen nebst ergänzenden Scholien. Philadelphia: Levy-
type Co., 1897. GSP, UC

2299 Theisz, J. W. Gepflückt am Wege, Lieder und Gedichte.
St. Louis, 1897. UC

2300 Keilmann, Wilhelm. Palla Toa, Epos. Heiligenstadt, 1898.
UC

2301 Kenkel, F. Der Schädel der Secundus Arbiter, Novelle.
Chicago, 1898. UC

2302 Kirchhoff, Theodor. Hermann, ein Auswandererleben, Ep.-
lyr. Dichtung. Leipzig, 1898. UC

2304 Saur, Rudolph. Gedichte. Washington, D. C.: Selbstverlag,
1898. GSP

2305 Vogel, Hedwig. Eva-Lieder. Berlin: Issleib, 1898. GSP

2306 Ernst, Friedrich. Peter Muehlenberg, oder Bibel und Schwert
Drama. New York, 1899. UC

2307 Haimbach, Philipp. Poetische Blätter. Philadelphia: Selbstverlag, 1899. GSP, UC

2308 Thiersch, Curt. Briefe des Mr. Schorsch Dobbeljuh Hutzel-
berger an die Mississippi Blätter, O tempora o moves,
Gedichte. St. Louis, 1899. UC

2309 Gugler, Julius. Der Stern des Westens, Episches Gedicht.
Milwaukee, 1900. UC

2310 Nies, Konrad. Deutsche Gaben, Ein Festspiel zum Deutschen
Tag. St. Louis: Witter, 1900. GSP

2311 _____. Funken, Gedichte. New York: Verlag der Deutsc
Amerikanischen Dichtung, 1900. GSP, UC

2312 _____. Rosen im Schnee: Ein deutsch-amerikanisches
Weihnachtsspiel in vier Bildern. St. Louis: Witter, 1900.
GSP, UC

2313 Reitzel, Robert. Mein Buch, Einem Vielgeliebten zum Ge-
dächtnis. Detroit, 1900. UC

2314 Rueckheim, Mathilde. Von seiner Fülle, Erbauungsverse.
Chicago, 1901. UC

2315   Steiner, Hans.   Blüten und Ranken, Gedichte.   Dresden, 1902.
       UC

2316   Baer, B. A.   Herzens-Angelegenheiten, amerikanische Hu-
       moresken.   Leipzig: Seemann, 1903.   GSP

2317   Giorg, Kara.   Skanderberg.   Cincinnati, 1903.   UC, GSP

2318   Pfaefflin, Hermann.   Harano, Eine Volksage aus der Irokesen-
       Zeit.   Rochester, New York: Abendpost, 1903.   GSP, UC

2319   Rothensteiner, John.   Hoffnung und Erinnerung, Lieder aus
       Amerika.   St. Louis, 1903.   UC

2320   Zschiesche, Eduard.   Neue Blätter zu "Tausend und eine
       Nacht, Zukunftsträume.   n. p. :   Roesch, 1903.   GSP

2321   Baumgarten, Julius.   Messias, Schauspiel.   Wissen nicht
       Glauben.   Philosophische Betrachtung.   New York, 1904.   UC

2322   Henrici, Ernst.   Dramatische Werke.   Baltimore: Schnei-
       dereith, 1904-05.   DLC, MHS, NN, UC

2323   Kloss, Waldemar.   Lyra Germanica-Latina.   St. Louis, 1904.
       UC

2324   Rattermann, Heinrich A.   Nordamerikanische Vögel in Liedern.
       Cincinnati, 1904.   UC

2325   Viereck, Georg Sylvester.   Gedichte.   New York: New York
       Progressive Printing Co., 1904.   GSP, UC

2326   Benignus, Wilhelm.   Weltstromlieder.   Baltimore: Schnei-
       dereith, 1905.   PPCS

2327   Bertsch, Hugo.   Die Geschwister.   Stuttgart, 1905.   UC

2328   Ilgen, Pedro.   Tiefgluth.   St. Louis, 1906.   UC

2329   Bertsch, Hugo.   Bilderbogen aus meinem Leben.   Stuttgart,
       1906.   UC

2330   Dreisel, Hermann.   Gesammelte Schriften.   Milwaukee, 1905.
       UC

2331   Heischmann, John.   Beim Kaiser zu Gast: Zur Erinnerung
       an die Einweihung des Domes in Berlin am 27. Febr. 1905.
       New York, 1905.   GSP

2332   Hoffman, Emile.   Veilchen und rothe Nelken, Gedichte.   In-
       dianapolis, 1905.   UC

2333   Mueller. A.   Muellerlieder: Lieder und Gedichte von Mueller von Davenport. Davenport, Iowa: Selbstverlag, 1905. GSP, UC

2334 Nies, Konrad. Die herrlichen Drei. Festspiel. Indianapolis: Nordamerikanischer Turnerbund, 1905. GSP

2335 Kohlsaat, T. Herzensklänge, Gedichte. Cincinnati, 1906. UC

2336 Lochemes, M. Gedichte eines Deutschamerikaners. Milwaukee, 1906. UC

2337 Michel, Friedrich. Asraklänge und andere Gedichte. New York: Schlesier & Schweikardt, 1906. GSP, UC

2338 Wienand, Paul. Oelzweige, Geistliche Lieder und Gedichte. Cleveland: Central Publishing House, 1906. GSP, UC

2339 Hofmann, Jule. Gedichte. Marburg: Ebel, 1907. GSP

2340 Zagel, Hermann. Reisebilder aus den Vereinigten Staaten. St. Louis: Louis Lange, 1907. GSP

2341 Andriessen, Hugo. Poetische Auslese. Pittsburgh, 1908. UC

2342 Hubel, Henni. Belauscht, Gedichte und Sprüche. New York, 1908. UC

2343 Ilgen, Pedro. Sulamith. St. Louis, 1908. GSP

2344 Knortz, Karl. Das Buch des Lebens: Sprüche der Weisheit für Freie und Unfreie. Leipzig: Klinkhard & Biermann, 1908. DLC

2345 Rauser, Friedrich. Siegfried Bergmann: Ein dramatisches Volkstück. Philadelphia: Schaefer & Koradi, 1908. GSP

2346 Schlapp, George. Erzählende Dichtungen. Milwaukee: Caspar, 1908. GSP, UC

2347 Toeplitz, Martha. Kleine Geschichten für grosse Leute. Berlin, 1908. GSP

2348 Wahlde, Hermann von. Neue Gedichte. Cincinnati, 1908. UC

2349 Wienand, Paul. Musenblüten, Gedichte. Washington, D.C., 1908. GSP

2350 Drescher, Martin. Gedichte. Chicago, 1909. UC

2351 Etzelmueller, Herman. Die Mutter, ihr Glauben, Hoffen,

Lieben in Gedichten.   Maperville, Illinois, 1909.   UC

2352   Hempel, Max.   Gedichte.   St. Louis: Co-Operative Printing, 1909.   GSP, UC

2353   Zagel, Hermann.   Jack Roostand.   St. Louis: Lange, 1909-12.   GSP

2354   Kirchstein, Anna.   Herzenstöne, Gedichte.   Chicago, 1910.   UC

2355   Laubengeiger, W.   Die Mutter in deutschem Liede.   Berlin/Dubuque, Iowa, 1910.   UC

2356   Raible, Marie.   Deutsch-Amerika.   St. Louis: Meyer, 1910.   GSP

2357   Sattler, Otto.   Stille und Sturm, Gedichte.   New York, 1910.   UC

2358   Wienand, Paul.   Orientalische Reisebilder.   Utica, New York: American Authors Agency, 1910.   GSP

2359   Bode, August.   Aus meiner Reisemappe.   Cincinnati, 1911.   UC

2360   Braun, Oscar.   Wir Deutsch-Amerikaner, Gedichte.   Cincinnati, 1911.   UC

2361   Hartung, Carl.   Fliegende Gedanken, Gedichte.   Chicago, 1911.   UC

2362   Rosen, Erwin.   Der deutsche Lausbub in Amerika.   Stuttgart, 1911.   GSP

2363   Augustin, A.   Ernste und heitere Bilder aus einem deutsch-amerikanischen Pastorenleben.   Breklum: Jensen, 1912.   GSP

2364   Brachvogel, Udo.   Gedichte.   Leipzig, 1912.   UC

2365   Benignus, Wilhelm.   Lieder eines Pilgers.   New York: Schmetterling, 1912.   GSP

2366   Baltzer, Friedrich.   Gedichte.   Pittsburgh, 1913.   UC

2367   Lange, August.   Walpurgisnacht, Eine nordische Fantasie.   Philadelphia: Selbstverlag, 1913.   GSP

2368   Lienhard, Heinrich.   Blumen am Wege, Gedichte.   Milwaukee, 1913.   UC

2369   Reitzel, Robert.   Des armen Teufel: Gesammelte Schriften.   Detroit: Reitzel-Klub, 1913.   GSP

152   German-Americana

2370   Keidel, Heinrich.   Die Flucht, dramatisches Spiel.   Columbus,
       1914. UC

2371   Rattermann, Heinrich A.   Gesammelte ausgewählte Werke.
       Cincinnati: Selbstverlag, 1914. UC, UM

2372   Rosenberg, Wilhelm.   Die Geisterschlacht.   Cincinnati, 1914-
       15. UC

2373   Brodt, Herbert.   Ist auch ein Unglück in der Stadt, das der
       Herr nicht tut? Predigt. Erie, Pa., 1915. UC

2374   Baltzer, Friedrich.   Ergo Terbalz, Erzählung.   Pittsburgh,
       1915. UC

2375   Hoepli, J.   Erlebtes und Erstrebtes, Tagebuchblätter.   Frauen
       feld, 1915. UC

2376   Keidel, Heinrich.   Die grossen Illusionen des amerikanischen
       Volkes. Berlin, 1915. UC

2377   Klaeber, Friedrich.   Deutsche Kriegsgedichte.   St. Paul,
       1915. GSP, UC

2378   Rehbach, Rudolf.   Meine Höllenfahrt und andere Gedichte.
       New York: Stechert, 1915. GSP

2379   Sattler, Otto.   Krieg: Gedichte der Zeit.   New York: Ro-
       chow, 1915. GSP

2380   Voges, G.   Deutscher Humor am Mississippi.   St. Louis,
       1915. UC

2381   Germanistic Society of Minnesota.   Zur Kriegszeit.   Min-
       neapolis/St. Paul, 1915. UC

2382   Gompertz, Hans and Max Schmetterling.   Gedichte aus gros-
       ser Zeit. New York, 1916. GSP, UC

2383   Jürgensen, Mathilde.   Ein schlichtes Saitenspiel.   New York,
       1916. UC

2384   Rosenberg, Wilhelm.   Liebesglück und Liebesleid.   Cleveland
       1916. UC

2385   Vogel, Rev.   Das Pfarrhaus auf der Prairie.   Milwaukee:
       Northwestern Publishing House, 1916. GSP

2386   Rennert, Hans.   Gedichte und Übersetzungen.   Philadelphia,
       1917. GSP

2387   Gillhoff, Johannes.   Juernjakob Swehn, der Amerikafahrer.
       Berlin, 1918. GSP

Language and Literature   153

2388   Segall, Julius.   Gedichte.   Milwaukee, 1920.   UC

2389   Zimpel, Theodor.   Ut'n Harten. Hoch- und plattdeutsche Ge-
       dichte.   New York: Selbstverlag, 1920.   GSP, UC

2390   Heeren, Wilhelm.   Blätter und Blüthen, Gedichte.   Pittsburgh,
       1921.   UC

2391   Juergensen, Mathilde.   Heimatliebe, Gedichte.   3 Aufl.   New
       York, 1921.   GSP

2392   Nies, Konrad.   Welt und Wildnis, Gedichte und Lieder aus
       vier Erdteilen.   Leipzig: Haertel, 1921.   GSP, UC

2393   Doernenburg, Emil.   De Profundis, Gedichte.   Braunschweig:
       Goeritz, 1922.   GSP, UC

2394   Lafrentz, F. W.   Nordische Klänge, plattdeutsche Gedichte.
       Hamburg: Hermes, 1922.   GSP

2395   Siff, Heinrich.   Aus der Wüste, Gedichte.   2. Aufl.   New
       York: Stuyvesant, 1922.   GSP

2396   Bertsch, Hugo.   Der Tramp, Roman.   Dresden, 1923.   UC

2397   Zegel, H. H.   Aus Frühlingstagen, Geschichte.   Peioria, 1923.
       UC

2398   Scheurmann, Erich.   Als Landstreicher durch Amerika.   Kon-
       stanz, 1923.   UC

2399   Roda, Roda.   Ein Frühling in Amerika.   Munich, 1924.   UC

2400   Michel, Friedrich.   Deutsche und englische Gedichte.   New
       York: Verlag des Deutschen geselligwissenschaftlichen Ver-
       eins, 1924.   GSP

2401   Willram, B. J.   Rothensteiner: Ausgewählte Dichtungen.
       Innsbruck, 1924.   UC

2402   Benignus, Wilhelm.   Melodien vom Rhein, Neckar, Hudson
       und Niagara.   n. p., 1924.   UC

2403   Wicke, Victor.   Gedichte.   Leipzig: Hesse & Becker, 1924.
       GSP

2404   Benignus, Wilhelm.   Epik und Lyrik.   n. p., 1926.   UC

2405   Kollbrunner, Oskar.   Die Schenke des Mister Bucalo.   Frauen-
       feld: Huber, 1927.

2405A Doernenburg, Emil.   Lieder eines Einsamen.   Leipzig, 1928.
       UC

2406   Edward, Georg. Passatwind. Munich: Drei-Masken-Verlag,
       1928. DLC, MHS, NN, ICU, OCI

2407   Herzberger, F. Onkel David, Eine Erzählung. 2. Aufl.
       St. Louis: Lange, 1928. GSP

2408   Nix, Robert. Poems. Spokane: Elsie M. Nix, 1930.

2409   Alfredo, Waldemar. Wie ich die Welt sah. Philadelphia:
       Reports Publishing Co., 1931. GSP

2410   Schmidt, Felix. Entwurzelt: Roman aus dem deutschameri-
       kanischen Leben der Nachkriegszeit. Cleveland: Wächter und
       Anzeiger, 1932. GSP

2411   Hammerstein-Illing, Caecilie. Weisse Flieder, Novellen.
       Chicago: Gutenberg, 1933. GSP

2412   Voigt, Rudolf. 12 Gedichte. Chicago, 1934. GSP

2413   Racine, Eva. Ausgewählte Gedichte. Philadelphia: Charles
       J. Racine, 1935. GSP

2414   Leineweber, C. H. Liebe und Tod. Milwaukee: Gutenberg,
       1937. GSP

2415   Mirbach, Henry. Gedichte. Syracuse, New York: Syracuse
       Union Deutsche Zeitung für Central New York, 1939. GSP

2416   Hirsch, Helmut. Amerika: Du Morgenröte, Verse eines
       Flüchtlings: 1939-42. New York: Willard, 1939-42. DLC,
       NN, NNC, ICU, MHS, ICN, PPCS

2417   Jockers, Ernst. Wandlungen. New York: Westermann, 1940.
       GSP, UC

2418   Marx, Karl Theodor. Der Feigling. New York: Stuyvesant,
       1942. DLC, NN, MKUK, GSP

2419   Sahl, Hans. Die hellen Nächte, Gedichte aus Frankreich.
       New York: Spiral Pr., 1942. DLC

2420   Scheibe, Fred Karl. Dem Licht entgegen. Philadelphia:
       Graf, 1942. Printed by the last German-American printer in
       Philadelphia. DLC

2421   _____. Wiskonsin Erlebnis. New York, 1942. DLC

2422   Siefkes, Siegfried. Erinnerungen und Gedanken von Pastor
       S. H. Siefkes. Columbus: Lutheran Book Concern, 1942.
       GSP

2423   Tippmann, H. K. Amerikanische Balladen und andere

Gedichte. New York: Arrowhead Pr., 1942. GSP

2424 Yoder, Joseph. Amische Lieder. Huntington, Pa.: Yoder
Publishing Co., 1942.

2425 Friedrich, Gerhard. When Quakers Meet and Other Poems.
Guilford College, North Carolina: Guilford College, 1943.
Collection of German poems.

2426 Marx, Karl Theodor. Nachdenkliches. New York: Baker &
Brooks, 1943.

2427 Wolff, Hans. Lied des Lebens, Gedichte. New York: Willard, 1945. GSP

2428 Farau, Alfred. Wo ist die Jugend, die ich rufe? New York:
Willard, 1946. DLC, InU, MHS

2429 Leineweber, Clemens. Wünsche und Weisen. Washington,
D. C., 1946.

2430 Waldinger, Ernst. Die kühlen Bauernstuben. New York:
Aurora, 1946. UM

2431 Bierwirth, Heinrich. Aus dem Leben eines Deutsch-Amerikaners. Yarmouth, Mass., 1947. DLC, KMK, PPULC,
MeB, OCU, TNJ, CU, MHS, ICU, TxU

2432 Stern Luitpold, Josef. Das Josef-Luitpold-Buch: Lyrik und
Prosa aus vier Jahrzehnten. Wien: Wiener Volksbuchhand-
lung, 1948. DLC

2433 Ascher, Franzi. Bilderbuch aus der Fremde. Wien: Wiener
Verlag, 1948. OCI

2434 Runes, Dagobert. Jordan Lieder: Frühe Gedichte. New
York: Philosophical Library, 1958. DLC, UK

2435 Richter, Fritz. Wenn du drüben bist: Geschichte eines
Schlesiers in Amerika. Stuttgart: Behrendt Verlag, 1949.

2436 Klatt, Margarete. Brücke zur Heimat. Arolsen: Weizacker,
1950.

2437 Cohn, Ruth. Inmitten aller Sterne. 2 Aufl. New York:
Peter Thomas Fisher, 1952. DLC, MiU, MHS, CoU, OU,
CLSU, IU, NIC, NcU, CST, CtY

2438 Waldinger, Ernst. Glück und Geduld. New York: Ungar,
1952. DLC, PST, NcD, NN, UM

2439 Senn, Alfred. Aus meinem Leben. Bala-Cynwyd, Pa., 1952.

2440   Birmelin, John. The Poems of John Birmelin. (Yearbook of
        the Pennsylvania German Folklore Society, 16). Allentown:
        Schlechter, 1953.

2441   Muller, Olga. German Poems. West Nyack, New York:
        Gaus, 1953.

2442   Voigt, Rudolf. Das sehnsüchtige Herz: Gedichte eines
        Deutschen in Amerika. Osterode: Giebel & Ohlenschläger,
        1953.

2443   Zucker, A. E. Amerika und Deutschland. New York: Ap-
        pleton-Century-Crofts, 1953.

2444   Kaufmann, Eduard. O höre: Gedanken, die immer wieder
        auferstehen. New York: Rosenberg, 1953. OCH

2445   Bergammer, Friedrich. Von Mensch zu Mensch. München:
        Desch, 1955. IEN, NN, PU, NCD

2446   Sauder, Ben. Der Nachbar an de Schtroas. Norristown, Pa.:
        Pennsylvania German Society, 1955.

2447   Wood, Ralph Charles. Klumpendal, Ernstes und Heiteres
        aus dem Leben einer deutschen Gemeinde in den USA. Wolf-
        shagen-Scharbeutz: Franz Westphal Verlag, 1955. Con-
        sidered "the best" German-American novel of the twentieth
        century, according to Heinz Kloss.

2448   Paulus, Helmut. Geliebte Heimat: Vier Erzählungen. Stutt-
        gart: Verlag Silberburg, 1956. DLC

2449   Van der Berg, Rose. Gedichte: Aus dem Leben für das
        Leben. Baltimore: Selbstverlag, 1956. About the German-
        Americans in Baltimore.

2450   Wood, Ralph Charles. Es Evangelium vum Mattheus aus der
        griechischen Schprooch ins Pennsilvendeitsch iwwersetzt.
        Stuttgart: Steinkopf, 1956. Translation of the Gospel Matthew
        into the Pennsylvania German dialect by a fifth- generation
        Pennsylvania German.

2451   Clausen, Emma. Im Vorübergehen, Gedichte. Los Angeles:
        Selbstverlag, 1956.

2452   Marx, Karl Theodor. Deutschamerikanische Aphorismen.
        München: Gabeva, 1957. MKUK, NN, GSP

2453   Stein, Herbert. New York. (Serie Mais Auslandstaschen-
        bücher, 8). München: Volk und Heimat, 1957.

2454   Clausen, Emma. Kleinigkeiten, Gedanken in Vers und Spruch.
        Los Angeles: Commonwealth Pr., 1958.

2455 Waldinger, Ernst. Zwischen Hudson und Donau: Gedichte. Wien: Bergland, 1958.

2456 Wolff, Hans. Auch der Herbst kommt wieder. New York: Gaus, 1958.

2457 Graf, Oskar Maria. Die Flucht ins Mittelmässige. Frankfurt: Nest, 1959. About the New York Germans in the 1950's.

2458 Saenger, Eduard. Die fremden Jahre: Gedichte aus der Emigration. Heidelberg, 1959.

2459 Birmelin, John. E bissel vun dem en e bissel vun sellum: Mundartverse aus Pennsylvanien. Kaiserslautern: Heimatstelle Pfalz, 1960.

2460 Kollisch, Margarete. Wege und Einkehr. Wien: Bergland, 1960. DLC

2461 Schmidt-Barrien, Heinrich. De Spaassmaker. Hamburg: Fehrs-Gilde, 1960. About the New York Germans.

2462 Gong, Alfred. Manifest Alpha: Gedichte. Wien: Bergland, 1961. NN, Cty, MHS, DLC

2463 Grunewald, Dora. Gedichte. Milwaukee, 1967. MilPL

2464 Frey, Egon. Werktagslied. Wien: Europäischer Verlag, 1968.

2465 Funk, Ralph. The Dialect Poems. (Publications, Pennsylvania German Society, 2.) Allentown, Pa., 1968.

2466 Scheibe, Anna Katarina. Die verborgene Welt: Geschichten, Gedanken und Gedichte einer deutschamerikanischen Hausfrau. Wien: Europäischer Verlag, 1968. DLC

2467 Wood, Ralph Charles. The Four Gospels Translated into the Pennsylvania German Dialect. (Publications, Pennsylvania German Society, 1.) Allentown, Pa., 1968.

2468 Gong, Alfred. Happening in der Park Avenue: New Yorker Geschichten. München: Piper, 1969.

2469 Grossberg, Mimi. Gedichte und kleine Prosa. Wien: Bergland, 1972. DLC

2470 Tolzmann, Don Heinrich. Handbuch eines Deutschamerikaners, Gedichte. Gordonville, Pa.: Andrew S. Kinsinger, 1973. GSP, MKUK, MHS, MPL, TxU, NUPL, SCC, CC, DU, CCHS,

2471 Ascher-Nash, Franzi. Gedichte eines Lebens: Poems of a

Lifetime. Wien: Europäischer Verlag, (In press).

2472   Brause, Herman. Auf fernen Wegen, Gedichte. Wien: Europäischer Verlag, (In press).

2473   Förster de J., Maria. Heiter-besinnlich-wähle- und stimm dich. Wien: Europäischer Verlag, (In press).

III. THE GERMAN-AMERICAN PRESS AND BOOK TRADE

German-American Newspapers and Periodicals

2474 Abendpost. 223 W. Washington St., Chicago, Ill. 60606.

2475 American Turner Topics. 1550 Clinton Ave. N., Rochester, New York 14621.

2476 Amerika-Herold-Lincoln Freie Presse. 2002 N. 16 St., Omaha, Neb. 68101.

2477 Amerika-Schweizer Zeitung. 1 Union Sq. West, Room 410, New York, N. Y. 10003.

2478 Aufbau. 2121 Broadway, New York, N. Y. 10023.

2479 Bahn Frei. Lexington Ave. & 85th St., New York, N. Y. 10028.

2480 Baltimore Correspondent. 2002 N. 16 St., Omaha, Neb. 68101.

2481 Bay Area International Monthly. Box 322, San Jose, Cal. 94133.

2482 Black and Red. Northwestern College, Watertown, Wisconsin 53094.

2483 Der Buchwurm. Box 1403, Thousand Oaks, Cal. 91360. The only German-American book trade journal.

2484 Buffalo Volksfreund. 3614 S. Creek Rd., Hamburg, New Jersey 14075.

2485 Bulletin of the Home for the Aged Lutherans. 7500 W. North Ave., Wauwatosa, Wisconsin 53213.

2486 California Freie Presse. 149 California St., Room 224, San Francisco, Cal. 94111.

2487 California Staats-Zeitung. 221 E. Pico Blvd., Los Angeles, Cal. 90015.

2488   Cincinnati Kurier.   432 Walnut St., Cincinnati, Ohio 45202.

2489   Detroiter Abend-Post.   1436 Brust St., Detroit, Michigan
       48226.

2490   Der Deutsch-Amerikaner.   4740 N. Western Ave., Chicago,
       Ill. 60625.

2491   Deutsche Wochenschrift.   2507 S. Jefferson Ave., St. Louis,
       Missouri 63104.

2492   Deutscher Wochenspiegel.   74 Hillcrest Dr., Penfield, New
       York 14526.

2493   Eintracht.   9456 N. Lawler St., Skokie, Ill. 60076.

2494   Evangeliumsposaune.   4912 N. W. Ave., Racine, Wisconsin
       53406.

2495   Florida Staats-Zeitung und Herold.   60-20 Broadway, Wood-
       side, New York 11377.

2496   Freiheit.   35 E. 12 St., New York, N. Y. 10003.

2497   G. B. U. Reporter.   4254 Clairton Blvd., Pittsburgh, Pa.
       15227.

2498   German-American Trade News.   606 Fifth Ave., New York,
       N. Y. 10019.

2499   Der Harugari.   114-40 122nd St., South Ozone Park, New
       York 11420.

2500   Die Hausfrau.   1517 W. Fullerton Ave., Chicago, Ill. 60614.

2501   Herold der Wahrheit.   R. 2, Kalona, Iowa 52247.

2502   International Monthly.   Box 8522, San Jose, Cal. 95125.

2503   Internationale Bibellektionen.   4912 N. W. Ave., Racine,
       Wisconsin 53406.

2504   Katholischer Jugendfreund.   20001 Devon Ave., Chicago, Ill.
       60645.

2505   Katholisches Wochenblatt und der Landsmann.   Box 1071,
       Omaha, Neb. 68101.

2506   Kinder Journal.   41 Union Sq., New York, N. Y. 10003.

2507   Kinder Zeitung.   175 E. Broadway, New York, N. Y. 10002.

2508   Kirchliches Monatsblatt für das Evangelisch-Lutherische

Haus.   584 E. Geneva Ave., Philadelphia, Pa. 19120.

2509   Kolping Banner. 125 N. Stratton Lane, Mt. Prospect, Ill.

2510   Kultur und Leben. 175 E. Broadway, New York, N.Y. 10002.

2511   Los Angeles Kurier. 5858 Hollywood Blvd., Los Angeles, Cal. 90028.

2512   Der Lutheraner. 3440 Tedmar, St. Louis, Mo. 63139.

2513   Luxembourg News of America. 201 Sunset Dr., Wilmette, Ill. 60091.

2514   Lyrik und Prosa. Dept. of Germanic and Slavic, 240 Crosby Hall, State University of New York, Buffalo, New York 14214.

2515   The Melting Pot. 630 N. Van Buren St., Milwaukee, Wisconsin 53202.

2516   The Mennonite. 722 Main St., Box 347, Newton, Kansas 67114.

2517   Milwaukee Deutsche Zeitung. 223 W. Washington St., Chicago, Ill. 60606.

2518   Milwaukee Herold. 2002 N. 16 St., Omaha, Neb. 68101.

2519   Morgen Freiheit. 35 E. 12 St., New York, N.Y. 10003.

2520   Nachrichten der Donauschwaben in Amerika. 4219 N. Lincoln Ave., Chicago, Ill. 60618.

2521   Neue Zeitung. 9471 Hidden Valley Pl., Beverly Hills, Cal. 90210.

2522   New Jersey Freie Zeitung. Box 167, Irvington, New Jersey 07111.

2523   New Yorker Staats-Zeitung und Herold. 60-20 Broadway, Woodside, New York 11377.

2524   Ninth Manhattan Masonic News. 220 E. 15 St., New York, N.Y. 10003.

2525   Der Nordamerikanische Calender. Baltic, Ohio 43804.

2526   Ostfriesen Zeitung. Wall Lake, Iowa 51466.

2527   Philadelphia Gazette-Democrat. 1838 Reading Terminal Arcade, Room 217, 12th & Market Streets, Philadelphia, Pa.

2528   Plattdeutsche Post. 91 New Dorp Plaza, Staten Island, New York 10306.

2529   Rundschau. 339 Walnut St., Philadelphia, Pa. 19104.

2530   Saenger Zeitung. 1832 Hillsdale Ave., Dayton, Ohio 45414.

2531   St. Josephs Blatt. Mount Angel Abbey, Benedict, Oregon
       97373.

2532   Schwenkfeldian. 1 Seminary St., Pennsburg, Pa. 18073.

2533   Der Sendbote. 7308 Madison St., Forest Park, Ill. 60130.

2534   Shmuessen mit Kinder un Yungt. 770 E. Parkway, Brooklyn,
       New York 11213.

2535   Siebenbürgisch-Amerikanisches Volksblatt. 1436 Brush St.,
       Detroit, Michigan 48226.

2536   Solidarity. 714 Seneca Ave., Ridgewood, New York 11227.

2537   Sonntagspost. 2002 N. 16 St., Omaha, Neb. 68101.

2538   Staats-Anzeiger. 622-12 St., Bismarck, N. Dak. 58501.

2539   Steuben News. 369 Lexington Ave., Suite 2003, New York,
       N. Y. 10017.

2540   Swiss-American. 603 Forest Ave., Paramus, New Jersey
       07652.

2541   Tägliche Andachten. 3558 S. Jefferson Ave., St. Louis,
       Missouri 63118.

2542   Together. 1661 N. Northwest Highway, Park Ridge, Ill.
       60068.

2543   Unser Tsait. 25 E. 78 St., New York, N. Y. 10021.

2544   Unser Veg. 305 Broadway, Room 910, New York, N. Y.
       10007.

2545   Unser Veg. 166 West Washington, Chicago, Ill. 60602.

2546   Unterrichtspraxis. 339 Walnut St., Philadelphia, Pa. 19106.

2547   Voice of the Federation of American Citizens of German De-
       scent. 460 Chapman St., Irvington, New Jersey 07111.

2548   Volkszeitung-Tribüne. Box 1071, Omaha, Neb. 68101.

2549   Wächter und Anzeiger. 4164 Lorain Ave., Cleveland, Ohio
       44113.

2550   The Wanderer. 128 E. 10th St., St. Paul, Minnesota 55101.

2551 Washington Journal. 3132 Main St. N. W. , Washington, D. C.
      20007.

2552 Der Wecker. 175 E. Broadway, New York, N. Y. 10002.

2553 Die Weltpost. Box 1071, Omaha, Neb. 68101

2554 Der Yid. 134 Broadway, Brooklyn, New York 11211.

2555 Di yiddische Heim. 770 E. Parkway, Brooklyn, New York
      11213.

2556 Yiddishe Kultur. 1133 Broadway, Suite 1023, New York,
      N. Y. 10010.

2557 Das yiddishe Vort. 5 Beekman St. , New York, N. Y. 10038.

2558 Der yiddisher Kwal. 545 Bedford Ave. , Brooklyn, New York
      11211.

2559 Yiddisher Kemfer. 45 E. 17th St. , New York, N. Y. 10003.

2560 Yidishe Shprakh. 1048 Fifth Ave. , New York, N. Y. 10028.

2561 Yugntruf. 3328 Bainbridge Ave. , Bronx, New York 10467.

2562 Zamlungen. 35 E. 12 St. , New York, N. Y. 10003.

2563 Zein. 144 W. 73d St. , New York, N. Y. 10023.

2564 Zukunft. 25 E. 78th St. , New York, N. Y. 10021.

Newspaper Histories

2565 Arndt, Karl. The Ernst Steiger Collection of German-Ameri-
      can Newspapers and Periodicals in Heidelberg and Vienna Dili-
      gently Compared and Catalogued for Cooperating Libraries as
      a Guide to Microfilm Copies of the Heidelberg Collection.
      Worcester, Mass.: The Author, 1964.

2566 _____. Microfilm Guide and Index to the Library of Con-
      gress Collection of German Prisoners of War Camp Papers
      Published in the U. S. of North America from 1943 to 1946.
      Worcester, Mass.: The Author, 1965.

2567 _____. and May E. Olson. Die deutschsprachige Presse
      der Amerikas 1732-1968: Geschichte und Bibliographie. Pul-
      lach bei München: Verlag Dokumentation, 1973.

2568 _____. _____. German-American Newspapers and
      Periodicals 1732-1955: History and Bibliography. Heidelberg:

Quelle & Meyer, 1961. Lists 5,000 German-American newspapers and locations of files.

2569   Berg, P. H. "Mennonite Brethren Press," ML. 6 (1951): 38-41.

2570   Bockstahler, Oscar. "The German Press in Indiana," IMH. 48 (1952): 161-68.

2571   Bressler, Leo. "The Pennsylvania German," AGR. 18, iv (1952): 11-14; v (1952): 13-15.

2572   Breychs-Vauthier, A. C. Die Zeitungen der österreichischen Emigration 1934-66. (Biblos-Schriften, 26.) Wien: Österreichische Nationalbibliothek, 1960.

2573   Broadbent, T. L. "A Goethe House Note from the San Francisco Sonntagspost: Implications and Deductions," CQ. 44 (1971): 168-71.

2574   _____. "The Salt Lake City Beobachter: Mirror of an Immigration," UHQ. 26 (1958): 329-50.

2575   Cazden, Robert E. "Free German and Free Austrian Newspapers and Periodicals in the United States, 1933-50; A Checklist," in German Exile Literature in America 1933-50. Chicago: ALA, 1970, pp. 178-89.

2576   Cunz, Dieter. "Die deutsche Presse in Amerika," D. Rundschau. 84 (1958): 204-07.

2577   _____. "Die historische Rolle der deutschen Presse in Amerika," W-J. (Apr. 17, 1959; Oct. 17, 1969).

2578   _____. "John Gruber and his Almanac," Eck. (Dec. 10, 17, 1955).

2579   _____. "Schuricht's Virginia-German Weekly," AGR. 18, i (1951): 14-16.

2580   Downs, Lynwood. "The German Musical Journal," AGR. 22, v (1956): 8-9, 35.

2581   Dunson, Alvis. A Checklist of German Newspapers in Missouri up to 1940. Ohio State University: Dissertation, 1959.

2582   Dyck, Henry. "The New Ulm Pioneer," AGR. 18, iii (1952): 18, 35.

2583   Etzler, T. Herbert. "German-American Newspapers in Texas With Special Reference to the Texas Volksblatt, 1877-79," SwHQ. 57 (1954): 423-31.

2584   _____. "Texas Volksblatt, 1877-89, " AGR. 19 (1953): 16-
          17.

2585   Flack, James. "The Press in Detroit, 1880-1900, " MichH.
          50 (1966): 76-87.

2586   Frantz, Clair. The Religious Teachings of the German Al-
          manacs Published by the Sauers in Colonial Pennsylvania.
          Temple University: Dissertation, 1955.

2587   Gilbert, Russell. "Sower's Almanac as an Advertising Medi-
          um, " AGR. 15, i (1948): 9-12.

2588   Godcharles, Frederic. "The Collection of the Issues of the
          German Presses, Charter, Treaties etc. at the Pennsylvania
          State Library, " PGS: P&A. 40 (1932): 11-14.

2589   Groen, H. J. "A Note on the German-American Newspaper
          of Cincinnati, 1860, " MDU. 37 (1945): 67-71.

2590   Gruber, John. "The Farmer's Bible: John Gruber's Al-
          manac, " Valleys of Hist. 2 (1966): 6-9.

2591   Hanhardt, Arthur. "Jugendpost, " AGR. 21, iv (1953): 22, 31.

2592   Hofacker, Erich. "Das Westland, an American Periodical for
          Germany, " AGR. 19, i (1952): 19-22.

2593   Johnson, Warren. The Content of American Colonial News-
          papers Relative to International Affairs, 1704-63. University
          of Washington: Dissertation, 1962.

2594   Kalbfleisch, Herbert. The History of the Pioneer German
          Language Press of Ontario, 1835-1918. Toronto: University
          of Toronto Pr., 1968.

2595   Kisler, Mark. "The German Language Press in Michigan:
          A Survey and Bibliography, " MichH. 44 (1960): 302-23.

2596   Knoche, Carl. The German Immigrant Press in Milwaukee.
          Ohio State University: Dissertation, 1969.

2597   Koester, Leonard. "An Amusing Description of the Pioneer
          Press in Kentucky, " KyHS. 54 (1956): 214-220.

2598   _____. "German Newspapers Published in Louisville, "
          AGR. 20, v (1954): 24-27.

2599   Korman, Gerd. "Political Loyalties, Immigrant Traditions,
          and Reform: The Wisconsin German-American Press and
          Progressivism, 1909-12, " WMH. 40 (1957): 161-68.

2600   Lang, Elfrieda. "The Germans of Dubois County: Their

Newspapers, Their Politics and Their Part in the Civil War, "
IMH. 42 (1946): 229-48.

2601   "Ein Loblied auf den Aufbau: Kölner Stadt-Anzeiger über die
       deutsche Presse in den USA, " Aufbau. (May 25, 1973).

2602   Massmann, John. Friedrich Orthwein: A Case Study in
       Historical Investigation. University of Minnesota: Disserta-
       tion, 1959.

2603   Metzenthin-Raunick, Selma. "One Hundred Years New-Braun-
       felser Zeitung, " AGR. 19, vi (1953): 15-16.

2604   Miller, Edmund. The Hundred Year History of the German
       Correspondent. Baltimore, 1941.

2605   Moore, Powell. "The Newspaper Press of the Calumet Re-
       gion, 1836-1933, " IMH. 52 (1956): 111-40.

2606   Norden, Rudolph. "Zur Fürsprache für den Lutheraner, " DL.
       128 (1973): 93.

2607   Owens, Lilliana. "St. Louis Catholic Journalism Prior to
       the Civil War, " SJR. 57 (1965): 200-07.

2608   Pochmann, Henry. "Early German-American Journalistic
       Exchanges, " HLQ. 11 (1948): 161-79.

2609   "Propaganda für den Lutheraner, " DL. 128 (1973): 21.

2610   Rippley, LaVern. "Notes About the German Press in the
       Minnesota River Valley, " RJGAH. 35 (1972): 37-45.

2611   Saalberg, Harvey. "The Westliche Post of St. Louis: Ger-
       man Language Daily, 1857-1938, " JQ. 45 (1968): 452-56, 472.

2612   Scheu, Friedrich. Die Emigrationspresse der Sozialisten,
       1938-45. (Monographien zur Zeitgeschichte.) Wien: Europa,
       1968.

2613   Schultz, Ferdinand. History of the New Yorker Staatszeitung.
       Columbia University: Dissertation, 1950.

2614   Shoemaker, Alfred L. "German Newspapers of Central Penn-
       sylvania, " PD. 5, xii (1954): 10-11; xiii (1954): 14.

2615   _____. German Newspapers of the Coal Regions, " PD. 5,
       xiv (1954): 10-11.

2616   _____. "Hanover Newspapers, " PD. 4, iv (1953): 15.

2617   _____. "Union County German Newspapers, " PD. 4, xiii
       (1953): 12, 14.

2618 _____. "Westmoreland County German Newspapers, " PD. 4, xi (1953): 15.

2619 _____. "York County Checklist, " PD. 5 (1954): 10.

2620 Smith, E. and J. G. Stewart. "Gruber's Hagerstown Almanac, " Eck. (Jan. 9, 1965).

2621 Spritz, L. W. "Der Lutheraner, ein treuer Zeuge der Wahrheit, " DL. 129 (1973): 57-58.

2622 Suren, Victor. "Der Wanderer Arrives at Journey's End, " SJR. 50 (1957): 124-25.

2623 Swope, E. Pierce. "Der Libanoner Morgenstern, " Eck. (June 13, 1964).

2624 Tolzmann, Don Heinrich. "The German Language Press in Minnesota, 1855 to 1955, " GAS. 5 (1972): 169-78.

2625 United States. Library of Congress. List of Newspapers Principally Representative of German Groups Outside Germany. Washington, D. C., 1946.

2626 Waldenrath, Alexander. "The German Language Newspress of Pennsylvania During the American Revolution, " GAS. 6 (1973): 43-56.

2627 Weisert, John. "The Limping Messenger, " AGR. 27, iii (1961): 8-10.

2628 Wittke, Carl. The German Language Press in America. Lexington: University of Kentucky, 1957.

2629 Wust, Klaus G. "German Immigrants and their Newspapers in the District of Columbia, " RJGAH. 39 (1959): 26-66.

2630 _____. "Items on Maryland in Early Pennsylvania-German Newspaper, " RJGAH. 32 (1966): 59-60.

2631 _____. "Matthias Bartigs' Newspapers in Virginia, " AGR. 18, i (1951): 16-18.

2632 Wuttge, Frank. "Aus den Annalen des Staats-Herold, " NYSZH: Sonderbeilage. (Dec. 28, 1969): 30-34.

2633 Zucker, A. E. "Die Abendschule, 1852-1940: A Pioneer Weekly, " AGR. 8 (1942): 14-17.

2634 _____. "Two German-American Periodicals, " AGR. 10 (1943): 26-27.

German-American Journalists

2635   August, Ruth. "Val J. Peter, Publisher," AGR. 27, i (1960):
       16-18.

2636   Barba, Preston. "Sim Schmalzgsicht's Own Magazine," Eck.
       (Oct. 27, 1956).

2637   "Biographien von einigen der früheren Redakteuer und Eigen-
       thümer der Belleviller Zeitung," B. Post & Z. (Jan. 11,
       1899): 12-20.

2638   Cunz, Dieter. "John Gruber and His Almanac," MHM. 47
       (1952): 89-102.

2639   Durnbaugh, Donald. "The German Journalist and the Dunker
       Love Feast," PFI. 18 (1968): 40-48.

2640   Fornell, Earl. "Ferdinand Flake: German Pioneer Journal-
       ist of the Southeast," AGR. 21, iii (1955): 25-28.

2641   Grossmann, Kurt. Michael Wurmbrand: The Man and His
       Work. New York: Philosophical Library, 1956.

2642   Hirsch, Helmut. "Tribun und Prophet: Moses Hesse als
       Pariser Korrespondent der Illinois Staats-Zeitung," Int. Rev.
       of Soc. Hist. 2 (1957): 209-30.

2643   Institut für Auslandsbeziehungen. "Ehrung für Otto Lohr,"
       ZKA. 12 (1962): 257-59.

2644   Kehres, Gregory. "Carl Neurer, Pioneer Editor," SJR. 53
       (1961): 349-52, 385-88.

2645   [Kenkel.] "Frederick Philip Kenkel," MHR. 46 (1952): 307.

2646   Kloss, Heinz. "James C. Lins: Political Columnist," Eck.
       (Aug. 25, 1951; Nov. 13, 1965).

2647   Massmann, John. "Friedrich Orthwein: Minnesota's First
       German Editor," AGR. 26, iv (1960): 16-17, 38.

2648   Michaelis, Richard. Nach vierzig Jahren: Erinnerungen
       eines Zeitungsleiters. Midford, Wisconsin, 1907. UC

2649   Raschen, J. "American-German Journalist a Century Ago,"
       AGR. 12, v (1946): 13-15.

2650   Rosenberger, Arthur. "N. B. Grubb, Editor and Minister,"
       ML. 6 (1951): 42-45.

2651   Rothfuss, Herman. "Westward with the News," AGR. 20,
       iii (1954): 22-25.

2652   Saalberg, Harvey. "Dr. Emil Preetorius, Editor-in-Chief
        of the Westliche Post 1864-1905, " MHS Bul. 24 (1968): 103-
        112.

2653   Schellenberg, T. "Editor Abraham L. Schellenberg, " ML.
        9 (1954): 19-28.

2654   Schlicher, J. J. "Bernhard Domschke: The Editor and the
        Man, " WMH. 29 (1946): 319-332, 435-56.

2655   Shoemaker, Alfred L. "Henry Dulheuer: The Old Traveler, "
        PD. 3 (1952): 1, 3.

2656   Schoenke, F. L. Aus längstvergangenen Tagen: Erinnerungen
        eines Journalisten. n. p., n. d. UC

2657   Vagts, Alfred. "Heinrich Boernstein, Ex- and Repatriate, "
        MHS Bul. 12 (1956): 105-12.

2658   Weisert, John. "Dr. Anthony Hunn, Medical Friend of the
        People, " AGR. 23, v (1957): 28-31.

2659   "Johann Georg Wesselhöft, " Mitteilungen d. DPV von Phil.
        9 (1908): 12-19.

German-American Printing & Publishing History

2660   Arnold, Edmund. "The Mergenthaler Story, " AGR. 21, ii
        (1954): 16-18.

2661   Barba, Alvaro. "Gründlicher Unterricht von den Metallen:
        In zwey Büchern. Vormals im Spanischen beschrieben, " PAAS.
        60 (1960): 92-93. About a German imprint from Ephrata.

2661A   Barba, Preston. "Carl A. Bruckman: Printer and Publish-
        er, " HRBC. 9 (1944): 81-83.

2662   _____. "Christopher Sauer, Senior, " ECK. (Dec. 4, 11,
        18, 1943).

2663   _____. "The First Printer in the Lehigh Valley, " Eck.
        (Jan. 18, 1958).

2664   Bargen, G. "General Conference Mennonite Press, " ML. 6
        (1951): 35-37, 48.

2665   Benz, Ernst. "Franklin and the Mystic Rocket, " AGR. 29
        (1963): 24-26.

2666   Berg, P. H. "Mennonite Brethren Press, " ML. 6 (1951):
        38-39.

2667   Beswick, J. The Work of Friedrich Leypoldt, Bibliographer
       and Publisher. New York: Bowker, 1942.

2668   Bock, Eve. "Contributions of the German Reformed Church
       to American Culture, " GAS. 6 (1973): 57-67.

2669   Bornemann, Henry. Pennsylvania German Bookplates. Phila-
       delphia: Pennsylvania German Society, 1953.

2670   Boyer, Walter. "Adam und Eva im Paradies, " PD. 8, ii
       (1957): 14-18.

2671   Brandt, Harry. Meet Henry Kurtz: Editor, Publisher,
       Preacher, Clerk of Annual Conferences. Elgin, Ill.: Breth-
       ren Publishing House, 1841.

2672   Bristol, Roger. Index of Printers, Publishers and Booksell-
       ers indicated by Charles Evans in His American Bibliography.
       Charlottesville: Bibliographical Society of the University of
       Virginia, 1961.

2673   Brumder, Herbert. The Life Story of George Brumder and
       Henriette Brumder. Milwaukee: The Author, 1960.

2674   Buten, Harry. "Charles Magnus: Versatile Printer, " AGR.
       20, iii (1954): 26-27.

2675   Classen, Johann. "Editions of Ein schön Gesangbüchlein, "
       ML. 12 (1957): 47-48, 96.

2676   Colket, Meredith. "Family Records Printed During the Co-
       lonial Period, " Papers. Bibliographical. S. of A. 57 (1963):
       61-67.

2677   Cowen, David. "Deigendesch's Nachrichten Rossartzney-
       büchlein, " J. Amer. Vet. Med Assoc. 139 (1961): 359-66.

2678   Davenport, F. G. "John Henry Rand and Public Health in
       Illinois, 1877-91, " ISHS. 1 (1958): 277-93. About printing
       of medical pamphlets.

2679   Dorn, O. A. "Early Printing in the Missouri Synod, " CHIQ.
       24 (1951): 1-23.

2680   Dreis, Hazel. "Lancaster, Pennsylvania, Bookbindings: A
       Historical Study, " PBSA. 42 (1948): 119-28.

2681   Dunson, Alvis. German Publications in Missouri. Ohio
       State University: Dissertation, 1954.

2682   Durnbaugh, Donald.. "Christopher Sauer: Pennsylvania-Ger-
       man Printer: His Youth in Germany and Later Relationships
       with Europe, " PMBH. 82 (1958): 316-40.

2683   . "Was Christopher Sauer a Dunker?" PMHB. 93
(1969): 383-91.

2684   Eberly, William. "The Printing and Publishing Activity of
Henry Kurtz," Brethren Life & Thought. 8 (1964): i.

2685   Fielding, Mantle. American Engravers Upon Copper and
Steel: Biographical Sketches and Checklists of Engravings,
A Supplement to David McNeely Stauffer's American En-
gravers. Philadelphia: Private Pr., 1917.

2686   Finckh, Alice. "A Year is Born: A Calendar is Made,"
AGR. 15, ii (1948): 26-27.

2687   Fisher, Nevin. The History of Brethren Hymnbooks. Bridge-
water, Va.: Beacon Publishers, 1950.

2688   Foltz, M. A. "A Notable Publication House in Chambersburg,
1835-64," KHSP. (1908): 183-99.

2689   Friedel, F. "Lieber's Contribution to the International Copy-
right Movement," HLQ. 8 (1945): 200-06.

2690   Friedrich, Gerhard. "Three Anecdotes about Christopher
Sower," Eck. (Sept. 17, 1955).

2691   Fritsch, W. A. Deutsche Bücher im Staate Indiana. Jeffer-
sonville, Indiana, n.d. UC

2692   Galen, Albert. "Concordia Publishing House's One Hundred
Years," CHIQ. 42 (1969): 157-70.

2693   German-American Typographia. Buchdrucker-Zeitung. Chicago, 1873-1940.

2694   Hamilton, M. W. "A Veteran Printing Press," HRBC. 7
(1941-42): 85-86.

2695   Hocker, Edward. "The Sower Printing House of Colonial
Times," PGSP. 53 (1948): 1-125.

2696   Hollyday, Guy. "The Ephrata Wall-Charts and Their Inscriptions," PFL. 19 (1970): 34-46.

2697   Horst, Irvin. "Joseph Funk, Early Mennonite Printer and
Publisher," MQR. 31 (1957): 260-77.

2698   Hostetler, John. God Uses Ink: The Heritage and Mission
of the Mennonite Publishing House After Fifty Years. Scottdale, Pa.: Mennonite Publishing House, 1958.

2699   . "The Mennonite Book and Tract Society, 1899-
1908," MQR. 31 (1957): 105-27.

2700   International Typographical Union.   Jahres-Bericht der deutsch-
       amerikanischen Typographia.   New York, 1894-1937.

2701   Jonas, Klaus.   "Kurt Wolff, Notes on a Creative Publisher,"
       AGR. 31, v (1965): 11-14.

2702   Landenberger, J. Louis.   "Ketterlinus, Lithographer," AGR.
       14, iv (1948): 26-28.

2703   Lange, Herman.   "History of the Text Book of the Moravian
       Church," MHS. 13 (1944): 133-62.

2704   Larremore, Thomas.   "An American Typographic Tragedy:
       The Imprints of Frederick Conrad Bursch," PBSA. 43 (1950):
       1-38.

2705   Lichten, Frances.   "Fractur from the Hostetter Collection,"
       PD. 6, i (1954): 11-13.

2706   Livengood, William.   "The First Bible West of the Alleghen-
       ies," Eck. (Oct. 23, 1954).

2707   Marty, Martin and John Deedy.   The Religious Press in Amer-
       ica.   New York: Holt, Rinehart and Winston, 1963.

2708   Mengel, Willi.   Ottmar Mergenthaler and the Printing Revo-
       lution.   Brooklyn: Mergenthaler Linotype Co., 1954.

2709   Minnick, Rachel.   A History of Printing in Maryland, 1791-
       1800.   Baltimore: Enoch Pratt Free Library, 1949.

2710   Moschzisker, Bertha von.   "Order is the First Law: John
       von Wicht," AGR. 20, iii (1954): 15-17.

2711   Murray, Dorothy.   "William John Henning: The Man--The
       Publisher," Richmond Cty. Hist. 2 (1970): 7-12.

2712   Nichols, Charles.   "Justus Fox: A German Printer of the
       18th Century," Proc. Amer. Antiq. Soc. 25 (1915): 55-69.

2713   Oda, Wilbur.   "Gabriel Miesse--Doctor and Engraver," PD.
       (Nov. 1, 1951).

2714   One Hundred Years of the Printing Firm of Schneidereith and
       Sons in the City of Baltimore.   Baltimore: Schneidereith,
       1949.

2715   Reger, Willy.   "The Pilger Publishing House," HRBC. 7
       (1941-42): 78-80.

2716   Reichmann, Felix.   "Christopher Sower Exhibition," AGR.
       10 (1944): 8-10, 29.

2717 _____. Christopher Sower, Sr., 1694-1758, Printer in Germantown. Philadelphia: Carl Schurz Memorial Foundation, 1943.

2718 _____. "Christopher Sower's Bible," GR. 19 (1944): 146-49.

2719 Romaker, A. J. "Developments of the Publication Interests," in The German Baptists in North America. Cleveland: German Baptist Publication Society, 1924, pp. 71-79.

2720 [Sauer.] "Christopher Sauer: One-Man Bible Society of Germantown (1694-1758)," Bible Soc Record. 113 (1968): 692.

2721 Scheer, G. F. "First Printing in the Valley of Virginia," PW. 150 (1947): 2891-2897.

2722 Schwarze, W. "Early Hymnals of the Bohemian Brethren," MHS. 13 (1944): 163-73.

2723 Seidensticker, Oswald. "Die beiden Christoph Sauer in Germantown," DDP. 12 (1880-81): 10-15, 47-51, 89-92, 178-82, 218-20, 305-10, 350-57, 389-93, 437-44; 13 (1881-82): 63-67, 114-18, 138-42.

2724 Shaffer, Ellen. "Illuminators, Scribes and Printers: A Glimpse of the Free Library's Pennsylvania Dutch Collection," PF. 9 (1958): 18-27.

2725 Shoemaker, Alfred L. "Adam and Eve Broadsides," PD. 4, vi (1952): 4-5.

2726 _____. "Adams County Printers," PD. 4, x (1953): 13-14.

2727 _____. "The Ephrata Printers," PD. 4, ix (1953): 11-13.

2728 Sommer, Roger. "Old German and English Baptismal Certificates," CHIQ. 31 (1958): 89-92.

2729 Smith, Elmer and John Stewart. "Peter Bernhart: Fraktur Artist," Eck. (May 7, 1966).

2730 Sower, Albert. "The Sower Bible," BHSM. 4 (1943): 33-38.

2731 Sower, Christopher. "The Last Will of Germantown Printer Christopher Sower of March 23, 1777," RJGAH. 32 (1966): 61-64.

2732 Standard, Paul. "Hermann Zapf in Amerika," BfddB. 17 (1961): 49-51.

2733   Stauffer, David.   American Engravers upon Copper and Steel.
        New York: Grolier Club, 1907. 700 biographies of American
        engravers before 1825.

2734   Stern, Madeline.   "Ernst Steiger: German-American Pub-
        lisher, " in Imprints on History. Bloomington: Indiana Uni-
        versity Pr., 1956, pp. 233-58.

2735   _____. "Henry Frank: Pioneer American Hebrew Pub-
        lisher, " AJA. 20 (1968): 163-68.

2736   Studer, Gerald.   Frederick Goeb: Master Printer.   Somer-
        set, Pa.: Goeb Bible Sesquicentennial, 1963.

2737   _____. "Master Printer Goeb: The Goeb Bible, " J. Alle-
        ghenies. 1 (1963): 6-10.

2738   Sutton, Walter.   "Cincinnati as a Frontier Publishing and
        Book Trade Center, 1796-1830, " OSAHQ. 56 (1947): 117-43.

2739   Taubert, Sigfred.   "Zur Geschichte des deutschen und deutsch
        sprachigen Buchdrucks und Buchhandels im Ausland, " BfddB.
        9 (May 5, July 28, Dec. 4, 1953).

2740   Thompson, D. W.   "Oldest American Printing Press, " PD.
        6, iii (1954): 28-33.

2741   Thompson, Lawrence.   "Victor Hammer of Kentucky, " AGR.
        20, v (1954): 13-15.

2742   Von Zeller, Bernhard and Ellen Otten.   Kurt Wolff: Brief-
        wechsel eines Verlegers. Frankfurt: Scheffler, 1966.

2743   Wayland, John.   "Literary Activities and Associations of the
        Shenandoah Co., Va. Henkel Press Bibliography, " in A His-
        tory of Shenandoah County, Virginia. Strasburg, Va., 1927,
        pp. 481-97.

2744   Wust, Klaus.   "The English and German Printing Office: Bi
        lingual Printers in Maryland and Virginia, " RJGAH. 32 (196(
        24-37.

2745   _____. "German Books and German Printers in Virginia,
        Rockingham Recorder. 2 (1958): 24-29.

2746   _____. "A Virginia-German Printer: Laurentz Wartman:
        (1775-1840), " AGR. 20, vi (1954): 29-30.

2746A   Zehner, Olive. "Ohio Fractur, " PD. 6, iii (1954): 13-15.

Bibliographical Guides to German-American Imprints

2747   American Catalog of Books, 1876-1910.   New York: Publish-
       ers' Weekly, 1876-1910.

2748   Arndt, Karl.   "Books Printed in the Harmony Society Press,"
       in George Rapp's Harmony Society 1785-1847.   Rutherford:
       Fairleigh Dickinson University Pr., 1972, pp. 629.

2749   Bender, Harold Stauffer.   Two Centuries of American Men-
       nonite Literature, A Bibliography of Mennonitica Americana,
       1727-1928.   Goshen, Indiana: Mennonite Historical Society,
       1929.   Indicates library locations.

2750   "Bibliography of German Printing in the US," AGR. 12-18
       (1946-51).

2751   Bristol, Roger.   Maryland Imprints, 1801-1810.   Charlottes-
       ville: University of Virginia Pr., 1953.

2752   Cappon, Lester and Irva Brown.   New Market, Virginia Im-
       prints 1806-76.   Charlottesville, 1942.   Lists imprints of
       the Henkel press.

2753   Cazden, Robert E.   "Free German Books and Pamphlets Pub-
       lished in the United States, 1933-54:   A Checklist," in Ger-
       man Exile Literature in America 1933-50.   Chicago: ALA,
       1970, pp. 190-215.

2754   _____ .   German Exile Literature: A Symposium and Ex-
       hibit.   24th University of Kentucky Foreign Language Confer-
       ence.   Lexington, 1971.   Lists 103 Exile imprints.

2755   Concordia Publishing House.   A Catalog of Concordia Publish-
       ing House.   St. Louis: Concordia, 1931.

2756   Croll, P. C.   "Lebanon County, Pa. Imprints and Bibliogra-
       phy," L. Cty. HS. 4 (1906-09): 153-99.

2757   Deutsche Bibliographie, 1945/50- .   Bücher und Karten.
       Frankfurt: Buchhändler-Vereinigung GMBH, 1952- .

2758   Deutsche Nationalbibliographie und Bibliographie des im Aus-
       land erschienenen deutschsprachigen Schrifttums.   Reihe A,
       Reihe B.   Leipzig: Verlag für Buch- und Bibliothekswesen,
       1931- .

2759   Deutsches Bücherverzeichnis.   Leipzig: Börsenverein der
       deutschen Buchhändler, 1916-43.

2760   Deutsches Bücherverzeichnis: Verzeichnis der in Deutschland,
       Österreich, der Schweiz und im übrigen Ausland herausgegeb-
       enen deutschsprachigen Verlagsschriften sowie der wichtigsten

Veröffentlichungen ausserhalb des Buchhandels.   Leipzig:
Verlag für Buch- und Bibliothekswesen, 1915- .

2761   Doll, Eugene and A. Funke.   The Ephrata Cloisters: An Annotated Bibliography.   Philadelphia: Carl Schurz Memorial
Foundation, 1944.

2762   Evans, Charles.   American Bibliography: A Chronological
Dictionary of all Books, Pamphlets and periodical Publications
Printed in the United States of America from the genesis of
Printing....   Chicago: The Author, 1903-59.   14 vol.

2763   Friedrich, Gerhard.   "A New Supplement to Seidensticker's
American-German Bibliography, " PH. 7 (1940): 213-24.
Lists 77 titles with library locations.

2764   The Genesis of Printing in 1639 down to and Including the
Year 1880; With Bibliographical and Biographical Notes.   Chicago: Printed for the Author, 1903-59.

2765   Gott, John.   Imprints of Winchester, Virginia, 1787-1876.
Catholic University: Dissertation, 1953.

2766   Guerra, Francisco.   American Medical Bibliography 1639-178:
New York: Lathrop C. Harper, 1962.   Includes Pennsylvania
German imprints.

2767   _____.   "Medical Literature in North America during the
Colonial Period and the Revolutionary War: A Summary, "
B. Hist. Med. 35 (1962): 149-55.

2768   Hammer, Carolyn Reading.   "A Victor Hammer Bibliography
(1930-55), " ABC. 6 (Dec.., 1955): 3-12; 6 (Jan., 1956): 6-
10.

2769   Heinsius, Wilhelm.   Allgemeines Bücher-Lexikon, 1700-1892.
Leipzig: Brockhaus, 1812-94.

2770   Hildeburn, Charles.   A Century of Printing: The Issues of
the Press in Pennsylvania, 1685-1784.   Philadelphia: Mat-
lack & Harvey, 1885-86.

2771   _____.   List of Publications Issues in Pennsylvania, 1685
to 1759.   Philadelphia: Collins, 1882.

2772   Historical Records Survey.   Bibliography of Research Projec⸢
Reports: A Check-List of Historical Records Survey Publica⸤
tions.   Washington: Federal Works Agency, W. P. A., 1943.

2773   _____.   Divisioh of Women's and Professional Projects.
Works Progress Administration.   American Imprints Inventory.   Washington: Historical Records Survey, 1937-42.

2774   Horsch, John. Kurzgefasste Geschichte und Lehren, sowie
       Verzeichnis der Literatur der Taufgesinnten. Elkhart, Indi-
       ana, 1890.

2775   Horst, Irvin. "Singers Glen, Virginia Imprints 1847-78: A
       Checklist," Eastern Mennonite Col. Bul. 44 (1965): 6-14.

2776   Kayser, Christian. Vollständiges Bücher-Lexikon, 1750-1910.
       Leipzig: Tauchnitz, 1834-1912.

2777   Kelly, James. American Catalogue of Books (Original and Re-
       prints), Published in the U. S. from Jan. 1861 to Jan. 1871,
       With Date of Publications, Size, Price, and Publisher's Name.
       New York: Wiley, 1866-71.

2778   Kloss, Heinz. "Deutsche und französische Drucke des ameri-
       kanischen Kontinental-Kongress," Nation und Staat. (Feb. 10,
       1937): 283-92.

2779   Kriebel, Howard. "Philadelphia Prints in the Schwenkfelder
       Historical Library," Perkiomen Region. 9, ii (1931): 42-48.

2780   McMurtrie, Douglas. "Locating the Printed Source Materials
       for United States History; With a Bibliography of Lists of
       Regional Imprints," MVHR. 31 (1944): 369-406.

2781   Meynen, E. "Deutsche Drucke, Verfasser und Drucker," in
       Bibliographie des Deutschtums der kolonialzeitlichen Einwan-
       derung in Nordamerika. Leipzig: Harrassowitz, 1937, pp.
       185-90.

2782   O'Callaghan, E. A List of Editions of the Holy Scriptures
       and Parts Thereof Printed in America Previous to 1860:
       With Introduction and Biographical Notes. Albany, New York:
       Munsell & Rowland, 1861.

2783   Oda, Wilbur. "A Check List of the German-Language Im-
       prints of America Through 1830," PD. 4, i (1952): 12-14;
       4, ii (1952): 12-14; 4, iii (1952): 12-14; 4, v (1952): 6-7,
       13; 4, viii (1952): 12-13.

2784   _____. "Ephrata German Imprints," PD. 9, ix (1953):
       10-12.

2785   _____. "German-Language Imprints of Harrisburg," PD.
       4, xiv (1953): 12-14.

2786   _____. "Gettysburg German Imprints," PD. 4, i (1953):
       14.

2787   _____. "Hanover German Imprints," PD. 4, xii (1953):
       14-15.

178   German-Americana

2788 _____. "New Berlin German Imprints, " __PD.__ 4, xiii (1953):
      13, 15.

2789 Publisher's Trade List Annual. New York: Bowker, 1873- .

2790 Reichmann, Felix. Christopher Sower, Sr., 1694-1758: Print-
      er in Germantown: An Annotated Bibliography. (Bibliogra-
      phies on German-American History, 2.) Philadelphia: Carl
      Schurz Memorial Foundation, 1943.

2791 _____. "German Printing in Maryland: A Check List,
      1768-1950, " RJGAH. 27 (1950): 9-70.

2792 Reinholdt, Georg Christoph. Georg Christoph Reinholdt, Buch-
      binder in der Markt-Strasse, neben dem Wirtshause zum
      Schwarzen Bären, zu Philadelphia, hat folgende Bücher zu
      verkaufen. Philadelphia: Miller, 1773. LCP

2793 Roorbach, Orville Augustus. Bibliotheca Americana, 1820-61.
      New York: Roorbach, 1852-61.

2794 Roy, Donald. "Selected Pittsburgh Imprints, 1807-60, in the
      Library of the Historical Society of Western Pennsylvania, "
      West. Pa. Hist. Mag. 44 (1961): 175-97.

2795 Seidensticker, Oswald. The First Century of German Print-
      ing in America, 1728-1830; Preceded by the Literary Work of
      Franz Daniel Pastorius. Philadelphia: Schäfer & Koradi,
      1893.

2796 Shaw, Ralph and Richard Shoemaker. American Bibliography:
      A Preliminary Checklist. New York: Scarecrow, 1958-65.
      Lists locations. Covers 1801-1819 in 19 vols. plus three vols.
      of indexes and corrections.

2797 Shoemaker, Alfred. "A Check List of Dialect Literature, "
      __PD.__ 4, i (1952): 6-10.

2798 _____. A Checklist of Imprints of the German Press of
      Lehigh County, Pennsylvania, 1807-1905, With Biographies
      of the Printers. Easton, Pa., 1943.

2799 _____. "A Checklist of Imprints ʻof the German Press of
      Lehigh County, Pennsylvania, 1807-1900, With Biographies of
      the Printers, " PLCHS. 16 (1947): 1-240.

2800 _____. "A Checklist of Imprints of the German Press of
      Northampton· County, Pennsylvania, 1766-1905, With Biogra-
      phies of the Printers, " NCHGS. 4 (1943): 1-162.

2801 Shoemaker, Richard H. Checklist of American Imprints,
      1820- . New York: Scarecrow, 1964- .

2802   Shuey, William.   "A Historical Catalog of the Publications,
       1834-92, " in Manual of the United Brethren Publishing House:
       History and Description.   Dayton: United Brethren Publish-
       ing House, 1892.

2803   Sower, Charles.   "The Sower Publications, " PG. 2 (1901):
       89-93.

2804   Stapleton, Ammon.   "Research in the First Century of Ger-
       man Printing in America, 1728-1830, " PG. 5 (1904): 81-89,
       183; (1905): 262-63.

2805   Tanselle, G. Thomas.   Guide to the Study of U.S. Imprints.
       Cambridge: Belknap Press of Harvard University Press, 1971.

2806   Ward, Robert Elmer.   "Bibliographie deutsch-amerikanischer
       Originalwerke im Besitz der deutschen Gesellschaft von Penn-
       sylvania, " GAS. 1, i (1969): 33-48.

2807   Warrington, James.   "A Bibliography of Church Music Books
       Issued in Pennsylvania, With Annotations, " PG. 1 (1912):
       170-77.

2808   Wolf, Edward.   "Chronological List of Helmuth Imprints Con-
       taining Hymns, Anthem, and Cantata Texts, " GAS. 5 (1972):
       129-46.

2809   Wust, Klaus.   "English and German Printing Office: Bilingual
       Printers in Maryland and Virginia, " RJGAH. 32 (1966): 24-
       37.

2810   _____.   "German Printing in Virginia: A Check List, 1789-
       1834, " RJGAH. 28 (1953): 54-66.

German-American Printers

2811   Bolk Printing Co.   4219 W. North Ave., Milwaukee, Wiscon-
       sin 53208.

2812   Garden City Printing Co.   2100 West Roscoe St., Chicago,
       Ill.

2813   Gordonville Print Shop.   Gordonville, Pa. 17529.   Prints with
       German Gothic type.

2814   William B. Graf & Sons.   1631 Germantown Ave., Philadel-
       phia, Pa. 19122.

2815   Graphic Sales Co.   Irvington, New Jersey 07111.

2816   Krause Printing Co.   5746 N. Western Ave., Chicago, Ill.
       60659.

2817   William B. Schwab Printing.   289 Campbell St., Rochester,
       New York.

2818   Segall Printing Co.   651 Turk St., San Francisco, Cal.

2819   Wisconsin Cuneo Press, Inc.   5400 W. Good Hope Rd., Mil-
       waukee, Wisconsin.

German-American Book Stores and Sellers

2820   Adressbuch des ausländischen Buchhandels: Verzeichnis aus-
       ländischer Buchhändler, die deutsche Literatur führen.   Leip-
       zig: Bibliographie des deutschen Buchhandels, 1925.

2821   Baker, Hugh and C. Sanford.   "The Book Trade in California,
       1849-59," CHSQ.   30 (1951): 97-116.

2822   Brown, H. Glenn.   A Directory of the Book-Arts and Book
       Trade in Philadelphia to 1820.   New York: New York Public
       Library, 1950.

2823   Cazden, Robert E.   "Karl Christoph Reiche (1740-1790) and
       America," GAS.   5 (1972): 56-67.

2824   _____.   "The Provision of German Books in America Dur-
       ing the Eighteenth Century," Libri.   23 (1973): 81-108.

2825   _____.   "Retail Distributors of Free German Publications
       in the U. S. 1933-70," in German Exile Literature in Amer-
       ica 1933-50.   Chicago: ALA, 1970, pp. 175-77.

2826   Grothe, M. Justina.   German Catholic Publishing and Book
       Distribution Within the United States From 1865 to 1880.
       Catholic University: Dissertation, 1950.

2827   Hoffman, Edwin.   "The Bookshops of New York City 1743-
       1948," NYH.   30 (1949): 53-65.

2828   Kloss, Heinz.   "Auslanddeutsches Buch und reichsdeutscher
       Buchmarkt," BfddB.   (April 3, 1934).

2829   Lehmann-Haupt, Hellmut.   The Book in America: A History
       of the Making and Selling of Books in the United States.   New
       York: Bowker, 1951.

2830   Ludwig, Herman.   "Die Organe der erscheinenden Literatur:
       Der Buchhandel: Was hat eine gute deutsche Buchhandlung in
       den Vereinigten Staaten zu hoffen," Serapeum.   7 (1846): 177-
       90.

2831   Marx, Hilde.   "Albert A. Phiebig: Buchsucher und Buchfind-
       er," Aufbau.   (Sept. 7, 1973).

2832 Pabel, Reinhold. Enemies are Human. Philadelphia: Winston, 1955. About a Chicago bookseller.

2833 Steiger, Ernst. Mitteilungen über den Betrieb deutscher Bücher und Zeitschriften in den Vereinigten Staaten. New York: Steiger, 1868. UM

2834 Stern, Madeline. "Anton Roman, Argonaut of Books," CHSQ. 27 (1949): 1-19.

2835 Sutton, Walter. The Western Book Trade: Cincinnati as a Nineteenth Century Publishing and Book Trade Center; Containing a Directory of Cincinnati's Publishers, Booksellers, and Members of Allied Trades and a Bibliography. Columbus: Ohio State University Pr., 1961.

2836 Taubert, Sigfrid. "Zur Geschichte des deutschsprachigen Buchdrucks und Buchhandels im Ausland: Friedrich Leypoldt, New York," BfddB. (1955): 216-18. About a New York bookseller and publisher.

2837 Tolzmann, Don Heinrich. "Deutschamerikanische Buchhandlungen," DMH. (Dec. 6, 1973). About present day German-American book shops.

2838 Wust, Klaus. "Jacob D. Dietrich (1778-1838): Publisher and Bookseller in Four States," Eck. (June 15, 1957).

German-American Book Stores and Distributors

2839 Adler's Foreign Books. 162 Fifth Ave., New York, N. Y. 10010.

2840 Anhalt's Book Store and Bindery. 1710 W. Belmont Ave., Chicago, Ill. 60657.

2841 Aufbau Bücherdienst. 2121 Broadway, New York, N. Y. 10023.

2842 Franz Bader, Inc. 2124 Pennsylvania Ave. N. W., Washington, D. C. 20037.

2843 Brentano's. 1326 Fifth St. N. W., Washington, D. C.

2844 Der Buchwurm/Buchhandlung. Box 1403, Thousand Oaks, Cal. 91360.

2845 Cafe Heidelberg. 7627-27 Pendleton Pike, Indianapolis, Indiana 46226.

2846 D. A. N. K. -Buchdienst. 4740 N. Western Ave., Chicago, Ill. 60625.

2847   Deutsche Buchhandlung.   4762 Melrose Ave., Los Angeles,
        Cal. 90029.

2848   Erich Drucker, Books.   Box 66, New York, N.Y. 10024.

2849   Ernie's Continental Imports.   8400 8th Ave., Inglewood, Cal.
        90305.

2850   European Book Co.   925 Larkin St., San Francisco, Cal.

2851   European Imports.   8900 N. Waukegan Rd., Chicago, Ill.

2852   Gerard Fuchs.   2061 Broadway, New York, N.Y. 10023.

2853   German Gift and Variety Shop.   202 Valencia, San Francisco,
        Cal. 94116.

2854   German News Co., Inc.   218 E. 86 St., New York, N.Y.
        10028.

2855   German Specialties.   1581 Church St., San Francisco, Cal.

2856   W. S. Heinman, Imported Books.   200 W. 72 St., New York,
        N.Y. 10023.

2857   L. Heymann.   Box 6448, Carmel, Cal. 92921.

2858   Walter Hoops, Book Service-AR.   5437 Enright Ave., St.
        Louis, Missouri 63112.

2859   House of Tyrol Imports.   Box 180, Helen, Georgia 30545.

2860   Kereke Bros., Inc.   215 E. 86 St., New York, N.Y. 10028.

2861   Andrew S. Kinsinger.   Gordonville, Pa. 17529.   An Amish
        bookseller.

2862   Kroch's and Brentano's Inc.   29 Wabasha Ave., Chicago, Ill.
        60603.

2863   Kurt B. Merlander.   626 N. Valley St., Burbank, Cal. 91505

2864   Mission Book Store/Tabor-Gemeinde.   Roosevelt Blvd. &
        Mascher St., Philadelphia, Pa. 19120.

2865   Pathway Books.   R. 4, Box 266, La Grange, Indiana 46761.
        An Amish bookstore.

2866   A. J. Phiebig.   Box 352, White Plains, New York 10602.

2867   Räber's Bookstore.   Baltic, Ohio 43804.   An Amish shop.

2868   Herbert Reichner.   Stockbridge, Mass. 01262.

2869 Mary S. Rosenberg, Inc. 100 W. 72 St., New York, N.Y.
      10023.

2870 Anton K. Rumpfs Buchhandlung. 5923 Twin Lakes Dr., Cleve-
      land, Ohio 44129.

2871 Schiller's Books. Garden State Plaza, Paramus, New Jersey
      07652.

2872 Schnell's Book Service. 524 Mayfair St., Box 303, Vineland,
      New Jersey 08360.

2873 Schoenhof's Foreign Books, Inc. 1280 Massachusetts Ave.,
      Cambridge, Mass. 02138.

2874 Schroeder's Book and News Store. 212 E. Superior Ave.,
      Cleveland, Ohio 44114.

2875 F. A. O. Schwarz. 745 Fifth Ave., New York, N.Y. 10022.

2876 Specialized Book Service. 35 Audrey Ave., Oyster Bay, New
      York 11771. Deals with scientific material.

2877 Stechert-Hafner, Inc. 31 E. 10 St., New York, N.Y. 10003.

2878 Womrath Bookshop. 229 Fulton Ave., Hempstead, New York
      11550.

German-American Reading Interests and Habits

2879 Arnold, Arnim. Heine in England and America: A Biblio-
      graphical Checklist. London: Linden, 1959.

2880 Blankenagel, John. "Early Reception of Hauptmann's Die
      Weber in the United States," MLN. 68 (1953): 334-40.

2881 Born, Jürgen. Die Aufnahme und der Einfluss Franz Kafkas
      in Amerika. Freie Universität, Berlin: Dissertation, 1958.

2882 Burkhard, Arthur. Franz Grillparzer in England and Amer-
      ica. Vienna: Berland, 1961.

2883 Cappel, Edith. Gerhart Hauptmann in America. Columbia
      University: Dissertation, 1952.

2884 Dietel, Günther. Studien zur Aufnahme der deutschen Litera-
      tur in Amerika, 1919-39. University of Jena: Dissertation,
      1952.

2885 Frese, Hans. Das deutsche Buch in Amerika: Übersetzungen
      der Jahre 1918-35. Zeulenroda: Sporn, 1937.

2886   Frey, John. "America and Franz Werfel, " GQ. 19 (1946):
        121-28.

2887   Friedrich, Gerhard. "Abraham H. Cassel Invents an Anec-
        dote, " AGR. 9 (1942): 19-20, 39.

2888   Gerhard, Elmer Schultz. "Library of the Davenport Turnge-
        meinde, " AGR. 12, v (1946): 33-35, 37.

2889   "German Bible Subscribers in Western Maryland in 1819, "
        RJGAH. 35 (1972): 57-59.

2890   Germania Männerchor. Catalog der deutsch-amerikanischen
        Bibliothek. Chicago: Germania Männerchor, 1894. UC

2891   Guggisberg, Hans. "Jacob Burckhardt und Amerika, " JA.
        13 (1968): 53-68.

2892   Hatfield, Henry and J. Merrick. "Studies of German Litera-
        ture in the United States, 1939-46, " MLR. 43 (1948): 353-92.

2893   Hatfield, James. "Götz von Berlichingen in America, " GR.
        24 (1949): 177-83.

2894   Henkels, Stan. The Extraordinary Library of Hon. Samuel
        W. Pennypacker, Governor of Pennsylvania. Philadelphia,
        1905-09. The library of a Pennsylvania-German bibliomaniac.

2895   Heydt, Alfred von der. Friedrich Bodenstedt in Amerika und
        sein Buch Vom Atlantischen zum Stillen Ozean. Cornell:
        Dissertation, 1949.

2896   Hirsch, Mildred and D. Harris. "From the Library of
        Pastorius, " BFHA. 42 (1953): 76-84.

2897   Hofacker, Erich. German Literature as Reflected in the
        German-Language Press of St. Louis Prior to 1898. (Wash-
        ington University Studies.) St. Louis: Washington Univer-
        sity, 1946.

2897A   Johnson, Hildegard B. "The Carver County German Reading
        Room Society, " MHist. 24 (1943): 214-26.

2898   Jonas, Klaus. "Franz Kafka: An American Bibliography, "
        Bul. of Bibliogr. 20 (1953): 212-16, 231-33.

2899   _____ . "Hermann Hesse in Amerika: Bibliographie, " MC
        44 (1952): 95-99.

2900   Kahn, Robert. "Seume's Reception in England and America,
        MLR. 52 (1957): 65-71.

2901   Kopp, W. L. German Literature in the United States, 1945-

60. Chapel Hill: University of North Carolina Pr., 1967.

2902   Kornbluth, Martin. "The Reception of Wilhelm Meister in America," SY. 13 (1959): 128-34.

2903   Kraus, Joe. Book Collections of Five Colonial College Libraries: A Subject Analysis. University of Illinois: Dissertation, 1960.

2904   Kulp, Roy. "Abraham Harley Cassel: Dunkard Bibliophile," PFL. 11 (1960): 34-37.

2905   LaBelle, M. "H. L. Mencken's Comprehension of Friedrich Nietzsche," Comp. Lit. Studies. 7 (1970): 43-49.

2906   Montgomery, John. "The Colonial Parish Library of Wilhelm Christoph Berkenmeyer," PBSA. 53 (1959): 114-49.

2907   Pabst, Carl. "Books of the Schwarzenau Church," Gospel Messenger. 34 (1952): 12-13.

2908   Palmer, P. B. "The Library Movement in Reading, 1820-60," HRBC. 7 (1941-42): 70-74.

2909   [Pennypacker.] Rare Books and Manuscripts, Autographs, also Rare Paintings by Benjamin West, and Other Historical Portraits: The Collection of the Late Hon. Samuel W. Pennypacker. Philadelphia: Freman, 1920.

2910   Pick, R. and Ann Weaver. "Hugo von Hofmannsthal in England and America: A Bibliography," in Hoffmannsthal Studies in Commemoration. London: University of London, 1963, pp. 119-47.

2911   Quynn, W. R. "Jacob Engelbrecht: Collector of Autograph Letters (1797-1878)," MHM. 56 (1961): 399-408.

2912   Raunick, S. M. "A Survey of German Literature in Texas," SWHQ. 33 (1929): 134-59.

2913   Reichart, Walter. "Gerhart Hauptmann: His Work in America," AGR. 29, ii (1962): 4-6, 31.

2914   _____. "Hauptmann Study in America: A Continuation Bibliography," Monatshefte. 54 (1962): 296-310.

2915   _____. "Hauptmann's Dramas on the American Stage," Maske und Kothurn. 8 (1962): 223-32.

2916   _____. "Hebbel in Amerika und England: Eine Bibliographie," Hebbel Jahrbuch. (1961): 118-35.

2917   Robacker, Earl. "Books Not for Burning," PFL. 9 (1957-58): 44-52.

2918   Rosenberger, H. T.   Intimate Glimpses of the Pennsylvania
       Germans. Gettysburg, 1965. Contains information on H. S.
       Heilman, a Pennsylvania-German bibliophile.

2919   Sander, Volkmar. "Der deutsche Bildungsroman in Amerika, "
       DR. 87 (1961): 1032-1038.

2920   Schneider, Franz. "Stifter im Westen der Vereinigten Staa-
       ten, " Adalbert Stifter-Institut des Landes Oberösterreich.
       9 (1961): 43-45.

2921   Schroeder, Adolf. "Rainer Maria Rilke in America, A Bib-
       liography, 1926-51, " MO. 44 (1952): 27-38.

2922   Straubinger, O. "The Reception of Raimund and Newstroy in
       England and America, " Hietsch. (1961): 481-94.

2923   Tecklin, Jerry. The Literature of the St. Louis Hegelians.
       University of Wyoming: Dissertation, 1963.

2924   Thomas, J. W. "German Literature in the Old South, " AGR.
       19, ii (1952): 8-10, 33.

2925   Tolzmann, Don Heinrich. "The St. Louis Freie Gemeinde:
       A Nineteenth Century German-American Library, " MHR. (In
       Press).

2926   Waidson, H. M. "Jeremias Gotthelf's Reception in Britain
       and America, " MLR. 43 (1948): 223-38.

2927   Ward, Robert Elmer. "The German-American Library of
       H. H. Fick: A Rediscovery, " GAS. 1, i (1969): 49-68; 2,
       i (1970): 2-39.

2928   Weiss, Gerhard. Die Aufnahme Heinrich Heines in Gross-
       britannien und den Vereinigten Staaten von Amerika (1828 bis
       1856): Eine Studie zur Rezeption des Menschen und Prosa-
       künstlers. University of Mainz: Dissertation, 1955.

2929   Wust, Klaus. "The Books of the German Immigrants in the
       Shenandoah Valley, " Eck. (Jan. 26, 1957).

2930   _____. "Jung-Stilling and the American Backwoods, "
       RJGAH. 34 (1970): 35-39.

IV. RELIGIOUS LIFE

Bibliographical and Introductory Material

2931   Allison, William.   Inventory of Unpublished Material for American Religious History in Protestant Church Archives and other Depositories. Washington, D. C.: Carnegie Institution,
1910.

2932   American Church History Series, Consisting of Denomina-
tional Histories Published Under the Auspices of the American Society of Church History. New York: Christian Literature Co., 1893-1901.

2933   Anderson, H. G.   "The European Phase of John Ulrich Gies-
sendanner's Life," SCHM. 67 (1966): 129-37.   Life of a German-American minister.

2934   Barba, Preston.   "Letters of a Rural Pennsylvania German
Pastor," Eck. (Mar. 3, 1965).

2935   _____.   "The Old Dutch Church in Lower Merion," BHSM.
9 (1954): 185-243; 281-346.

2936   Barrick, M.   "Folk-Beliefs of a Pennsylvania Preacher,"
KRQ. 10)1965): 191-93.

2937   _____.   "Pulpit Humor in Central Pennsylvania," PFL. 19
(1969): 28-36.

2938   Betterton, William.   "Early Church Groups," Palimpsest. 40
(1964): 283-92.

2939   Brendle, Thomas.   "Moses Dissinger, Evengelist and Patriot,"
PGS. 63 (1959): 91-192.

2940   Bridenbaugh, Carl.   Mitre and Sceptre: Transatlantic Faiths,
Idea, Personalities and Politics, 1689-1775.   New York: Oxford, 1962.

2941   Burr, Nelson Rollin.   A Critical Bibliography of Religion in
America.   (Princeton Studies in America, 5.)   Princeton:
Princeton University Pr., 1961.

2942   Deck, Elmer. "The North Heidelberg Church, " HRBC. 34
        (1969): 85, 101-04.

2943   Dilorio, Bob. "The Christmas Tree Church, " Herald Travel-
        er. (Dec. 20, 1970). About Karl Follen's church.

2944   Dodd, Gladys. "The Early Career of Abraham L. Eisenhower,
        Pioneer Preacher, " KHQ. 29 (1963): 233-49.

2945   Doll, Eugene. "Social and Economic Organization in two
        Pennsylvania German Religious Communities, " American J.
        Soc. 57 (1951): 168-77.

2946   Dunlap, Raymond. Churches of Today and Yesterday in South-
        ern Lancaster County. n. p. ; Fellowship of Solanco Churches,
        1968.

2947   Eisenach, Georg. Das religiöse Leben unter den Russland-
        deutschen in Russland und Amerika. Marburg: Spener, 1950.

2948   Fecher, V. J. A Study of the Movement for German National
        Parishes in Philadelphia and Baltimore, 1782-1802. (Analecta
        Gregoriana, 77.) Rome: Gregorian University, 1955.

2949   Fothergill, G. List of Emigrant Ministers to America, 1690-
        1891. New York: Public Library, 1904.

2950   Frank, Sam. "Samuel E. Hager: Kentucky Missionary to
        Japan, " KHSR. 58 (1960): 194.

2951   Frantz, John. "John C. Guildin: Pennsylvania-German Re-
        vivalist, " PMHB. 87 (1963): 123-38.

2952   Gilbert, Russell. "An All Pennsylvania-German Church Ser-
        vice, " AGR. 22, vi (1956): 15.

2953   Gleis, Paul. History of the Prospect Hill Cemetery Society
        of Washington, D. C. 1858-1950. Washington, D. C. : Winkler,
        1950.

2954   Haas, Oscar. The First Protestant Church: Its History and
        Its People. New Braunfels: New Braunfels Zeitung, 1955.

2955   Kauffman, Floyd. History of Fairview and Spring Valley Con-
        gregations in North Dakota. Minot: Author, 1953.

2956   Kelpius, Johannes. A Method of Prayer. New York: Harper
        1951.

2957   Klein, Martha. "The First German Church in New Orleans
        Celebrates 125th Birthday, " AGR. 17, vi (1951): 29-30.

2958   Kloss, Heinz. "Die Kirchendeutschen in den Vereinigten

Staaten, " Neue Zeit. (Oct. 13, 1931): 8-10.

2959 _____. "Zur Entwicklung des Protestantismus im Überseedeutschtum, " Mitt. d. Akad. z. wiss. Erforsch. u. Pflege
d. D. 6 (1930): 30-37.

2960 Kuhns, Frederick. "Religion on the Iowa Frontier, " IJHP.
51 (1953): 37-56.

2961 Lenhart, John. "Statistics of Pastoral Functions of the German-speaking Congregations of Wheeling W. Va., " SJR. 50
(1957): 61-63.

2962 McLoughlin, William. Billy Sunday was his Real Name. Chicago: University of Chicago Pr., 1955. Story of Billy Sonn-
tag.

2963 Malone, Henry. "The Early Nineteenth Century Missionaries
in the Cherokee Country, " THQ. 10 (1951): 127-39.

2964 Mayer, Frederick. The Religious Bodies of America. St.
Louis: Concordia Publishing House, 1956.

2965 Milhouse, Paul. Philip William Otterbein: Pioneer Pastor
to Germans in America. Nashville: Upper Room, 1968.

2966 Mode, Peter. Source Book and Bibliographical Guide for
American Church History. Menasha, Wis.: Collegiate Pr.,
1921.

2967 Müller, Wilhelm. Das religiöse Leben in Amerika. Jena,
1911.

2968 National Council of Churches of Christ in the U.S.A. Bureau
of Research and Survey. Churches and Church Membership in
the U.S.: An Enumeration and Analysis by Counties, States
and Regions. New York: The Council, 1956-58.

2969 Oberholtzer, Frank. "Die Schietze Kaerrich, " Eck. (Apr.
26, 1957).

2970 Petter, Rodolphe. "How I Became a Missionary, " ML. 10
(1955): 4-13.

2971 Quattlerbaum, Paul. "Some German Protestants in South
Carolina in 1794, " SCHGM. 51 (1950): 75-77.

2972 Rohr-Sauer, Philip von. "Elfrieda von Rohr-Sauer, Pioneer
Pastor's Daughter and Minister's Wife, " CHIQ. 33 (1960):
33-54.

2973 Runge, John. "Seedtime and Harvest-Pages from the Life of
a Pioneer Pastor, " CHIQ. 26 (1955): 145-55.

2974 Schaff, Philip. America: A Sketch of its Political, Social and Religious Character. Cambridge: Harvard University Pr., 1961.

2975 Schmid, F. Schmid Letters: A Translation of Letters Written Between the Years 1833 and 1879 by F. Schmid, Pioneer German Missionary from Ann Arbor, Michigan to His Seminary in Basel, Switzerland. St. Louis: E. E. Hutzel, 1953.

2976 Shoemaker, Alfred. "Andreas Bernhardus Smolnikar, God's Ambassador Extraordinary," PD. 3 (1952): 1-2.

2977 Smith, James and L. Jamison. Religion in American Life. Princeton: Princeton University Pr., 1961.

2978 Strauss, Felix. "A Brief Survey of Protestantism in Archiepiscopal Salzburg and the Emigration of 1732," GHQ. 43 (1959): 29-59.

2979 Streit, Robert and Johannes Dindinger. Bibliotheca Missionum. Rome: Herder, 1967.

2980 Sweet, William. Religion on the American Frontier: A Collection of Source Material. Chicago: University of Chicago Pr., 1931-46.

2981 Torrence, R. M. "The Rev. Philip Otterbein and Susan Leroy Otterbein," MdHM. 47 (1952): 264-66.

2982 Treher, Charles. "Snow Hill Cloister," PGS. 2 (1968).

2983 Tweedie, Stephen. The Geography of Religious Groups in Ohio Pennsylvania, and Upstate New York: Persistence and Change. Syracuse: Dissertation, 1969.

2984 Voigt, Gilbert. "Religious Conditions among German-speaking Settlers in South Carolina, 1732-74," SCHGM. 56 (1955): 59-66.

2985 Vollmar, E. R. "Writings in Church History for 1956," M. 1 (1957): 81-88. An annual bibliography.

2986 Weidhaas, Walther. "German Religious Influences on American Place Names," AGR. 23, vi (1957): 33-34.

2987 Weis, Frederick. The Colonial Clergy of Maryland, Delaware and Georgia. Lancaster, Mass., 1950.

2988 _____. "The Colonial Clergy of the Middle Colonies: New York, New Jersey and Pennsylvania, 1628-1776," AAS. 66 (1957): 167-351.

2989 Winters, R. L. "John Caspar Stoever, Colonial Pastor," PGSP. 53 (1948): 1-171.

2990   Witschey, Warren. "A Brief Biography of the Rev. John W.
Reger, D.D.," WVaH. 30 (1969): 548-58.

2991   Wust, Klaus. "German Mystics and Sabbatarians in Virginia,
1700-64," VMHB. 72 (1964): 330-47.

2992   _____. "John Peter Ahl (1748-1827), Ministerial Tramp
and Medical Pioneer in Seven States," Eck. (Oct. 31, 1964).

2993   Yearbook of American Churches. New York: National Council of Churches in the U.S.A., 1916- .

2994   Zelinsky, Wilbur. "An Approach to the Religious Geography
of the U.S.," Annals of Amer. Geographers. 51 (1961): 139-
93.

The Hutterites

2995   Allard, Albert. "The Hutterites, Plain People of the West,"
NGM. 138 (1970): 98-125.

2996   Cobb, Douglas. "The Jamesville Bruderhof: A Hutterian
Agriculture Colony," J. of the West. 9 (1970): 60-77.

2997   Conkin, Paul. Two Paths to Utopia: The Hutterites and the
Llano Colony. Lincoln: University of Nebraska Pr., 1964.

2998   Eaton, Joseph and Robert Weil. Culture and Mental Disorders,
A Comparative Study of the Hutterites and Other Populations.
Glencoe, Ill.: Free Pr., 1955.

2999   _____ and others. "The Hutterite Mental Health Study,"
MQR. 25 (1951): 47-59.

3000   Friedmann, Robert. "Bibliography of Works in the English
Language Dealing with the Hutterite Communities," MQR. 32
(1958): 237-38.

3001   _____. "A Comprehensive Review of Research on the Hutterites, 1880-1950," MQR. 24 (1950): 353-63.

3002   _____. "A Hutterite Census for 1969: Hutterite Growth in
One Century, 1874-1969," MQR. 44 (January, 1970).

3003   Goerz, H. "A Day with the Hutterites," ML. 8 (1953): 14-
16.

3004   Gross, Paul. The Hutterite Way. Saskatoon, Canada: Freeman, 1965.

3005   Peters, Victor. All Things Common: The Hutterian Way of

Life. Minneapolis: University of Minnesota Pr., 1966.

3006   Peterson, Hans. "Hilldale: A Montana Hutterite Colony in
       Transition," Rocky Mt. SSJ. 7 (Spring, 1970).

3007   Sawka, Patricia. "The Hutterian Way of Life," Can. Geogr.
       J. 77 (1968): 127-31.

3008   Schludermann, S. "Developmental Study of Social Role Per-
       ception Among Hutterite Adolescents," J. of Psych. 77 (1969):
       267-73.

3009   _____. "Social Role Perception of Children in Hutterite
       Communal Society," J. of Psych. 77 (1969): 183-88.

3010   Waltner, Gary. "Zu Besuch auf einem hutterischen Bruder-
       hof in Süddakota," Menn. Gemeinde-Kalender. (1969): 42-51.

3011   Zieglschmid, A. Die älteste Chronik der hutterischen Brü-
       der: Ein Sprachdenkmal aus früh neuhochdeutscher Zeit.
       Philadelphia: Carl Schurz Memorial Foundation, 1943.

3012   _____. "The Hutterian Chronicle," AGR. 8 (1942): 18-25.

3013   _____. "The Hutterians on the American Continent," AGR.
       8, iii (1942): 20-24.

3014   _____. Das klein-Geschichtsbuch der Hutterischen Brüder.
       Philadelphia: Carl Schurz Memorial Foundation, 1947.

3015   _____. "A Song of the Persecution of the Hutterites in
       Velke Valley," MQR. 17 (1943): 151-64.

The Amish

3016   Bachman, Calvin. The Old Order Amish of Lancaster County.
       Lancaster: Pennsylvania German Society, 1960.

3017   Barclay, Harold. "Plain and Peculiar People," Alberta An-
       thropologist. 1 (1967).

3018   _____. "The Plain People of Oregon," Rev. of Relig. Res.
       8 (1968): 140-65.

3019   Beachy, Alvin. "The Amish Settlement in Somerset County,
       Pennsylvania," MQR. 28 (1954): 263-92.

3020   _____. "The Rise and Development of the Beachy Mennon-
       ite Churches," MQR. 29 (1955): 118-40.

3021   Beiler, Joseph. Amish Farm and Home Directory of Lancaster and Lebanon Districts. Gordonville, Pa.: Kinsinger, 1966.

3022 Bender, Harold. "Documents Relating to Bishop Jacob Schwarzendruber (1800-68)," MQR. 20 (1946): 222-29.

3023 Borntreger, Hans. Eine Geschichte der ersten Ansiedlung der Amischen Mennoniten und die Gründung ihrer ersten Gemeinde im Staate Indiana, nebst einer kurzen Erklärung über die Spaltung, die in dieser Gemeinde geschehen ist. Shipshewana, Ind.: Reuben S. Borntreger, 1952.

3024 Buchwalter, Grace. "Modern Amana," AGR. 19, v (1953): 16-18.

3025 Carman, John. "Amish Bring New, Quieter Ways to Wadena, Minnesota," Mpls. Star. (Sept. 4, 1973).

3026 Christner, L. The Atlas of the Old Order Amish Church Districts of Indiana. Topeka, Indiana: Author, 1949.

3027 Clark, Allen. History of the Amish of Delaware. Dover, Del.: Author, 1964.

3028 _____. The Lord is my Shepherd: The Amish of Delaware. Dover, Del.: Author, 1963.

3029 "Communal Colony Changes," AI. 34 (1958): 227-28.

3030 Conners, Mary. "The Hook and the Eye People of Northern New York," NYFQ. 17 (1961): 63-69.

3031 Corrie, Walter. Work as a Central Life Interest: A Comparison of the Amana Colony Worker with the Non-Amana Colony Worker in a Given Industry. State Univ. of Iowa: Dissertation, 1958.

3032 Cunz, Dieter. "God's Plain People in Maryland," AGR. 14, iv (1948): 12-16.

3033 _____. "The Plain People Have Green Thumbs," Wash. Post. (Dec. 1, 1946).

3034 Denlinger, Donald. The Gentle People: A Portrait of the Amish. New York: Grossman, 1969.

3035 Dickel, Martin. "Communal Life in Amana," IJH. 59 (1961): 83-89.

3036 Freed, S. A. "Suggested Type Societies," Amer. Anthropologist. 59 (1957): 55-68.

3037 Gehmann, Richard. "Plainest of Pennsylvania's Plain People:

The Amish Folk, " NGM. 128 (1965): 226-53.

3038   Getz, Jane. "The Economic Organization and Practices of
       the Old Order Amish of Lancaster County, Pennsylvania, "
       MQR. 20 (1946): 53-80, 98-127.

3039   Gingerich, Ervin. Ohio Amish Directory: Holmes County
       and Vicinity. Millersburg, Ohio: Author, 1966.

3040   Hayes, Abner. The Old Order Amish Mennonites of Pennsyl-
       vania: Survival of Religious Fundamentalism in a New World
       Environment. Lewistown, Pa.: Mifflin County Historical
       Society, 1947.

3041   Heller, Harry. "The Sleeping Preachers: An Historical
       Study of the Role of Charisma in Amish Society, " PFL. 18
       (1969): 19-31.

3042   Horst, Mel and Elmer Smith. Among the Amish in Pennsyl-
       vania Dutchland. Akron, Pa.: Applied Arts Associates, 1959.

3043   Hostetler, John. "The Amish, Citizens of Heaven and Amer-
       ica, " PFL. 10 (1959): 32-37.

3044   . "Amish Family Life, A Sociologist's Analysis, "
       PFL. 12 (1961): 28-39.

3045   . "The Amish in America, " Amer. Heritage. 3, iv
       (1953): 4-8.

3046   . The Amish Life. Scottdale, Pa.: Mennonite Pub-
       lishing House, 1952.

3047   . "Amish Problems at Diener-Versammlungen, "
       ML. 4 (1949): 34-38.

3048   . Amish Society. Baltimore, 1963.

3049   . Annotated Bibliography on the Amish. Scottdale,
       Pa.: Mennonite Publishing House, 1951.

3050   . Children in Amish Society. New York: Holt,
       Rinehart and Winston, 1971.

3051   . "Old World Extinction and New World Survival of
       the Amish: A Study of Group Maintenance, " Rural Soc. 20
       (1955): 212-19.

3052   Kepler, Luther and Anne Fisher. "The Nebraska Old Order
       Amish, " ML. 16 (1961): 122-27.

3053   Landing, James. "The Amish and Mennonite Settlement at
       Nappanee, Indiana, " Family Life. 2 (1969): 38 ff.

3054 _____. "Geographic Models of Old Order Amish Settlements, " Prof. Georg. 21 (1969): 238-43.

3055 _____. The Spatial Development and Organization of an Old Amish-Beachy Amish Settlement: Nappanee, Indiana. Pennsylvania State: Dissertation, 1967.

3056 Longsdorf, Kenneth. "A Patchwork of Novels About the Plain People, " PD. (May 15, 1951).

3057 McKnight, Ruth. "The Quaint and the Devout: A Study of the Amish at Vilonia, Arkansas, " AHQ. 23 (1964): 314-28.

3058 Messerschmidt, H. Edgar. "Working with the Amish, " AGR. 12, vi (1946): 22-24.

3058A Miller, D. "The Amish in Kansas, " ML. 6 (1951): 20-23.

3059 "Minutes of the Amish Conference of 1809, " MQR. 20 (1946): iii.

3060 Moershel, Henry. "Historical Background of Amana, " IJH. 59 (1961): 78-82.

3061 Mook, Maurice. "The Amish Communities at Atlantic, Pennsylvania, " MQR. 28 (1954): 293-301.

3062 _____. "A Brief History of Former, Now Extinct Amish Communities in Pennsylvania, " WPHM. 38 (1955): 33-46.

3063 _____. "Crawford County Number Two: A Now Extinct Old Order Amish Community of the 1930's, " WPHM. 37 (1954): 33-46.

3064 _____. "Defense of the Dutch: The Amish Dutch, " Eck. (May 15, 1954).

3065 _____. "An Early Amish Colony in Chester County, " Eck. (Feb. 26, Mar. 5, 1955).

3066 _____. "Extinct Amish Mennonite Communities in Pennsylvania, " MQR. 30 (1956): 267-76.

3067 _____. "Joseph Johns: German Amish City Father, " Eck. (Apr. 16, 23, 1955).

3068 _____. "The Number of Amish in Pennsylvania, " Eck. (June 26, 1954).

3069 _____. "The Nebraska Amish of Pennsylvania, " ML. 17 (1962): 27-30.

3070 _____. "Pennsylvania Amish Communities that Failed, " Eck. (Aug. 21, 1954).

3071 _____ and John Hostettler. "The Amish and their Land,"
Landscape. 6 (1957): 21-29.

3072 Morton, John. "All Amish Lost a Little Ground in the Decision," National Observer. 6, iii (1967).

3073 Mullen, Patricia. The Plain People. Bethpage, Long Island:
C. M. Johnson, 1958.

3074 Newswanger, K. Amishland. New York: Hastings House,
1954.

3075 Rice, Charles and J. Shenk. Meet the Amish. New Brunswick: Rutgers University Pr., 1947.

3076 _____ and R. Steinmetz. The Amish Year. New Brunswick: Rutgers University Pr., 1956.

3077 Royer, Mary. "The Amish and Mennonite Theme in American Literature for Children," MQR. 19 (1946): 285-91.

3078 Schlabach, John. Begebenheiten in der Amischen Gemeinde
1850 bis 1898. Middlesburg, Ohio, 1963.

3079 Schreiber, William. "The Amish in The New Land," Midway.
12 (1962): 108-26.

3080 _____. "The Amish Sugarcreek Budget," Eck. (Jan. 5,
12, 1957).

3081 _____. "A Day with the Amish," AGR. 12, iii (1946): 12-
13.

3082 _____. "Hymns of the Amish Ausbund in Philological and
Literary Perspective," MQR. 36 (1962): 36-60.

3083 _____. Our Amish Neighbors. Chicago: University of
Chicago Pr., 1962.

3084 _____. "Volksreligisität und Lebenseinstellung der Amish-
Mennoniten," Sociologus. 19 (1969): 78-87.

3085 Schwartzberg, Joseph. A Geographical Analysis of Old Order
Amish and Stauffer Mennonite Communities in Southern Maryland. University of Maryland: Dissertation, 1951.

3086 Shambaugh, Bertha. "Amana That Was and Amana That Is,"
Palimpsest. 44 (1963): 89-124.

3087 Smith, Elmer. The Amish People: Seventeenth Century Trad
tion in Modern America. New York: Exposition Pr., 1958.

3088 _____. "The Amish Population in Southeastern Pennsylvania," Eck. (Aug. 22, 1959).

3089 _____. "The Amish Today, " PGFS. 24 (1960).

3090 Stoll, Joseph. The Amish-Mennonites in Davies County, Indiana. Aylmer, Canada: Author, 1959.

3091 Stoltzfus, Grant. "Amish Backgrounds in Berks County, " HRBC. 16 (1951): 38-42.

3092 _____. History of the First Amish Communities in America. Harrisburg, Va.: Eastern Mennonite College, 1958.

3093 _____. "History of the First Amish Mennonite Communities in America, " MQR. 28 (1954): 235-62.

3094 Stroup, Martin. The Amish of the Kishacoquilias Valley. Lewistown: Mifflin Co. Hist. Soc., 1967.

3095 Tice, George. The Amish Portfolio. Colonia, New Jersey: Author, 1968. Limited edition of twelve photographic prints.

3096 Tortora, Vincent. "The Amish at Play, " PD. 8 (1957): 14-34.

3097 _____. The Amish Folk of the Pennsylvania Dutch Country. Lancaster: Photo Arts Pr., 1958.

3098 Umble, John. "The Grove-Pleasant Hill Amish Mennonite Church in Wayne County, Ohio, in the Nineteenth Century, 1815-1900, " MQR. 31 (1957): 156-219.

3099 Yambura, Barbara. A Change and a Parting: My Story of Amana. Ames: Iowa State University, 1960.

3100 Yoder, Don. "What to Read on the Amish, " PFL. 18 (1969): 14-19.

3101 Yoder, Sanford. "The Amish in Wright County, " Palimpsest. 43 (1962): 401-32.

3102 _____. "My Amish Boyhood, " Palimpsest. 39 (1958): 109-44. Author born in Sharon Center, Iowa in 1870's.

The Mennonites

3103 Augsburger, Myron. Pilgrim Aflame. Scottdale: Herald, 1967.

3104 Baehr, Karl. "Secularization Among the Mennonites of Elkhart County, Indiana, " MQR. 16 (1942): 131-60.

3105 Bailes, Kendall. "The Mennonites Come to Kansas, " AH. 10 (1959): 30-33, 102-05.

3106   Bainton, Roland. "Harold S. Bender," CH. 31 (1963): 476.

3107   Bender, Elizabeth. "The Letters of Ludwig Keller to John
        Horsch," MQR. 21 (1947): 175-204.

3108   Bender, Harold. "The Elkhart County, Indiana Mennonites,"
        ML. 14 (1959): 71.

3109   _____. "The First Mennonite Minister in America," ML.
        13 (1958): 174-77.

3110   _____. "John Horsch, 1867-1941: A Bibliography," MQR.
        21 (1947): 131-44.

3111   _____. "Menno Simons and the North American Mennon-
        ites of Swiss-South German Background," MQR. 34 (1961):
        317-18.

3112   _____. The Mennonite Encyclopedia: A Comprehensive
        Reference Work on the Anabaptist-Mennonite Movement.
        Scottdale, Pa.: Mennonite Publishing House, 1955-59.

3113   _____. "Mennonite Inter-Group Relations," MQR. 32 (1958
        48-58.

3114   _____. "A Tribute to Robert Friedmann," MQR. 35 (1961)
        242-47. Bibliography of his work included.

3115   Boese, J. A. The Prussian-Polish Mennonites Settling in
        South Dakota. Freeman: Pine Hill Pr., 1967.

3116   _____. "The Story of the Mennonites at Avon, South Dako-
        ta," ML. 15 (1960): 39-45.

3117   Brackhill, Martin. "A Communication on the Origins of the
        Early Eighteenth Century Pennsylvania Mennonite Immigrants,'
        MQR. 27 (1953): 78-82.

3118   Braun, Fritz. "Auswanderer aus der Mennonitengemeinde
        Friedelsheim im 19. Jahrhundert," Mitt. z. Wanderungsges.
        d. Pfälzer. (1956): Folge 1-2.

3119   _____. "Nineteenth Century Emigrants from the Mennon-
        ite Congregation of Friedelsheim in the Palatinate," MQR.
        30 (1956): 133-54.

3120   Brunk, Harry. History of the Mennonites in Virginia. Har-
        risonburg, Va.: Author, 1959.

3121   Buller, Chris. "Fifty Years in Dawson County, Montana,"
        ML. 9 (1954): 110-117, 143.

3122   Classen, Daniel. "Meade, A Changed Community," ML. 6
        (1951): 14-17, 19.

3123   Correll, Ernst. "The Congressional Debates on the Mennon-
        ite Immigration from Russia 1873-74, " MQR. 20 (1946): 178-
        221.

3124   _____. "Notes on John Horsch as a Historian, " MQR. 21
        (1947): 145-50.

3125   Crockford, Hamilton. "Mennonites of Peninsula are Living
        in Smiling Land of Plenty, " Richmond Times Dispatch. (Nov.
        26, 1950). On Mennonites in Virginia.

3126   Dalke, Diedrich. "Mennonite Pioneers at Emid, " ML. 11
        (1965): 165-71.

3127   Dean, William. John F. Funk and the Mennonite Awakening.
        State University of Iowa: Dissertation, 1965.

3128   Dehnert, Celest. "Peter R. Schroeder, Pastor and Confer-
        ence Worker, " ML. 4 (1949): 38-41.

3129   Doremus, James. A Study of the Mennonites. Colgate Uni-
        versity: Dissertation, 1961.

3130   Dyck, Cornelius. An Introduction to Mennonite History.
        Scottdale, Pa.: Herald, 1967.

3131   "An 1875 Mennonite Evaluation of Kansas, " MQR. 4 (1954):
        307-09.

3132   Entz, J. "First Mennonite Church, Newton, 1878-1953, " ML.
        9 (1953): 153-58, 173.

3133   Epochs of History of First Mennonite Church of Pretty Prai-
        rie, Kansas, 1884 to 1954. Pretty Prairie, Kansas: Private
        Pr., 1955.

3134   Erb, Paul. Orie O. Miller: The Story of a Man and an Era.
        Scottdale, Pa.: Herald, 1969.

3135   Fretz, Herbert. The History of the Deep Run Mennonite Con-
        gregation of Bucks County, Pa. Bedminster, Pa.: Author,
        1949.

3136   Fretz, J. W. "The Apostolic Christian Church, " ML. 6
        (1951): 19-20.

3137   _____. "The Colfax Washington Community, " ML. 9 (1954):
        140-42.

3138   _____. "First Mennonites in Chicago, " ML. 8 (1953): 56-
        57.

3139   _____. "The Mennonite Community at Meade, " ML. 6
        (1951): 8-13.

3140   _____. "Planning a Christian Community, " ML. 6 (1951):
         34-35.

3141   _____. "A Western Kansas Mennonite Settlement, " ML.
         8 (1953): 174-77.

3142   Friedmann, Robert. "A. J. F. Zieglschmid, An Obituary, "
         MQR. 24 (1950): 364-65.

3143   _____. "John Horsch und Ludwig Keller, " MQR. 21 (1947):
         160-74.

3144   _____. Mennonite Piety Through the Centuries: Its Genius
         and Its Literature. Goshen, Indiana: Mennonite Historical
         Society, 1949.

3145   Friesen, Jacob. T. "A Rural Church: Beatrice, Nebraska, "
         ML. 8 (1953): 80-81.

3146   Funk, Ray. "Bruderthal, Seventy-Five Years Ago, " ML. 4
         (1949): 4-6.

3147   Gaeddert, Joyce. "From Danzig to Elbing, " ML. 25 (1970):
         62-64.

3148   Gingerich, Melvin. "The First Mennonite Settlement in Iowa, "
         MQR. 42 (1968): 193-202.

3149   _____. "A Guide to Maps in Mennonite Books and Peri-
         odicals, " MQR. 27 (1953): 345-48.

3150   _____. "An Iowa Mennonite Church Constitution of 1865, "
         MQR. 28 (1954): 224-27.

3151   _____. "John Carl Krehbiel, A Mennonite Pioneer in
         Iowa, " ML. 15 (1960): 57-59.

3152   _____. Mennonite Attire through Four Centuries. Breinigs
         ville, Pa.: Pennsylvania German Society, 1970.

3153   _____. "Mennonite Indentured Servants, " ML. 16 (1961):
         107-09, 128.

3154   _____. "The Mennonites in Iowa, " Palimpsest. 40 (1959):
         161-224.

3155   _____. "Mennonites in Lee and Davis Counties, Iowa, "
         ML. 15 (1960): 51-52.

3156   _____. "Russian Mennonites React to their New Environ-
         ments, " ML. 15 (1960): 175-80.

3157   _____. "Sebastian Irig: His Life and Times, " MQR. 35
         (1961): 297-308.

3158   Goering, John. "First Mennonite Church, McPherson," ML.
        12 (1958): 67-70.

3159   Graber, John. Fifty Years of the Salem Mennonite Church in
        Freeman, South Dakota. Freeman: Pine Hill Pub., 1958.

3160   Gracy, David. Littlefield Lands. Austin: University of
        Texas Pr., 1968.

3161   _____. "Mennonites at Littlefield: An Instance in the
        Colonization of the Texas Plains," MQR. 42 (1968): 184-92.

3162   Graeber, Arthur. "The Swiss Mennonites, Pretty Prairie,"
        ML. 5 (1950): 30-34.

3163   Graeff, Arthur. "Very Near the Truth," Penn. Traveler. 1
        (1958): 38-39, 66-69.

3164   Gratz, Delbert. "The Background of the Nineteenth Century
        Swiss Mennonite Immigrants," ML. 11 (1956): 61-64.

3165   _____. "Some Periodical Articles Concerning Anabaptists
        and Mennonite Periodicals," MQR. 28 (1954): 61-67.

3166   _____. "The Swiss Mennonites of Allen and Putnam Coun-
        ties," NOQ. 28 (1957): 126-36.

3167   Grunau, P. "North Enid Mennonite Church," ML. 9 (1954):
        176-77.

3168   Harder, Leland. "First Mennonite Church," ML. 8 (1953):
        58-59. A Chicago church.

3169   Harms, E. "John H. Harms, Pioneer Mennonite Doctor,"
        ML. 4 (1949): 13-15.

3170   Harms, Orlands and others. "The Mennonites of Wichita,"
        ML. 8 (1953): 4-13.

3171   Hartzler, Levi. "Bethel Mennonite Church," ML. 8 (1953):
        60-61.

3172   Hege, Christian and Christian Neff. Mennonitisches Lexikon.
        Frankfurt, 1913.

3173   Hershberger, Guy. "Harold S. Bender and his Time," MQR.
        38 (1964): 83-112.

3174   _____. "John Horsch: A Prophet of Biblical Non-Resist-
        ance," MQR. 21 (1947): 156-59.

3175   _____. "A Newly Discovered Pennsylvania Mennonite Peti-
        tion of 1755," MQR. 33 (1959): 143-51.

3176 _____. Recovery of the Anabaptist Vision: A Sixtieth
     Anniversary Tribute to Harold S. Bender. Scottdale, Pa.:
     Mennonite Publishing House, 1957.

3177 Hillsboro Johannestal Mennonite Church: Sixtieth Anniversary
     of the Johannesthal Church. Hillsboro, Kansas, n. d. Covers
     1882-1942.

3178 Hollenbach, Raymond. "Salford Mennonite Meeting House, "
     Eck. (Apr. 30, 1966).

3179 Hostetler, John. Mennonite Life. Scottdale, Pa.: Herald,
     1954.

3180 _____. "Religious Mobility in a Sect Group: The Men-
     nonite Church, " Rural Soc. 19 (1954): 244-55.

3181 _____. The Sociology of Mennonite Evangelism. Scott-
     dale, Pa.: Herald, 1954.

3182 In Commemoration of Seventy-Five Years in America. White-
     water, Kansas: Emmaus Mennonite Church, 1952.

3183 Kauffman, J. H. A Comparative Study of Traditional and
     Emergent Family Types Among Midwest Mennonites. Univer-
     sity of Chicago: Dissertation, 1960.

3184 Kaufman, Edmund. "Mennonite Missions among the Oklahoma
     Indians, " COO. 40 (1962): 41-54.

3185 Krahn, Cornelius. From the Steppes to the Prairies. Mor-
     ton, Kansas: Mennonite Publications Office, 1949.

3186 _____. "Mennonite Research in Progress, 1969, " ML. 25
     (1970): 90-92.

3187 _____. Mennonitisches Jahrbuch 1951. Newton, Kansas:
     Mennonite Publications Office, 1951.

3188 _____. "Die Verstädterung der Mennoniten, " M. Gesch-
     ichtsblätter. 26 (1969): 5-11.

3189 Kraus, C. Norman. "American Mennonites and the Bible,
     1750-1950, " MQR. 41 (1967): 309-29.

3190 Krehbiel, John. "Early Years at West Point, Iowa, " ML.
     15 (1960): 53-56.

3191 Kreider, Rachel. "One Hundred Years in Wadsworth, " ML.
     8 (1953): 161-66. An Ohio church.

3192 Landing, James. "Exploring Mennonite Settlements in Vir-
     ginia, " Va. Georgr. 4 (1969): 6-12.

3193 Landis, Ira. "Hans Herr: A Myth, " MRJ. 11 (1970): 25, 32.

3194 _____. "Mennonite Agriculture in Colonial Lancaster County, Pa., " ECK. (Aug. 24, 31, Sept. 7, 14, 1946).

3195 [No entry.]

3196 _____. "The Reply of the Lancaster Conference to the John H. Oberholtzer Constitution of 1847, " MQR. 29 (1955): 74-76.

3197 Lehman, James. Sonnenburg: A Haven and A Heritage. Kidron, Ohio: Kidron Community Council, 1969.

3198 Lohrentz, J. H. "Daniel F. Berghold 1876-1948, " ML. 6 (1951): 3, 44.

3199 Martin, Ernest. The Midway Story: The Life of a Congregation as Reflected in the History of a Building. Columbiana, Ohio: Midway Mennonite Church, 1969.

3200 Mennonite Life. "Index: 1946-55, Ten Years of Mennonite Life, " ML. 11 (1956): 33-48.

3201 Neufeld, I. "Jacob Stucky, Pioneer of Two Continents, " ML. 4 (1949): 46-47.

3202 Neufeld, Peter. "Inman Bethel Mennonite Church, " ML. 8 (1953): 132-35.

3203 Neufeld, Vernon. "Mennonites Settle in Lee County, Iowa, " ML. 8 (1953): 170-73.

3204 Pannabecker, S. "The Anabaptist Conception of the Church in the American Mennonite Environment, " MQR. 25 (1951): 34-36.

3205 _____. Faith in Ferment: A History of the Central District Conference. Newton, Kansas: Faith and Life Pr., 1968.

3206 _____. "Mennonite Seminar in Chicago, " ML. 8 (1953): 68-71, 88.

3207 _____. "The Nineteenth Century Swiss Mennonite Immigrants and their Adherence to the General Conference Mennonite Church, " MQR. 21 (1946): 64-102.

3208 Penner, Horst. Weltweite Bruderschaft. Karlsruhe: Schneider, 1955.

3209 _____. "West Prussian Mennonites through Four Centuries, " MQR. 23 (1949): 232-45.

3210 Peters, Frank. "The Early Mennonite Brethren Church:
      Baptist or Anabaptist," ML. 14 (1959): 176-78.

3211 Prentis, Noble. "As Others Saw Them," ML. 25 (1970): 59-
      62. Opinions on German-American Mennonites.

3212 Raid, Howard. "Donnellson Migrations Analyzed," ML. 15
      (1960): 62-63, 91. The Iowa Mennonites.

3213 _____. "Swiss Mennonites Plan a Museum," ML. 15
      (1960): 165.

3214 Redekop, Calvin. The Old Colony Mennonites: Dilemmas of Eth-
      nic Minority Life. Baltimore: Johns Hopkins Univ. Pr., 1968.

3215 Reiner, Gustav. Exiled by the Czar: Cornelius Jansen and
      the Great Mennonite Migration 1874. Newton, Kansas: Men-
      nonite Publishing House, 1956.

3216 Risser, Emma. History of the Pennsylvania Mennonite Church
      in Kansas. Hesston: Pennsylvania Mennonite Church, 1958.

3217 Sappington, Roger. "The Mennonites in the Carolinas," MQR.
      41 (1968): 96-116.

3218 Sawatzky, Heinrich. Templer mennonitischer Herkunft. (His-
      torical Series, 2.) Winnipeg: Echo-Verlag, 1957.

3219 Schelbert, Leo. "Eighteenth Century Migration of Swiss Men-
      nonites to America," MQR. 42 (1968): 285-300.

3220 Schmidt, John. "I was a Stranger," MQR. 33 (1959): 245-49.

3221 _____. "Mennonite Bibliography," ML. 20 (1965): 90-95;
      23 (1968): 138-41; 25 (1970): 93-96.

3222 _____. "When People Migrate: Footnote to the Mennonite
      Migration of the 1870's," MQR. 33 (1959): 152-55.

3223 Schneider, Hermann. Die Mennoniten von Kühbörncheshof bei
      Katzweiler und Umgebung. (Schriften zur Wanderungsgesch-
      ichte, 19.) Kaiseralautern, 1964.

3224 Schnell, K. "John F. Funk, 1835-1930, and the Mennonite
      Migration 1873-75," MQR. 24 (1950): 199-229.

3225 Schrag, Martin. "The Swiss-Volknian Mennonite Background,
      ML. 9 (1954): 156-61.

3226 Schreiber, William. The Fate of the Prussian Mennonites.
      Göttingen: Göttingen Research Committee, 1955.

3227 _____. "Mennonites of Wayne County, Ohio," Eck. (Aug.
      17-Sept. 21, 1957).

3228   Schroeter, Elizabeth. From Here to the Pinnacles: Memories
        of Mennonite Life in the Ukraine and in America. New York:
        Exposition Pr., 1956.

3229   Shaner, Richard. "Kutztown's Mennonites, " PFL. 14 (1965):
        21-30.

3230   Shank, Clarence. A Brief History of the Marion Mennonite
        Congregation. Marion: Mennonite Hist. Comm., 1968.

3231   Shelly, William. "Mennonite Landmarks in Germantown, "
        ML. 13 (1958): 170-73.

3232   Shipley, Helen. The Migration of the Mennonites from Russia
        1873-83, and their Settlement in Kansas. University of Min-
        nesota: Dissertation, 1954.

3233   Shoemaker, Alfred. "Team Mennonites, " PD. 8 (1957): 38-
        42.

3234   Simon, Grant. "Dissenters and Founders, " AGR. 25, i
        (1958): 17-19.

3235   Smith, Charles. Story of the Mennonites. Newton, Kansas:
        Mennonite Publication Office, 1957.

3236   Smith, Elmer. "The Wislerites: The Demographic and Geo-
        graphic Distribution of Old Order Mennonites, " Eck. (July 30-
        Aug. 27, 1960).

3237   Smith, Henry. The Story of the Mennonites. Newton, Kan-
        sas: Mennonite Publishing Office, 1950.

3238   Sprunger, Eva. "Samuel Ferdinand Sprunger, Pastor, Con-
        ference Worker, " ML. 8 (1953): 178-82.

3239   Stoll, Joseph. The Lord is my Shepherd: The Life of Eliza-
        beth Kemp Stutzman. Aylmer, Canada: Pathway, 1965.

3240   Stoltzfus, Grant. Mennonites of the Ohio and Eastern Con-
        ference. Scottdale, Pa.: Herald, 1970.

3241   Swope, Wilmer. "The Mennonites of Bristol Township, Trum-
        bull County, Ohio, " MHB. 23 (1962): 5-8.

3242   Toews, John. Lost Fatherland: The Story of the Mennonite
        Emigration from Soviet Russia, 1921-27. Scottdale, Pa.:
        Herald, 1968.

3243   _____. "Mennonite Brethren Church, Reedleym, Californ-
        ia, " ML. 9 (1954): 151-52.

3244   Umble, John. "David A. Schenk's Notes on the History of the Sonnenberg Swiss Mennonite Congregation, " MQR. 29 (1955): 276-99.

3245   . "John Samuel Coffman: His Life and Work," ML. 14 (1959): 110-16.

3246   . "The Mennonites in Florida, " ML. 12 (1957): 108-15.

3247   Unruh, B. Geschichte der Mennoniten-Brüdergemeinde, 1860-1954. Winnipeg: Christian Pr., 1954.

3248   . Die Niederländisch-niederdeutschen Hintergründe der Mennonitischen Ostwanderung im 16., 18. und 19. Jahrhundert. Karlsruhe: Selbstverlag, 1955.

3249   Unruh, Inez. "John Holdemann, Founder of the Church of God in Christ, Mennonite, " ML. 14 (1959): 123-24.

3250   Unruh, John. "The Burlington and Missouri River Railroad Brings the Mennonites to Nebraska, 1873-78, " NH. 45 (1964): 3-30, 177-206.

3251   Waltner, Erland. "Harold S. Bender: The Ecumenical Mennonite, " MQR. 38 (1964): 138-47.

3252   Wenger, Eli. The Weaverland Mennonites: Including a Biography of Bishop Benjamin W. Weaver. Ephrata, Pa.: Lester R. Sauder, 1969.

3253   Wenger, F. "The Mennonites of Aberdeen, Idaho, " ML. 12 (1957): 121-25.

3254   Wenger, Harry. "The Church of God in Christ, Mennonite," ML. 14 (1959): 122-23.

3255   Wenger, J. C. "Germantown, A Mennonite Gateway, " ML. 13 (1958): 175-77.

3256   . Glimpses of Mennonite History and Doctrine. Scottdale, Pa.: Herald, 1947.

3257   . "Jacob Wisler and the Old Order Mennonite Schism of 1872 in Elkhart County, Indiana, " MQR. 33 (1959): 108-31, 215-40.

3258   . The Mennonites in Indiana and Michigan. Scottdale, Pa.: Herald, 1961.

3259   . "The Theology of John Horsch, " MQR. 21 (1947): 151-55.

3260   Wiche, David. They Seek a Country, A Survey of Mennonite

Migrations with Special Reference to Kansas and Gnadenau.
Hillsboro, Kansas: Mennonite Brethren Publishing House,
1959.

German-American Sects

3264   Alderfer, O.   The Mind of the Brethren in Christ: A Syn-
thesis of Revivalism and the Church Conceived as Total Community.   Claremont Graduate School and University Center:
Dissertation, 1964.

3265   Bargen, Bernhard.   "A Christian Community is Born," ML.
11 (1956): 13-16, 30.

3266   Baugher, Norman.   "Their Faith and Ours," Gospel Messenger. 106 (1956): 3-4, 8-9.

3267   Berky, Andrew.   "The Schwenkfelders," HRBC. 27 (1961):
13-15.

3268   Beyreuther, Rich.   Der junge Zinzendorf.   Leipzig: Koehler
& Amelang, 1958.

3269   Brunk, Harry.   "The Kline-Funk Controversy," BLT. 9 (1964):
21-35.   About the Dunkers and Mennonites.

3270   Corder, A.   "Early Quakerism in Friedrichstadt," Friends In-
tell. (May 12, 1951): 270-72.

3271   Davis, James R.   A History of the Evangelical United Brethren Church in California 1849-1962.   Univ. of Southern California: Dissertation, 1963.

3272   Drury, A. W.   "The Historical Society Catalogue of the Historical Literature Concerning the United Brethren Church in
Christ being in Possession of the Historical Society, the Library of Bonebrake Seminary, or the Publishing House, Dayton, Ohio," Relig. Telescope. 98 (1932): 7-8.

3273   Durnbaugh, D. F.   European Origins of the Brethren: A
Source Book on the Beginnings of the Church of the Brethren
in the Early Eighteenth Century.   Elgin, Ill.: Brethren Pr.,
1958.

3274   _____.   "Relgionships of the Brethren with the Mennonites
and Quakers, 1708-1865," CH. 35 (1966): 35-59.

3275   _____.   "Supplement and Index to the Brethren Bibliography," BLT. 11 (1966): 37-54.

3276   _____   and L. W. Schultz.   "A Brethren Bibliography,
1713-1963," BLT. 9 (1964): 3-177.

3277   _____ and _____. A Brethren Bibliography, 1713-1963: 250 Years of Brethren Literature. Elgin, Ill.: The Brethren Pr., 1964.

3278   Ehlert, Arnold. Brethren Writers: A Checklist, With an Introduction to Brethren Literature and Additional Lists. Grand Rapids: Baker Book House, 1969.

3279   Evans, Theodore. The Brethren Pastor: Differential Conceptions of an Emerging Role. Ohio State Univ.: Dissertation, 1960.

3280   Flory, John. Literary Activity of the German Baptist Brethren in the Eighteenth Century. Elgin, Ill.: Brethren Publishing House, 1908.

3281   _____. "Our Literary Activity in the Twentieth Century," Gospel Messenger. 73 (1924): 598-99.

3282   Folkedahl, Beulah. "The Reorganized Church of Jesus Christ of Latter Day Saints in Southwestern Wisconsin," WMH. 36 (1953): 122-26.

3283   Friedmann, Robert. "Did Anabaptism of the Sixteenth Century Ever Contemplate Emigration to America," MQR. 37 (1963): 332-52.

3284   Fries, Adelaide. Records of the Moravians in North Carolina Raleigh: North Carolina Hist. Comm., 1922-47.

3285   Gapp, Samuel. "Philip Henry Gapp and the Philadelphia German Home Mission, 1850-64," Trans. Morav. Hist. Soc. 17, ii (1960).

3286   Gerhard, E. and S. S. Schultz. "The Schwenkfelders and the Moravians Two Hundred Years Ago, 1723-42," Schwenck. 1 (1944): 1-51.

3287   Gilbert, Russell. "Blooming Grove, the Dunker Settlement of Central Pennsylvania," PH. 20 (1953): 23-39.

3288   Glovier, David. Pictorial History of the Virginia Conference: The Church of the United Brethren in Christ. Staunton, Va.: The Conference, 1966.

3289   Gollin, G. "Bethlehem Transformed: The Secularization of a Moravian Settlement," PH. 37 (1970): 53-63.

3290   Graves, Arthur. The First Hundred Years: One Hundred Years of History of the First Baptist Church of Bethlehem, 1869-1969. Bethlehem, Pa.: E. Goepp, 1969.

3291   Gray, Elma and Leslie Robb. Wilderness Christians: The

Moravian Mission to the Delaware Indians. Ithaca: Cornell, 1956.

3292 Hamilton, J. Taylor and Kenneth Hamilton. History of the Moravian Church: The Renewed Unitas Fratrum, 1722-1957. Bethlehem: Moravian Church in America, 1967.

3293 Hamilton, Kenneth. Records of the Moravians in North Carolina. Raleigh: State Dept. of Archives and History, 1969.

3294 Hark, J. Max. "Gottfried Partsch: An Historical Romance of the Early Moravian Settlers in the Lebanon Valley," Eck. (July 5-Aug. 9, 1958).

3295 Heckewelder, John. Thirty Thousand Miles with John Hecke- welder. Pittsburgh: Univ. of Pittsburgh Pr., 1958. About a leading Moravian.

3296 Henry, James. "Moravian Manuscript Literature," Trans. Morav. Hist. Soc. 4 (1891-95): 15-25.

3297 Hogan, Herbert. The Intellectual Impact of the Twentieth Century on the Church of the Brethren. Claremont Graduate School: Dissertation, 1958.

3298 Hostetler, John. "Toward a New Interpretation of Sectarian Life in America," PD. (June 15, 1951).

3299 Kendall, D. H. A History of Bethel Evangelical United Breth- ren Church of Chewsville, Maryland. n. p.: Quincy Orphanage Pr., 1956.

3300 Kuehl, Henry. "The Beginnings and Development of the Mora- vian Settlement at Emmaus, Pa.," MHS. 14 (1947): 147-83.

3301 Langton, Edward. History of the Moravian Church: The Story of the First International Protestant Church. New York: Macmillan, 1956.

3302 Lantz, Philip. "The Influence of John Heckewelder, Moravian Missionary, on the Lives of Western Pennsylvania Indians and Settlers," WPHM. 38 (1955): 21-32.

3303 Luther, Leslie. Moravia (New York) and Its Past and the Ad- joining Townships. Indianapolis: Luther, 1966.

3304 McPherson, Kansas: First Church of the Brethren: Diamond Anniversary, 1885-1960. McPherson, 1960.

3305 Mahr, August. "Diary of a Moravian Indian Mission Migra- tion Across Pennsylvania in 1772," OSAHQ. 62 (1953): 247- 70.

3306   Malin, W. G. Catalog of Books Relating to or Illustrating
        the History of the Unitas Fratrum, or United Brethren. Phila-
        delphia: Collins, 1881.

3307   Moore, George. "Dunkard Life in Lebanon Valley Sixty Years
        Ago," PFL. 12 (1961): 20-13.

3308   The Moravian Contribution to the Town of Hope, New Jersey.
        Hope: Hope Hist. Soc., 1955.

3309   Neisser, Georg. History of the Beginnings of Moravian Work
        in America. Bethlehem, Pa.: Moravian Church Archives,
        1955.

3310   Nelson, Vernon and Lothar Madelheim. "The Moravian Set-
        tlements of Pennsylvania in 1757: The Nicholas Garrison
        Views," PFL. 19 (1969): 2-5.

3311   North Carolina Historical Records Survey. Guide to the Manu-
        scripts of the Moravian Church in America, Southern Province
        Raleigh: North Carolina Historical Records Survey, 1942.

3312   Ogden, Galen. "A Bibliography of Brethren Publications,"
        Schwarzenau. 3 (1942): 58-116.

3313   Raper, Horace. "Accounts of Moravian Mountain Excursions
        of a Hundred Years Ago," NCHR. 47 (1970): 281-316.

3314   Rights, Douglas. "Adelaide Lisetta Fries," NCHR. 29 (1952):
        1-7.

3315   Ronk, Albert. History of the Brethren Church. Ashland,
        Ohio: Brethren Publishing Co., 1968.

3316   Sappington, Roger. Courageous Prophet: Chapters from the
        Life of John Kline. Elgin, Ill.: Brethren Pr., 1966.

3317   _____. "Dunker Beginnings in North Carolina in the
        Eighteenth Century," NCHR. 46 (1969): 214-38.

3318   _____. "Two Eighteenth Century Congregations in North
        Carolina," NCHR. 47 (1970): 176-204.

3319   Sawyer, Edwin. The Religious Experience of the Colonial
        American Moravians. Columbia University: Dissertation,
        1956.

3320   Schaefer, Richard. "The Union Church in Pennsylvania,"
        Eck. (Apr. 7, 1951).

3321   Schreiber, William. "The Swiss Brethren in Ohio," AGR.
        12, v (1946): 22-24.

3322   Schultz, Selina.   Caspar Schwenckfeld von Ossig.   n. p.:
       Board of Publication, Schwenckfelder Church, 1946.

3323   _____.   "The Schwenckfelders of Pennsylvania, " PH. 24
       (1957): 293-320.

3324   Schulz-Behrend, Georg.   "The Swedenborgians at Jasper,
       Iowa: The Disappointment of Hermann Diekhöner, " AGR. 12,
       iv (1946): 27-28.

3325   Schwarze, W. N.   "Consecration of the Moravian Church,
       Bethlehem, Pa., " MHS. 14 (1947): 133-39.

3326   Smith, Elmer and John Stewart.   "The 100th Anniversary of
       an Assassination and Death of the Dunkard Elder John Kline
       Recounted, " Eck. (Nov. 28, 1964).

3327   Spangler, D. W.   "The Dunkard Church at Hygiene, Colorado, "
       CM. 27 (1950): 110-18.

3328   Spencer, Claude.   An Author Catalog of Disciples of Christ
       and Related Religious Groups.   Canton, Missouri: Disciples
       of Christ Historical Society, 1946.

3239   Starr, Ed.   A Baptist Bibliography: Being a Register of
       Printed Material by and about Baptists; Including Works Writ-
       ten Against the Baptists.   Rochester: American Baptist His-
       torical Society, 1947-64.   Lists locations.

3330   Stein, Kenneth.   Church Unity Movements in the Church of
       the United Brethren in Christ until 1946.   Union Theological
       Seminary: Dissertation, 1965.

3331   Stoudt, John.   "Die Ausstrahlung der Marburger theologischen
       Fakultät auf das geistige Leben Amerikas im 18. Jahrhundert, "
       ZRG. 15 (1963): 35-54.

3332   _____.   "Evangelische Bruderschaften im Pennsylvanien
       der Kolonialzeit, " ZRG. 12 (1960): 346-60.

3333   Surratt, Jerry.   From Theocracy to Voluntary Church and
       Secularized Community: A Study of the Moravian Church in
       Salem, North Carolina.   Emory: Dissertation, 1968.

3334   Sutton, Traver.   The Merger of the Evangelical and United
       Brethren in Christ Churches.   Ball State Teacher's College:
       Dissertation, 1965.

3335   Tillson, David.   A Pacifist Community in Peacetime: An In-
       troductory Description of the Woodcrest Bruderhof at Rifton,
       New York.   Syracuse: Dissertation, 1958.

3336   Towlson, C.   Moravian and Methodist Relationships and

Influences on the Eighteenth Century.   London: Epsworth,
1957.

3337   Wach, Joachim.   "Caspar Schwenkfeld, A Pupil and a Teacher
in the School of Christ, " JR. 26 (1946): 1-29.

3338   Weinlick, John.   "Colonial Moravians: Their Status among
the Churches, " PH. 26 (1959): 213-25.

3339   _____.   Count Zinzendorf.   New York: Abingdon, 1956.

3340   Yoder, Don.   "Into the Indian Country with Brother Schmick:
A Moravian Diary of 1797, " PD. 5 (1953): 2-3, 10.

3341   _____.   "Zinzendorf and Moravian Research, " PD. 8 (1957)
43-44.

3342   Zorb, Elizabeth.   "Reflections on Moravian Pietism, " PH. 25
(1959): 115-21.

The Lutherans

3343   A. L. C. Yearbook.   Minneapolis: Augsburg Publishing House,
1960-

3344   Ackermann, Adolph.   "Pioneer Pastor and Lutheran Missionary: J. C. F. Heyer, " CHIQ. 39 (1966): 31-41.

3345   Allbeck, Willard.   "A Binocular View of Lutheranism in
America, " LuthQ. 14 (1962): 206 ff.

3346   _____.   A Century of Lutherans in Ohio.   Yellow Springs:
Antioch Pr., 1966.

3347   _____.   "John Stough: Founder of Ohio Lutheranism, "
LuthQ. 12 (1960): 25-43.

3348   _____.   "Journal of John Samuel Mau, 1794-95, " LuthQ.
13 (1961): 155-64.

3349   _____.   "Lutheran Separation: The Ohio Story, " LuthQ.
11 (1959): 28-41.

3350   Anderson, Hugh.   Lutheranism in the Southeastern States,
1860-86:   A Social History.   The Hague: Mouton, 1969.

3351   Anderson, Joseph Lawrence.   The Role of the Confessional
Writings in the Formation of the Lutheran Church in America.
Boston University: Dissertation, 1966.

3352   Bachmann, E. Theodore.   "S. S. Schmucker, " in Sons of the

Religious Life   213

Prophets: Leaders in Protestantism from Princeton Seminary.
Princeton: Princeton University Pr., 1963.

3353 Behnken, John. This I Recall. St. Louis: Concordia, 1964.

3354 Bertram, Elizabeth. The History of the Lutheran Children's
      Friend Society of Missouri, 1903-47. St. Louis University:
      Dissertation, 1950.

3355 Biegener, E. "Heinrich Bernhard Koester," CHIQ. 22 (1949):
      158-66.

3356 _____. "Karl Georg Stoeckhardt, D. Theol., 1842-1913,"
      CHIQ. 21 (1948): 154-66.

3357 _____. "The Rev. C. L. Janzow, 1847-1911," CHIQ. 21
      (1948): 30-35.

3358 Blum, William. "Hebron Evangelical Lutheran Church, Inter-
      mont, W. Va.," NGSQ. 38 (1950): 6-8.

3359 Bodensieck, Julius. The Encyclopedia of the Lutheran Church.
      Minneapolis: Augsburg, 1965.

3360 Boerger, J. F. "Autobiography," CHIQ. 30 (1957): 26-37.

3361 Bowden, Henry. "Philip Schaff and Sectarianism: The Ameri-
      canization of a European Viewpoint," J. of Ch. & State. 8, i
      (Winter 1966).

3362 Brauer, Jerald. "Lutheranism in American Theological Edu-
      cation," Con. Theol. M. 36 (1965): 373-84.

3363 Caemmerer, Richard and A. Fuerbringer. Toward a More
      Excellent Ministry. St. Louis: Concordia, 1964.

3364 "Deutsche Gemeinden in der Prairie," DL. 129 (1973): 34-35.

3365 Diller, Nebraska Zion Evengelical Lutheran Church: Fiftieth
      Anniversary. Diller: Zion, 1960.

3366 Drach, George. "Christian Frederick Welden," LCQ. 19
      (1946): 79-83.

3367 DuBrau, Richard. "The Gold Lure and the Coming of Luther-
      anism to California," CHIQ. 32 (1959): 65-78.

3368 Ehlers, Karl. "Six Feet Plus and Every Inch a Missionary:
      The Life and Ministry of Dr. Carl Manthey Zorn," CHIQ. 44
      (1971): 122-29.

3369 Eifert, William. "I Would Do it Again," CHIQ. 37 (1965):
      143-69.

3370   Eikmeier, Hermann. "The Lutheran Proseminar in Steeden,"
        CHIQ. 29 (1957): 137-53.

3371   "Einige Mitteilungen über die ersten Anfänge der lutherischen
        Mission in Montana," DL. 129 (1973): 38-39.

3372   Eisenberg, William. This Heritage: The Story of Lutheran
        Beginnings in the Lower Shenandoah Valley, and of Grace
        Church, Winchester. Winchester, Va.: Trustees of Grace
        Evangelical Lutheran Church, 1954.

3373   Engelbert, E. "Martin Luther Church in Baltimore," RJGAH.
        26 (1945): 30-32.

3374   Evers, Fritz. "Unterwegs," Kirch. Monatsblatt. 13 (1956):
        42-43. About three German Lutheran churches.

3375   Forster, Walter. Zion on the Mississippi: The Settlement
        of the Saxon Lutherans in Missouri. St. Louis: Concordia,
        1953.

3376   Franzmann, Martin and Alfred Fuerbringer. "The Lutheran
        Council in the United States of America," Con. Theol M. 35
        (1965): 219 ff.

3377   Frost, Elizabeth. The Men of Wurtemburg and their House
        of God, 1760-1960. Rhinebeck, New York: St. Paul's Evan-
        gelical Lutheran Church of Wurtemburg, 1961.

3378   Fry, C. George. "Matthias Loy, Leader of Ohio's Lutherans,"
        OH. 76 (Autumn 1968).

3379   _____. Matthias Loy: Patriarch of Ohio Lutheranism,
        1828-1915. Ohio State Univ.: Dissertation, 1965.

3380   [Fuerbringer.] "Obituary for Ludwig Ernst Fuerbringer,"
        MHR. 41 (1947): 424. An important Michigan German Luth-
        eran.

3381   Fuerbringer, Ludwig E. Eighty Eventful Years: Reminis-
        cences of Ludwig Ernest Fuerbringer. St. Louis: Concordia,
        1944.

3382   Gaines, William. "A Place Fitted for Praise," Va. Caval-
        cade. 5 (1956): 38-41.

3383   Goetsch, Ronald. "Mission Expansion and Outreach in the
        North Wisconsin District: An Historical Evaluation," CHIQ.
        35 (1962): 18 ff.

3384   Good, William. A History of the General Council of the
        Evangelical Lutheran Church in North America. Yale: Dis-
        sertation, 1967.

3385   Grabau, Johann. "Johann Andreas August Grabau: A Bio-
        graphical Sketch, " CHIQ. 23 (1950): 10-17, 66-74.

3386   [Graebner.] "Theodore Graebner, " MHR. 45 (1950): 201.

3387   Grauer, Gerhard. "St. Paul's Church Chicago, " AGR. 19,
        iii (1953): 18-19.

3388   Groh, John. "Revivalism Among Lutherans in America in
        the 1840's, " CHIQ. 43 (Feb. & May, 1970).

3389   Grueber, Henry. "Guided by God's Counsel, " CHIQ. 30
        (1957): 84-92, 118-29.

3390   "Die Gründung der Synode vor 125 Jahren, " DL. 128 (1973):
        75-78. About the Missouri Synod.

3391   Hammer, Carl. "Late German Documents from Organ
        Church, " AGR. 17, iv (1951): 14-16.

3392   Haney, James. The Religious Heritage and Education of
        Samuel Simon Schmucker: A Study in the Rise of American
        Lutheranism. Yale: Dissertation, 1968.

3393   Harjunpaa, Toivo. "The Lutherans in Russian Alaska, " Pac.
        Hist. Rev. 37 (1969): 123-46.

3394   Hattstaedt, Otto. "The Life and Works of Pastor Frederick
        Lochner, " CHIQ. 21 (1948): 166-74.

3395   Haug, Hans. "Aufruf des Präsidenten der Deutschen Interes-
        sen-Konferenz der L. K. A. , " Kirch. Monatsblatt. 30 (1973):
        214.

3396   Hine, Ruth. "The Lutheran Movement in Berks County, "
        HRBC. 15 (1950): 202-03.

3397   Hook, Wade. "The Lutheran Church in the Carolinas, " LuthQ.
        11 (1959): 60-67.

3398   Huffman, Charles. The St. Michaels Story. Staunton, Va. :
        McClure Printing, 1964.

3399   Jabker, Paul. Holy Cross Lutheran Church: A Typical
        Lutheran Parish in the Growth of St. Louis. St. Louis Uni-
        versity: Dissertation, 1951.

3400   Jenssen, J. C. American Lutheran Biographies: Or Histori-
        cal Notices of Over 350 Leading Men of the American Luther-
        an Church from its Establishment to 1890. Milwaukee, 1890.

3401   Kang, Wi Jo. "Why Was John Peter Gabriel Muhlenberg, a
        Lutheran Pastor, Ordained in the Anglican Church?" CHIQ.
        34 (1962): 22-27.

3402   Kantomen, T. "Lutheranism as a Cultural Force in Europe
        and America," in The Church and Modern Culture. Valparai-
        so: Valparaiso University Pr., 1954.

3403   Kavasch, Paul. "The Lutheran Church-Missouri Synod during
        the Early Years of the Civil War," CHIQ. 31 (1959): 104-09.

3404   Keever, Homer. "A Lutheran Preacher's Account of the 1801-
        02 Revival in North Carolina," Meth. Hist. 7 (1968): 38-55.

3405   Keffer, Marion. "The Early Days of Zion Evangelical Luth-
        eran Church, Founded 1806 at Sherwood, York County," York
        Pion. & Hist. Soc. (1960): 12-22.

3406   Kersten, Lawrence. The Lutheran Ethic and Social Change.
        Wayne State University: Dissertation, 1968.

3407   [Kionka.] "H. C. Kionka," CHIQ. 25 (1952): 92.

3408   Kluender, Paul. "Beginning a Prairie Ministry," CHIQ. 35
        (1962): 67 ff.

3409   Knudsen, Gunnar. "Trinity Lutheran Church: The First Two
        Hundred Years," HRBC. 16 (1951): 66-72, 93.

3410   Koch, J. B. "Frankenmuth Marker," CHIQ. 32 (1960): 105-
        06.

3411   Koehneke, Paul. "Joint Mission Festivals in the Lutheran
        Church-Missouri Synod till 1868," CHIQ. 24 (1951): 23-24.

3412   Koenig, Emilie. "As Thou Leadest Me," CHIQ. 28 (1956):
        166-67; 29 (1956): 1-29.

3413   Koenig, Paul. "C. C. Schmidt, D. D. November 8, 1843-
        Oct. 12, 1925," CHIQ. 26 (1953): 36-45.

3414   Koerner, Gustave. "The Old Lutherans and Bishop Stephan,"
        CHIQ. 33 (1960): 81-84.

3415   Kreider, Harry. The Beginnings of Lutheranism in New York.
        New York: Carroll Good, 1949.

3416   _____. "Justus Falckner," CHIQ. 27 (1955): 86-93.

3417   _____. "Lutheran Church Life in New York City in the
        First Half of the Eighteenth Century," NYPL. 62 (1958): 610-
        14.

3418   Kretzmann, Karl. "An Adventure of Dr. Walther in 1856,"
        CHIQ. 19 (1946): 9-15.

3419   _____. "Francis Arnold Hoffman," CHIQ. 18 (1945): 35-
        54.

3420 _____. "The Men of 1847," CHIQ. 19 (1946): 3-9.

3421 _____. "That Log Cabin in Perry County," CHIQ. 19 (1946): 152-60.

3422 Kuegele, Martin. "The First Lutheran in the State of Missouri," CHIQ. 25 (1952): 125-41.

3423 _____. "Rev. Frederick Gottlob Kuegele of Crimora, Va.," CHIQ. 19 (1946): 145-51.

3424 Laer, Arnold. "The Lutheran Church in New York, 1649-1772: Records in the Lutheran Church Archives at Amsterdam, Holland," BNYPL. 50 (1946): 409-27, 830-37.

3425 Lang, Marcus. The Relationship of Church Progress in Missouri Synod Lutheran Churches of the St. Louis Metropolitan District to the Status of the Communities in which They are Located. Washington University: Dissertation, 1946.

3426 Linke, Marian. "A Hundred Years St. Thomas Lutheran Church, Germantown," AGR. 22, v (1956): 28-29.

3427 "List of Publications by Lutherans in the United States," Evang. Rev. 12 (1860-61): 542-74.

3428 Loehner, Louis. "Lutheran Parsonage Life Seventy Years Ago," CHIQ. 34 (1962): 35-44.

3429 Luebke, Frederick. "The Immigrant Condition as a Factor Contributing to the Conservatism of the Lutheran Church-Missouri Synod," CHIQ. 38 (1965): 19-28.

3430 Luecking, F. D. Mission in the Making. St. Louis: Concordia, 1964.

3431 Luecke, W. H. "A Half Century of Testimony of Staunch Lutheranism in New York City," CHIQ. 32 (1959): 2-14.

3432 Lueker, Erwin. Lutheran Encyclopedia. St. Louis: Concordia, 1954.

3433 Luessenhop, William. "Early Lutheranism in Colorado," ColM. 38 (1961): 131-34.

3434 Lutheran Church. New York. Protocol of the Lutheran Church in New York City, 1702-1750. New York: The Synod, 1958.

3435 The Lutheran Historical Conference. St. Louis: Concordia, 1964. Articles on Lutheran history, libraries and research.

3436 McCartney, James. "Sectarian Strife in Dundas County: A Lutheran-Episcopalian Land Endowment Controversy, 1784-1846," CH. 54 (1962): 69-86.

3437   Marth, Elmer. "Gustav Adolph Kindermann: Leader of a
       German Lutheran Immigration and Pioneer Southeastern Wis-
       consin Pastor, " CHIQ. 38 (1965): 135-45; 38 (1966): 168-88.

3438   Mauelshagen, Carl. Salzburg Lutheran Expulsion and its Im-
       pact. New York: Vantage Pr. , 1963.

3439   Maxwell, Jack. The Liturgical Lessons of Mercersburg: An
       Examination of the Issues Which Emerged During the Mercers-
       burg Liturgical Controversy. Princeton Theological Seminary:
       Dissertation, 1969.

3440   Mayer, H. A. "Die Frankenkolonie, die Freude brachte, "
       DL. 129 (1973): 81.

3441   _____ . "Krisen in der Geschichte der Missouri-Synode, "
       DL. 128 (1973): 82-83.

3442   Meier, Everette. "The Life and Work of Henry C. Schwan
       as Pastor and Missionary, " CHIQ. 24 (1951): 132-39; 25
       (1952): 72-85, 97-121.

3443   Meyer, Carl. Log Cabin to Luther Tower. St. Louis: Con-
       cordia, 1966.

3444   _____ . "Lutheran Immigrant Churches Face the Problems
       of the Frontier, " CH. 29 (1960): 440-62.

3445   _____ . "Some Aspects of the Observances of the Reforma-
       tion Quadricentennial by American Lutherans, " CHIQ. 41
       (1968): 14-34.

3446   _____ . "Walther Bibliography, " Con. Theol. M. 32 (1961)
       658-63.

3447   Meyer, John. "The Men of Cleveland, " Con. Theol M. 33
       (1962): 5, 30 ff.

3448   Meyer, Ruth. "A Man Sent From God, " CHIQ. 35 (1962):
       6 ff. About Rev. J. Fritz.

3449   Mishra, Vishwa. "The Lutheran Standard: 125 Years of
       Denominational Journalism, " JQ. 45 (1968): 71-76.

3450   Molnar, Kenneth. "Johann Friedrich Bünger, " CHIQ. 30
       (1957): 1-25.

3451   Morgan, Jacob and others. History of the Lutheran Church
       in North Carolina. n. p. : United Evengelical Lutheran Synod
       of North Carolina, 1953.

3452   Morris, John Gottlieb. Bibliotheca Lutherana: A Complete
       List of the Publications of all the Lutheran Ministers in the

U.S. Philadelphia: Lutheran Board of Pub., 1876.

3453   Muhlenberg, Henry. The Journals of Henry Melchior Muhlenberg. Philadelphia: Muhlenberg Pr., 1945.

3454   _____. Notebook of a Colonial Clergyman. Philadelphia: Muhlenberg, 1959.

3455   Mundinger, Carl. Government in the Missouri Synod. St. Louis: Concordia, 1947.

3456   Nau, John. "The Lutheran Church in Louisiana," CHIQ. 25 (1952): 1-48.

3457   Neve, Herbert. American Lutheran Evangelism: Its Historical Perspective and Its Confessional Basis. University of Heidelberg: Dissertation, 1959.

3458   Ortner, Donald. A Centennial History of St. John's Evangelical Lutheran Church at Waltz, Michigan. Waltz, 1958.

3459   Ottersberg, Gerhard. "Wilhelm Loehe," LuthQ. 4 (1952): 170-90.

3460   Owen, Ralph. "The Old Lutherans Come," CHIQ. 20 (1947): 3-56.

3461   Pannkoke, O. A Great Church Finds Itself: The Lutheran Church between the Wars. n.p.: Private Pr., 1966.

3462   Perrin, Richard. "A Fachwek Church in Wisconsin," WMH. 43 (1962): 239-44.

3463   Pfeiffer, J. Auf Luthers Spuren in Amerika. Berlin, 1954.

3464   Pieper, Walter. "C. F. W. Walther Revealed in His Letters," CHIQ. 34 (1962): 5-16.

3465   Plehn, Herbert. "Oscar Adelbert Sauer," CHIQ. 42 (1969): 41-46.

3466   [Polack.] "William Gustave Polack," CHIQ. 23 (1950): 87-88.

3467   Polack, William G. "Autobiographical Sketch of Herman Ruhland, 1865-1948," CHIQ. 21 (1948): 151-54.

3468   _____. "Karl Kretzmann, D.D., 1877-1949," CHIQ. 22 (1949): 49-55.

3469   _____. "Wyneken Paintings," CHIQ. 20 (1947): 2.

3470   Rattermann, Heinrich. Geschichte der deutschen Gemeinde

der Hoffnungsvollen Kirche in Boone County, Kentucky. Cincinnati, 1880.

3471   Rehmer, Rudolph. "Founding of Lutheran Congregations in
Indiana to 1861," CHIQ. 42 (1969): 90 ff.

3472   Reimann, Henry. "C. F. W. Walther's 1879 Edition of
Baier's Compendium," CHIQ. 34 (1962): 86 ff.

3473   "Report of the Executive Committee of the Missionary Society
of the Synod of Pennsylvania, Containing Brother Wynecken's
Report," CHIQ. 20 (1947): 124-35.

3474   Repp, Arthur. "Beginnings of Lutheranism in Houston, Texas," CHIQ. 26 (1953): 49-77.

3475   _____. "Daughters of Serbin, 1870-1905: History of the
Lutheran Churches at Fedor and Warda, Texas," CHIQ. 21
(1948): 49-67.

3476   _____. "History of Holy Cross, Warda, Texas, Daughter
of Serbin, 1873-1905," CHIQ. 26 (1953): 1-16.

3477   _____. "The Lutheran Church in America a Century Ago,"
CHIQ. 20 (1947): 63-79.

3478   Rightmeyer, Thomas. "The Holy Orders of Peter Muhlenberg," Hist. Mag. Prot. Episc. Ch. 30 (1961): 183-97.

3479   Rudnick, Milton. Fundamentalism and the Missouri Synod:
A Historical Study of their Interaction and Mutual Influence.
St. Louis: Concordia, 1966.

3480   "St. Paul's Church, New York," AGR. 18, iv (1952): 26-27.

3481   St. Paul's Lutheran Church: 93 Year History, 1871-1964.
Albert, Kansas: St. Paul's, 1964.

3482   Sauer, Alfred. "The Autobiography of John Jacob Sauer,"
CHIQ. 22 (1949): 3-36.

3483   Sauer, O. A. Centennial 1852-1952: Bethlehem Lutheran
Church. Richmond, Va., 1952.

3484   Schabacker, Martin. St. Paul Lutheran Church 1878-1953.
Minden, Nebraska: Warp, 1953.

3485   Schild, Karl. "Muhlenberg as Revealed in His Diary," AGR.
9 (1942): 33.

3486   _____. "75 Jahre der Tabor-Gemeinde in Philadelphia,"
Kirch. Monatsblatt. 30 (1973): 210-11.

3487   Schmelder, William. "Walther at Altenburg, " CHIQ. 34
       (1961): 65 ff.

3488   Schneider, Carl. The German Church on the American Fron-
       tier: A Study in the Rise of Religion among the Germans of
       the West. Based on the History of the Evangelischer Kirchen-
       verein des Westens, 1840-66. St. Louis: Eden, 1939.

3489   Schoenfuhs, Walter. "Eduard Raimund Baierlein: Lutheran
       Missionary to the Indians in America and Asia, " CHIQ. 27
       (1955): 133-40, 145-60; 28 (1955): 1-26.

3490   Schuetze, Otto. History of the Christ Lutheran Church.
       Bethesda, Maryland: Christ Lutheran, 1960.

3491   Sihler, W. "Eine Reise zur ersten Synode, " DL. 128 (1973):
       86.

3492   Smith, C. E. "Henry Muhlenberg (1753-1815): Botanical
       Pioneer, " PAPS. 106 (1962): 443-60.

3493   Smylie, James. "Philip Schaff: Ecumenist, " Encounter. 28
       (1967): 3-16.

3494   Sommer, Roger. "Martin Samuel Sommer, " CHIQ. 23 (1950):
       123-31.

3495   Spitz, Lewis. Life in Two Worlds: Biography of William
       Sihler. St. Louis: Concordia, 1968.

3496   Stallmann, Reinhold. "Warum verliessen die Väter Europa?"
       DL. 129 (1973): 105-07.

3497   Stange, Douglas. "Frederick Henry Quitmann, D. D. The
       Flowering of Rationalism in the American Lutheran Church, "
       CHIQ. 39 (1966): 67-76.

3498   Stecher, Robert. "The Life and Times of Anton Daniel
       Stecher: German-American, Lutheran Missionary, " CHIQ.
       42 (1969): 51-78.

3499   Suelflow, August. "Blicke in die 125 Jahre, " DL. 129 (1973):
       103-05.

3500   _____. "The Father's Faith: The Children's Language, "
       CHIQ. 30 (1957): 130-41.

3501   _____. The Heart of Missouri. St. Louis: Concordia,
       1954.

3502   _____. "The Life and Work of Georg Ernst Christian
       Ferdinand Sievers, " CHIQ. 20 (1947): 135-41, 180-87; 21
       (1948): 36-41, 75-87, 100-14, 175-80; 22 (1949): 43-48, 77-
       84.

3503   . "The Men Who Founded the Institute, " CHIQ. 30
(1957): 59-69.

3504   . A Plan for Survival. New York: Greenwich Book
Publishing, 1965. On the Milwaukee Lutherans.

3505   . "Planting of Lutheranism in Detroit, " CHIQ. 39
(1966): 77-89.

3506   . "Trinity Parish, Wisconsin Territory, " CHIQ. 23
(1950): 1-9.

3507   . "William Gustave Polack, " CHIQ. 23 (1950): 97-
122.

3508   Suelflow, Roy. "First Years of Trinity Congregation, Frie-
stadt, Wisconsin, " CHIQ. 18 (1945): 2-12, 55-62, 83-99.

3509   . "The Relations of the Missouri Synod with the Buffalo Synod up to 1866, " CHIQ. 27 (1955): 1-19, 57-73, 97-
132.

3510   Sunderman, Otto. "A Blessed Life of Service, " CHIQ. 36
(1963): 90-94.

3511   Swihart, Altman. Luther and the Lutheran Church, 1483-
1960. New York: Philosophical Library, 1960.

3512   Tappert, Theodore. "The Date of Henry Melchior Muhlenberg's Birth, " CHIQ. 42 (1969): 91 ff.

3513   . "Helmuth and the Fries Rebellion in 1799, " LuthQ
17 (1965): 265-69.

3514   . "John Caspar Stoever and the Ministerium of
Pennsylvania, " LChQ. 21 (1948): 180-84.

3515   Thiele, Gilbert. "Glimpses of One Hundred Years of Missouri Synod Lutheranism in Minnesota, " CHIQ. 29 (1956):
89-102.

3516   . "To Theodore Hoyer: A Tribute, " Con. Theol M.
34 (1963): 392-94.

3517   Thorkelson, Willmar. Lutherans in the USA. Minneapolis:
Augsburg, 1969.

3518   Tietjen, John. Which Way to Lutheran Unity? A History
of Efforts to Unite the Lutherans of America. St. Louis:
Concordia, 1966.

3519   Umbach, Walter. "The Heritage of Mother Trinity, " CHIQ.
38 (1965): 73-83. About a St. Louis church.

3520   Umbeck, S. Social Adaptations of a Selected Group of Ger-
       man Background Protestant Churches in Chicago. Chicago,
       1944.

3521   Uplegger, Francis. "A Brief Review of Nearly 90 Years of
       Life by the Grace of God, " CHIQ. 38 (1965): 146-50.

3522   Vesper, Herman. "Lutheran Church Life in the Mohawk Val-
       ley in Colonial Days, " Schoharie Co. HR. (1963): 3-6, 23-
       24.

3523   Wade, William. Historical Sketch of New Jerusalem Lutheran
       Congregation. Lovettsville, Va.: New Jerusalem Church,
       1950.

3524   Wagner, Hans-Ludwig. "The Bicentennial of Zion in Balti-
       more, " RJGAH. 29 (1950): 61-67.

3525   Walker, H. H. "Carl Ferdinand Wilhelm Walther, D. D.:
       The Luther of America, " CHIQ. 29 (1957): 171-80.

3526   [Walther.] "C. F. W. Walther, " Con Theol. M. 32 (1961):
       581-664.

3527   Walther, C. F. W. Letters of C. F. W. Walther: A Selec-
       tion. Philadelphia: Fortress Pr., 1969.

3528   _____. "Thesis on the Question of Church Polity, " CHIQ.
       34 (1961): 33-35.

3529   Wambsganss, Fred. "Five Decades of Pastorial Activities, "
       CHIQ. 30 (1958): 145-54.

3530   Ward, Gordon. "The Formation of the Lutheran General
       Synod, South, During the Civil War, " LuthQ. 13 (1961): 132-
       54.

3531   Weiser, Frederick. "The Muhlenberg Way, " CHIQ. 34 (1961):
       45-53.

3532   Wentz, Abdel. A Basic History of Lutheranism in America.
       Philadelphia: Muhlenberg Pr., 1955.

3533   Wiederaenders, Robert. Correspondences of Wilhelm Loehe
       in American Repositories. Dubuque, Iowa: ALC, 1969.

3534   _____. "The Lutheran Church in North America: A Bib-
       liography, " LuthQ. 10 (1959): 339-51.

3535   _____ and Walter Tillmanns. The Synods of American
       Lutheranism. St. Louis: Lutheran Historical Conference,
       1968.

3536   Wight, Willard. "The Journals of the Rev. Robert J. Miller,
        Lutheran Missionary in Virginia, 1811 and 1813," VMHB. 61
        (1953): 141-66.

3537   _____. "Two Lutheran Missionary Journals, 1811, 1813,"
        SCHGM. 55 (1954): 7-14.

3538   Wolf, Richard. Documents of Lutheran Unity in America.
        Philadelphia: Fortress Pr., 1966.

3539   Wust, Klaus. Zion in Baltimore, 1755-1955: The Bicenten-
        nial of the Earliest German-American Church in Baltimore.
        Baltimore: Zion Church, 1955.

3540   Yoder, Don. "The Bench Versus the Catechism: Revivalism
        and Pennsylvania's Lutheran and Reformed Churches," PF. 10
        (1959): 14-23.

3541   _____. "A Lutheran Minister Rides the Tennessee Fron-
        tier: The Ministerial Diary of John George Butler, 1805,"
        PD. 3 (1952): 1-7.

3542   Zorn, Hans. "Carl Manthey-Zorn in India and His Coming
        to America," CHIQ. 32 (1960): 1-2, 23-29, 57-61.

3543   _____. "Carl Manthey-Zorn's Theological Preparations
        for Service in God's Kingdom," CHIQ. 32 (1959): 39-47.

3544   _____. "The Early Years of Carl Manthey-Zorn," CHIQ.
        31 (1959): 79-87, 110-16; 32 (1959): 23-29.

The Jews

3545   Aberbach, Moses. "The Early German Jews of Baltimore,"
        RJGAH. 35 (1972): 21-36.

3546   Adler, Selig and T. Connolly. From Ararat to Suburbia:
        The History of the Jewish Community of Buffalo. Philadel-
        phia: Jewish Publication Society of America, 1960.

3547   American Federation of Jews from Central Europe. Twenty
        Years: 1940-60. New York: The Federation, 1961.

3548   Bernard, Martin. "The Religious Philosophy of Emil G.
        Hirsch," AJA. 4 (1952): 61-82.

3549   Bernstein, M. "A Note on Altenmuhr Jews," AJHS. 49
        (1959): 53-55.

3550   Blau, J. L. and W. S. Baron. The Jews of the U.S., 1790-
        1840: A Documentary History. New York: Columbia, 1963.

3551 Boroff, David. "A Little Milk, A Little Honey," AH. 17
      (1966): 12-14. German Jews in New York.

3552 Brandes, Joseph. Immigrants to Freedom: Jewish Com-
      munities in Rural Jersey Since 1882. Philadelphia: Univer-
      sity of Pa. Pr., 1970.

3553 Cogan, Sara. Pioneer Jews of the California Mother Lode,
      1849-80: An Annotated Bibliography. Berkeley: Western
      Jewish Hist. Center, 1968.

3554 Cohen, Naomi. A Dual Heritage: The Public Career of Os-
      car S. Straus. New York: Jewish Publication Society of
      America, 1969.

3555 Cohon, Samuel. "The History of the Hebrew Union College,"
      PAJHS. 40 (1950): 17-55.

3556 Cushmore, Joyce. "Abraham Jacobi: Father of American
      Pediatrics," AGR. 25, vi (1959): 29-31, 37.

3557 Davis, Moshe. Yahadut Amerika Be-Hitpathutah. New York:
      Jewish Theological Seminary, 1951.

3558 DeSola Pool, D. "Religious and Cultural Phases of Ameri-
      can Jewish History," PAJHS. 39 (1950): 291-301.

3559 Dickinson, John. German and Jew: The Life and Death of
      Sigmund Stein. Chicago: Quadrangle Books, 1967.

3560 Dobert, Eitel Wolf. "Einhorn and Szold: Two Liberal Ger-
      man Rabbis in Baltimore," RJGAH. 29 (1956): 51-57.

3561 Drachman, Bernard. The Unfailing Light: Memoirs of an
      American Rabbi. New York: Rabbinical Council of America,
      1948.

3562 Dubow, Sylvan. "Identifying the Jewish Serviceman in the
      Civil War: A Re-Appraisal of Simon Wolf's 'The American
      Jew as Patriot, Soldier and Citizen'," AJHQ. 59 (March 1970).

3563 Fein, Isaac. The Making of an American Jewish Community:
      The History of Baltimore Jewry from 1773 to 1920. Phila-
      delphia: Jewish Publication Soc. of America, 1970.

3564 Fierman, Floyd. Some Early Jewish Settlers on the South-
      western Frontier. El Paso: Texas Western Pr., 1960.

3565 Fleishaker, Oscar. The Illinois-Iowa Jewish Community on
      the Banks of the Mississippi River. Yeshiva University:
      Dissertation, 1957.

3566 Frank, Fedora. Five Families and Eight Young Men: Nash-

ville and Her Jewry, 1850-61. Nashville: Tennessee Book
Co., 1962.

3567   Frank, Helmut. "As a German Rabbi to America," in Paul
       Lazarus Gedenkbuch. Jerusalem, 1961, pp. 135-42.

3568   Freund, Miriam. "Make My Eyes Look to the Future,"
       PAJHS. 49 (1960): 159-72.

3569   Friedman, Lee. "The Problems of Nineteenth Century Amer-
       ican Jewish Peddlers," PAJHS. 44 (1954): 1-7.

3570   German Jewish Publishers of New York. A Bibliographical
       Essay, Containing an Account of Books, Treatises, Essays
       and Articles Written by Willy Aron. New York: German
       Jewish Publishers of America, 1935.

3571   Ginsberg, Louis. "Two Streams Become One," Va. Caval-
       cade. 7 (1958): 23-29.

3572   Glanz, Rudolph. The German Jew in America: An Annotated
       Bibliography Including Books, Pamphlets and Articles of Spe-
       cial Interest. New York: Ktav Publishing Co., 1970.

3573   _____. "The German Jewish Mass Emigration: 1820-80,"
       AJA. 22 (1970): 49-66.

3574   _____. "German-Jewish Names in America," JSS. 23
       (1962): 143-69.

3575   _____. "The Immigration of German Jews up to 1880,"
       YIVO Annual of J. Soc. Sci. 4 (1947): 81-89.

3576   _____. Jew and Irish: Historic Group Relations and Im-
       migration. New York: Author, 1966.

3577   _____. Jews in Relation to the Cultural Milieu of the
       Germans in America up to the Eighteen Eighties. New York:
       Yiddish Scientific Institute, 1947.

3578   _____. The Jews of California from the Discovery of
       Gold Until 1880. New York: Author, 1962.

3579   _____. "The Rise of the Jewish Club in America," JSS.
       31 (1969): 82-99.

3580   Glazer, Nathan. American Judaism: A Historical Survey of
       the Jewish Religion in America. Chicago: University of
       Chicago Pr., 1957.

3581   Goodman, Abram. American Overture: Jewish Rights in
       Colonial Times. Philadelphia: Jewish Publication Soc.,
       1947.

3582 _____. "A German Mercenary Observes American Jews During the Revolution," AJHQ. 59 (1969): 227.

3583 _____. "A Jewish Peddler's Diary 1842-43," AJA. 3 (1951): 81-111.

3584 Gordon, Albert. Jews in Transition. Minneapolis: University of Minnesota Pr., 1949.

3585 Grollman, Earl. "Dictionary of American Jewish Biography in the Early Seventeenth Century," AJA. 3 (1950): 3-10.

3586 Handlin, Oscar. "American Views of the Jews at the Opening of the 20th Century," PAJHS. 40 (1951): 323-44.

3587 Hebrew Union College. Jewish Institute of Religion. Jewish Americana: A Supplement to A. S. W. Rosenbach, An American Jewish Bibliography. Cincinnati: American Jewish Archives, 1954.

3588 Heller, James. Isaac M. Wise: His Life, Work and Thought. New York: Union of American Hebrew Congregations, 1965.

3589 Hellman, George. "Joseph Seligman: American Jew," PAJHS. 41 (1951): 27-40.

3590 Hirschler, Eric. Jews from Germany in the United States. New York: Farrar, Straus and Cudahy, 1956.

3591 Jonas, Harold. "American Jewish History as Reflected in General American History," PAJHS. 39 (1950): 283-90.

3592 Kaganoff, Nathan. "Judaica Americana," AJHQ. 56 (1967): 457-65; 57 (1967): 254-62.

3593 Karp, A. The Jewish Experience in America: Selected Studies. New York: Ktav, 1969.

3594 Kaup, Leo. The Story of Radical Reform Judaism. Los Angeles: Private Pr., 1951.

3595 Kisch, Guido. In Search of Freedom: A History of American Jews from Czechoslovakia. London: Edward Goldston, 1949.

3596 Kober, Adolf. "Jewish Emigration from Würtemberg to the United States of America, 1848-55," PAJHS. 41 (1952): 225-73.

3597 _____. "Jewish Religious and Cultural Life in America as Reflected in the Felsenthal Collection," PAJHS. 45 (1955): 93-127.

3598   Kohn, S. Joshua. The Jewish Community of Utica, New York,
        1847-1948. New York: American Jewish Historical Soc.,
        1959.

3599   Korn, Bertram. American Jewry and the Civil War. Phila-
        delphia: Jewish Publication Soc., 1952.

3600   _____. The Early Jews of New Orleans. Waltham: Amer-
        ican Jewish Historical Soc., 1969.

3601   _____. Eventful Years and Experiences: Studies in Nine-
        teenth Century American Jewish History. Cincinnati: 1954.

3602   Lazar, Robert. "Jewish Communal Life in Fargo, North
        Dakota: The Formative Years, " N. Dak. Hist. 36 (1969):
        347-55.

3603   Levine, A. E. American Jewish Bibliography. Cincinnati:
        American Jewish Archives, 1959.

3604   [Lewisohn.] "Ludwig Lewisohn: in Memoriam, " AJA. 17
        (1965): 109-13.

3605   Maass, Ernest. "Integration and Name Changing among Jew-
        ish Refugees from Central Europe in the United States, " NA.
        6 (1958): 129-71.

3606   McKelvey, Blake. "The Jews of Rochester: A Contribution
        to their History During the Nineteenth Century, " PAJHS. 40
        (1950): 57-73.

3607   Mandel, Irving. "Attitudes of the American Jewish Commun-
        ity toward East-European Immigration, " AJA. 3 (1950): 11-34.

3608   Marcus, Jacob. American Jewry: Documents-Eighteenth
        Century, Primarily Hitherto Unpublished Manuscripts. Cin-
        cinnati, 1959.

3609   _____. "A Selected Bibliography of American Jewish His-
        tory, " PAJHS. 51 (1961): 97-134.

3610   _____. "Selma Stern-Täubler, Archivist, Retires, " AJA.
        8 (1956): 132.

3611   Marcus, Robert. Memoirs of American Jews, 1775-1865.
        Philadelphia: 1955.

3612   Meissner, Frank. "German Jews of Prague: A Quest for
        Self-Realization, " AJHS. 50 (1960): 98-120.

3613   Michael, Deborah. The Cincinnati Jewish Community Before
        1860. University of Cincinnati: Dissertation, 1970.

3614   Newmark, Leo. California Family Newmark: An Intimate
       History. Santa Monica: Stern, 1970.

3615   New York Public Library. Jewish Collection. Dictionary
       Catalog of the Jewish Collection. Boston: Hall, 1960.
       250,000 entries.

3616   Nodel, Julius. The Ties Between: A Century of Judaism on
       America's Last Frontier, 1858-1958. Portland: Nodel &
       Apsler, 1959.

3617   Parish, William. "The German Jew and the Commercial
       Revolution in Territorial New Mexico, " NMHR. 35 (1959): 1-
       23.

3618   _____. "The German Jew and the Commercial Revolution
       in New Mexico, 1850-1900, " NMQ. 29 (1960): 307-32.

3619   Plant, Gunther. "Jewish Colonies at Painted Woods and Devil's
       Lake, " NDH. 32 (1965): 59-70.

3620   _____. The Jews in Minnesota: The First Seventy-Five
       Years. New York: American Jewish Historical Soc., 1959.

3621   Proctor, Samuel. "Jewish Life in New Orleans, 1718-1860, "
       LHQ. 40 (1957): 110-32.

3622   Raisin, Max. Great Jews I Have Known. New York: Philo-
       sophical Library, 1952.

3623   Reissner, Hanns. "Ganstown, USA: A German-Jewish
       Dream, " AJA. 14 (1962): 20-31.

3624   _____. "The German-American Jews, 1800-50, " Yearbook
       LBI. 10 (1965): 57-116.

3625   Reznikoff, Charles. The Jews of Charleston. Philadelphia:
       Jewish Publication Soc., 1950.

3626   Rhodes, Irwin. "Early Records of Jews of Lancaster County,
       Pa., " AJA. 12 (1960): 96-108.

3627   Rockaway, R. A. "Ethnic Conflict in an Urban Environment:
       The German and Russian Jew in Detroit, " AJHQ. 60 (1970):
       133-50.

3628   Rosenbach, Abraham. An American Jewish Bibliography:
       Being a List of Books and Pamphlets by Jews or Relating to
       them Printed in the U.S. from the Establishment of the Press
       in the Colonies until 1850. Baltimore: Lord Baltimore Pr.,
       1926.

3629   Rosenbaum, Jeanette. "Hebrew German Society Rodeph

Shalom in the City and County of Philadelphia, 1800-1950,"
PAJHS. 41 (1951): 83-93.

3630 Rosenberg, Stuart. The Jewish Community in Rochester,
1843-1925. New York: Columbia Univ. Pr., 1954.

3631 _____. "Some Sermons in the Spirit of the Pittsburgh
Platform, " HJ. 17 (1956): 59-76.

3632 Rosenbloom, Joseph. A Biographical Dictionary of Early
American Jews: Colonial Times through 1800. Lexington:
University of Kentucky Pr., 1960.

3633 Rosenswaiker, Ira. "An Estimate and Analysis of the Jewish
Population in the U.S. in 1790, " AJHS. 50 (1960): 23-67.

3634 _____. "The Jewish Population of the U.S. as Estimated
from the Census of 1820, " AJHQ. 53 (1963): 131-78.

3635 Rothkoff, Aaron. "The American Sojourns of Ridbaz Jacob
David Wiloski, 1845-1913: Religious Problems within the
Immigrant Community, " AJHQ. 57 (1968): 557 ff.

3636 Roundtree, Moses. Strangers in the Land. Philadelphia:
Dorrance, 1970.

3637 Rudolph, B. From a Minyan to a Community: A History of
the Jews of Syracuse. Syracuse: Syracuse University Pr.,
1970.

3638 Ryback, Martin. "The East-West Conflict in American Reform Judaism, " AJA. 4 (1952): 3-25.

3639 Sachs, Howard. "Development of the Jewish Community of
Kansas City, 1864-1908, " MHR. 60 (1966): 350-60.

3640 Schwartz, Lois. "Early Jewish Agricultural Colonies in North
Dakota, 1882, " NDH. 32 (1966): 216-32.

3641 Seller, Maxine. "Isaac Leeser: A Jewish-Christian Dialogue
in Antebellum Philadelphia, " PH. 35 (1968): 231-42.

3642 _____. "Isaac Leeser's Views on the Restoration of a
Jewish Palestine, " AJHQ. 58 (1969): 118-35.

3643 Siegel, Burt. "The Little Jew was There: A Bibliographical
Sketch of Sigmund Shlesinger, " AJA. 20 (1968): 16-32.

3644 Standard Jewish Encyclopedia. Garden City, New York:
Doubleday, 1959.

3645 Sulzberger, Mayer. "No Better Jew, No Purer Man: Mayer
Sulzberger on Isaac Leeser, " AJA. 21 (1969): 140-48.

3646 Szajkowski, Zosa. "A Note on the American-Jewish Struggle
       Against Nazism and Communism in the 1930's," AJHQ. 59
       (1970): 272-89.

3647 "Trail Blazers of the Trans-Mississippi West," AJA. 8 (1956):
       59-130.

3648 Turner, Justin. "The First Decade of the Los Angeles Jewry:
       A Pioneer History, 1850-60," AJHQ. 54 (1964): 123-64.

3649 Whiteman, Maxwell. "Isaac Leeser and the Jews of Phila-
       delphia: A Study in National Jewish Influence," AJHS. 48
       (1959): 207-44.

3650 Wilder-Okladek, F. The Return Movement of Jews to Aus-
       tria after the Second World War. The Hague: Nijhoff, 1969.

3651 Wilhelm, Kurt. "Benjamin Szold," HJ. 15 (1953): 49-58.

3652 Wischnitzer, Mark. To Dwell in Safety: The Story of Jewish
       Migration since 1800. Philadelphia: Jewish Publication Soc.,
       1948.

The Catholics

3653 Arnold, Robert. "The Krauss Organ and Church of the Most
       Blessed Sacrament," HRBC. 33 (1968): 98-101.

3654 Barry, Colman. "Boniface Wimmer, Pioneer of the American
       Benedictines," CHR. 41 (1955): 272-96.

3655 _____. The Catholic Church and German Americans. Mil-
       waukee: Bruce, 1953.

3656 _____. "The German Catholic Immigrant," in Roman
       Catholicism and the American Way of Life. Notre Dame,
       1960, pp. 188-203.

3657 _____. Worship and Work: St. John's Abbey and Univer-
       sity, 1856-1956. Collegeville, Mn., 1956.

3658 Binsfeld, Edmund. "Francisca Bauer: The Sister of the
       Woods," OHQ. 69 (1960): 353-66.

3659 Blecker, Paulin. One Hundred Years in Christ, 1857-1957.
       St. Cloud, Minnesota, 1957. The story of a church in New
       Munich, Minnesota.

3660 Blied, Benjamin. Austrian Aid to American Catholics, 1830-
       60. Milwaukee: Author, 1944.

3661   _____. "Bishop Messmer comes to Green Bay, " Salesianum. 50 (1956): 1-7.

3662   _____. Three Archbishops of Milwaukee: Michael Heiss,
Frederick Katzer, Sebastian Messmer. Milwaukee: Author,
1955.

3663   Boeddeker, Alfred. 100th Anniversary: St. Boniface Parish,
San Francisco, 1860-1960. San Francisco, 1960.

3664   Browne, Henry. "Peter E. Dietz, Pioneer Planner of Catholic Social Action, " CHR. 33 (1948): 448-56.

3665   Casper, Henry. History of the Catholic Church in Nebraska.
Milwaukee: Bruce, 1961.

3666   Catholic Encyclopedia. New York: Catholic Encyclopedia Pr.,
1907-22.

3667   Costello, Frank. "Kohlmann and Fenwick: Two New York
Jesuits and a Treatise on Penance, " Archivum Historicum Soc.
Jesu. 23 (1956): 334-44.

3668   Curley, Michael. Cheerful Ascetic: The Life of Francis
Xavier Seelos, C. S. S. R. New Orleans: Seelos Center, 1969.

3669   _____. Venerable John Newmann, C. S. S. R., Fourth
Bishop of Philadelphia. Washington: Catholic University Pr.,
1951.

3670   Curran, Francis. "The Buffalo Mission of German Jesuits,
1869-1907, " U. S. Cath. Hist. Soc. Recs. and Stud. 43 (1955).

3671   Day, Edward. "They Came to St. Michaels: First Redemp-
tionist Beginnings in Chicago, " SJR. 54 (1961): 25-30, 59-64.

3672   Dengler, Theobald. "Frederick Kenkel, " AGR. 28, i (1961):
6-7.

3673   Doerfler, Bruno. "Father Bruno's Narrative Across the
Boundary, " Saskatchewan Hist. 9 (1956): 26-31, 70-74; 10
(1957): 11-26, 55-62. Travels of Minnesota Germans in
Canada.

3674   Duker, Abraham. "Emerging Culture Patterns in American
Jewish Life, " PAJHS. 39 (1950): 351-88.

3675   Ellerkamp, Alphonse. "The Kolping Society in America, "
AGR. 23, iii (1957): 25-27.

3676   Ellis, John. A Guide to American Catholic History. Milwaukee: Bruce, 1959.

3677   Furlan, W.   In Charity Unfeigned: The Life of Father Fran-
       cis Xavier Pierz.   Paterson, New Jersey: St. Anthony Guild
       Pr., 1952. A Minnesota German priest.

3678   Gellner, Charles. "Ecclesiastical History of the Catholic
       Germans in Maryland," RJGAH. 26 (1945): 37-48.

3679   Gleason, Philip. The Conservative Reformers: German-
       American Catholics and the Social Order. Notre Dame: Notre
       Dame University Pr., 1968.

3680   _____. The Central Verein, 1900-17: A Chapter in the
       History of the German-American Catholics. Notre Dame Uni-
       versity: Dissertation, 1960.

3681   _____. "German Catholic Missionaries in Maryland during
       the 18th Century," RJGAH. 26 (1945): 33-36.

3682   _____. "The Social Reform Activities of the Central
       Bureau, 1909-17," SJR. 54 (1961): 263-67, 301-04.

3683   Guide to Catholic Literature, 1888-1940. Detroit: Romig,
       1940.

3684   Hanousek, Mary. A New Assisi, The First Hundred Years
       of the Sisters of St. Francis of Assisi. Milwaukee: Bruce
       1948.

3685   Hodges, Joseph. St. Mary's Church Cemetary, 1851-1951.
       Richmond, Va., 1951.

3686   Hogan, Peter. "Americanism and the Catholic University of
       America," CHR. 33 (1947): 158-90.

3687   Howard, Brice. A History of St. Joseph, 1856-1956. St.
       Cloud, Minnesota, 1956.

3688   Inama, Fr. Adalbert. "The Letters of Fr. Adalbert Inama,"
       SJR. 54 (1961): 237-43, 276-82, 314-17, 352-53, 384-87;
       55 (1962): 26-30, 61-64, 94-96, 133-36, 166-69, 203-05, 242-
       44, 279-81, 312-16, 352-53, 390-93; 56 (1963): 27-30, 63-66,
       130-33, 171-72, 204-05.

3689   Janssen, Hans. "Benedictine Nuns in South Dakota," AGR.
       28, iv (1962): 32-34.

3690   Johnson, Peter. Crosier on the Frontier: A Life of John
       Martin Henni: Archbishop of Milwaukee. Madison: State
       Hist. Soc., 1959.

3691   Kleber, Albert. History of St. Meinrad Archabbey. St.
       Meinrad, Indiana: Grail, 1954.

3692   Kohler, Mary. Rooted in Hope: The Story of the Dominican
        Sisters of Racine, Wisconsin. Milwaukee: Bruce, 1962.

3693   Lenhart, John. "Beginnings of German Congregations in and
        around St. Louis 1838-44," SJR. 54 (1961): 163-65, 202-08.

3694   _____. "Beginnings of the Diocese of Milwaukee," SJR.
        60 (1967): 397-400, 423-27; 61 (1968): 26-30, 62-65, 98-105,
        170-75, 205-09, 240-42, 277-81, 396-400, 431-38; 62 (1969):
        27-32, 63-65.

3695   _____. "The Catholic Church in the State of Virginia,
        1785-1843," SJR. 49 (1956): 274-78.

3696   _____. "The Debt of Catholic American to Catholic Aus-
        tria," SJR. 58 (1965): 63-65.

3697   _____. "Economic Valuation of the German Catholic Con-
        gregation in Wheeling, W. Va., 1856-1955," SJR. 49 (1956):
        240-43.

3698   _____. "Ethnic Groups of the German Congregation of
        the Wheeling District, 1820-1949," SJR. 49 (1956): 96-101,
        130-33.

3699   _____. "German-American Catholics in Boston, 1846,"
        SJR. 36 (1943-44): 167-68, 207-08.

3700   _____. "German Catholic Congregations in the Wheeling,
        W. Va., District, 1820-1955: Statistics," SJR. 49 (1956):
        96-99.

3701   _____. "The German Catholic Orphanage in Wheeling,
        W. Va., 1886-1954," SJR. 49 (1956): 204-07.

3702   _____. "German-speaking Catholic Congregations Begin-
        nings, Alton, Illinois, 1836-94," SJR. 63 (1970-71): 280-83,
        385-88.

3703   _____. "A Guide for Catholic German Immigrants, 1869,"
        SJR. 52 (1960): 132-35, 166-68.

3704   _____. "Order of Services in German Congregations in
        Wheeling, W. Va., 1858-1956," SJR. 49 (1957): 312-14.

3705   _____. "Pioneer German Priests: Indiana, 1834-40,"
        SJR. 52 (1960): 26-28, 179-82, 214-17, 236-40; 53 (1961):
        26-28, 61-64, 132-34, 164-67, 200-03, 234-40, 272-75.

3706   _____. "Reconciliation of a Fallen-Away Parish in Wis-
        consin, 1852," SJR. 51 (1958): 24-29.

3707   _____. "Report of Rev. Francis Xavier Paulhuber, Mis-

sionary, on his Labors in America, 1851-56, " SJR. 50 (1957):
276-79, 311-15, 381-85.

3708   _____. "Report of the Missionary P. F. X. Weniger, S. J. ,
to the Ludwig-Missions-Verein in Munich on the Missions
Preached During 1869 in the United States, " SJR. 51 (1958):
96-101, 128-32, 236-38.

3709   _____. "Ursuline Beginnings in St. Louis, " SJR. 57
(1965): 275-76, 350-53, 384-86.

3710   Ludwig, M. A Chapter of Franciscan History: The Sisters
of the Third Order of Saint Francis of Perpetual Adoration,
1849-1949. New York: Bookman Associates, 1950.

3711   _____. Right-Hand Glove Uplifted: A Biography of Archbishop Michael Heiss. New York: Pageant, 1968.

3712   _____. "Sources for the Biography of Michael Heiss,
Bishop of La Crosse, 1868-80, and Archbishop of Milwaukee,
1881-90, " Recs. Amer. Cath. Hist. Soc. of Phila. 79 (1968):
195-222.

3713   McAndrews, Dunstan. Father Joseph Kundek, 1810-57: A
Missionary Priest of the Diocese of Vincennes. St. Meinrad,
Indiana: Grail, 1955.

3714   McCauley, Janet. "Pioneering German Jesuits in Colonial
Pennsylvania, 1741-81, " SJR. 58 (1965): 269-72, 304-08,
342-44; 58 (1966): 379-82, 414-18, 451-56; 59 (1966): 25-
27, 62-65, 99-101, 145-47.

3715   McGloin, John. "European Archival Resources for the Study
of California Catholic History, " CH. 30 (1961): 103-05.

3716   Mellon, Knox. "Christian Priber and the Jesuit Myth, "
SCHM. 61 (1960): 75-81.

3717   Meng, John. "Cahenslyism: The First Stage, 1883-91, "
CHR. 31 (1945): 389-413: 32 (1946): 302-40.

3718   Mulcahy, George. "Catholic Backgrounds in Lewisburg,
Union County, Pa. , " ACHS. 61 (1950): 98-100.

3719   Official Catholic Directory. New York: Kennedy, 1886-

3720   Parsons, Wilfrid. Early Catholic Americana: A List of
Books and other Works by Catholic Authors in the U. S.,
1729-1830. New York: Macmillan, 1939.

3721   "The Pastors of Conewago, 1750-1880, " ACHS. 60 (1949):
144-46.

3722   Pfaller, Louis. "Abbot and Bishop Wehrle: A Benedictine on the Old Frontier," Amer. Ben. Rev. 12 (1961): 461-84; 13 (1962): 71-122.

3723   _____. "Bishop Wehrle and the German Immigrants in North Dakota," NDQ. 29 (1961): 93-97.

3724   "Problems of a German-American Country Pastor in 1886," SJR. 50 (1957): 63-65.

3725   Prokop, D. "Der Aufstieg einer amerikanischen Benediktinerabtei deutscher Gründung: Ein Beitrag zum hundertjährigen Jubiläum der Abtei St. John's, Collegeville, Minnesota," Christ Unterwegs. 11 (1957): 8-16.

3726   Rattermann, Heinrich A. Dr. Johann Martin Henni, erster Bischof und Erzbischof von Milwaukee. Cincinnati, 1882.

3727   Regnert, Henry. "The Buffalo Mission," SJR. 52 (1961): 384-86.

3728   Rothan, Emmet. German Catholic Immigrant in the U. S. Catholic University of America: Dissertation, 1947.

3729   Scheper, Francis. "German Pioneers of the Faith," SJR. 47 (1955): 386-88; 48 (1956): 26-27, 217-19, 250-51, 288-89, 324-26; 49 (1956): 26-27, 59-62.

3730   _____. "Pioneers of the Faith: Rev. Francis Xavier Pierz," SJR. 48 (1956): 360-62, 396-98, 433-34.

3731   Shannon, James. Catholic Colonization on the Western Frontier. New Haven: Yale University Pr., 1957.

3732   "Sisters of St. Francis Centenary," AGR. 17, iii (1951): 27-28.

3733   Stauffer, Elmer. "Conewago Chapel," PD. 7 (1965): 28-33.

3734   Stoew, Walter. "John Cross, First Bishop of New Jersey," Hist. Mag. Prot. Episc. Ch. 35 (1966): 221-30.

3735   Tegeder, Vincent. "The Benedictines in Frontier Minnesota," MH. 32 (1951): 34-43.

3736   _____. "Pioneering Monks," MH. 33 (1952): 53-60. German monks in Minnesota.

3737   Thauren, Johannes. Ein Gnadenstrom zur Neuen Welt und seine Quelle: Die Leopoldinen Stiftung zur Unterstützung der amerikanischen Missionen. Wien: St. Gabriel, 1940.

3738   Thomas, M. Evangeline. "The Rev. Louis Dumortier, S. J.,

Itinerant Missionary to Central Kansas, 1859-67," KHQ. 20
(1952): 252-70.

3739   Treutlein, Theodore. "Father Gottfried Bernhardt Midden-
dorff, S. J. , Pioneer of Tucson," NMHR. 32 (1957): 310-18.

3740   Trisco, Robert. The Holy See and the Nascent Church in
the Middle Western U. S. , 1826-50. (Analecta Gregoriana,
125.) Rome: Gregorian University, 1962.

3741   Ursala, Mary. "Changing Patterns of Catholic Population in
Eastern U. S. ," AAG. 49 (1959): 197.

3742   Vollmar, Edward. "The Archives of the Missouri Province
of the Society of Jesus," Manuscripta. 12 (1968): 179-89.

3743   _____. The Catholic Church in America: An Historical
Bibliography. New Brunswick, New Jersey: Scarecrow, 1963.

3744   Weber, Ralph. The Life of Rev. John A. Zahm, C. S. C. :
American Catholic Apologist and Educator. University of
Notre Dame: Dissertation, 1956.

3745   Westermeier, Therese. "St. Walburga in America," AGR.
18, iv (1952): 19, 31.

Other Groups

3746   Beck, Clara. "History of Whitpain Township," BHSM. 5
(1946): 106-17, 179-218. About the Reformed Church.

3747   Bruyn, Kathleen. "Matthias Klaiber, Physician and Minister, "
CM. 33 (1956): 197-208. A German Methodist.

3748   Corwin, C. E. Manual of the Reformed Church in America,
1628-1933. New York: Reformed Church in America, 1922-
33.

3749   Dauerty, J. S. "The Source of Reformed Worship," JPHS.
36 (1958): 217-53.

3750   Dunn, David. A History of the Evengelical and Reformed
Church. Philadelphia: Christian Education Pr. , 1961.

3751   Fox, H. Clifford. German Presbyterians in the Upper Mississippi Valley. State University of Iowa: Dissertation, 1941.

3752   Frantz, John. "The Return to Tradition: An Analysis of the
New Measure Movement in the German Reformed Church, "
PH. 31 (July, 1964).

3753 _____. Revivalism in the German Reformed Church in
America to 1850, With Emphasis on the Eastern Synod. University of Pennsylvania: Dissertation, 1961.

3754 Frick, Willis. "John R. Kooken: Minister, Educator, Diplomat and Soldier, " BHSM. 15 (1966): 5-13.   German Reformed
minister.

3755 Glatfelder, Charles. "The Eighteenth Century German Lutheran and Reformed Clergymen in the Susquehanna Valley, "
PH. 20 (1953): 57-68.

3756 Hinke, William. Bibliography of the Reformed Church of the
U. S. Lancaster, Pa.: New Era Printing Co., 1902.

3757 _____. Ministers of the German Reformed Congregations
in Pennsylvania and other Colonies in the Eighteenth Century.
Philadelphia: Heidelberg Pr., 1951.

3758 Lang, Elfrieda. The History of Trinity Evangelical and Reformed Church, 1853-1953. Mount Vernon, Indiana. St.
Louis: Eden Publishing House, 1953.

3759 Merkle, Grace and Ardeth Mengs. "After Ninety Years: Immanuel Evangelical and Reformed Church of Orangeville, "
Hist. Wyoming. 13 (1960): 97-102.

3760 Muelder, Herman. The Early History of the German Methodist Conference of the Midwest. University of Minnesota:
Dissertation, 1928.

3761 O'Malley, John. The Otterbeins: The Postlude of Pietism.
Drew University: Dissertation, 1970. German Reformed
pastors.

3762 Rapp, David. "The Attitude of the Early Reformed Church
Fathers toward Worldly Amusements, " PF. 9 (1958): 40-53.

3763 Snyder, Charles. "The Beginnings of the Reformed Church in
Northumberland and Nearby Counties, NCHSP. 15 (1946): 37-
122.

3764 Weaver, Glenn. "The German Reformed Church and the Home
Missionary Movement before 1863: A Study in Cultural and
Religious Isolation, " CH. 22 (1953): 298-313.

3765 Weis, James. "The Presbyterian Mission to German Immigrants, " JPH. 43 (1965): 264-94.

3766 Weiser, Frederick. "Parochial Register of the Indian Creek
Reformed Church, 1753-1851," PGSP. 3 (1970): 117-79.

3767 Wetzel, Daniel. "First Reformed Church: 1753-1953, " HRBC
19 (1953): 46-50, 57-61.

3768   Wittke, Carl. William Nast: Patriarch of German Methodism.
        Detroit: Wayne State University Pr., 1959.

3769   Yoder, Don. "James Ross Reily, 1788-1844, Reformed Pas-
        tor on the Frontier," PD. 4 (1953): 9.

3770   _____. "Pastor Reily Rides the Lykens Valley Circuit,
        1812-15," PD. 4 (1953): 6-9.

The Freethinkers and Freie Gemeinden

3771   American Secular Union. Report of the International Congress
        for Progressive Thought and of the 27th Annual Congress of
        the American Secular Union and Freethought Federation. New
        York: The Truth Seeker Co., 1904. This meeting was held
        in 1904 in the St. Louis Freie Gemeinde.

3772   Cooper, Berenice. "Die Freie Gemeinde: Freethinkers on
        the Frontier," MH. 41 (1968): 53-60.

3773   Hoops, Walter. Our Rationalist Heritage: An Anthology for
        Freethinkers. Chicago: CF Printing Service, n.d.

3774   Johnson, Hildegard B. "List of Lectures and Debates Given
        Before the Davenport Turngemeinde," IJHP. 44 (1946): 54-60.

3775   Klemp, Friedrich. Denken und Freidenken: Vortrag. n.p.,
        1889. UC

3776   Knortz, Karl. Die Notwendigkeit einer Organisation der
        Freidenker. Milwaukee: Verlag des Bundes der Freien
        Gemeinden und Freidenker-Vereine von Nord-Amerika, 1910.
        DLC

3777   Kottinger, H. M. Leitfaden für den Unterricht in den Sonn-
        tags-Schulen freier Gemeinden, sowie überhaupt für die Ge-
        mütbildung und religiöse Aufklärung der Jugend. Milwaukee:
        G. P. Roth, 1871. DLC

3778   Muench, Friedrich. Gesammelte Schriften. St. Louis: C.
        Witter, 1902. GSP, DLC

3779   Schneider, Heinrich. "D. Karl Friedrich Bahrdt's Letter to
        George Washington," GR. 29 (1954): 230-33.

3780   Vonnegut, Clemens. Versuch eines Leitfadens zum Unterricht
        in der Sittenlehre im freidenkerischen Sinne. Milwaukee,
        1890. UC

3781   Weisert, John. "Eduard Mühl's Lichtfreund," AGR. 22, iv
        (1956): 30-31.

V. EDUCATION

A List of German-American Schools

3782   German-American School. c/o Dr. H. Ebenhoech, 3191
Waverly St., Palo Alto, Cal. 94306.

3783   German-American Schulabteilung. First Baptist Church of
Van Nuys, 14800 Sherman Way, Van Nuys, Cal.

3784   German-American Schulverein. 704 So. Spring St., No. 205,
Los Angeles, Cal. 90014.

3785   German-American Schulverein. 207 E. 84th St., New York,
N. Y.

3786   German-American Schulverein. 755 Channing Ave., Palo
Alto, Cal. 94301.

3787   German Educational Society. 3167 Kennedy Blvd., North
Bergen, New Jersey.

3788   German Language and Schulverein. Steubenhalle, 2924 W.
North Ave., Milwaukee, Wisconsin.

3789   German Language Bible Studies. Evengelical Mennonite
Brethren Church, Mountain Lake, Minnesota 56159.

3790   German Language School. St. Lukes Kirche, Boulder Hill,
Aurora, Ill.

3791   German Language School. Faith Church, Fairview & 59th,
Downers Grove, Ill.

3792   German Language School. Grace Lutheran School, 7310 W.
Division St., River Forest, Ill.

3793   German Language School. St. Timothy Church, 9000 N. Kil-
dare, Skokie, Ill.

3794   German Language School. Deutsches Haus, 2651 Pipestone
Rd., Benton Harbor, Michigan.

3795   German Language School. John E. Riley School, South Plain-
field, New Jersey.

3796   German Language School.   Farchers Grove, Springfield Rd.,
        Union, New Jersey.

3797   German Language School.   1154 Washington Ave., Westwood,
        New Jersey.

3798   German Language School.   Deutsch-Amerikanischer Kultur-
        verein, Jefferson Hall, 2617 W. Fond du Lac Ave., Milwaukee,
        Wisconsin.

3799   German Saturday School.   29 Crestview Rd., Manchester, New
        Hampshire.

3800   German School.   Box 26, Oakland, Cal. 94604.

3801   German School.   Box 5545, Redwood City, Cal.

3802   German School.   Marina Jr. High School, Chestnut & Filmore
        Streets, San Francisco, Cal.

3803   German School.   566 Cottonwood St., Vacaville, Cal. 95688.

3804   German School-D. A. N. K.   2517 N. 49th St., Milwaukee,
        Wisconsin 53210.

3805   German School-D. A. N. K.   Albright United Methodist Church,
        5555 W. Capitol, Milwaukee, Wisconsin.

3806   German Schulverein.   c/o D. Philippi, 409 Sunset Rd., Ala-
        meda, Cal. 94501.

3807   German Schulverein.   c/o V. Silversides, 126 Endeavor Dr.,
        Corte Madera, Cal. 94925.

3808   German Schulverein.   c/o H. Erdmann, 1850 San Anselmo,
        Fairfield, Cal.

3809   German Schulverein.   Walters School, 39600 Logan Dr., Fre-
        mont, Cal.

3810   German Schulverein.   1849 Fordham Way, Mt. View, Cal.
        94040.

3811   German Schulverein.   Oakland High School, Park & MacArthur
        Blvd., Box 26, Oakland, Cal. 94604.

3812   German Schulverein.   c/o S. Fiolka, 1196 Grand Teton,
        Pacifica, Cal. 94044.

3813   German Schulverein.   c/o G. Brugger, Kennedy School, Good-
        win Ave. & Connecticut Ave., Redwood City, Cal.

3814   German Schulverein.   California-Halle, Polk & Turk St., San
        Francisco, Cal.

3815 German Schulverein. Monroe School, 1055 S. Monroe St.,
      San Jose, Cal.

3816 German Schulverein. Box 4172, San Rafael, Cal.

3817 German Schulverein. Santa Venetia Middle School, No. San
      Pedro Rd., San Rafael, Cal.

3818 German Schulverein. Box 2491, Santa Clara, Cal. 95051.

3819 German Schulverein. c/o Dr. Hans Schneider, Potomas,
      Maryland.

3820 German Schulverein. St. Pius School, Utah & Grand St., S
      Louis, Missouri.

3821 Tri-State German-American School Society. c/o Dr. W.
      Kraeling, McMickan Hall, University of Cincinnati, Cincinna
      Ohio.

Teachers

3822 Barba, Preston. "The Pennsylvania German Who Conquered
      Paris, " Eck. (Feb. 8, 1958).

3823 Bixler, Miriam. "Ellen A. Brubaker, Pioneer Free Kinder
      gartner, " J. Lanc. Co. Hist. Soc. 71 (1967): 165-75.

3824 Emerson, Haven. "Health Education in Three Dimensions, "
      AGR. 12, v (1946): 4-7.

3825 Freund, Elisabeth. Crusader for Light: Julius R. Fried-
      lander: Founder of the Overbrook School for the Blind, 183
      Philadelphia: Dorrance, 1959.

3826 Gillan, Dennis. Some American Uses of Froebel. Rutgers
      State University: Dissertation, 1969.

3827 Gutek, Gerald. "An Examination of Joseph Neef's Theory o
      Ethical Education, " Hist. of Ed. Q. 9 (1969): 187-201.

3828 Hummel, William. "Abraham Reincke Beck: Portrait of a
      Schoolmaster, " J. Lanc. Co. Hist. Soc. 60 (1964): 1-40.

3829 Hunsicker, Robert. "Christopher Dock: Early American
      School Master, " Bul. HS. Mont. Co. 13 (1961): 25-46.

3830 Kistler, Richard. "The Professor is Busy, " Eck. (August
      7, 1948).

3831 Kreider, Carl. "Harold S. Bender: The Educator, " MQR.
      38 (1964): 121-29.

3832   Kretzmann, Karl. "The Rev. Dr. Augustus Lawrence Graebner, 1849-1904," CHIQ. 20 (1947): 79-93.

3833   Lazenby, M. C. "German Class on TV," AGR. 21, vi (1955):
30-31. About Ralph Wood's class.

3834   Leatherman, Quintus. "Christopher Dock, Mennonite Schoolmaster," MQR. 16 (1943): 32-44.

3835   McDonald, Grace. "Pioneer Teachers: The Benedictine
Teachers at St. Cloud," MH. 35 (1957): 263-71.

3836   Max Leopold: Scholar and Teacher. Philadelphia: Alumni
Association, Dropsie College for Hebrew and Cognate Learn-
ing, 1952.

3837   Mayer, Herbert. "Hoyer on History," CTM. 34 (1963): 395-
400.

3838   Milnes, Humphrey. "Hermann Boeschenstein," GLL. 23
(1969): 1-6.

3839   Morris, Monica. "Teacher Training in Missouri Before 1871,"
MHR. 43 (1948): 18-37.

3840   Munehrath, M. Bibliography of the Works of the School Sisters of St. Francis, Milwaukee, Wisconsin. Catholic University of America: Dissertation, 1965.

3841   Navall, Lotte. "Dedrich Navall: Writer and Teacher," ML.
24 (1969): 161-63.

3842   Owen, Ralph. "John Eiselmeier, 1861-1947," AGR. 13, iv
(1947): 34.

3843   Schley, John. Schley Letters Found in Speyer Archives,"
SHGM. 30 (1959): 112-14. Schley was the first Maryland
German schoolmaster.

3844   Shoemaker, Alfred. "Barring out the Schoolmaster," PD.
7 (1956): 14-17.

3845   Shriver, George. "Philip Schaff as a Teacher of Church History," J. Presby. Hist. 47 (1969): 74-92.

3846   Studer, Gerald. Christopher Dock: Colonial Schoolmaster.
Scottdale: Herald, 1967.

3847   Wegener, M. "Short Biographies of Some Outstanding Teachers of the Missouri Synod," CHIQ. 20 (1947): 170-80.

3848   Wegener, Wilhelm. "My Biography," CHIQ. 21 (1948): 6-26.

3849 _____. "Reminiscences of an Old Teacher, " CHIQ. 23
(1950): 59-65.

3850 White, Mary. "Madame Sophie Sosnowski, Educator of
Young Ladies, " CHQ. 50 (1966): 283-87.

Schools, Colleges and Seminaries in German-America

3851 Allgemeiner Schulverein zur Erhaltung des Deutschtums in
Amerika. Handbuch des Deutschtums in Amerika, Nebst
einem Adressbuch der deutschen Auslandschulen. Leipzig:
Reimer, 1906.

3852 Bachmann, E. Theodore. "Curricular Offerings on the History of Lutheranism, " CHIQ. 38 (1966): 197-203.

3853 Baltimore. Zions Schule. Jahresbericht des Inspectors bei
der Jahresversammlung des Schulvereins am 23. Juni 1872.
Baltimore: Schneidereith, 1872. MdBZ

3854 Becker, Ernest. "History of the English-German Schools in
Baltimore, " RJGAH. 25 (1942): 13-17.

3855 Bell, Whitfield. "Benjamin Franklin and the German Charity
Schools, " Proc. Amer. Phil. Soc. 99 (1956): 381-87.

3856 Berky, Andrew. "The Schoolhouse Near the Spring: A History of the Union School and Church Association, Dillingers-
ville, Pa., 1835-1955, " PGSP. 56 (1955): 173 pp.

3857 Beutler, Albert. The Founding and History of Bethel College
of Indiana. University of Michigan: Dissertation, 1970.

3858 Birkner, Elsa. "Lutheran Secondary Education in Chicago, "
CHIQ. 32 (1959): 70-86.

3859 Blied, Benjamin. "From Munich to Milwaukee by Way of
Pennsylvania, " AGR. 14, i (1947): 21-23, 37.

3860 Bosse, Richard. Origins of Lutheran Education in Ohio.
Ohio State University: Dissertation, 1969.

3861 Bowman, Paul. Brethren Education in the Southeast. Elgin,
Ill.: Brethren Publishing House, 1955.

3862 Buehring, Paul. "Wilhelm Schmidt: Founder of Columbia
Seminary, " LuthQ. 7 (1955): 348-57.

3863 Buerger, E. "History of the Lutheran High School in Milwaukee, Wisconsin, " CHIQ. 33 (1961): 107-20.

3864   Butterfield, L. A Letter by Dr. Benjamin Rush Describing
       the Consecration of the German College at Lancaster in June,
       1787. Lancaster: Franklin and Marshall College, 1945.

3865   Clauser, Jerome. Comenian Pedagogy and the Moravian
       School Curriculum, 1740-1850. Pennsylvania State University:
       Dissertation, 1961.

3866   Damm, Helmut. The University of Michigan from 1850 to
       1917 as a Leading Center of German Influences During the
       Nation's Economic Take-Off Period. University of Michigan:
       Dissertation, 1970.

3867   Deutsch-Amerikanischer Lehrerseminar. Jahrbuch. Milwau-
       kee: Lehrerseminar, 1915-18. UC

3868   Deutsch-Englische Akademie: Kurzgefasste Geschichte der-
       selben und des Nordamerikanischen Lehrerseminars. Mil-
       waukee, 1901. UC

3869   "Deutsche hohe Schule in Lancaster, Pennsylvania," Allg.
       Lit-Z. 1 (1788): Col. 143. NYPL

3870   "Deutsche Schule des D. A. N. K. -Gruppe Milwaukee," DMH.
       (Sept. 27, 1973).

3871   Die deutsche Schule in Amerika: Organ des Verein deutscher
       Lehrer in Amerika: Monatsschrift für Nationale Erziehung in
       den deutschen Schulen und Familien. Wolfenbüttel, 1902- .

3872   Dibelius, W. and G. Lenz. "Adressbuch der deutschen Aus-
       landschulen," in Handbuch des Deutschtums in Amerika. Ber-
       lin, 1904.

3873   Doerksen, John. Mennonite Berthren Bible College and Col-
       lege of Arts: Its History, Philosophy and Development. Uni-
       versity of North Dakota: Dissertation, 1968.

3874   Dulon, Rudolf. Aus Amerika: Über Schule, deutsche Schule,
       an Schulen und deutsch-amerikanischen Schulen. Leipzig:
       Winter, 1866. DLC

3875   Dunson, Alvis. "Notes on the German Influence on Education
       in Early Missouri," AGR. 25, v (1959): 17-19.

3876   Emrick, Howard. The Role of the Church in the Development
       of Education in Pennsylvania, 1638 to 1834. University of
       Pittsburgh: Dissertation, 1959.

3877   Erickson, D. Public Controls for Nonpublic Schools. Chi-
       cago: University of Chicago Pr., 1969.

3878   Fick, H. H. Die Poesie in der deutschamerikanischen Schule.
       Cincinnati, 1883. UC

3879 Finckh, Alice. "Lankenau School Sixty Years," AGR. 16, iv
      (1950): 9-11.

3880 Fraser, Stewart. "Some Foreign Views of American Educa-
      tion: The Nineteenth Century Background," Compar. Ed. Rev.
      12 (1968): 300-09.

3881 Freidel, Frank. "A Plan for Modern Education in Early
      Philadelphia," PH. 14 (1947): 175-84.

3882 Freitag, Alfred. A History of Concordia Teachers College:
      1864-1964. University of Southern California: Dissertation,
      1965.

3883 Frentz, Clarence. "A History of the Winter Bible Schools of
      the Mennonite Church," MQR. 16 (1942): 51-81, 178-95.

3884 Das Gemeinschulwesen von Cincinnati: Jahresbericht. Cin-
      cinnati, 1870. UC.

3885 "German at Thiel College," AGR. 24 (1958): 25-26.

3886 Goebel, Julius. Zur deutschen Frage in Amerika: Ein Wort
      über Schule, Seminar und Schulverein. New York, 1886. UC

3887 Gohla, Kurt. "Die Schultätigkeit des Deutsch-Amerikanischen
      Schulverein von New York," ZKA. 14 (1964): 79-83.

3888 Griebsch, Max. Nationale Erziehung in den Vereinigten
      Staaten von Nordamerika. München, 1907.

3889 Grunewald, Dora. "Vom Deutschen Tag und von der Deutsche
      Sprachschule," DMH. (Aug. 23, 1973).

3890 Haller, Mabel. Early Moravian Education in Pennsylvania.
      Bethlehem: Times Publishing Co., 1953.

3891 _____. "Moravian Influence on Higher Education in Colon-
      ial America," PH. 25 (1959): 205-22.

3892 Harbold, P. "Schools and Education in the Borough of Lan-
      caster," LCHP. 46 (1942): 1-44.

3893 Harmon, John. "Foreign Languages in Independent Secondary
      Schools, Fall, 1959," MLA Report. (1961): 35-42.

3894 Haselmayer, Louis. "Das deutsche Kollegium: Wesleyan's
      Teutonic Past," Ala. 35 (1960): 206-15.

3895 Die hauptsächlichen deutschen Vereinigungen, Kirchen, Schu-
      len und sonstigen deutschen Einrichtungen in Amerika. Ber-
      lin: Zentralverlag, 1932.

3896   Hendrickson, Walter. "St. Louis Academy of Science: The Early Years, " MHR. 61 (1966): 83-94.

3897   Henry, Thomas. "The Singing School at the Ephrata Cloister, " KFQ. 11 (1966): 203-06.

3898   Hertzler, Silas. "Attendance in Mennonite Secondary Schools and Colleges, 1949-50, " MQR. 26 (1952): 48-62.

3899   _____. "Attendance in Mennonite Secondary Schools and Colleges, 1950-51, " MQR. 26 (1952): 280-97.

3900   _____. "Attendance in Mennonite Colleges, 1959-60, " MQR. 35 (1961): 238-41; 36 (1962): 276-79.

3901   Hollenbach, Raymond. "The Early Schools of Heidelberg Township, " Eck. (May 14-June 18, 1960).

3902   _____. "The Heidelberg School Board in the Civil War, " Eck. (July 16, 1960).

3903   Hostetler, John. Conference on Child Socialization. Philadelphia: Temple University, 1969.

3904   _____. Educational Achievements: Achievement and Life Styles in a Traditional Society, the Old Order Amish. Washington: HEW, 1969.

3905   _____. "Old Order Amish Child Rearing and Schooling Practices: A Summary Report, " MQR. 44 (April 1970).

3906   _____. "Total Socialization: Modern Hutterite Educational Practices, " MQR. 44 (Jan., 1970).

3907   Huebener, Theodore. "The German School of the New York Turn-Verein, " AGR. 16, vi (1950): 14-15.

3908   _____. "Private German Language Schools, " GQ. 23 (1950): 221-22.

3909   Johnson, Peter. Halcyon Days: Story of St. Francis Seminary in Milwaukee, 1856-1956. Milwaukee: Bruce, 1956.

3910   Keefer, Daryle. The Education of the Amish Children in Lagrange County, Indiana. Carbondale: Southern Illinois University Pr., 1969.

3911   Keiter, Kenneth. "Early Lutheran Primary Education in Pennsylvania, " Eck. (Mar. 26-Apr. 2, 1949).

3912   Kloss, Heinz. "Die deutschamerikanische Schule, " JAS. 7 (1962): 141-75.

3913 _____. "Die privaten Schulen der führenden weiseen Zuwanderer-Volksgruppen in den Vereinigten Staaten," Volksforsch. 4 (1940): 161-75.

3914 Landis, Elizabeth. "The Schwenkfelders and their School System, 1764-1842," HRBC. 35 (1970): 99-102, 111-16.

3915 Lenhart, John. "German Catholic Schools in Wheeling, W. Va., 1846-1955," SJR. 49 (1956): 168-69.

3916 _____. "Promoters of the German School Sisters of Notre Dame," SJR. 58 (1965): 29-30.

3917 _____. "The State of U.S. Catholic Schools in 1855," SJR. 56 (1963): 239-43, 278-281, 315-16, 349-52, 358.

3918 Leutheuser, Arthur. "The Founding, Rise and Extinction of Walther College," CHIQ. 31 (1958): 33-38.

3919 McLain, William. "The Julius K. Hofmann Memorial Fund in Baltimore," AGR. 26 (1959): 7-9.

3920 Madeira, Sheldon. A Study of the Education of the Old Order Amish Mennonites of Lancaster County, Pennsylvania. University of Pennsylvania: Dissertation, 1955.

3921 Merkens, Albert. "Early Lutheran Settlers and Schools in Northern Illinois," CHIQ. 21 (1948): 68-74, 128-35, 180-86; 22 (1949): 37-42, 89-94.

3922 Meyer, Adolphe. Educational History of the American People New York: McGraw-Hill, 1957.

3923 Meyer, Carl. "Concordia Seminary: For 125 Years Toward a More Excellent Ministry," MHR. 59 (1965): 210-222.

3924 _____. "Teacher Training in the Missouri Synod to 1864,' CHIQ. 30 (1957): 97-110, 157-66.

3925 Münnich, U. "Der Deutschunterricht in Fort Wayne, Indiana, USA," Muttersprache. 79 (1969): 20-25.

3926 Mustard, Helen. "A Survey of Language Schools Not Under Academic Auspices," MLA Report. (1961): 187-96.

3927 New York. Deutsch-Amerikanischer Schulverein. Deutsch-Amerikanischer Schulverein von New York: Festschrift zur silbernen Jubelfeier. New York: Goldman, 1908.

3928 Niermann, Henry. "History of Concordia College, New Orleans," CHIQ. 36 (1963): 65-89.

3929 Norwood, F. A. "Frankfurt-am-Main and Baldwin-Wallace College," OSAHQ. 60 (1951): 20-27.

3930   Ohio. German Teacher's Association. Jahrbuch. Cincinnati:
       Deutscher Lehrerverein des Staates Ohio, 1893-95.

3931   Pellman, Hubert. Eastern Mennonite College, 1917-67. Har-
       risonburg: Eastern Mennonite College, 1967.

3932   Rattermann, Heinrich A. "Die Pioniere des deutschen Schul-
       system in den V. S.: August Renz, Dr. Friedrich Rölker, und
       Joseph A. Hermann, " in Gesammelte Ausgewählte Werke.
       Cincinnati: Selbstverlag, 1914, vol. 12: 108-16.

3933   Richards, George. History of the Theological Seminary of the
       Reformed Church in the United States 1825-1934: Evengelical
       and Reformed Church 1934-1952. Lancaster: Rudisill, 1952.

3934   Roberts, Clarence. North Central College: A Century of
       Liberal Education 1861-1961. Naperville, Ill.: North Central
       College, 1960.

3935   Rohrbach, Heinrich. "Lawrence's German School, " AGR. 24
       (1958): 26-27.

3936   Romig, Edgar. "The English and Low Dutch Schoolmaster, "
       NYHS. 43 (1959): 149-60.

3937   Rosewall, Richard. Singing Schools of Pennsylvania, 1800-
       1900. University of Minnesota: Dissertation, 1969.

3938   Savage, Doris. "The Rochester Theological Seminary in the
       Old U. S. Hotel, " Roch. Hist. 31 (1969): 1-23.

3939   Schmidt, Wayne E. Wisconsin Synod Lutheran Parochial
       Schools: An Overview of the Years 1850-90. University of
       Wisconsin: Dissertation, 1968.

3940   Schoff, Kitt. and E. Haines. "German Sectarian and British
       Friend, " AGR. 26, ii (1959): 17-19. About a bilingual school.

3941   "Schulwesen der Deutschen in Pennsylvania, " in A. L. Schloe-
       zer, Stats-Anzeiger. 12 (1788): 471-80. NYPL

3942   Schuricht, Hermann. Geschichte der deutschen Schulbestre-
       bungen in Amerika. Leipzig, 1884.

3943   Stach, John. "The Changing Character of Concordia College,
       Ft. Wayne, Indiana, as Reflected in Synodical Resolutions,
       1847-1953, " CHIQ. 26 (1953): 115-19.

3944   _____. A History of the Lutheran Schools of the Missouri
       Synod in Michigan, 1845-1940. Ann Arbor: Edwards, 1942.

3945   Suelflow, Roy. The History of Concordia Seminary, St. Louis,
       1839-1865. Washington University: Dissertation, 1946.

3946   _____. "The History of Concordia Seminary, St. Louis,
            1847-65," CHIQ. 24 (1951): 49-68, 97-124.

3947   Tortora, Vincent. "The Amish and their School Problem,"
            Eck. (Oct. 8, 1955).

3948   _____. "The Amish in their One-Room Schoolhouses,"
            PFL. 11 (1960): 42-46.

3949   Umble, John. Goshen College, 1894-1954: A Venture in
            Christian Higher Education. Goshen, Indiana: Goshen Col-
            lege, 1955.

3950   Viereck, Louis. Zwei Jahrhunderte deutschen Unterrichts in
            den Vereinigten Staaten. Braunschweig: Friedrich Vieweg,
            1903.

3951   Voigt, Frieda. The Engelmann Heritage. Milwaukee: Mil-
            waukee Alumni Association of the National Teacher's Seminary,
            1951.

3952   _____. "The National Teacher's Seminary, 1878-1919,"
            Hist. Messenger Mil. Co. HS. 25 (1969): 137-39.

3953   Voigt, Harry. Concordia, Missouri: A Centennial History.
            Concordia: Centennial Committee, 1960.

3954   Vonderlage, E. "The American Luther-League," CHIQ. 36
            (1963): 33-42.

3955   _____. "The Michigan Storm Center in the School Ques-
            tion," CHIQ. 35 (1962): 37 ff.

3956   Waite, Frederick. "American Sectarian Medical Colleges,"
            BHM. 19 (1946): 148-66.

3957   Wallace, Paul. Lebanon Valley College: A Centennial His-
            tory. Annville, Pa.: Lebanon Valley College, 1966.

3958   Wedel, P. "Beginnings of Secondary Education in Kansas,"
            ML. 3 (1948): 14-17.

3959   _____. The Story of Bethel College. North Newton, Kan-
            sas: Bethel College, 1954.

3960   Wentz, Frederick. "Evangelical Academies and America's
            Lutherans," LuthQ. 14 (1962): 126 ff.

3961   Willibrand, W. "When German Was King," GQ. 30 (1957):
            254-61.

3962   Woolverton, John. "William Augustus Muhlenberg and the
            Founding of St. Paul's College," Hist. Mag. Prot. Episc.
            Ch. 29 (1960): 192-218.

3963   Zeydel, Edwin.   "New Light on the Early Teaching of German
        in Cincinnati, " BCHS. 22 (1964): 257-58.

3964   _____.   "The Teaching of German in Cincinnati: An His-
        torical Survey, " HPSQ. 20 (1962): 29-37.

3965   _____.   "The Teaching of German in the U. S. From Co-
        lonial Times to Present, " GQ. 37 (1964): 315-92.

VI. CULTURAL LIFE

<u>Art</u>

3966   Adams, Ruth. <u>Pennsylvania Dutch Art.</u> Cleveland: World Publishing, 1950.

3967   Alderfer, William. "The Artist Gustav Pfau, " J. Ill. State HS. 60 (1968): 383-90.

3968   Allen, George. "A Note on Pennsylvania Dutch Art, " Eck. (Mar. 19, 1949).

3969   "An American Artist, " AGR. 16, iv (1950): 28. About S. Kempf.

3970   Andrews, Katherine. "Walter von Gunten: Scherenschnitte Artist, " Wisc. Tales & Trails. 7 (1966): 23-25.

3971   Art Index: A Cumulative Author and Subject Index to a Selected List of Fine Arts Periodicals. New York: Wilson, 1933- .

3972   "An Artist at Ninety, " AGR. 19, iii (1953): 20. On J. Otto Schweizer.

3973   B., L. "Swiss Painters of the American Indians, " SAHS. 1 (1965): 7-9.

3974   Baker, Adelaide. "The Work of Margaret Seeler, " AGR. 28 (1962): 10-12.

3975   Barba, Preston. "Folk Art on Pennsylvania German Tombstones, " HRBC. 20 (1955): 42-47.

3976   _____. "Pennsylvania German Tombstones, " AGR. 20, vi (1954): 24-28.

3977   _____. "Pennsylvania German Tombstones: A Study in Folk Art, " PGFS. 18 (1954): 1-228.

3978   _____. "Symbols and Stones, " PH. 23 (1956): 241-47.

3979   Beal, Rebecca. Jacob Eichholtz, 1776-1842: Portrait

Painter of Pennsylvania. Philadelphia: Hist. Soc. of Pa.,
1969.

3980 Bender, Harold. "Mennonites in Art," MQR. 27 (1954): 187-
203.

3981 Benisovich, Michael and Anna Heilmaier. "Peter Rindisbacher, Swiss Artist," MH. 32 (1957): 155-62.

3982 Benson, Evelyn. "Gilbert and Mason: Pennsylvania Wood
Engravers," PD. 7 (1956): 9-13.

3983 Bier, Justus. "Stefan Hirsch's Old World Trilogy," AGR.
19, iv (1953): 18-19, 30.

3984 Bixler, Leo. "Pine Tar and its Uses," PFL. 13 (1963): 18-
23.

3985 "Bodmer-Miller Bonanza Comes to Omaha's Joslyn Art Museum," MMH. 12 (1962): 75.

3986 Boyer, Walter. "The Meaning of Human Figures in Pennsylvania Dutch Folk Art," PFL. 11 (1960): 5-23.

3987 Brand, Millen. Fields of Peace: A Pennsylvania German Album. New York: Doubleday, 1970.

3988 [Brehme.] "Claire Eichbaum Brehme," AGR. 22, vi (1956):
29.

3989 Brown, Mark. "Some Reflections on a Threatened Treasure,"
Montana: Mag. West. Hist. 20 (1970): 55-58.

3990 Caumann, Samuel. The Living Museum: Experiences of an
Art Historian, Alexander Dorner. New York: New York
University Pr., 1957.

3991 Cotton, Bruce. "A Southern Artist on the Civil War," AH.
9 (1958): 117-20. On Adalbert Volck.

3992 Davidson, Marshall. "Carl Bodmer's Unspoiled West," AH.
14, iii (1963): 43.

3993 De Francesco, I. Art of the Pennsylvania Germans. American Crayon Co., 1947.

3994 Dennis, James. Karl Bitter (1867-1915), Architectural Sculptor. University of Wisconsin: Dissertation, 1963.

3995 Dielmann, Henry. "Elisabeth Ney, Sculptor," SHQ. 45
(1961): 157-83.

3996 Dresser, Louisa. "The Background of Colonial American

Portraiture: Some Pages from a European Notebook, " Amer.
Antiq. Soc., Proc. 76 (1966): 19-58.

3997 [Ehrlich.] "William Ehrlich, " AGR. 17, iv (1951): 10.

3998 Engel, Lorenz. Among the Plains Indians. Minneapolis:
Lerner, 1970. Paintings of Karl Bodmer.

3999 Ernst, Jimmy and F. du Plessix. "The Artist Speaks: My
Father Max Ernst, " Art in Amer. (Nov. -Dec., 1968): 54-61.

4000 Ferris, Edythe. "Karl Rungius, Artist, " AGR. 18, iv (1952):
9-10.

4001 Finckh, Alice. "Friend of the Blackfeet, " AGR. 17, vi
(1951): 12-13. About W. Reiss.

4002 Finkelstein, I. The Life and Art of Josef Albers. New York
University: Dissertation, 1968.

4003 Francis, Henry. "Early German Paintings in the Cleveland
Museum of Art, " AGR. 21, ii (1954): 4-9.

4004 Gerdts, William. "Edward Kranich, 1826-1891, " NJHS. 79
(1961): 16-20.

4005 Gomersall, R. "A Father and Son Paint, " AGR. 17, i (1950):
10-13. On the Newswangers.

4006 Goosman, Mildred. "Karl Bodmer: Earliest Painter in Montana, " Montana: Mag. of West. Hist. 20 (1970): 36-41.

4007 Grafly, Dorothy. "Fritz Janschka, " AGR. 20, i (1953): 6-8.

4008 _____. "Paula Himmelsbach Balano, " AGR. 22, i (1955):
26-28.

4009 Grosz, George. A Little Yes and a Big No. New York:
Dial, 1947.

4010 Grunewald, Dora. "Kunst und Leben, " DMH. (Oct. 18, 1973).

4011 Gürster, Eugen. "Anne Marie Jauss, An American German
Painter, " AGR. 17, v (1951): 8-12.

4012 Heintzelman, Arthur. "Woodcuts by Karl Friedrich Zahring-
er, " Boston PLQ. 8 (1956): 204-08.

4013 Herbatschek, Heinrich. "George Peter: Ein deutschameri-
kanischer Maler, " AGR. 13 (1946): 32.

4014 Hilmer, George. "A Painter of Saxon Immigration Scenes, "
CHIQ. 28 (1955): 27-34.

4015   Hollyday, Guy. "The Ephrata Codex: Relationships Between
       Text and Illustration, " PFL. 20 (1970): 28-43.

4016   Horan, James. The Life and Art of Charles Schreyvogel:
       Printer-Historian of the Indian Fighting Army of the Ameri-
       can West. New York: Crown, 1969.

4017   Kaiser, Leo. "Seven Upon the Green: German Bronzes of
       St. Louis, " MIA. 12 (1962): 15-20.

4018   [Kaufman.] "Enit Kaufman, " AGR. 23, iv (1957): 27.

4019   Kaufman, Henry. Pennsylvania Dutch American Folk Art.
       New York: American Studio Books, 1946.

4020   Kieffer, Elizabeth. "Penmanship: The Art of the Scrivener, "
       PD. 5 (1954): 3, 12.

4021   Koenig, Karl. "Otto Georg Hitzberger, " AGR. 19, v (1953):
       24-26.

4022   Kriebel, Lester. "Irwin Peter Mensch: Last of the Pennsyl-
       vania Dutch Fraktur Artists, " HRBC. 18 (1953): 40-46.

4023   Kurtz, Wilbur. "How the Cyclorama was Painted, " AH. 7
       (1956): 45. About W. Wehner.

4024   Lichten, Frances. Folk Art Motifs of Pennsylvania. New
       York: Hastings, 1954.

4025   _____. Folk Art of Rural Pennsylvania. New York:
       Scribners, 1963.

4026   _____. Fraktur: The Illuminated Manuscripts of the
       Pennsylvania Dutch. Philadelphia: Free Library, 1958.

4027   [Linke.] "Conrad J. Linke, " AGR. 22, iii (1956): 20-21.

4028   Loggins, Vernon. Two Romantics and Their Ideal Life. New
       York: Odyssey, 1947. About Elisabet Ney.

4029   "The Lost Art of Fractur Painting: Pennsylvania German De-
       sign, " Design. 61 (1959): 72.

4030   Maass, Joachim. "The Work of the Sculptor: Henry Rox, "
       AGR. 12, iii (1946): 23-27.

4031   McAllister, William. Pennsylvania German Wood Carving.
       (Home Craft Course, 13.) Keyser, 1945.

4032   Matthey, Horst. "Indianermaler und posthumer Botschafter:
       Charles Wimar, " ZKA. 19 (1969): 250-52.

4033   Maxwell, E. "Max Wieczorek," AGR. 18, iv (1952): 15-18.

4034   Meuli, Karl. "Peter Rindisbacher, der Indianermaler aus
        dem Emmental," in Beiträge zur Volkskunde. Basel, 1960,
        200 pp.

4035   Middleton, Margaret. "Jeremiah Theüs," AGR. 19, ii (1952):
        11-13.

4036   Moscanyi, Paul. Karl Knaths. Washington: Phillips Gal-
        lery, 1957.

4037   Mook, Maurice. "S. Roesen: The Williamsport Painter,"
        Eck. (Dec. 3, 1955).

4038   "Nature in Art: The Grofes," AGR. 13, iv (1947): 24-28.

4039   Newton, Earle. "Jacob Eichholtz," PH. 26 (1959): 103-18.

4040   New York. Historical Society. Dictionary of Artists in
        America, 1564-1860. New Haven: Yale University Pr., 1957.

4041   Norman, John. "The Painting Preacher: John Valentine
        Haidt," PH. 20 (1953): 18-86.

4042   Patrick, Ransom. The Early Life of John Neagle: Philadel-
        phia Portrait Painter. Princeton University: Dissertation,
        1958.

4043   Pennsylvania German Fraktur and Color Drawings ... Ex-
        hibited at Pennsylvania Farm Museum of Landis Valley, Lan-
        caster, Pa. Lancaster: Landis Valley Associates, 1969.

4044   Pinckney, Pauline. Painting in Texas: The Nineteenth Cen-
        tury. Austin: University of Texas Pr., 1967.

4045   Purnell, M. A. "Fritz Eichenberg," AGR. 16, iii (1950): 7-
        12, 26.

4046   Richter, F. "The Art of the Miniature," AGR. 16, vi (1950):
        20-22.

4047   Robacker, Earl. "Major and Minor in Fractur," PD. 7
        (1956): 2-7.

4048   _____ and Ada Robacker. "Floral Motifs in Dutchland's
        Art," PFL. 17 (1968): 2-7.

4049   Roessler, Hermann. "An American German Primitive Paint-
        er," AGR. 26, iv (1960): 29.

4050   Rox, Henry. "Eric Isenburger's Paintings," AGR. 13, i
        (1946): 14-17.

4051 Runes, Dagobert David and H. Schrickel. Encyclopedia of the Arts. New York: Philosophical Library, 1946.

4052 Rutledge, Anna. "Portraits in Varied Media in the Collections of the Maryland Historical Society," MdHM. 41 (1946): 282-326.

4053 _____. "Portraits Painted Before 1900 in the Collection of the Maryland Historical Society," MdHM. 41 (1946): 11-50.

4054 "Samson Schames," AGR. 22, iv (1956): 28-29.

4055 [Schrag.] Exhibition of Paintings and Drawings by Karl Schrag. New York: Kraushaar Galleries, 1969.

4056 Schreiber, Theodore. "German Art in the City Art Museum of St. Louis," AGR. 13, iii (1947): 19-23.

4057 Shelley, Donald. "The Fraktur-Writings or Illuminated Manuscripts of the Pennsylvania Germans," PGFS. 23 (1958-59): 373 pp.

4058 Shiffman, Joseph. "The Alienation of the Artist: Alfred Stieglitz," Amer. Q. 3 (1951): 244-58.

4059 Smith, Ophia. "A Survey of Artists in Cincinnati: 1789-1830," BCHS. 25 (1967): 3-20.

4060 Smith, Ralph. A Biographical Index of American Artists. Baltimore: Williams & Wilkins, 1930.

4061 Sommer, Frank. Pennsylvania German Prints, Drawings, and Paintings: A Selection from the Winterthur Collection. Winterthur, Del.: Winterthur Museum, 1965.

4062 Spawn, Willman. "To Many Lands," AGR. 14, i (1947): 25-28.

4063 Stehle, R. "Ferdinand Pettrich in America," PH. 33 (1966): 389-411.

4064 Steinitz, Kate. "Kurt Schwitters and America," in Kurt Schwitters: A Portrait From Life. Berkeley: University of California Pr., 1968, pp. 110-21.

4065 Stoudt, John. Early Pennsylvania Arts and Crafts. New York: Barnes, 1964.

4066 _____. Pennsylvania German Folk Art. Allentown, Pa.: Schlechters, 1948.

4067 Taft, Robert. "The Pictorial Record of the Old West:

Heinrich Balduin Möllhausen, " KHQ. 16 (1948): 225-44.
About his sketches of America.

4068 _____. "The Pictorial Record of the Old West, " KHQ. 19
(1951): 225-53.

4069 Taylor, David. Lights Across the Delaware. Philadelphia:
Lippincott, 1954. On E. Leutze.

4070 Thieme, Ulrich and F. Becker. Allgemeines Lexikon der
bildenden Künstler von der Antike bis zur Gegenwart. Leipzig: Seeman, 1907-50. Lists locations of art works.

4071 Trump, Richard. The Life and Work of Albert Bierstadt.
Ohio State University: Dissertation, 1963.

4072 Vagts, Alfred. "Wilhelm Heine: Traveler Artist, " AGR. 22,
i (1955): 9-13.

4073 [van Loen.] "Alfred van Loen, " AGR. 26, iii (1960): 28.

4074 Vanstone, James. "An Early Nineteenth Century Artist in
Alaska: Louis Choris and the First Kotzebue Expedition, "
PNQ. 51 (1960): 145-58.

4075 Villard, Oswald. "Karl Bitter, Sculptor, " CG. 5 (1945): 40-
44.

4076 Vollmar, Hans. Allgemeines Lexikon der bildenden Künstler
des XX. Jahrhunderts. Leipzig: Seemann, 1953-62.

4077 [Vorst.] "Joseph P. Vorst, " MHR. 42 (1948): 198.

4078 Wagner, William. "George Rackelmann, Iowa Artist, " Annals
of I. 37 (1966): 275-91.

4079 Wainwright, Nicholas. "Augustus Kollner, Artist, " PMHB.
84 (1960): 325-35.

4080 "Water Colors by Fritz Richter, " AGR. 17, iv (1951): 18-19,
51.

4081 Weiner, Egon. "Anton Grauel: The Sculptor, " AGR. 20, v
(1954): 19, 31.

4082 Weisert, John. "Carl Brenner's Polimosorama, " FCHQ. 30
(1956): 315-18.

4083 Werner, Alfred. "Painter With X-Rays Eyes, " AGR. 22, iii
(1956): 9-13. On O. Kokoschka.

4084 Weygandt, Cornelius. "Beasts in Dutchland, " PD. 6 (1955):
10-15. Depiction of animals in folk art.

4085 _____. "Dutch Folk Art, " PD. 5 (1954): 12-15.

4086 Who's Who in American Art. New York: Bowker, 1935- .

4087 Wight, Frederick. Hans Hofmann. Berkeley: University of California Pr., 1957.

4088 _____. "Lyonel Feininger, " AGR. 20, vi (1954): 18-19.

4089 Wust, Klaus. Folk Art in Stone: Southwest Virginia. Edinburgh: Shenandoah History, 1970.

4090 Wyneken, H. "A Memorial to Gustav Pfau: Artist, " CHIQ. 21 (1948): 149-51.

4091 Zehner, Olive. "Harry S. High Folk Art Collection, " PD. 6 (1954): 16-19.

4092 Zieglschmid, A. "Petri and Lungkwitz, Pioneer Artists in Texas, " AGR. 9 (1942): 4-6.

Architecture

4093 Barba, Preston. "Unser Scheiere, " Eck. (Aug. 6, 1949).

4094 Becker, Carl and W. Daily. "Some Architectural Aspects of German-American Life in Nineteenth Century Cincinnati, " HPSQ. 20 (1962): 75-88.

4095 Bucher, Robert. "The Swiss Bank House in Pennsylvania, " PFL. 18 (1968-69): 3-11.

4096 "Chicago: Metropole der Architektur, " DMH. (Sept. 13, 1973). German architects in Chicago.

4097 Davis, Mary. "The History of the Hain Houses, " HRBC. 33 (1968): 122-24, 137, 146.

4098 Dieffenbach, Victor. "Building a Pennsylvania Barn, " PFL. 12 (1961): 20-24.

4099 Dornbusch, Charles. Pennsylvania German Barns. Allentown, Pa.: Schlechters, 1958.

4100 "Early Middle-Western Buildings: Drawings by Kenneth Becker, " AGR. 14, v (1948): 42-43.

4101 "Evangelisch-Reformirter Kirchenbau: 1773, " Eck. (Aug. 13, 1966).

4102 Frank, John. "Adolphus Heiman: Architect and Soldier, " THQ. 5 (1946): 35-57.

4103   Graeff, Arthur. "The Graeff House," Eck. (May 1, 1965).

4104   Horst, Melville and E. Smith. Covered Bridges of Pennsyl-
        vania Dutchland. Akron, Pa.: Applied Arts, 1960.

4105   Howland, Garth. "An Architectural History of the Moravian
        Church, Bethlehem, Pa.," MHS. 14 (1947): 51-132.

4106   Hurwitz, Elizabeth. "Decorative Elements in the Domestic
        Architecture of Eastern Pennsylvania," PD. 7 (1955): 6-29.

4107   Johnson, Hildegard B. "Immigrant Traditions and Rural Mid-
        western Architecture," AGR. 9 (1943): 17-20.

4108   Jordan, Terry. "German Houses in Texas," Landscape. 14
        (1964): 24-26.

4109   Jordy, William. "The Aftermath of the Bauhaus in America:
        Gropius, Mies and Breuer," in The Intellectual Migration:
        Europe and America, 1930-60. Cambridge: Harvard Univer-
        sity Pr., 1969, pp. 485-544.

4110   [No entry]

4111   Kauffman, Henry. "Church Architecture in Lancaster County,"
        PD. 6 (1955): 16-27.

4112   _____. Golden Stars on the Barn. Allentown, Pa.: Author,
        1965.

4113   _____. "Moravian Architecture in Bethlehem," PD. 6
        (1955): 12-19.

4114   _____. "Of Bells and Bell Towers," PD. 6 (1954): 24-25.

4115   _____. "The Summer House," PD. 8 (1956): 2-7.

4116   Krahn, Cornelius. "Developments and Trends: Mennonite
        Church Architecture," ML. 12 (1957): 19-27, 34.

4117   Kramer, Ellen. "The Domestic Architecture of Detlef Lienau:
        A Conservative Victorian. New York University: Disserta-
        tion, 1961.

4118   Kuhn, Charles. "America and the Bauhaus," AGR. 15, ii
        (1949): 16-22.

4119   Lawton, Arthur. "The Pre-Metric Food and Its Use in Penn-
        sylvania German Architecture," PFL. 19 (1969): 37-45.

4120   Lerch, Lila. "Hex Signs or Fire Marks?" Eck. (Dec., 10,
        1949).

4121 Lewis, Arnold. "Karl Hinckeldeyn: Critic of American
      Architecture, " AGR. 27, ii (1960): 10-13, 37.

4122 Long, Amos. "Bank Structures in Rural Pennsylvania, "
      PFL. 20 (1970-71): 31-39.

4123 _____. "Dryhouses in the Pennsylvania Folk-Culture, "
      PFL. 13 (1962-63): 16-23.

4124 _____. "Farmstead Arches in Berks, " HRBC. 30 (1965):
      116-17, 124-25.

4125 _____. "Outbuildings on the Early Pennsylvania German
      Farmstead, " AGR. 29 (1963): 18-21.

4126 _____. "Outdoor Privies in the Dutch Country, " PFL. 13
      (1963): 33-38.

4127 _____. "The Woodshed, " PFL. 16 (1966-67): 38-45.

4128 Mahr, Augustus. "Origin and Significance of Pennsylvania
      Dutch Barn Symbols, " OSAHQ. 54 (1946): 1-32.

4129 Massey, James. "The Bertolet-Herbein Cabin, " AGR. 26
      (1960): 12-14.

4130 Montgomery, Richard. "Houses of the Oley Valley, " PD. 6
      (1954): 16-26.

4131 Murtagh, William. "Half-Timbering in American Architecture, "
      PFL. 9 (1958): 2-11.

4132 Neutra, Richard. Auftrag für Morgen: Rückblick auf ein
      Leben für die Architektur. Hamburg: Classen, 1962.

4133 Parrent, H. C. "Adolphus Heiman and the Building Methods
      of Two Centuries, " THQ. 12 (1953): 204-12.

4134 Perrin, Richard. "German Timber Farm Houses in Wiscon-
      sin: Terminal Examples of a Thousand Year Building Tradi-
      tion, " WMH. 44 (1961): 199-202.

4135 _____. Historic Wisconsin Buildings: A Survey of Pioneer
      Architecture, 1835-70. Milwaukee: Public Museum, 1962.

4136 Remak, Joachim. "The Bauhaus Long Shadow: Some Thoughts
      about Weimar and Us, " Pacific NWQ. 61 (1970): 201-11.

4137 Roos, Frank. Writings on Early American Architecture: An
      Annotated List of Books and Articles on Architecture Con-
      structed Before 1860 in the Eastern Half of the U. S. Colum-
      bus: Ohio State University Pr., 1943.

4138   Schmidt, Mildred and Joseph Schmidt. "German Influences
        on Hermann Houses, " AGR. 20, iv (1954): 13-17.

4139   Schreiber, William. "The Pennsylvania Dutch Bank Barn in
        Ohio, " OFL. 2 (1968): 5-30.

4140   Shoemaker, Alfred. The Pennsylvania Barn. Lancaster:
        Pennsylvania Dutch Folklore Center, 1956.

4141   _____. "Pennsylvania German Barns, " ML. 6 (1951): 6-
        11.

4142   Spring, Agnes. "Boettcher Mansion Becomes a New Execu-
        tive Residence, " COL. M. 37 (1960): 199-206.

4143   Stauffer, Harry. "The Trail of the Stone Arched Bridges in
        Berks County, " PD. 8 (1957): 20-31.

4144   Stoltzfus, Grant. "Cooperation Builds a Barn in a Day, "
        AGR. 16, vi (1950): 18-19.

4145   Stoudt, John. Decorated Barns of Eastern Pennsylvania.
        (Homecraft Series, 15.) Keyser, 1945.

4146   Tortora, Vincent. "Amish Barn Building, " PFL. 12 (1962):
        14-19.

4147   Wacker, Peter and Roger Trindell. "The Log House in New
        Jersey: Origins and Diffusions, " Keystone FQ. 13 (1969):
        248-68.

4148   Withey, Henry and Elsie Rathburn. Biographical Dictionary
        of American Architects. Los Angeles: New Age Pub. Co.,
        1956.

4149   Wolfe, Beatrice. "The Geesey Collection, " AGR. 20, vi
        (1954): 14-17.

Crafts

4150   Berky, Andrew. "Buckskin or Sackcloth: A Glance at the
        Clothing Once Worn by the Schwenkfelders in Pa., " PFL. 9
        (1958): 50-52.

4151   Bridenbaugh, Carl. The Colonial Craftsman. New York:
        New York University Pr., 1950.

4152   Clark, Roger. "Cincinnati Coppersmiths, " BCHS. 23 (1965):
        257-72.

4153   Coumans, C. "Ornamental Iron Grave Markers, " Waterloo
        HS. 49 (1962): 72-75.

4154   Cummings, John.   "Painted Chests from Bucks County," PFL.
9 (1958): 20-23.

4155   Dreppard, Carl.   American Clocks and Clockmakers.   Boston:
Branford, 1958.   Pp. 196-293 list the makers.

4156   Dyke, Samuel.   "The Bachman Family of Cabinetmakers, 1766-
1894," LCHS.   69 (1965): 168-80.

4157   _____.   "The Beck Family of Gunsmiths, Lancaster County, Pa.," LCHS.   72 (1969): 28-49.

4158   _____.   "List of Gunsmiths of Lancaster County, Pa.,
Period: 1728-1863," LCHS.   72 (1969): 50-60.

4159   Eckhardt, George.   Pennsylvania Clocks and Clockmakers
An Epic of Early American Science, Industry and Craftsman-
ship.   New York: Devin-Adair, 1955.

4160   Frey, H. C.   "The Conestoga Wagon," LCHP.   51 (1947): 62-
91.

4161   Frey, J. William and H. C. Frey.   The Conestoga Wagon:
A Pennsylvania Dutch Product.   Lancaster: Authors, 1947.

4162   Gluckman, Arcadi and L. Sattlerlee.   American Gun Makers.
Harrisburg: Stackpole, 1953.

4163   Graeff, Marie.   Pennsylvania German Quilts.   (Homecraft
Course, 14.)   Keyser, 1946.

4164   Hollenbach, R. E.   "Der Blechschmidt," Eck.   (May 8, 1964).

4165   _____.   "The Blue Dyer: Der Blo Farrewer," Eck.   (June
22, 1968).

4166   _____.   "Gottschalk Gottschalk: An Old-Time Weaver,"
Eck.   (Mar. 16, 1968).

4167   _____.   "The Harness-Maker: Der Saddeler," Eck.   (Feb.
9, 1957).

4168   _____.   "In der Schmid: 1836-40," Eck.   (Oct. 5, 12,
1957).

4169   _____.   "Peter Wotring: Sein Schreib Buch, 1799," Eck.
(Mar. 7, 1964).   On a cabinet maker.

4170   _____.   "Wagons and Carriages," Eck.   (Mar. 8, 1957).

4171   Hopf, Carroll.   "Decorated Folk Furniture," PFL.   20 (1970):
2-8.

4172   James, A. E.   Potters and Potteries of Chester County, Pa.
       Westchester, Pa.:   Chester County Historical Society, 1945.

4173   Kauffman, Henry.   "Coppersmithing in Pennsylvania," PGFS.
       11 (1948): 82-153.

4174   _____.   Early American Gunsmith.   Harrisburg: Stackpole,
       1952.

4175   _____.   Early American Ironware, Cast and Wrought.   Rut-
       land, Vermont: Tuttle, 1966.

4176   _____.   Pennsylvania German Copper and Brass.   (Home-
       craft Course, 25.)   Keyser, 1947.

4177   _____.   Pennsylvania Kentucky Rifle.   Harrisburg: Stack-
       pole, 1960.

4178   _____.   "Rifles in Berks County," HRBC.   (Winter 1965-
       66): 12-13.

4179   Kettermann, Marie.   Two Hundred Years of Pennsylvania
       Dolls.   Plymouth Meeting, Pa., 1949.

4180   Kiebach, R. E.   "Fences in Pennsylvania German Land,"
       Eck.   (Sept. 18, 1954).

4181   Landis, Henry and George Lands.   "Lancaster Rifle Acces-
       sories," PGFS.   9 (1946): 113-84.

4182   Lerch, Lila.   "Berks County Box Chests," HRBC.   28 (Fall
       1963).

4183   _____.   "Early (Pennsylvania German) Clocks," Eck.   (Aug.
       21, 28, 1965).

4184   Lichten, Frances.   "Pennsylvania Dutch Needlework," PD.   7
       (1956): 18-21.

4185   McPharlin, Paul.   The Puppet Theatre in America: A History
       New York, 1949.

4186   Natzler, Otto.   Gertrud and Otto Natzler: Ceramics.   Los
       Angeles: County Museum of Art, 1968.

4187   Nutting, Wallace.   Furniture Treasury: All Periods of Amer-
       ican Furniture with Some Foreign Examples in America, Also
       American Hardware and Household Utensils.   Framington,
       Mass.:   Old America, 1928-33.

4188   "The Old Coppershop," AGR.   12 iv (1946): 10-11.

4189   Pennsylvania German Arts and Crafts.   New York: Museum
       of Art, 1949.

4190   Poole, Earl. "Joseph Lehn: Driven to Design," AGR. 15,
        i (1948): 12-14.

4191   Reibel, Daniel. "The Kunstfest at Old Economy," PFL. 20
        (1970): 23-27.

4192   Reichmann, Felix. "Pennsylvania Dutch Furniture," BHSMCo.
        3 (1942): 84-97.

4193   Reinert, Guy. "Henry Dreihaus: Wrought Iron Craftsman,"
        AGR. 12, vi (1946): 7-11.

4194   _____. "Isaac Stahl: One of the Last Pennsylvania Dutch
        Potters," HRBC. 15 (1950): 242 ff.

4195   _____. Pennsylvania German Coverlets. Plymouth Meet-
        ing, Pa., 1947.

4196   _____. Pennsylvania German Splint and Straw Baskets.
        (Home Craft Course, 22.) Plymouth Meeting, Pa., 1946.

4197   Robacker, Earl. "Antiques for Fancy and for Fun," PD. 6
        (1955): 2-6.

4198   _____. "Antiques in Dutchland," PFL. 12 (1962): 2-7.

4199   _____. "Basketry: A Pennsylvania Dutch Art," PD. 7
        (1955): 2-5.

4200   _____. "Butter Molds," PD. 6 (1954): 6-8.

4201   _____. "The Dutch Touch in Iron," PD. 8 (1957): 2-6.

4202   _____. "Like the One Grandma Had," PFL. 14 (1965):
        14-20.

4203   _____. "Paint Decorated Furniture of the Pennsylvania
        Dutch," PFL. 13 (1962): 2-8.

4204   _____. "Pennsylvania Chalkware," PFL. 9 (1958): 2-7.

4205   _____. "Pennsylvania Pewter and Pewterers," PFL. 13
        (1962-63): 2-6.

4206   _____. "Pennsylvania Redware," PD. 8 (1957): 2-7.

4207   _____. "Piece Patch Artistry," PFL. 13 (1963): 2-10.

4208   _____. "The Rise of Interest in Pennsylvania Dutch An-
        tique," PD. 8 (1956): 18-22.

4209   _____. "Stitching for Pretty," PFL. 15 (1966): 2-9.

4210   _____. "Such Fancy Boxes, Yet," PD. 8 (1957): 3-8.

4211   _____. "Tick Tock Time in Old Pennsylvania," PFL. 9 (1958): 32-37.

4212   _____. "Tim With Holes In," PFL. 12 (1961): 2-7.

4213   _____. "The Township Weavers of Pennsylvania," PFL. 12 (1961): 3-7.

4214   Sackett, S. "The Hammered Dulcimer in Ellis County, Kansas," J. Int. Folk Music Council. 14 (1962): 61-64.

4215   Savage, R. Pennsylvania German Wrought Ironwork. (Homecraft Course, 10.) Plymouth Meeting, Pa., 1947.

4216   Schiffer, Margaret. Historical Needlework of Pennsylvania. New York: Scribner's, 1968.

4217   Seitz, Albert. "Furniture Making by the Slaugh Family of Lancaster," LCHS. 63 (1969): 1-25.

4218   Shoemaker, Alfred. "Scratch-Carved Eggs," PD. 6 (1955): 20-23.

4219   Shumway, George. Conestoga Wagon. New York, 1964.

4220   Smith, Elmer. Arts and Crafts of the Shenandoah Valley: A Pictorial Presentation. Witmer, Pa.: For the Shenandoah Valley Folklore Society, 1968.

4221   _____. "Shenandoah Pottery," Eck. (Feb. 15, 1969).

4222   _____. "Strasburg Pottery," Eck. (Mar. 1, 1969).

4223   Smith, G. Hubert. "Minnesota Potteries," MH. 33 (1953): 229-35.

4224   Smith, Ray. "The Kentucky Rifle and Its Snyder County Makers," Eck. (July 13, 20, 1946).

4225   Steinmetz, Rollin and C. Rice. Vanishing Crafts and Their Craftsmen. New Brunswick: Rutgers University Pr., 1960.

4226   Stephens, W. B. "Hermann Wenzel and His Air Clock," CHSQ. 27 (1948): 1-7.

4227   "What Has Become of the Pennsylvania German Antiques?," Eck. (Mar. 15, 1947).

4228   Wust, Klaus. "German Craftsmen in Jamestown," AGR. 23 (1957): 10-11.

Music

4229   Adler, Samuel. "Music In the American Synagogue, " Amer.
        Choral Rev. 6 (1964): 7-9.

4230   Arndt, Karl. "The First Wabash Song, " IMH. 38 (1942): 80-
        82.

4231   _____. "Mozart and Schiller on the Wabash, " MO. 38
        (1946): 244-48.

4232   Babow, Irving. "The Singing Societies of European Immigrant
        Groups in San Francisco: 1851-1953, " J. Beh. Sci. 5 (Jan.
        1969).

4233   Barba, Preston. "In Polen steht ein Haus, " Eck. (Apr. 3,
        1948).

4234   Bellinger, Martha. "Music in Indianapolis, 1900-44, " LMH.
        42 (1946): 47-65.

4235   Benton, Rita. "Early Musical Scholarship in the U.S., "
        Fontes Artis Musicae. 9 (1964): 12-21.

4236   Berger, David. "Music from Germany: Birth and Justifica-
        tion of a Radio Program, " AGR. 35 (1969): 11-13.

4237   Berges, Ruth. "Bruno Walter: Striver for Perfection, " AGR.
        27, i (1960): 7-9.

4238   _____. "The Glory around His Head, " AGR. 23, iv (1957):
        4-7. On J. Meyerowitz.

4239   _____. "Mahler in America, " AGR. 26, iv (1960): 12-13.

4240   Betterton, William. "Music in Early Davenport: Bands and
        Orchestras, " Palimpsest. 40 (1964): 27-82.

4241   _____. "The Sängerfest of 1898, " Palimpsest. 40 (1964):
        293-300.

4242   Bittinger, Emmert. "More on Brethren Hymnology, " B. Life
        and Thought. 8 (1963): 11-16.

4243   Blakely, Lloyd. "Johan Conrad Beissel and Music of the
        Ephrata Cloister, " J. Res. Music Ed. 15 (1967): 120-38.

4244   Boatwright, Howard, "Paul Hindemith as a Teacher, " Mus.
        Q. 50 (1964): 279-89.

4245   Boyer, Walter. "The Folksong Tradition in the Mahantongo
        Valley, " NCoHS. 21 (1957): 148-62.

4246 _____. "The German Broadside Songs of Pennsylvania,"
PFL. 10 (1959): 14-19.

4247 _____. Songs Along the Mahantongo: Pennsylvania Folksongs. Hatboro, Pa.: Folklore Associates, 1964.

4248 Brand, Hans. Centennial Year Syracuse Liederkranz, 1855-
1955. Syracuse, 1955.

4249 Brendle, Thomas. "Collecting Dialect Folk Songs," PFL. 11
(1961): 50-52.

4250 Britton, George. Pennsylvania Dutch Folk Songs. Folkways
Records in German: FA 2215, 1962.

4251 Brown, Robert and F. Braun. "The Tunebook of Conrad
Doll," PBSA. 42 (1948): 229-38.

4252 Buffington, Albert. Dutchified German Spirituals. (Pennsylvania German Society, 62.) Lancaster, 1965.

4253 Burkhart, Charles. "The Church Music of the Old Order
Amish and Old Colony Mennonites," MQR. 27 (1953): 34-54.

4254 Carlson, Charles. "The Ephrata Cloister's Music of Yesteryear," Mus. J. 22 (1964): 52, 118-20.

4255 Clark, Robert. "A Bavarian Organist Comes to New Orleans,
LHQ. 29 (1946): 14-42.

4256 Cone, John. Oscar Hammerstein's Manhattan Opera Company.
Norman: University of Oklahoma Pr., 1966.

4257 Danek, Victor. A Historical Study of the Kneisel Quartet.
Indiana University: Dissertation, 1962.

4258 David, Hans. "Musical Life in the Pennsylvania Settlement
of the Unitas Fratrum," Moravian Hist. Soc., Trans. (1942):
44 pp.

4259 Davis, Ronald. A History of Resident Opera in the American
West. University of Texas: Dissertation, 1962.

4260 DeChant, Aliene. Of the Dutch I Sing. Kutztown, Pa., 1951.

4261 Dichter, Harry and E. Shapiro. Early American Sheet Music
Its Lure and Lore, 1768-1889; Including a Directory of Early
American Music Publishers. New York: Bowker, 1941.

4262 Downs, Lynwood. "Music Moves West," MH. 20 (1951): 239-
42.

4263 Draegert, Eva. "Cultural History of Indianapolis: Music,

1875-1890, " IMH. 53 (1957): 265-304.

4264   Eitner, Robert. Bio-bibliographisches Quellen-Lexikon der
        Musiker und Musikgelehrten der christlichen Zeitrechnung bis
        zur Mitte des neunzehnten Jahrhunderts. Leipzig: Breitkopf,
        1900-04.

4265   Eskew, Harold. "Joseph Funk's Allgemein Nützliche Choral
        Music (1816), " RJGAH. 32 (1966): 38-46.

4266   Farlee, L. A History of the Church Music of the Amana So-
        ciety: The Community of True Inspiration. Iowa State Uni-
        versity: Dissertation, 1968.

4267   Fornell, Martha and Earl Fornell. "A Century of German
        Song in Texas, " AGR. 24, i (1957): 29-31.

4268   Forster, William. "The Liederkranz of New York, " AGR. 10
        (1944): 10-13.

4269   Frantz, Edna. "One Man's Musical Family, " AGR. 12, iii
        (1946): 417.

4270   French, John. "Otto Sutro and Music in Baltimore, " MdHM.
        47 (1952): 260-62.

4271   Furness, Marion. "Childhood Recollections of Old St. Paul, "
        MH. 29 (1948): 114-29. On C. Schurz.

4272   Gladych, Elizabeth. "Madame Schumann-Heink and the Lark, "
        R. Digest. (Feb. 1957): 53-56.

4273   Goetsch, Bertha. "John Wendel Eysenbach, Pioneer Musician
        and Teacher, " NOQ. 29 (1957): 194-205.

4274   Goleeke, Wallace. A History of the Male Chorus Singing
        Movement in Seattle. University of Washington: Dissertation,
        1969.

4275   Gombosi, Marilyn. Catalog of the Johannes Herbst Collection.
        Chapel Hill: University of North Carolina Pr., 1970.

4276   Hall, James. The Role of the Tune Book in American Cul-
        ture, 1800-20. University of Pennsylvania: Dissertation,
        1966.

4277   Hamilton, Kenneth. "The Bethlehem Christmas Hymn, " MHS.
        14 (1947): 11-23.

4278   Hamm, Charles. "Folk Hymns of the Shenandoah Valley, "
        V. Cavalcade. 6 (1956): 14-19.

4279   Hammer, Carl. "Organ Church and the Broken Key, " AGR.
        13, v-vi (1947): 33-36.

270   German-Americana

4280   Hark, Ann. "Trauer-Lieder, " AGR. 27, i (1960): 27-30.

4281   Hatch, Christopher. "Music for America: A Critical Con-
        troversy of the 1850's, " AQ. 14 (1962): 578-86.

4282   Hausman, Ruth. Sing and Dance with the Pennsylvania Dutch.
        New York: Marks Music Corp., 1953.

4283   Hewitt, Theodore. "German Hymns in American Hymnals, "
        GQ. 21 (1948): 37-50.

4284   Hill, Thomas. Ernest Schelling: His Life and Contributions
        to Music Education Through Educational Concerts. Catholic
        University of America: Dissertation, 1970.

4285   Hogue, A. R. "Carl Schurz: A Wagnerian Enthusiast, " AGR.
        16, iii (1949): 3-6.

4286   Holliday, Joseph. "Cincinnati Opera Festivals in the Gilded
        Age, " BCHS. 24 (1966): 131-49.

4287   _____. "The Cincinnati Philharmonic and Hopkins Hull
        Orchestras, 1856-68, " BCHS. 26 (1968): 158-73.

4288   _____. "The Musical Legacy of Theodore Thomas, " BCHS.
        27 (1969): 191-205.

4289   Huneker, Erik. "The Big Four, " Opera News. 30 (1965): 8-
        13.

4290   "Hymn of the Moravian Nuns of Bethlehem, " Eck. (Mar. 19,
        1966).

4291   Jackson, George. "The American Amish Sing Medieval Folk
        Tunes Today, " SFQ. 10 (1946): 151-57.

4292   Jahresverzeichnis der deutschen Musikalien und Musikschriften
        Leipzig: Hofmeister, 1852- .

4293   Jost, Walter. "A Mennonite Hymn Tradition, " ML. 21 (1966)
        126-28.

4294   Kendall, John. "New Orleans Musicians of Long Ago, " LHQ.
        31 (1948): 130-49.

4295   King, Rolf. "The Significance of Hans Gram for Early Amer-
        ican Musical Development, " AGR. 12, iii (1946): 17-22.

4296   Korson, George. Pennsylvania Songs and Legends. Phila-
        delphia: University of Pennsylvania, 1949.

4297   Krohn, Ernst. "A Beethoven First in St. Louis, " BMHS. 23
        (1966): 59-64.

4298   Lawson, Charles. Musical Life in the Unitas Fratrum Mission at Springplace, Georgia, 1800-1936. Florida State University: Dissertation, 1970.

4299   Lendrim, Frank. Music for Every Child: The Story of Karl Wilson Gehrkens. University of Michigan: Dissertation, 1962.

4300   Lenhart, Charmenz. Musical Influence on American Poetry. Athens: University of Georgia Pr., 1956.

4301   Lowen, Irving. Music and Musicians in Early America. New York: Norton, 1964.

4302   _____. Music in American Civilization, 1770-1820. University of Maryland: Dissertation, 1961.

4303   Lumpkin, Ben. "Der Traum des Baumes: A Religious Song from the Middle Ages," JAF. 78 (1965): 66-68.

4304   McCorkle, Donald. "The Collegium Musicum Salem: Its Music, Musicians and Importance," NCHR. 33 (1956): 483-98.

4305   _____. "Musical Instruments of the Moravians in North Carolina," AGR. 21, iii (1955): 12-17.

4306   Mangler, Joyce. Rhode Island Music and Musicians, 1773-1850. Detroit: Information Service Inc., 1965.

4307   Martens, Helen. Hutterite Songs: The Origins and Aural Transmission of their Melodies from the Sixteenth Century. Columbia University: Dissertation, 1969.

4308   Mattfeld, Julius. A Handbook of American Operetic Premieres, 1731-1962. (Detroit Studies in Music Bibliography, 5.) Detroit: Information Service Inc., 1963.

4309   Maurer, J. "America's Heritage of Moravian Music," Eck. (May 21, 28, 1955).

4310   _____. "America's Heritage of Moravian Music: Contributions of Early Pennsylvania Composers," HRBC. 18 (1953): 66-70, 87-91.

4311   _____. "The Moravian Trombone Choir," HRBC. 20 (1954): 2-8.

4312   _____. "Music in Wachovia, 1753-1800," WMQ. 8 (1951): 214-27.

4313   Mencken, H. L. H. L. Mencken on Music: A Selection of His Writings on Music; Together With an Account of H. L. Mencken's Musical Life and a History of the Saturday Night Club. New York: Knopf, 1961.

4314   Mussulman, J.   "Mendelssohnism in America, " MusQ. 53
        (1967): 335-46.

4315   Nau, John.   "The History of the German Song in New Or-
        leans, " In The 43d National Saengerfest of the North Ameri-
        can Singer's Union.   New Orleans: Deutsches Haus, 1958,
        pp. 13-17.

4316   Nettl, Paul.   "German Melodies in American College Songs, "
        AGR. 13, v-vi (1947): 21-23.

4317   Neve, Paul.   The Contribution of the Lutheran College Choirs
        to Music in America.   Union Theological Seminary: Disserta-
        tion, 1967.

4318   Nitz, Donald.   "The Norfolk Musical Society, 1814-20: An
        Episode in the History of Choral Music in New England, " J.
        Res. in Mus. Ed. 16 (1968): 319-28.

4319   Pfatteicher, Carl.   "The Hymns of the Bohemian Brethren, "
        AGR. 21, iii (1955): 35.

4320   _____.   "Music and the Carl Schurz Foundation, " AGR. 13,
        iii (1947): 40-41.

4321   Pleasants, Henry.   "The Golden Era: When the Met was a
        German Opera House, " AGR. 33, ii (1966): 18-20.

4322   Poladian, Sirvart.   "Paul Aron and the New Music in Dres-
        den, " BNYPL. 66 (1962): 297-315.

4323   Pruett, James.   "Francis F. Hagen: American Moravian
        Musician, " AGR. 24, ii (1957): 15-17.

4324   Reese, Gustave.   "A Tribute to Manfred Bukofzer, " J. Amer.
        Mus. Soc. 8 (1955): 163-64.

4325   Robertson, Elizabeth.   "Singing Wood: Moennig Violin, " AGR.
        21, iii (1955): 18-19.

4326   Rubin, Ruth.   "Nineteenth Century History in Yiddish Folk-
        song, " NYFQ. 15 (1959): 220-28.

4327   _____.   Voices of a People: The Story of Yiddish Folk
        Song.   New York, 1963.

4328   _____.   "Yiddish Folksongs of Immigration and the Melting
        Pot, " NYFQ. 17 (1961): 173-82.

4329   Russell, Theodore.   Theodore Thomas: His Role in the De-
        velopment of Musical Culture in the United States, 1835-1905.
        University of Minnesota: Dissertation, 1969.

4330   Sachse, Julius. Music of the Ephrata Cloister. Repr.: New
       York: AMS Pr., 1971.

4331   Schulze, E. "Johann Georg Kunz, " CHIQ. 30 (1957): 40-44.

4332   Seltsam, William. Metropolitan Opera Annals: A Chronicle
       of Artists and Performances. New York: Wilson, 1947.

4333   Sendry, Alfred. Bibliography of Jewish Music. New York:
       Columbia University Pr., 1951.

4334   Sherman, John. "The Birth of a Symphony Orchestra, " MH.
       33 (1952): 3, 93-104. On E. Oberhoffer in Minnesota.

4335   Smith, Carleton. "America in 1801-25: The Musicians and
       the Music, " BNYPL. 68 (1965): 483-92.

4336   Smith, Elmer and John Stewart. "Memorial to a Mennonite
       Musician, " Eck. (Nov. 24, 1963).

4337   Sonneck, Oscar. A Bibliography of Early Secular Music:
       18th Century. New York: DaCapo, 1964.

4338   Spell, Lota. "The Early German Contributions to Music in
       Texas, " AGR. 12, iv (1946): 8-10.

4339   Stoudt, John. "The Pennsylvania Christmas Hymn of 1742, "
       PH. 22 (1955): 69-73.

4340   Tauber, Violetta. "Elizabeth Gyring: Profile in Music, "
       AGR. 28, vi (1963): 30-32.

4341   Thomas, Arnold. The Development of Male Glee Clubs in
       American Colleges and Universities. Columbia University:
       Dissertation, 1962.

4342   Tuckman, William. "Sigmund and Jacob Schlesinger and
       Joseph Block: Civil War Composers and Musicians, " AJHQ.
       53 (1963): 70-75.

4343   Warrington, James. "A Bibliography of Church Music Books
       Issued in Pennsylvania With Annotations, " Penn Germania. 1
       (1912): 170-77, 262-68, 371-74, 460-65, 627-31, 755-59.

4344   Wechsberg, Joseph. "Trustee in Fiddledale: Profile of
       Emil Hermann, " New Yorker. 29, no. 35 (1953): 38-59; 29,
       no. 36 (1953): 39-55.

4345   Werner, Heinz. "Die Opa Hirchleitner Story, " Schlagzeug.
       3 (1958): xiii, 24-26; xiv, 25-26; xv, 25-27; xvi, 26-29.

4346   Wessling, Berndt. Lotte Lehmann: Mehr als eine Sängerin.
       Salzburg: Residenz, 1969.

4347   Wolf, Edward. "Justus Henry Christian Helmuth: Hymnodist
       <u>GAS.</u> 5 (1972): 117-47.

4348   Wolf, Edwin. <u>American Song Sheets.</u> Philadelphia: Library
       Company of Philadelphia, 1963.

4349   Wolfe, Richard. <u>Secular Music in America, 1801-25: A Bib</u>
       <u>liography.</u> New York: Public Library, 1964.

4350   Wunderlich, Charles. <u>A History and Bibliography of Early</u>
       <u>American Musical Periodicals, 1782-1852.</u> University of
       Michigan: Dissertation, 1962.

4351   Yoder, Don. <u>Pennsylvania Spirituals.</u> Lancaster, Pa.: Foll
       life Society, 1961.

4352   _____. "Spirituals From the Pennsylvania Dutch Country,"
       <u>PD.</u> 8 (1957): 22-33.

4353   _____. "The Themes of the Pennsylvania Dutch Spiritual,"
       <u>PD.</u> (Sept. 1, 1951).

4354   _____. "Willy Brown of Mahantongo: Our Foremost Folk-
       singer," <u>PD.</u> 4 (1952): 1-3.

4355   Yoder, Paul. <u>Nineteenth Century Sacred Music of the Men-</u>
       <u>nonite Church in the U.S.</u> Florida State University: Disserta
       tion, 1961.

4356   Zucker, A. E. "Adolf Gustav Steinmann," <u>RJGAH.</u> 30 (1959)
       29-35.

Theatre

4358   Andriessohn, J. "Die literarische Geschichte des Milwaukee
       deutschen Bühnenwesens, 1850-1911," <u>GAA.</u> 10 (1912): 65-88,
       150-70.

4359   Arrington, Joseph. "John Maelzel: Master Showman of Auto
       mata and Panoramas," <u>PMHB.</u> 84 (1960): 56-92.

4360   Behrmann, Alfred. "Kotzebue on the American Stage," <u>Ar-</u>
       <u>cadia.</u> 4 (1969): 274-84.

4361   Bowen, Elbert. "The German Theatre of Early Rural Mis-
       souri," <u>MHR.</u> 46 (1952): 157-61.

4362   _____. <u>Theatrical Entertainment in Rural Missouri Before</u>
       <u>the Civil War.</u> (University of Missouri Studies, 32.) Colum
       bia: University of Missouri Pr., 1959.

4363   Bruning, Eberhard. "Die amerikanische Arbeiter-Theater-
        bewegung der 30er Jahre, " ZAA. 9 (1961): 341-409.

4364   Bryson, A. "German Theatre Methods and Theory in Texas, "
        AGR. 28, v (1962): 26-29.

4365   Evans, Thomas. Piscator in the American Theatre: New
        York, 1939-51. University of Wisconsin: Dissertation, 1968.

4366   Frenz, Horst. "The German Drama in the Middle West, "
        AGR. 8 (1942): 15-17, 37.

4367   Frey, John. "Maria Stuart Off Broadway, " AGR. 24, vi
        (1958): 6-8, 27.

4368   Gaiser, Gerhard. The History of the Cleveland Theatre from
        the Beginning until 1854. State University of Iowa: Disserta-
        tion, 1953.

4369   German Theatre Association. Mitteilungen des deutschen
        Theater-Verbandes von New York. New York: Der Verband,
        1926-29.

4370   "German Theatre in Milwaukee, " Th. Arts. 28 (1944): 465-74.

4371   Guertler, Siegfried. Der Turm: Eine Schrift des deutschen
        Theaters des Kulturkreises Salt Lake City. Salt Lake City:
        German Theatre, 1959.

4372   Hauser, Edel. "Freischütz ohne Schützenhilfe, " DMH. (Aug.
        16, 1973).

4373   Herbatschek, Heinrich. "Die Anfänge des deutschen Theaters
        in Milwaukee, " AGR. 13, iii (1947): 17-18.

4374   Heuck, Robert. "Show Business Over-The-Rhine, " HPSO. 16
        (1958): 121-42.

4375   Kieffer, Elizabeth. "John Durang: The First Native Ameri-
        can Dancer, " PD. 6 (1954): 26-38.

4376   Kistler, Mark. "The German Theater in Detroit, " MichH.
        47 (1963): 289-300.

4377   Knepler, Henry. "Schiller's Maria Stuart on the Stage in
        England and America, " Crosscurrents. 2 (19): 5-31.

4378   Kopp, W. Lamarr. "Das klassische deutsche Drama an den
        New Yorker Bühnen seit dem Zweiten Weltkrieg, " ZKA. 20
        (1970): 289-96.

4379   Kosch, Wilhelm. Deutsches Theater-Lexikon: Biographisches
        und Bibliographisches Handbuch. Klagenfirt: Kleinmayr, 1951-
        60.

4380   Kracauer, Siegfried. Von Caligari bis Hitler: Ein Beitrag
        zur Geschichte des deutschen Films. Hamburg: Rowohlt,
        1958.

4381   Leuchs, Fritz. The Early German Theatre in New York.
        New York: AMS Pr., 1928.

4382   Ley-Piscator, Maria. The Piscator Experiment: The Politi-
        cal Theatre. New York: Heinemann, 1967.

4383   Londre, Felicia. A Guide to the Productions of Plays in
        Foreign Language in American Colleges and Universities.
        University of Wisconsin: Dissertation, 1969.

4384   Loomis, Grant. "The German Theatre in San Francisco,
        1861-64," In Honorem Lawrence Marsden Price. Berkeley:
        University of California Pr., 1954.

4385   McDermott, Douglas. "The Odyssey of John Bonn: A Note
        on German Theatre in America," GQ. 38 (1965): 325-34.

4386   Moehlenbrock, Arthur. "The German Drama on the New Or-
        leans Stage," LHQ. 26 (1943): 361-627.

4387   Morrill, Reed and Joanne Morrill. "Deutsches Theater in
        Salt Lake City," AGR. 24, ii (1957): 26-27.

4388   Morrish, Ray. "Sells Brothers Circus," AGR. 21, v (1955):
        25-26.

4389   _____. "The German Drama on the Charleston Stage,"
        Furman Studies. 1 (1954): 32-39.

4390   Nolle, Alfred. "The German Drama on the St. Louis Stage,"
        GAA. 15 (1917): 29-65, 73-112.

4391   Odell, George. Annals of the New York Stage. New York:
        Columbia University Pr., 1927-49.

4392   Patel, Karl. "Deutsches Theater in Amerika," D. Rundschau
        81 (1955): 271-75.

4393   [Reinhardt.] "Max Reinhardt, 1873-1943," Th. Arts. 28 (194·
        36-52.

4394   Rippley, LaVern. "German Theatre in Columbus, Ohio,"
        GAS. 1, ii (1970): 78-100.

4395   Rothfuss, Hermann. "The Beginnings of the German-Ameri-
        can Stage," GQ. 24 (1951): 93-102.

4396   _____. "Criticism of the German-American Theatre in
        Minnesota," GR. 27 (1952): 124-30.

4397 _____. "The Early German Theatre in Minnesota, " MH.
32 (1951): 100-05, 164-73.

4398 _____. "Gustav Amberg: German-American Theatre
Promoter, " MO. 44 (1952): 357-65.

4399 _____. "Plays for Pioneers: German Dramas in Rural
Minnesota, " MH. 34 (1955): 239-42.

4400 _____. "Theodor Steidle: German Theatre Pioneer, " AGR.
17, iii (1951): 17-19, 33.

4401 Soellner, Ludwig. "Guter Besuch bei der Wilhelm Tell Auf-
führung, " DMH. (Sept. 13, 1973).

4402 _____. "Wilhelm Tell Spiele in New Glarus, Wisconsin, "
DMH. (Aug. 30, 1973).

4403 Stadelmann, Egon. "Deutsches Theater in New York, " NYSZH.
(Dec. 28, 1969).

4404 Steinitz, Hans. "Ein Kabarett-Abend mit Wolfgang Roth, "
Aufbau. (Oct. 19, 1973).

4405 Ward, Robert Elmer. "Deutsches Bühnenwesen in Amerika, "
GAS. 5 (1972): 53-54.

4406 Weisert, John. "Beginnings of German Theatricals in Louisville, " FCHQ. 26 (1952): 347-59.

4407 _____. "The First Decade at Sam Drake's Louisville
Theatre, " FCHQ. 39 (1965): 287-310.

4408 _____. "Some Characters of the German-American Stage, "
AGR. 24, iv (1958): 12-15.

4409 _____. "A Trinkspruch from Louisville's Bohemia, " AGR.
18, iii (1952): 16-17, 35. German-American plays in Cincinnati and Louisville.

4410 West, William. The Legitimate Theatre in Rural Missouri
from the Beginning of the Civil War Through 1872. University of Missouri: Dissertation, 1964.

4411 Youngerman, Henry. "Theatre Buildings in Madison, Wisconsin, 1836-1900, " WMH. 30 (1947): 273-88.

4412 Zeydel, Edwin. "The German Theatre in New York City, "
DAGB. 15 (1915): 255-309.

4413 Zucker, A. E. "Bibliographical Notes on the German Theatre in the U.S., " Monatshefte. 35 (1943): 255-64.

German-American Theatres

4414   Bayrische Volksbühne: Bauerntheater. Evergreen Lodge,
        Evergreen Road, Springfield, New Jersey.

4415   Deutsch-Dramatischer Verein. 687 Harris Ave., Providence,
        Rhode Island.

4416   Deutsches Theater. 1600 No. Wilcox Ave., Hollywood, Cal.
        90028.

4417   Deutsches Theater des Kulturkreis Salt Lake City. 1007-
        First Ave., Salt Lake City, Utah.

4418   Theatergruppe des Deutsch-Amerikanisches Klub. California-
        Halle. 625 Polk & Turk St., San Francisco, Cal.

Intellectual History

4419   Adorno, Theodor. "Scientific Experiences of a European
        Scholar in America, " In The Intellectual Migration: Europe
        and America, 1930-60. Cambridge: Harvard University Pr.,
        1969, pp. 338-70.

4420   Appel, John. Immigrant Historical Societies in the U.S.,
        1880-1950. University of Pennsylvania: Dissertation, 1960.

4421   _____. "Marion Dexter Learned and the German American
        Historical Society, " PMHB. 86 (1962): 287-318.

4422   Barba, Preston. "A Tribute to Arthur D. Graeff," HRBC.
        34 (1969): 82-84.

4423   Baumgaertel, Gerhard. "Hegel in der Philosophie von St.
        Louis, " Z. f. Phil Forsch. 14 (1960): 285-91.

4424   Becker, Ernest. "The Society for the History of the German
        in Maryland: A Chronicle, " RJGAH. 28 (1953): 9-20.

4425   Berger, David. "The Brain Drain: A Documentation, " AGR.
        25, ii (1969): 30-33.

4426   Bestor, Arthur. "The Transformation of American Scholar-
        ship, 1875-1917," LQ. 23 (1953): 164-79.

4427   Bonn, Moritz. Wandering Scholar. New York: Day, 1948.

4427A   Come, Donald. "The Social Gospel of Walter Rauschenbusch,
        SAQ. 49 (1950): 345-58.

4428   [Cunz.] "Auzzeichnung für Dieter Cunz, " ZKA. 12 (1962):
        371.

4429   [Cunz.] "Dieter Cunz (1910-1969): Tributes and Memories, "
       RJGAH. 34 (1970): 9-18.

4430   Cunz, Dieter. "Die wissenschaftliche Arbeit der Carl Schurz
       Foundation, " Schweizer B. z. Allg. Ges. 7 (1949): 206-12.

4431   "Deutschstämmige Pioniere der Weltraumforschung, " DDA.
       (March, 1973).

4432   Duggan, Stephen and Betty Drury. The Rescue of Science and
       Learning: The Story of the Emergency Committee in Aid of
       Displaced Foreign Scholars. New York: Macmillan, 1948.

4433   Easton, Lloyd. "Hegelianism in Nineteenth Century Ohio, "
       JHI. 23 (1962): 353-78.

4434   . Hegel's First American Followers: The Ohio
       Hegelians: John B. Stallo, Peter Kaufmann, Monscure Con-
       way and August Willich; With Key Writings. Athens: Ohio
       University Pr., 1966.

4435   Egle, William. "The First Historian of the Pennsylvania
       Germans, " PFL. 18 (1969): 46-49.

4436   [Einstein.] "In Memoriam: Albert Einstein, " AGR. 21, v
       (1955): 32.

4437   Ekirch, Arthur. "Frederick Grinke: Advocate of Free Insti-
       tutions, " JHI. 11 (1950): 75-92.

4438   Falk, Gerhard. The Immigration of the European Professors
       and Intellectuals to the U. S. and Particularly the Niagara
       Frontier During the Nazi Era, 1933-41. State University of
       New York at Buffalo: Dissertation, 1970.

4439   Faust, Albert. "German-American Historical Societies:
       Their Achievements and Limitations, " RJGAH. 28 (1953): 21-
       28.

4440   Fermi, Laura. Illustrious Immigrants: The Intellectual Mi-
       gration from Europe: 1930-41. Chicago: University of Chi-
       cago Pr., 1968.

4441   Fleming, Donald and Bernard Bailyn. The Intellectual Migra-
       tion: Europe and America, 1930-60. Cambridge: Harvard
       University Pr., 1969.

4442   Freidel, Frank. Francis Lieber. Baton Rouge: Louisiana
       State University Pr., 1947.

4442A Goetzmann, William. The American Hegelians: An American
       Intellectual Episode in the History of Western America. New
       York: Knopf, 1973.

4443   Goldschmidt, Walter.   The Anthropology of Franz Boas: Essays on the Centennial of His Birth.   San Francisco: Chandler, 1959.

4444   Greene, John.   "American Science Comes of Age: 1780-1820, JAH.   55 (1968): 22-41.

4445   Haines, George and Frederick Jackson.   "A Neglected Landmark in the History of Ideals, " MVHR.   34 (1947): 201-20.   A 1904 congress of German-American intellectuals.

4446   Harmon, Frederick.   The Social Philosophy of the St. Louis Hegelians.   Columbia University: Dissertation, 1943.

4447   Hofstadter, Richard and Walter Metzger.   The Development of Academic Freedom in the U.S.   New York: Columbia University Pr., 1955.

4448   Holborn, Louise.   "Deutsche Wissenschaftler in den Vereinigten Staaten in den Jahren nach 1933, " JAS.   10 (1965): 15-26.

4449   Jackson, Carl.   "The Meeting of East and West: The Case of Paul Carus, " JHI.   29 (1968): 73-92.

4450   Kaufman, Martin.   Homeopathy and the American Medical Profession, 1820-1960.   Tulane University: Dissertation, 1969

4451   Kaufmann, Peter.   Der Tempel der Wahrheit.   Cincinnati, 1858.

4452   Kent, Donald.   The Refugee Intellectual.   New York: Columbia University Pr., 1953.

4453   Klinger, H.   "Deutscher Anteil an Amerikas Medizin, " Z. f. ärztliche Fortbildung.   51 (June, 1962).

4454   Knoche, Walter.   "A. E. Zucker, " RJGAH.   35 (1972): 16-18.

4455   [Landsteiner.]   "Karl Landsteiner, M.D., " ACHS.   58 (1947): iii.

4456   Lasby, Clarence.   "Project Paperclip: German Scientists Come to America, " Va. Q. Rev.   42 (1966): 366-77.

4457   Lund, Gene.   "The Lutheran Scholar and Theology in America LuthQ.   12 (1960): 242-48.

4458   Marcuse, Herbert.   "Der Einfluss der deutschen Emigration auf das amerikanische Geistesleben: Philosophie und Soziologie, " JAS.   10 (1965): 27-33.

4459   "Oesterreichische Gelehrte im Ausland: Franz H. Mautner, USA, " O. Hochschulzeitung.   (Oct. 1, 1963).

4460   Meyer, Donald. "Paul Carus and the Religion of Science, "
        AQ. 14 (1962): 597-607.

4461   Mills, Donald. "Scientific Personnel and the Professions, "
        APSS. 367 (1966): 33-42.

4462   Murphy, C. "Augustus J. Prahl, " RJGAH. 35 (1970): 9-15.

4463   Murphy, Murray. "Kant's Children: The Cambridge Pragma-
        tists, " Trans. C. S. Peirce Soc. 4 (1968): 3-33.

4464   Nichols, James. The Mercersburg Theology. New York:
        Oxford University Pr., 1966.

4465   Penzel, Klaus. Church History and the Ecumenical Quest:
        A Study of the German Background and Thought of Philip
        Schaff. Union Theological Seminary: Dissertation, 1962.

4466   Plessner, Monika. "Die deutsche University in Exile in New
        York und ihr amerikanischer Gründer, " Frank. Hefte. 19
        (1964): 181-86.

4467   Pochmann, Henry. German Culture in America, 1600-1900:
        Philosophical and Literary Influences. Madison: University
        of Wisconsin Pr., 1957.

4468   _____. "The Hegelization of the West, " AGR. 9 (1943):
        24-31, 37.

4469   _____. New England Transcendentalism and St. Louis
        Hegelianism. Philadelphia: Carl Schurz Memorial Founda-
        tion, 1948.

4470   Prahl, Augustus. "German Scholars at the John Hopkins Uni-
        versity, " RJGAH. 30 (1959): 67-72.

4471   "Professor Guy Stern wird Universitätsdekan, " Aufbau. (Oct.
        12, 1973).

4472   Pross, Helge. Die Deutsche Akademische Emigration in den
        Vereinigten Staaten, 1933-41. Berlin: Duncker & Humbolt,
        1955.

4473   Richards, George. "The Mercersburg Theology: Its Pur-
        pose and Principles, " CH. 20 (1951): 42-55.

4474   Schaber, Will. Aufbau: Reconstruction: Dokumente einer
        Kultur im Exil, Mit einem Geleitwort von Hans Steinitz.
        Woodstock, New York: Overlook Pr., 1972.

4475   Schelbert, Leo. "The Swiss-American Historical Society, "
        IMR. 3 (1969): 64-66.

4476   Shriver, George.   Philip Schaff's Concept of Organic Histori-
        ography Interpreted in Relation to the Realization of an Evan-
        gelical Catholicism Within the Christian Community.   Duke
        University: Dissertation, 1961.

4477   Smith, Wilson.   "Francis Lieber's Moral Philosophy, " HLQ.
        18 (1955): 395-408.

4478   Stallo, Johann Bernhardt.   The Concepts and Theories of
        Modern Physics.   Cambridge: Harvard University Pr., 1960.

4479   _____. Reden, Abhandlungen, Briefe.   New York: Steiger,
        1893.   GSP

4480   Steinitz, Hans.   "Vierzig Jahre Universität im Exil: Ein
        Jubiläum der New Yorker New York School for Social Re-
        search, " Aufbau. (Sept. 14, 1973).

4481   Toms, Victoria.   The Intellectual and Literary Background of
        Francis Daniel Pastorius.   Northwestern University: Disser-
        tation, 1953.

4482   Vogel, Stanley.   German Literary Influences on American
        Transcendentalists.   New Haven: Yale University Pr., 1955.

4483   Wach, Joachim.   Comparative Study of Religion.   New York:
        Columbia University Pr., 1958.

4484   Walz, John.   German Influence in American Education.   Phila-
        delphia: Carl Schurz Memorial Foundation, 1936.

4485   Ward, Robert Elmer.   General Proposal for the Creation of
        an American Foundation for the Preservation of German Cul-
        ture in America.   Parma, Ohio: Society for German-Ameri-
        can Studies, 1973.

4485A   _____. A Proposal on Behalf of the Preservation of Ger-
        man Culture in the U. S.   Parma, Ohio: Society for German-
        American Studies, 1973.

4486   _____. "Symposium über deutsche Kultur in den Vereinig-
        ten Staaten, " DDA. (December, 1973).

4487   Weber, Evelyn.   The Kindergarten: Its Encounter with Edu-
        cational Thought in America.   New York: Teachers College
        Pr., 1969.

4488   Wentz, Abdel.   "The Philosophic Roots of S. S. Schmucker's
        Thought, " LuthQ. 18 (1966): 245-59.

4489   Wish, Harvey.   Society and Thought in Early America: A
        Social and Intellectual History of the American People Through
        1865.   New York: Longmans, Green & Co., 1950.

4490   Wüst, Julia. Karl Follen: Seine Ideenwelt und ihre Wirklich-
       keit. University of Erlangen: Dissertation, 1935.

4491   Wust, Klaus. "Johannes Braun (1771-1850): Ein geistiger
       Führer der Virginia-Deutschen, " Europa & die Niederdeutsche
       Welt. 9 (1955): 120-23.

Customs

4492   Alderfer, Gordon. "The Pioneer Culture of the Plain People, "
       ML. 5 (1950): 30-34.

4493   Alderfer, Harold. "On the Trail of the Hex Signs, " AGR. 19,
       vi (1953): 4-8.

4494   Aurand, A. M. Child Life of the Pennsylvania Germans.
       Harrisburg, Pa.: Aurand, 1947.

4495   _____ . Home Life of the Pennsylvania Germans. Harris-
       burg, Pa.: Aurand, 1947.

4496   _____ . Social Life of the Pennsylvania Germans. Harris-
       burg, Pa.: Aurand, 1947.

4497   Baldwin, S. "Amish Plain Costume: A Matter of Choice, "
       PFL. 19 (1970): 10-17.

4498   Banks, Betty. "Local Powwow Rituals, " HRBC. 33 (1967-68):
       15-17, 28-32.

4499   Barba, Preston. "Cherry Bounce, " Eck. (Mar. 15, 1969).

4500   _____ . "Great Affliction and Frontier Life in Northampton
       County, " Eck. (June 1, 8, 1957).

4501   _____ . "Greens, " Eck. (Mar. 27, 1954).

4502   _____ . "Himmelsbriefe or Talismanic Letters, " Eck.
       (Aug. 13, 1942).

4503   _____ . "Lichtmess, " Eck. (Feb. 2, 1957; Feb. 1, 1969).

4504   _____ . "Es Neiyaahr Aaschiesse, " Eck. (Dec. 31, 1949).

4505   _____ . "Old Time Christmas Baking, " Eck. (Dec. 8,
       1956).

4506   _____ . "Pie and the Pennsylvania Germans, " Eck. (Feb.
       24, 1951).

4507   Bayer, Russel. "Golden Fields in the Golden Years, " PFL.
       9 (1958): 12-17.

4508   Behrendt, Richard. "Deutscher Geist and American Way of
        Life: Gemeinsames und Unterschiedliches, " Vorträge anläss-
        lich der Hess. Hochschulwochen für staatswissen. Fortbildung.
        23 (1959): 206-26.

4509   Berkey, Andrew. "Christmas Customs of the Perkiomen Val-
        ley, " PD. 4 (1952): 1-2, 7.

4510   Bister, A. K. "Christmas with the Engelmann Family, " AGR.
        17, ii (1950): 20-22.

4511   Breen, Robert. "Merry Christmas, Happy New Year, " AGR.
        20, ii (1953): 22-23.

4512   Brendle, Thomas. "Customs of the Year in the Dutch Coun-
        try, " PD. (Nov. 15, 1951).

4513   _____. "Witchcraft in Cow and Horse, " PD. 8 (1956):
        28-31.

4514   Byington, Robert. "Popular Beliefs and Superstitions from
        Pennsylvania, " Keystone FQ. 9 (1964): 3-12.

4515   Cabaniss, Allen. "The Mississippi Jus Sacra: A Note, "
        JMH. 12 (1950): 169-73.

4516   Condit, William. "Christopher Ludwick: The Patriot Ginger-
        bread Baker, " PMHB. 81 (1957): 365-90.

4517   DeChant, Alliene. Seed Time to Harvest. Kutztown: Kutz-
        town Publishing Co., 1957.

4518   Dieffenbach, Victor. "Cabbage in the Folk-Culture of My
        Pennsylvania Dutch Elders, " PD. 3 (1952): 1-2.

4519   Dinkel, Phyllis. "Old Marriage Customs in Herzog, Kansas, "
        WF. 19 (1960): 99-105.

4520   Estep, Glenn and W. Pietchke. "A Study of Certain Aspects
        of Spiritualism and Pow-wow in Regard to the Folklore of
        Lancaster County, " PD. 5 (1954): 10-11, 15.

4521   Finckh, Alice. "In the Candle's Glow, " AGR. 14, ii (1947):
        4-6.

4522   Gapp, Samuel. "The Moravian Use of the Lot in Marriage, "
        PGFS. 22 (1958): 151-54.

4523   Gerhard, Elmer. "Pennsylvania Germans not Alone Supersti-
        tious, " Eck. (Nov. 25, 1950).

4524   Gilbert, Russell. "The Pennsylvania German in His Will, "
        AGR. 17, iii (1951): 24-26.

4525 _____. "Pennsylvania German Wills," PGFS. 15 (1951):
1-107.

4526 _____. Pennsylvania German Wills. Allentown, Pa.:
Schlechter, 1951.

4527 _____. "Pennsylvania German Wills in Berks County,"
HRBC. 21 (1955): 8-12.

4528 _____. "The Pennsylvania German Wills of Northumberland
County," NCoHSP. 17 (1949): 123-53.

4529 _____. "Some Characteristics of Pennsylvania German
Wills," Eck. (Sept. 18, 25, 1948).

4530 Gourley, J. F. Regional American Cookery, 1884-1934: A
List of Works on the Subject. New York: Public Library,
1936.

4531 Gourley, Norma. "About Powwowing," PD. 5 (1954): 7-8.

4532 Grey, Sara. "Children's Games Among Lancaster County
Mennonites," PFL. 16 (1967): 46 ff.

4533 Gröber, Karl. "Christkind, Krippe und Christbaum," AGR.
14, ii (1947): 15-21.

4534 Gunther, Gertrude. American Social History as Recorded
by German Travellers, 1783-1860. Columbia University:
Dissertation, 1950.

4535 Hand, Wayland. "A German House-Raiding Ceremony in
California," WF. 13 (1954): 199-202.

4536 Hark, Ann. Blue Hills and Shoofly Pie. Philadelphia: Lippincott, 1952.

4537 _____ and Preston Barba. Pennsylvania German Cookery.
Allentown, Pa.: Schlechter, 1950.

4538 Heffenger, Scott. "The Pennsylvania Dutch and their Queer
Ways," Eck. (Oct. 17-Nov. 7, 1959).

4539 Heller, Edna. "Drinks in Dutchland," PD. 8 (1956): 8-9.

4540 _____. "Pennsylvania Dutch Cooking Today and Yesterday,"
PFL. 17 (1968): 38 ff.

4541 _____. "Pies in Dutchland," PFL. 9 (1958): 44-45.

4542 Henry, James. "Christmas with the Moravians," AGR. 27
(1960): 4-7.

4543   Hershey, Mary. "A Study of the Dress of the Old Mennonites of the Franconia Conference, 1700-1953," PFL. 9, iii (1958): 24-27.

4544   Hollenbach, Raymond. "Account of a Hired Girl in a Pennsylvania German Family One Hundred Years Ago," Eck. (May 23, 1964).

4545   _____. "Ausschteir," Eck. (Dec. 5, 1964).

4546   _____. "Aussteuer-Dowries," Eck. (Mar. 23-Apr. 6, 1968).

4547   _____. "Fasenacht Kuche," PD. 5 (1954): 5.

4548   _____. "Hollerbeere-Elderberries," Eck. (July 10, 1965).

4549   _____. "Mer gehne fische," Eck. (May 2, 4, 1959).

4550   _____. "Mush," Eck. (Apr. 18, 1964).

4551   _____. "Neinuhrschdick un Fieruhrschdick," Eck. (June 29, 1957).

4552   _____. "Sheep and Wool on Local Farms in Bygone Days," Eck. (Feb. 29, 1964).

4553   Hostetler, John. "Amish Costume: Its European Origins," AGR. 22 (1956): 11-14.

4554   Hottenstein, Mary. "Traditional Pennsylvania German Christmas Cookies," HRBC. 35 (1970): 14-16.

4555   Howard, Dorothy. Traditional Play Customs of Amish and Mennonite Children in the Yoder School, Garret Co., Md. State Teacher's College, Frostburg, Md.: Dissertation, 1961.

4556   Hutchison, Ruth. Christmas in Bethlehem. New York: Oxford University Pr., 1958.

4557   _____. New Pennsylvania Dutch Cook Book. New York: Harper, 1958.

4558   Impink, Anne. "Transplanted Customs of the Pennsylvania Dutch," HRBC. 35 (1969): 17, 38 ff.

4559   Jones, Louis. "The Evil Eye Among European Americans," WF. 10 (1951): 11-25.

4560   Kaufman, David. "German and Pennsylvania German Surnames," Eck. (May 21, 28, June 4, 1966).

4561   _____. "A Minister's Son Attends a Frolic," Eck. (Mar. 2, 1968).

4562 Kemble, Howard and Harry Weiss. "The Forgotten Water-Cures of Brattleboro, Vermont," V. Hist. 37 (1969): 165-76.

4563 Keyser, Alan. "Nineteenth Century Shooting Matches," PFL. 12 (1961): 8-9.

4564 Kieffer, Elizabeth. "The Cheese Was Good," PFL. 19 (1970): 27-29.

4565 Klees, Fredric. "The Christmas Present and the Pennsylvania Dutch," HRBC. 18, ii (1953): 34-36.

4566 _____. "The Christmas Present and the Pennsylvania Dutch," Eck. (Dec. 4, 1954).

4567 Knortz, Karl. Nachklänge germanischen Glaubens und Brauchs in Amerika: Ein Beitrag zur Volkskunde. Halle: Peter, 1903. DLC

4568 Korson, George. "Courtship and Marriage Customs Among the Hard Coal Region Pennsylvania Dutch," Keystone FQ. 6 (1961): 2-16.

4569 Kramer, Gerhardt. Heritage of Cooking: A Collection of Recipes From East Perry County, Missouri. St. Louis: Concordia Historical Institute, 1966.

4570 Kulp, Clarence. "A Dunker Weekend Love Feast of 100 Years Ago," PFL. 11 (1960): 2-9.

4571 Kulp, Isaac. "Christmas Customs of the Goshenhoppen Region," Gosh. Region. 1 (1968): 4-11.

4572 Lincoln, Waldo. American Cookery Books, 1742-1860. Worcester: American Antiquarian Society, 1954.

4573 Long, Amos. "Dutch Country Scarecrows," PFL. 12 (1961): 54-59.

4574 Ludwig, G. M. "The Influence of the Pennsylvania Dutch in the Middle West," PGFS. 10 (1947): 1-101.

4575 Martin, Aaron. "Courtship and Marriage Practices," ML. 17 (Jan. 1962).

4576 "Matrimonial Bar," MMH. 8 (1958): 61-62.

4577 Meyer, Frederick. "The Forest Preacher on the Schoharie: An Historical Tale of the Life and Customs of the German Americans of the Eighteenth Century," Eck. (June 28-Sept. 6, 1952).

4578 Mook, Maurice. "Nicknames Among the Amish," ML. 16 (1961): 129-31.

4579   _____. "Nicknames Among the Amish," Names. 15 (1967):
111-18.

4580   _____. "Old Fashioned Bread Baking in Rural Pennsylvania," Eck. (Feb. 19, 1966).

4581   _____ and John Hostetler. "The Amish and Their Land,"
Eck. (July 8-29, 1961).

4582   Nolan, J. B. "Pennsylvania Sunday Best," AH. 8 (1957): 48-
51.

4583   The Pennsylvania Dutch Cook Book. Reading, Pa.: Culinary
Arts Pr., 1936.

4584   "Plattdeutsche Feiern in Amerika," Europa & die Niederdeutsche Welt. 19 (1955): 131-36.

4585   Polt, H. K. "Die Schlaraffia," AGR. 20, ii (1953): 16-19.

4586   Rippley, LaVern. Of German Ways. Minneapolis: Dillon,
1970. Excellent introduction to German-American customs.

4587   Robacker, Earl. "Art in Christmas Cookies," PD. 6 (1954):
3-7.

4588   _____. "Christmas," PFL. 16 (1966): 2-13.

4589   _____. "Knife, Fork and Spoon: A Collector's Problem,"
PFL. 9 (1958): 28-33.

4590   _____. "Search for a Long Lost Friend." Eck. (June 9,
1956).

4591   Robbins, Walter. "The North Carolina New Year's Shoot,"
Eck. (Jan. 3, 1959).

4592   Rush, Benjamin. "An Account of the Manners of the German
Inhabitants of Pennsylvania," Eck. (Sept. 22-Oct. 27, 1962).

4593   Sachse, Julius. "Excorcism of Fire," PD. 5 (1954): 6-9.

4594   Schreiber, William. "The Amish Way of Life," Eck. (Mar.
1-22, 1958).

4595   _____. "Amish Weddings Days," JAF. 73 (1960): 12-17.

4596   _____. "Wie der Weihnachtsbaum nach Amerika kam,"
Christ Unterwegs. 11 (1957): 2-4.

4597   Scribner, Robert. "Virginia's German' Tree," Va. Caval-
cade. 6 (1956): 4-7.

4598   Shaner, Richard. "Living Occult Practices in Dutch Pennsyl-
        vania Country, " PFL. 12 (1961): 62-63.

4599   _____. "Powwow Doctors, " PFL. 12 (1961): 72.

4599A   Shoemaker, Alfred. "Barricading the Road, " PD. 5 (1954): 2.

4600   _____. Christmas in Pennsylvania: A Folk-Cultural Study.
        Kutztown, Pa.: Pennsylvania Folklore Society, 1959.

4601   _____. "Church and Meetinghouse Stables and Sheds, "
        PFL. 11 (1960): 22-33.

4602   _____. Eastertide in Pennsylvania: A Folk-Cultural Study.
        Kutztown, Pa.: Pennsylvania Folklore Society, 1959.

4603   _____. "Whit-Monday: Dutch Fourth of July, " PD. 5
        (1954): 5, 12.

4604   Showalter, M. E. "Christmas Cookery and Customs from
        Greatgrandmother's Day, " AGR. 17, ii (1950): 7-9.

4605   _____. Mennonite Community Cookbook. Philadelphia:
        Winston, 1957.

4606   Shumway, George. Longrifles of Note, Pennsylvania. York,
        Pa.: Author, 1968.

4607   Single, Erwin. "Deutsch-Amerikanische Vereine: Teil unseres
        Lebens, " NYSZH. (May 13, 1973).

4608   Smith, Elmer. "The Amish Marriage Age, " Eck. (Aug. 1,
        1959).

4609   _____. "Amish Names, " Names. 16 (1968): 105-10.

4610   _____. "The Amish System of Nomenclature, " Eck. (Aug.
        8, 1959).

4611   _____. "The Amish Wedding Season, " Eck. (Jan. 17,
        1959).

4612   _____. "Belling, " Eck. (Jan. 23, 1965).

4613   _____. Bundling Among the Amish. Akron, Pa.: Applied
        Arts, 1961.

4614   _____. "A Dutch Get-Together, " Eck. (Oct. 24, 1964).

4615   _____. "Family Harvest: The Amish Wedding, " HRBC.
        26 (1960): 6-12.

4616   Smith, George. "The Trade and Mystery of Farming, " HP.
        20 (1968): 40-49.

4617   Soldner, Dora.   "Serenading on the New Year's Eve," AGR.
        18 (1951): 26-28.

4618   Staebler, Edna.   Food That Really Schmecks: Mennonite
        Country Cooking.   Chicago: Follett, 1968.

4619   Stauffer, Eva.   "Pennsylvania German Cooking," Eck. (Mar.
        20, 1948).

4620   Stewart, John and Elmer Smith.   "An Occult Remedy Manu-
        script from Pendleton County, West Virginia," Bul. Madison
        College. 22 (1964): 77-85.

4621   Tolles, Frederick.   "The Culture of Early Pennsylvania,"
        PMHB. 81 (1957): 119-37.

4622   Tortora, Vincent.   "Amish Funerals," PFL. 12 (1961): 8-13.

4623   _____.   "The Courtship and Wedding Practices of the Old
        Order Amish," PFL. 9 (1958): 12-21.

4624   Vogt, Evon and Hyman Ray.   Water Witching U.S.A.   Chi-
        cago: University of Chicago Pr., 1959.

4625   Weiser, Daniel.   "Braucherei," PD. 5 (1954): 6, 14.

4626   Westkott, Marcia.   "Powwowing in Berks County," PFL. 19
        (1970): 2-9.

4627   Wieland, P. R.   Outdoor Games of the Pennsylvania Germans.
        Plymouth Meeting, Pa., 1950.

4628   Wilson, Marian.   "Present Day Food Habits of the Pennsyl-
        vania Dutch," PFL. 9 (1958): 38-39.

4629   Wood, R. Charles.   "Life, Death and Poetry as Seen by the
        Pennsylvania Dutch," Monatshefte. 37 (1945): 453-65.

4630   Yeich, Edwin.   "Essen, oder Fressen," HRBC. 21 (1956):
        91-93.

4631   Yoder, Don.   "The Costumes of the Plain People," PD. 4
        (1953): 6-7.

4632   _____.   "Harvest Home," PFL. 9 (1958): 2-11.

4633   _____.   "Love Feasts," PD. 7 (1956): 34-37.

4634   _____.   "Men's Costumes Among the Plain People," PD.
        4 (1953): 6-9.

4635   _____.   "The Strauss Dance of the Dutch Country: A Lost
        German Dance of Our Forefathers?" PD. 5 (1954): 6-7.

4636   Zehner, Olive.   "Christmas in Dutch Country, " AGR. 20, ii
        (1953): 7-9.

4637   Zimmerman, Thomas.   "Ancestral Virtues of the Pennsyl-
        vania Germans, " Eck. (Dec. 7, 1968).

4638   _____.   "Puritan and Cavalier: Why Not the Pennsylvania
        German?" Eck. (Nov. 23, 1968).

Folklore

4639   Aurand, A. M.   Quaint Idioms and Expressions of the Penn-
        sylvania Germans.   Harrisburg, Pa.: Aurand, 1939.

4639A   Barba, Preston.   "Christmas Lore, " Eck. (Jan. 13, Dec. 21,
        1968).

4640   _____.   "Notes on Matteis Daag, " Eck. (Apr. 5, 1947).

4640A   _____.   "Der Tambour Yockel, " Eck. (July 16, 1949).

4641   Baver, Mrs. Russell.   "Washday Lore, " PD. 5 (1953): 6-7,
        15.

4642   Beam, C. Richard.   "Eulenspiegel in Pennsylvania, " Der
        Reggeboge. 5 (1971): 3-6.

4643   Boggs, Ralph.   "Folklore Bibliography for 1951, " SFQ. 16
        (1952): 1-78.

4643A   Bressler, Leo.   "Pennsylvania German Wit and Humor, "
        Eck. (Mar. 23-May 25, 1957).

4644   Buffington, Albert.   "Pennsylvaanischdeitscher Gschpass, a
        Collection of Pennsylvania German Anecdotes, Jokes and
        Stories, " Eck. (Aug. 5-Sept. 23, 1961).

4645   _____.   "Pennsylvania German Humor: Some Representa-
        tive Examples, " Keystone FQ. 8 (1963): 75-80.

4646   Burress, Lee.   "Folklore of Collecting in Wisconsin, " OFL.
        2 (1967): 125-33.

4647   DeChant, Alliene.   "Sixteen Years of the Folk Festival, "
        PFL. 14 (1965): 10-13.

4647A   Dorson, Richard.   American Folklore.   Chicago: University
        of Chicago Pr., 1959.

4648   Evans, E. E.   "The Pennsylvania Dutch Folk Festival: A
        European Report, " PFL. 12 (1961): 44-48.

4649   Gerberich, Albert. "Inscriptions from Graveyard on Harry
        Lantz Fehl Farm," NGSQ. 39 (1951): 71-72.

4650   Gerhard, Elmer. "Pennsylvania German Weather Lore,"
        HRBC. 18 (1952): 2-7; Eck. (Jan. 22-Feb. 5, 1955).

4651   _____. "Some Pennsylvania German Proverbs," HRBC.
        20 (1955): 71-75, 93-95.

4652   Graeff, Arthur. "1950 in Pennsylvania German Folklore,"
        PGFS. 15 (1951): 129-34. This annual bibliography appeared
        until 1955.

4653   _____. "Pennsylvania German Humor," Eck. (Nov. 12-
        Dec. 3, 1949).

4654   _____. "Stoy's Remedy," Eck. (Feb. 22, 1969).

4655   Hand, Wayland. North Carolina Folklore: Popular Beliefs
        and Superstitions. Durham: Duke University Pr., 1961.

4656   Haywood, Charles. A Bibliography of North American Folk-
        lore and Folksong. New York: Dover, 1961.

4657   Heilbron, Bertha. "North Star Folklore in Minnesota History:
        A Bibliography," WF. 9 (1951): 366-71.

4658   Heisey, M. L. "Stories Radiating from Conestoga Centre,"
        LCHP. 56 (1952): 1-19.

4659   Hering, Irwin. "Folklore and Superstitions Among the Penn-
        sylvania Germans," Eck. (Sept. 7-Oct. 19, 1968).

4660   Hoffman, W. "Folklore of the Pennsylvania Germans," Eck.
        (Mar. 28-Apr. 25, 1959).

4661   Hollenbach, Raymond. "Gwidde," Eck. (Oct. 9, 1954).

4662   _____. "Welschkarn," Eck. (Apr. 28, May 5, 1951).

4663   "Humorous Tales Told by Contemporary Pennsylvania Ger-
        mans," PGFS. 15 (1951): 109-28.

4664   Internationale volkskundliche Bibliographie. Bonn: Robert
        Hobelt, 1949- .

4665   Kaiser, Leo. "German Verse in American Cemetaries,"
        AGR. 26 (1960): 25-28.

4666   _____. "German Verse in Missouri Churchyards," ZKA.
        12 (1962): 319-22.

4667   Kieffer, Elizabeth. "Joseph Henry Dubbs as a Folklorist,"
        PFL. 9 (1958): 32-35.

4668 Korson, George. Black Rock: Mining Folklore of the Penn-
      sylvania Dutch. Baltimore: John Hopkins University Pr.,
      1960.

4669 _____. Pennsylvania Songs and Legends. Baltimore:
      John Hopkins University Pr., 1960.

4670 Kring, Hilda. The Harmonists: A Folk-Cultural Approach.
      University of Pennsylvania: Dissertation, 1969. Metuchen,
      New Jersey: Scarecrow Press, 1973.

4671 "Kutztown: Program 15th Annual Pennsylvania Dutch Folk
      Festival, July 3-11, 1964, Kutztown, " PFL. 13 (1964): 32-39.

4672 Lomax, Alan and Sidney Robertson. American Folksong and
      Folklore: A Regional Bibliography. New York: Progressive
      Ed. Assoc., 1942.

4673 Mankin, Carolyn. "Tales the German Texans Tell, " Singers
      & Storytellers. 30 (1961): 260-65.

4674 Nielson, George. "Folklore of the German-Wends in Texas, "
      Singers and Storytellers. 30 (1961): 244-59.

4675 Reichard, Harry. "Die Wedderberichte, " Eck. (Feb. 27,
      1954).

4676 Riedl, Norbert. "Folklore vs. Volkskunde, " Tenn. FSQ. 31
      (1965): 47-53.

4677 Rosenberger, Homer. "The Hex Doctor and the Witch of Far-
      randsville, " Keystone FQ. 3 (1958): 42-45.

4678 Shoemaker, Alfred. "Belsnickel Lore, " PD. 6 (1954): 34-38.

4679 _____. "D is for Dutch, " PD. 5 (1953): 5, 15.

4680 _____. "February Lore, " PD. 5 (1953): 11.

4681 _____. "Folklore on Snow, " PD. 5 (1953): 5.

4682 _____. "The Glingelsock, " PFL. 12 (1961): 53-55.

4683 _____. "Good Friday and Easter Lore, " PD. 4 (1953):
      2-3, 5, 11.

4683A _____. "The Last Five Years, " PD. 5 (1953): 3, 6.

4684 _____. "March Lore, " PD. 5 (1954): 9.

4685 _____. "Shrove Tuesday Lore, " PD. 5 (1954): 5.

4686 _____. "Water Witching, " PFL. 12 (1961): 25-27.

4687   Smith, Elmer and J. Stewart. "The Black Walnut," Eck.
        (Dec. 19, 1964).

4688   _____. "Grundsau Dag," Eck. (Jan. 30, 1965).

4689   _____. "Hydrophobia and the Madstone," Eck. (July 17,
        1965).

4690   _____. "Pennsylvania German Folklore in the Shenandoah
        Valley," Eck. (Apr. 7-Dec. 14, 1963).

4691   _____. "Shenandoah Valley Sayings," Eck. (June 5, 1965).

4692   Starr, Frederick. "Some Pennsylvania German Lore," Eck.
        (Aug. 15, 1959).

4693   Stoudt, John. "Folklore," HRBC. 17 (1952): 66-74.

4694   "Pennsylvania German Folklore," PGFS. 16 (1953): 157-70.

4695   Strong, Leah. "Humor in the Lehigh Valley," NYFQ. 15
        (1959): 126-30.

4696   Terbovich, John. "Religious Folklore among the German-
        Russians in Ellis County, Kansas," WF. 22 (1963): 79-88.

4697   Ver Nooy, Amy. "Place Names and Folklore in Dutchess
        County," NYFQ. 20 (1964): 42-46.

4698   Weigel, Lawrence. "German Proverbs From Around Fort
        Hays, Kansas," WF. 18 (1959): 98.

4699   Williams, Maynard. "Pennsylvania Dutch Folk Festival,"
        NGM. 102 (1952): 503-16.

4700   Wust, Klaus. "Folklore, Customs and Crafts of the Valley
        Settlers," HP. 20 (1968): 28-39.

4701   Yoder, Don. "Folklife Studies Bibliography, 1964: Peri-
        odicals," PFL. 14 (1965): 60-64.

4702   _____. "Folklore From the Hegins and Makontongo Val-
        leys," Eck. (Oct. 4-Nov. 22, 1947).

4703   _____. "Newspaper and Folklife Studies," PFL. 15 (1966):
        16-23.

4704   _____. "Notes and Documents," PFL. 16 (1966): 44-48.

4705   _____. "Sauerkraut in the Pennsylvania Folk-Culture,"
        PFL. 12 (1961): 56-69.

4706   _____. "Schnitz in the Pennsylvania Folk-Culture," PFL.
        12 (1961): 44-53.

4707   _____. "The Snake Bitten Dutchman," PFL. 16 (1966): 42-
          43.

4708   "Zeecheglaawe un Braucherei: Was der Mond dutt, was die
          Zeeche bedeite, un wie mer Krankheete los watt," Eck.
          (June 25, 1966).

VII. BUSINESS AND INDUSTRY

Histories and Individual Studies

4709   Adler, Cyrus. Jacob H. Schiff: His Life and Letters.
        Grosse Point: Scholarly Pr., 1968.

4710   Adler, Jacob. Claus Spreckels: The Sugar King in Hawaii.
        Honolulu: University of Hawaii Pr., 1965.

4711   Amelung, John. "Remarks on Manufactures, Principally on
        the New Established Glass-House Near Frederick-Town, in
        the State of Maryland," PAAS. 60 (1950): 101.

4712   Appelmann, Anton. Der Kaufmann als Vertreter des Deutsch-
        tums im Ausland, Nebst Richtlinien für Auswanderer und
        einem Verzeichnis der deutschen Handels- und diplomatischen
        Vertretungen in Amerika. Hamburg: Hanseatische Verlag-
        sanstalt, 1925.

4713   Baluyut, Fernando. Anheuser-Busch: A Study in Firm
        Growth. St. Louis University: Dissertation, 1961.

4714   Barba, Preston. "Distilleries, Cider Presses, etc., Among
        Our Early German Settlers," Eck. (Sept. 28, 1957).

4715   Baron, Stanley. Brewed in America: A History of Beer and
        Ale in the U.S. Boston: Little, Brown & Co., 1962.

4716   Bean, Geraldine. Charles Boettcher: A Study in Pioneer
        Western Enterprise. University of Colorado: Dissertation,
        1970.

4717   Beck, Herbert. "Elizabeth Furnace Plantation," LCHS. 69
        (1965): 25-41.

4718   Berky, Andrew. An Account of Some Hosensack Valley Mills.
        Pennsburg, Pa.: Schwenkfelder Library, 1958.

4719   Bining, Arthur. "Early Ironmasters of Pennsylvania," PH.
        18 (1951): 93-103.

4720   Bleyle, Carl. Georg Andreas Sorge's Influence on David Tan-
        nenberg and Organ Building in America during the Eighteenth

Century. University of Minnesota: Dissertation, 1969.

4721   Brady, John. "Emile Berliner: Microphone and Gramophone, "
        AGR. 27, i (1960): 33-35.

4722   Brause, Dolly. "History of German Mutual Insurance Com-
        pany of Eldora, " Cedar R. Gaz. (Apr. 1951).

4723   Brown, R. W. Friedrich List: The Father of German Rail-
        roads: His Residence in Dauphin and Schuylkill Counties.
        Harrisburg, Pa.: Dauphin Historical Soc., 1950.

4724   Brown, Seletha. "Dallas Wilson Spangler: Three Career
        Man, " CM. 32 (1955): 63-71.

4725   Carosso, Vincent. The California Wine Industry, 1830-95:
        A Study of the Formative Years. Berkeley: University of
        California Pr., 1951.

4726   "Carpenter Named John Scholl Left the World a Legacy of
        Charming Toys and Beautiful Fantasies, " Amer. Her. 20
        (1968): 19-23.

4727   Chickering, Allen. "In Memoriam C. O. G. Miller, " CHSQ.
        31 (1952): 176. A leading California businessman.

4728   Clark, Victor S. History of Manufactures in the U. S.
        Washington: Carnegie Institute, 1929.

4729   Cochran, Thomas. The Pabst Brewing Company: The History
        of an American Business. New York: New York University
        Pr., 1948.

4730   Cohen, Nathan. "William Volker: Mr. Anonymous, " AGR.
        25, v (1959): 12-15.

4731   Cornuelle, Herbert. Mr. Anonymous: The Story of William
        Volker. Chicago: Regnery, 1961.

4732   Counter, Margarete. "Pioneer Canning Industry in Colorado, "
        CM. 30 (1953): 37-48.

4733   Cunz, Dieter. "Amelung's Old Frederick Glass, " AGR. 12,
        v (1946): 16-19.

4734   _____. "Christian Meyer, Baltimore Merchant, " AGR.
        10 (1944): 11-13, 35.

4735   _____. "Maryland's First Paper Maker, " AGR. 12 (1945):
        21-23.

4736   Derleth, August. The Milwaukee Road. New York: Creative
        Age Pr., 1948.

4737   Documentary History of American Industrial Society. New
       York: A. H. Clark, 1910-11. Contains extensive bibliogra-
       phies.

4738   Dohme, Alfred. "Early History of Drug Business," AGR.
       13, i (1946): 24-26.

4739   Donovan, Frank. "Henry Villard," AGR. 19, vi (1953): 25-
       29.

4740   Eader, Thomas. "Baltimore Organs and Organ Building,"
       MHM. 65 (1970): 263-82.

4741   Elkinton, Howard. "Greiner and Mueller: Makers of Eyes
       for Humanity," AGR. 13, v-vi (1947): 28-32, 40.

4742   _____. "The Wandering Glass-Makers of Gablonz," AGR.
       15, iv (1949): 20-21.

4743   Erickson, Charlotte. American Industry and the European
       Immigrant, 1860-85. Cambridge: Harvard University Pr.,
       1957.

4744   Evers, Fritz. "Albert L. Heil," RJGAH. 28 (1953): 91.
       Insurance businessman.

4745   _____. "Henry L. Wienefeld," RJGAH. 29 (1956): 79-80.
       Manufacturer of cigars.

4746   _____. "J. George Mohlheinrich," RJGAH. 25 (1942): 40.
       Manufactured furniture.

4747   _____. "John G. Tjarks," RJGAH. 26 (1945): 52-53. A
       Maryland businessman.

4748   Ewan, Joseph. "Silk Culture in the Colonies, with Particu-
       lar Reference to the Ebenezer Colony and the First Local
       Flora of Georgia," Ag. Hist. 43 (1969): 129-47.

4749   Ferris, Raymond. "F. L. Maytag," AGR. 24, v (1958): 17-
       19.

4750   Fierman, F. "Samuel J. Freudenthal: Southwestern Mer-
       chant and Civic Leader," AJHQ. 57 (1968): 352-435.

4751   _____. "The Spiegelbergs: Pioneer Merchants and Bank-
       ers in the Southwest," AJHQ. 56 (1967): 371-451.

4752   Flanagan, John. "Theodore Hamm Founds a Brewery," AGR.
       27 (1960): 25-28.

4753   Ford, Edward. David Rittenhouse: Astronomer-Patriot, 1732-
       96. Philadelphia: University of Pennsylvania Pr., 1946.

4754   Gallegos, Rene. "Ferd Meyer, Early Trader," CM. 28 (1951):
       94-96.

4755   Gemmell, Alfred. "The Charcoal Iron Industry in the Perko-
       men Valley," BHSM. 6 (1948): 186-258.

4756   Gerhard, Elmer. "Frederick Graff and the Philadelphia Wa-
       terworks," AGR. 13, iii (1947): 30-34.

4757   German-American Technicians Association. Verbands-Statuten
       und Mitglieder Listen des Deutsch-Amerikanischen Techniker-
       Verbandes. Baltimore: Schneidereith, 1899. DLC, MB

4758   German Publishing Company. Das Neue Baltimore, Mit be-
       sonderer Berücksichtigung der Deutsch-Amerikaner im Gesch-
       äftsleben. Baltimore: Schneidereith, 1905. MdHi, MdBE,
       PPCS

4759   Gill, Larry. "From Butcher Boy to Beef King," MMH. 8
       (1958): 40-55.

4760   Gleis, Paul. "Ignaz W. Diepgen," RJGAH. 29 (1956): 79.
       An import-export businessman.

4761   Goodwyn, Frank. Life on the King Ranch. New York:
       Crowell, 1951.

4762   Hasse, Adelaide. Index of Economic Material in Documents
       of the States of the United States: Pennsylvania, 1790-1904.
       Washington: Carnegie Inst., 1919-22.

4763   Heiges, George. "Apothecaries of Lancaster County, 1760 to
       1900," LCHP. 50 (1946): 33-69.

4764   _____. Henry William Stiegel and His Associates: A
       Story of Early American Industry. Manheim, Pa.: Author,
       1948.

4765   _____. "Henry William Stiegel: Man of Vision," LCHS.
       72 (1968): 1-11.

4766   Hellstrom, O. H. "The Brewing Industry in Reading until
       1880," HRBC. 7 (1941): 39-43.

4767   Herndon, Booton. Bergdorf's on the Plaza. New York:
       Knopf, 1956.

4768   Hollenbach, Raymond. "Die Bittner's Corner Miehl," Eck.
       (Aug. 30, Sept. 6, 1947).

4769   _____. "The Old Tannery: Die alt Garwerei," Eck.
       (Feb. 23, Mar. 2, 1957).

4770   Hubbard, Donald and others. "Amelung Glasses and Modern
       Commercial Glasses, " Sci. Monthly. 75 (1952): 327-38.

4771   Hunter, D. Papermaking in Pioneer America. Philadelphia:
       University of Pennsylvania Pr., 1952.

4772   Hunter, Frederick. Stiegel Glass. New York: Dover, 1950.

4773   Kantor, Harvey. "The Barth Family: A Case Study of Pio-
       neer Immigrant Merchants, " MHR. 62 (1968): 410-30.

4774   Kinsey, Ralph. "The Wilhelms: Reading Industrialists, "
       HRBC. 31 (1965): 42-47.

4775   "Klieg-Light Kliegl, " New Yorker. 33 (1957): 20-21.

4776   Kloss, Heinz. Geschichte der landwirtschaftlichen Zusam-
       menschlüsse der Sprachdeutschen im Uebersee. Braunsch-
       weig: Westermann, 1958.

4777   Landing, James. American Essence: A History of the Pep-
       permint and Spearmint Industry in the U. S. Kalamazoo:
       Public Museum, 1969.

4778   Lenhart, John. "Andrew Kloman, " SJR. 35 (1942-43): 314-
       16, 351-53, 387-89; 36 (1943-44): 23-25, 58-60, 94-96, 104.
       About the steel industry.

4779   Loth, David. Swope of G. E. : The Story of Gerard Swope
       and General Electric in American Business. New York:
       Simon & Schuster, 1958.

4780   Lynch, Charles and others. "A History of Brewing in Lan-
       caster County: Legal and Otherwise, " LCHS. 70 (1966): 1-
       100.

4781   Lyon, Peter. "Isaac Singer and the Wonderful Sewing Ma-
       chine, " AH. 9 (1958): 34-38, 103-09.

4782   McKeen, John. "Pfizer: 110 Years of Service to Medicine
       and Industry, " Trade World. 2 (1960): 95-98.

4783   McNeilis, Sarah. "F. Augustus Heinze: An Early Chapter
       in the Life of a Copper King, " MMH. 2 (1952): 25-32.

4784   Milford, Harriet. "Amelung and His New Bremen Glass
       Wares, " MdHM. 47 (1952): 1-10.

4785   Miller, Robert. "Herman Sturm: Hoosier Secret Agent for
       Mexico, " IMH. 58 (1962): 1-15. Ran a munitions factory.

4786   Palut, James. Steuben Glass: A Monograph. New York:
       Bittner, 1948.

4787   Parish, William. The Charles Ilfeld Company: A Study of
        the Rise and Decline of Mercantile Capitalism in New Mexico.
        (Harvard Studies in Business History, 20.) Cambridge:
        Harvard University Pr., 1961.

4788   Parris, John. "Die ersten Golddollars, " ZKA. 19 (1969): 25.

4789   Parsons, John. Henry Deringer's Pocket Pistol. New York:
        William Morrow, 1952.

4790   Patzman, S. "Louis John Frederick Jaeger: Entrepreneuer
        of the Colorado River, " Arizona. 4 (1964): 31-36.

4791   Popham, Donald. "The Early Activities of the Guggenheims
        in Colorado, " CM. 27 (1950): 263-69.

4792   Purrington, Philip. "German Traders in New Bedford, " AGR.
        20, vi (1954): 2023.

4793   Quynn, Dorothy. "Johann Friedrich Amelung at New Bremen, "
        MdHM. 43 (1948): 155-79.

4794   Raid, Howard. "Farming and Industry in the Bluffton-Pan-
        dora Area, " ML. 11 (1956): 53-56.

4795   Rice, William. "Mount Hope Furnace, " AGR. 17, v (1957):
        28-29.

4796   Riebel, R. Louisville Panorama. Louisville: Liberty Nation-
        al Bank & Trust Co., 1954. Contains much detail on the
        Louisville Germans.

4797   Riebling, Frederick. "Charles A. Riebling, " RJGAH. 29
        (1956): 81-82. About an insurance businessman.

4798   Rosenwald, Emmanual. "Reminiscences of Emmanual Rosen-
        wald, " NMHR. 37 (1962): 110-31.

4799   Rubincam, Milton. "William Rittenhouse, American Pioneer
        Paper Manufacturer and Mennonite Minister, " PGS. 63 (1959):
        1-89.

4800   Schaeffer, A. "The United States-German Chamber of Com-
        merce, " AGR. 24, i (1957): 11-12, 17.

4801   Schenck, Carl. The Biltmore Story. St. Paul: Minnesota
        Historical Society, 1955.

4802   Schrag, Robert. "Newton, Kansas: A Center of Mennonite
        Businesses, " ML. 15 (1960): 64-67.

4803   _____. "The Story of a Mennonite Millionaire: Jacob
        Showalter, 1879-1953, " ML. 12 (1957): 64-69.

4804   Schultz, George.   "William Schultz: Pioneer Locomotive
       Builder, " AGR. 13, iv (1947): 19-20.

4805   Seitz, May.   The History of the Hoffman Paper Mills in Mary-
       land.   Towson, Md.:   Author, 1946.

4806   Shaner, Richard.   "Distillation and Distilleries among the
       Dutch, " PFL. 13 (1963): 39-42.

4807   Shannon, Harold.   "The Pauly Cheese Company, " WMH. 38
       (1955): 234-36.

4808   Smith, Elmer L.   "James A. Kline, 1877-1944:   Pioneer
       Auto Builder, " Eck. (Dec. 12, 1964).   Manufacturer of Pull-
       man autos.

4809   Steinman, D. B.   Brücken für die Ewigkeit.   Düsseldorf:
       Werner-Verlag, 1956.   On John Roebling.

4810   Stewart, Robert and Mary Stewart.   Adolph Sutro: A Biogra-
       phy.   Berkeley: Howell-North, 1962.   On a railroad builder
       and financier.

4811   Stolper, Toni.   Ein Leben in Brennpunkten unserer Zeit:
       Wien, Berlin, New York: Gustav Stolper, 1888-1947.   Tübin-
       gen: Wunderlich, 1960.

4812   Supplee, Barry.   "A Business Elite: German-Jewish Finan-
       ciers in Nineteenth Century New York, " Bus. Hist. Rev. 31
       (1957): 143-78.

4813   Suydam, F.   Christian Dorflinger: A Miracle of Glass.
       White Mills, 1950.

4814   Teesdale, Jerald.   "The Gunmaking Industry in Wisconsin, "
       WMH. 32 (1949): 302-11.

4815   Trachtenberg, Alan.   Brooklyn Bridge: Fact and Symbol.
       New York: Oxford University Pr., 1965.

4816   Treadwell, Edward.   The Cattle King: A Dramatized Biogra-
       phy.   Boston: Christopher Publishing, 1950.   On Heinrich
       Kreiser.

4817   Turner, Charles.   "An Immigrant Butcher's Diary, " WPHM.
       34 (1951): 135-44.

4818   Vitz, Carl.   "Martin Baum, " Museum Echo. 33 (1960): 35-3
       A Cincinnati merchant.

4819   _____.   "Martin Baum: Pioneer Cincinnati Entrepreneur,
       HPSO. 16 (1958): 215-39.

4820   Watkins, Lura. American Glass and Glassmaking. New York:
       Chanticleer Pr. , 1950.

4821   _____ . "Robert E. Dietz: From Burning Fluid to Kero-
       sene, " Rushlight. 22, iv (1956): 10-20.

4822   Webber, F. R₀ "Gemshorn and Klingel, " CHIQ. 29 (1956):
       41-47. On organ builders.

4823   _____ . "Worship by Machinery, " CHIQ. 33 (1961): 97 ff.

4824   Weiss, H. B. and G. Weiss. The Early Breweries of New
       Jersey. Trenton: Agricultural Soc. , 1963.

4824A Weslager, C. The Garrett Snuff Fortune. Wilmington, Del.:
       Knebels Pr. , 1965.

4825   Westermeier, Therese. "A Baltimore Pioneer in Proprietary
       Medicine, " JGAH. 28 (1953): 67-71.

4826   White, Margaret. "Germanic Glass, " AGR. 21, vi (1955):
       11-15.

4827   "Wie wir hören, " Aufbau. (Sept. 14, 1973). On Stauffer
       Chemical Co.

4828   Wilkins, Zora. "Henry Harnischfeger: Industrialist, " AGR.
       19, ii (1952): 26-28, 33₀

4829   Williams, Samuel. "Early Ironworks in the Tennessee Coun-
       try, " THQ. 6 (1949): 39-46.

4830   Winters, Shirley. "From a Small Apothecary, " AGR. 21, i
       (1954): 16-18.

4831   Wolf, Edward. "Adam Hoffmann: Master Brewer, " Bronx
       CHSQ. 5 (1968) : 65-73₀

4832   Yoder, Ida. "The Story of a Mill, " ML. 11 (1956): 21-24.

The Labor Movement

4833   Dayton, Eldorous. Walter Reuther: Autocrat of the Bar-
       gaining Table. New York: Devin-Adair, 1958.

4834   Dulles, Foster. Labor in America: A History. New York:
       Crowell, 1960.

4835   Epstein, Melech. Jewish Labor in USA: An Industrial, Po-
       litical and Cultural History of the Jewish Labor Movement,
       1882-1914. New York: Trade Union Sponsoring Committee,
       1950.

4836   Hollander, Jay.   "Prelude To a Strike, " NJHS. 79 (1961): 161
68.

4837   Hollenbach, Raymond. "George Washington and Thomas Jefferson and Their Plans for Using German Farm Labor, " Eck.
(Feb. 21, 28, 1959).

4838   Laslett, John. Labor and the Left: A Study of Socialist and
Radical Influences in the American Labor Movement, 1881-
1924. New York: Basic Books, 1970.

4839   Lowitt, Richard. "Frostburg 1882: German Strikers vs.
German Strikebreakers, " RJGAH. 28 (1953): 72-79.

4840   Madison, Charles.   American Labor Leaders.   New York:
Harper, 1950.

4841   Naas, Bernard and C. S. Sakr.   American Labor Union Periodicals.   Ithaca: Cornell University Pr., 1956.

4842   Neufeld, Maurice.   A Representative Bibliography of American Labor History. New York: Cornell University Pr.,
1964.

4843   Rayback, Joseph.   A History of American Labor.   New York,
1959.

4844   Reese, James.   "The Early History of Labor Organizations
in Texas, 1838-76, " SwHQ. 72 (1968): 1-20.

4845   Schieder, Wolfgang.   Die Anfänge der deutschen Arbeiter-
bewegung: Die Auslandsvereine im Jahrzehnt nach der Juli-
revolution von 1830.   Stuttgart, 1963.

4846   Schlüter, Hermann.   Die Anfänge der deutschen Arbeiter-
bewegung.   Stuttgart, 1907.

4847   _____ .   Die Brau-Industrie und Brauarbeiter-Bewegung in
Amerika.   Cincinnati: Internationaler Verband der Vereinigten Brauerei-Arbeiter von Amerika, 1910.

4848   _____ .   Lincoln, Labor and Slavery: A Chapter from the
Social History of America.   New York: Socialist Lit. Co.,
1913. DLC

4849   Taft, Philip.   Organized Labor in American History.   New
York: Harper, 1964.

4850   Wenk, M. and others.   Pieces of a Dream: The Ethnic
Worker's Crisis with America.   Staten Island: CMS, 1972.

4851   Wisconsin Historical Society.   Labor Papers on Microfilm: A
Combined List. Madison, 1960.   Covers the filming of most
of the labor papers in the U. S.

VIII. GERMAN-AMERICAN RADICALISM

The Forty-Eighters

4852　Bühler, Ottmar. "Carl Schurz and the Revolution of 1848, " AGR. 14, v (1948): 3-4.

4853　Cunz, Dieter. "Die Achtundvierziger in Amerika, " Schweizer B. z. Allg. Ges. 8 (1950): 215-19.

4854　＿＿＿＿＿. "Mit Heckerhut und Federkiel: Die Schriften der deutsch-amerikanischen Achtundvierziger, " D. Rundschau. 87 (1961): 782-85.

4855　Danton, George. "A Smart Flippant Fellow: Johann Ludwig Tellkampf, " NYH. 27 (1946): 458-75.

4856　Dobert, Eitel. Deutsche Demokraten in Amerika: Die Achtunvierziger und ihre Schriften. Göttingen: Vandenhoeck & Rupprecht, 1958.

4857　Edinger, Dora. "Christian Esselen: Citizen of Atlantis, " MH. 34 (1950): 133-43.

4858　＿＿＿＿＿. "A Feminine Forty-Eighter, " AGR. 8 (1942): 18-19, 38.

4859　Elkinton, Howard. "Four Forty-Eighters: Lindlheimer, Englemann, Hecker and Ulke, " AGR. 13 (1946) : 17-18, 30.

4860　＿＿＿＿＿. "If Carl Schurz Were Alive Today: Observations on Liberty and Freedom, " AGR. 13, v-vi (1947): 3-4.

4861　Eyck, F. G. "Franz Schneeweiss: A 48er in New Brunswick, " J. of Rutgers Univ. Lib. 19 (1956): 37-48.

4862　Feininger, T. Lux. "Lyonel Feininger's Heritage, " AGR. 32, v (1966): 9-12.

4863　Finckh, Alice. "Baltimore 1861: We Want Rapp, " RJGAH. 28 (1953): 79-82.

4864　Freidel, Frank. "A German-American Observer at the Frankfurt Parliament of 1848, " AGR. 15, iv (1949): 7-9.

4865   Hecker, Friedrich. "A Hecker Letter," AGR. 26, iv (1960):
        18-19.

4866   Heuss, Theodor. "Hans Kudlich," AGR. 19, iv (1953): 7-9,
        33.

4867   Hirsch, Helmut. "Die beiden Hilgards: Ein biographischer
        Beitrag zur Geschichte der Achtundvierziger Revolution und
        des Deutschamerikanertums," Z. f. d. Ges. d. Oberrheins.
        98 (1950): 486-97.

4868   _____. "Die beiden Hilgards: Zur Geschichte des Deutsch-
        amerikanertums und der Revolution von 1848," In Denker und
        Kämpfer. Frankfurt: Europäische Verlagsanstalt, 1955, pp.
        1-17.

4869   House, Roy. "1853 Looks Forward to 1953," AGR. 20, i
        (1953): 24-25.

4870   Johnson, Hildegard B. "German Forty-Eighters in Davenport, '
        IJHP. 44 (1946): 3-53.

4871   _____. "Hans Reimer Claussen," AGR. 10 (1944): 30-33.

4872   Kaiser, Bruno. Die Achtundvierziger: Ein Lesebuch für
        unsere Zeit. Weimar: Thüringer Volksverlag, 1955.

4873   Kaiser, Leo. "Granite, Bronze and Letters," ZKA. 13 (1963)
        15-16. On F. Hecker.

4874   Kistler, Mark. "German-American Liberalism and Thomas
        Paine," AQ. 14 (1962): 80-91.

4875   Koester, Leonard. "Latin Farmers in Indiana," IMH. 45
        (1950): 413-20.

4876   _____. "Latin Farmers in Northwestern Ohio," NwOQ. 21
        (1950): 113-19.

4877   Korn, Bertram. "Jewish Forty-Eighters in America," AJA.
        2 (1950): 3-20.

4878   Legge, Robert. "Hans Hermann Behr," CHSQ. 32 (1953):
        243-62.

4879   Meinecke, F. "The Year 1848 in German History: Reflec-
        tions on a Centenary," Rev. of Politics. 10 (1948): 475-92.

4880   Overmoehle, M. H. The Anti-Clerical Activity of the Forty-
        Eighters in Wisconsin, 1848-60: A Study in German Ameri-
        can Liberalism. St. Louis University: Dissertation, 1941.

4881   Pfund, Harry. "A Letter From Kinkel to Schurz's Father,"
        AGR. 23, vi (1957): 25-27.

4882 Reynolds, Alice. "Friedrich Hecker," AGR. 12, iv (1946): 4-7.

4883 _____. "Hecker Lore," AGR. 14, v (1948): 7-11.

4884 Robertson, Priscilla. Revolutions of 1848. Princeton: Princeton University Pr., 1952.

4884 Rothfels, Hans. "1848: One Hundred Years After," JMH. 20 (1948): 291-319.

4886 Schulte, Wilhelm. Fritz Anneke: Ein Leben für die Freiheit in Deutschland und in den USA. Dortmund: Historischer Verein, 1961.

4887 Schurz, Carl. Die Briefe von Carl Schurz an Gottfried Kinkel. Heidelberg: Winter, 1965.

4888 "Schurz-Kinkel Correspondence with Friedrich Krüger," AGR. 14, v (1948): 32-33.

4889 Siemering, A. "Die lateinische Ansiedlung in Texas: The Latin Settlement in Texas," Texana. 5 (1967): 126-31.

4890 Ulke, Heinrich. "Pages from the Record of a Forty-Eighter," AGR. 12, vi (1946): 29-32.

4891 Wittke, Carl. Against the Current: The Life of Karl Heinzen. Chicago: University of Chicago Pr., 1945.

4892 _____. "Friedrich Hassaurek: Cincinnati's Leading Forty-Eighter," OHQ. 68 (1959): 1-17.

4893 _____. "The German Forty-Eighters in America: A Centennial Appraisal," AHR. 53 (1948): 711-25.

4894 _____. Refugees of Revolution: The German Forty-Eighters in America. Philadelphia: University of Pennsylvania Pr., 1952.

4895 Zucker, A. E. "Carl Schurz' Escape from Rastatt," AGR. 14, iv (1948): 3-6.

4896 _____. "The Centennial of the Forty-Eighters," AGR. 14, ii (1947): 22-24.

4897 _____. The Forty-Eighters: Political Refugees of the German Revolution of 1848. New York: Columbia University Pr., 1950.

4898 _____. "Refugees of 1848 and 1944," AGR. 20, i (1953): 22-24.

4899 _____. "Roesler, Doughty Forty-Eighter, " AGR. 24, vi
      (1958): 25-27.

Communists, Socialists and Anarchists

4900   Andreas, Bert and W. Mönke. "Ein unbekannter Brief von
       Karl Marx an Joseph Weydemeyer, " Beitr. z. Ges. d. deut-
       schen Arbeiterbeweg. No. 1 (1968).

4901   Baxandall, Lee. Marxism and Aesthetics: A Selective Bib-
       liography. New York: Humanities Pr., 1968.

4902   Becker, Gerhard. "Die Agitationsreise Wilhelm Liebknechts
       durch die USA 1886; Ergänzendes zu einer Dokumentation von
       Karl Obermann, " Z. f. Geschichtswiss. 15 (1967): 842-62.

4903   Bruncken, Ernst. German Political Refugees in the US dur-
       ing the Period from 1815-1860. Repr.: San Francisco:
       R & E Associates, 1970.

4904   Burbank, David. "The First International in St. Louis, "
       MHSB. 18 (1962): 163-72.

4905   Busch, Francis. "The Haymarket Riot and the Trial of the
       Anarchists, " JillHS. 48 (1955): 247-70.

4906   Carter, Everett. "The Haymarket Affair in Literature, " AQ.
       2 (1951): 270-78.

4907   Corker, Charles. A Bibliography on the Communist Problem
       in the U. S. New York: Fund for the Republic, 1955.

4908   Foner, Philip. The Autobiographies of the Haymarket Mar-
       tyrs. New York: Humanities Pr., 1969.

4909   _____. "Marx's Capital in the U. S., " S&S. 31 (1967):
       461-66.

4910   Fried, Albert. Socialism in America. Garden City: Double-
       day, 1960.

4911   Goldberg, Harvey. American Radicals: Some Problems and
       Personalities. New York: Monthly Review Pr., 1957.

4912   Herreshoff, David. American Disciples of Marx: From the
       Age of Jackson to the Progressive Era. Detroit: Wayne
       State University Pr., 1967.

4913   Johnson, Oakley. The Day Is Coming: The Biography of
       Charles E. Ruthenberg. New York: International Publishers,
       1957.

4914   Krahn, Cornelius. "Abraham Thiessen: A Mennonite Revolutionary," ML. 24 (1969): 73-77.

4915   Mann, Arthur. "Solomon Schindler: Boston Radical," NEQ. 23 (1950): 453-76.

4916   Nash, Roderick. "Victor L. Berger: Making Marx Respectable," WMH. 47 (1964): 301-08.

4917   Obermann, Karl. Joseph Wedemeyer: Pioneer of American Socialism. New York: International Publishers, 1947.

4918   Preston, William. Aliens and Dissenters: Federal Suppression of Radicals, 1903-33. Cambridge: Harvard University Pr., 1963.

4919   Quint, Howard. "American Socialists and the Spanish-American War," AQ. 10 (1958): 131-41.

4920   Schlüter, Hermann. Die Internationale in Amerika. Chicago: Deutsche Sprachgruppe der Sozialistischen Partei, 1918. DLC

4921   Seidman, Joel. Communism in the U.S.: A Bibliography. Ithaca: Cornell University Pr., 1969.

4922·   Solle, Zdenek. "Die tschechischen Sektionen der Internationale in den VS," Historica. 8 (1964): 101-34.

4923   Stammhammer, Josef. Bibliographie des Socialismus und des Communismus. Repr.: Aaler: Otto Zelle Verlagsbuchhandlung, 1963.

4924   Tenney, Paul. The Socialist Movement in America to 1919: Some Problems, Personalities and Programmes. Tufts: Dissertation, 1966.

4925   Wittke, Carl. "Marx and Weitling." In Essays in Political Theory: Published in Honor of George H. Sabine. Ithaca: Cornell University Pr., 1948, pp. 179-193.

4926   _____. The Utopian Communist: A Biography of Wilhelm Weitling, Nineteenth Century Reformer. Baton Rouge: Louisiana State University, 1951.

4927   _____. "Wilhelm Weitling's Literary Efforts," MO. 40 (1948): 63-68.

4928   Zornow, W. "Hermann Kriege: Apostle of Young Americanism," AGR. 22, v (1956): 24-27.

Utopianists

4929   Alderfer, E. G. "Conrad Beissel and the Ephrata Experi-
        ment, " AGR. 21, vi (1955): 23-25.

4930   Andressohn, John. "Another Rappite Letter, " IMH. 51 (1955):
        359-60.

4931   Arndt, Karl. "The Effect of America on Lenau's Life and
        Work, " GR. 33 (1958): 125-42. His contact with the Harmony
        Settlement.

4932   _____. George Rapp's Harmony Society, 1785-1847.
        Philadelphia: University of Pennsylvania, 1965.

4933   _____. "The Harmony Society and Wilhelm Meisters
        Wanderjahre, " CL. 10 (1958): 193-202.

4934   _____. "New Light on the Harmonists, " WPHM. 25 (1942)
        168-74.

4935   _____. "Three Hungarian Travelers Visit Harmony, "
        PMHB. 79 (1955): 197-216.

4936   _____ and others. "Pragmatists and Prophets: George
        Rapp and Count Leon, " WPHM. 52 (1969): 1-27, 171-98.

4937   Bek, William. "From Bethel, Missouri to Aurora, Oregon:
        Letters of William Keil, 1855-70, " MHR. 48 (1953): 23-41,
        141-53.

4938   Bestor, Arthur. Backwoods Utopias: The Sectarian and
        Owenite Phases of Communitarian Socialism in America,
        1663-1829. Philadelphia: University of Pennsylvania Pr.,
        1950.

4939   Biever, Dale. "A Report of Archaeological Investigations
        at the Ephrata Cloister, 1963-66, " PGSP. 3 (1970): 1-53.

4940   Bridenstine, A. G. "The Restoration of the Ephrata Clois-
        ters, " Gospel Messenger. 100 (1951): 10-14.

4941   Brostowin, Patrick. John Adolphus Etzler: Scientific Utopia
        During the 1830's and 1840's. New York University: Dis-
        sertation, 1970.

4942   Crowe, Charles. George Ripley: Transcendentalist and
        Utopian Socialist. Athens: University of Georgia, 1967.

4943   Doll, Eugene. The Ephrata Cloister: An Introduction.
        Ephrata: Cloister Associates, 1958.

4943A   _____. "Historical Guide to the Seventh Day German

Baptist Cloister at Ephrata, Pennsylvania, " Pub. Instruction.
9 (1942): 22-26.

4944   Duss, John. The Harmonists: A Personal History.   Harrisburg: Pennsylvania Book Service, 1943.

4945   Ernst, James. Ephrata: A History.   (Pennsylvania German
Folklore Society, 25.) Allentown, 1963.

4946   Holloway, Mark. Heavens On Earth: Utopian Communities
in America, 1680-1880. New York: Library Publishers,
1951.

4947   Kamman, William. "Communia, " MO. 40 (1948): 423 ff.

4948   Klein, Walter. Johann Conrad Beissel, Mystic and Martinet,
1690-1768. Philadelphia: University of Pennsylvania Pr.,
1942.

4949   Lawson, Donna. Brothers and Sisters All Over the Land:
America's First Communes. New York: Praeger, 1972.

4950   McClary, Ben. "Not for the Moment Only: Eduard Bertz
to Mary Percival, Feb. 18, 1886, " THQ. 24 (1965): 54-62.

4951   Meyer, Lysle. "Radical Responses to Capitalism in Ohio
Before 1913, " OH. 79 (1970): 193-208.

4952   Miller, Ernest. "Utopian Communities in Warren County,
Pa., " WPHM. 49 (1966): 301-17.

4953   Nordhoff, Charles. Communistic Societies of the U.S.   New
York: Hillary House, 1960.

4954   Oda, Wilbur. "The Rev. Henry Kurtz and His Communal
Plans, " PD. 3 (1952): 6.

4955   Polt, H. K. "The Rappists and New Harmony, Indiana, "
AGR. 10 (1943): 17-20.

4956   Reichmann, Felix. "Exechial Sangmeister's Diary, " PMHB.
68 (1944): 292-313.   On Ephrata.

4957   _____ and Eugene Doll. Ephrata as Seen by Contem-
poraries. (Pennsylvania German Folklore Society, 17.) Allentown, 1953.

4958   Schulz-Behrend, George. "Communia, Iowa: A Nineteenth
Century German-American Utopia, " IJHP. 48 (1950): 27-54.

4959   Seagle, Gladys. The Rappist Revolt Against Lutheranism,
1804-1904. New York University: Dissertation, 1963.

4960   Shambaugh, Bertha. Amana That Was and Amana That Is.
       New York: Benjamin Blom, 1971.

4961   Singmaster, Elsie. "The Great Book," ECK. (Mar. 9, 1963).
       On Ephrata.

4962   Webber, Everett. Escape to Utopia: The Communal Move-
       ment in America. New York: Hastings House, 1959.

4963   Whitney, Norman. Experiments in Community: Ephrata,
       Amish, Doukhobors, Shakers, Bruderhof and Monteverde.
       Wallington, Pa.: Pendle Hill, 1966.

4964   Wilson, William. The Angel and the Serpent: The Story of
       New Harmony. Bloomington, 1964.

4965   Wittke, Carl. "Ora et Labora: A German Methodist Utopia,"
       OHQ. 57 (1958): 129-40.

4966   Yanosko, Michael. "John Chooses a Mill Site," AGR. 21, v
       (1955): 12-15. On the Harmony Society.

4967   Young, Arthur. The Letters of George Gissing to Edward
       Berta, 1887-1903. New Brunswick: Rutgers University Pr.,
       1961. On a Tennessee utopia.

4968   Young, Otis. "Personnel of the Rappite Community of Har-
       mony, Indiana in the Year 1824," IMH. 47 (1951): 313-19.

4969   Zieglschmid, A. "Dr. Wilhelm Keil's Communal Enterprises:
       Bethel, Missouri and Aurora, Oregon," AGR. 14, ii (1947):
       28-31.

Radical Literature from German-America

4970   Arbeiter-Zeitung. Constitution and Minutes. New York,
       1872-73. TIL

4971   _____. Protokoll-Buch des Verwaltung-Raths der Arbeiter
       Zeitung. New York: 1872-74. TIL

4972   Communisten Club. Protocolle des Communisten Clubs. New
       York, 1857-58. TIL

4973   Douai, Karl. ABC des Wissens für die Denkenden. Zürich:
       Genossenschaftsbuchdruckerei, 1884. DLC

4974   _____. Kindergarten und Volksschule als sozialdemo-
       kratische Anstalten. Leipzig: Genossenschaftsbuchdruckerei,
       1876. DLC

4975 Dulon, Rudolph. Der Tag ist angebrochen: Ein prophetisches Wort. Bremen: Geisler, 1852. DLC

4976 Faraday Club. Minutes of the Faraday Club. New York, 1888-89. TIL

4977 Fröbel, Julius. Amerika, Europa und die politische Gesichtspunkte der Gegenwart. Berlin: Springer, 1859. DLC

4978 _____. System der socialen Politik. Leipzig: Verlagsbureau, 1950. DLC

4979 _____. Theorie der Politik, als Ergebnis einer erneuerten Prüfung demokratischer Lehrmeinungen. Wien: C. Gerald, 1861-64. DLC

4980 _____. Die Wirtschaft des Menschengeschlechts auf dem Standpunkte der Einheit idealer und realer Interessen. Leipzig: Wigand, 1870. DLC

4981 General German Labor Association. Protokoll-Buch des Allgemeinen Deutschen Arbeiter-Vereins. New York, 1867-71. TIL

4982 General Labor Union. Protokoll-Buch des Centralvereins des Allgemeinen Arbeiter-Bundes. New York, 1853-55. TIL

4983 Hecker, Friedrich. Die Erhebung des Volkes in Baden für die deutsche Republik im Frühjahr 1848. Basel: Schabelitz, 1848. DLC

4984 _____. Reden und Vorlesungen. St. Louis: C. Witter, 1872. DLC

4985 Heinzen, Karl. Erlebtes: Nach meiner Exilierung. Boston, 1874. GSP

4986 _____. Erlebtes: Vor meiner Exilierung. Boston, 1864. GSP

4987 Kriege, Hermann. Die Väter unserer Republik in ihrem Leben und Wirken. New York: Uhl, 1847. DLC

4988 Ludvigh, Samuel. Alt und Neu: Uebungen für geistiges Turnen. Cincinnati, 1868. DLC

4989 _____. Frisch und frei: Eine Sammlung prosaischer Aufsätze. Cincinnati: Verlag des Verfassers, 1866. DLC

4990 _____. Reden, Vorlesungen und prosaische Aufsätze im Gebiete der Religion, Philosophie und Geschichte. Baltimore: Verlag des Verfassers, 1850. DLC, MnHi, PPMerc

314   German-Americana

4991   _____. Der Roman meines Lebens in Europa. Baltimore:
       Verlag des Verfassers, 1858. DLC, LNH, MnHi, PPL, WLac

4992   Most, Johann. Der Kleinbürger und die Socialdemokratie.
       Augsburg: Volksbuchhandlung, 1876. DLC

4993   _____. Memoiren, Erlebtes, Erforschtes und Erdachtes.
       New York: Selbstverlag, 1903. DLC

4994   _____. Die Pariser Commune vor den Berliner Gerichten.
       Braunschweig: Bracke, 1875. DLC

4995   Mueller, Jacob. Aus den Erinnerungen eines 48ers: Skizzen
       aus der deutsch-amerikanischen Sturm und Drang Periode der
       50er Jahre. Cleveland: Schmidt, 1896. GSP

4996   New Yorker Volkszeitung. Clippings on Labor Matters. New
       York, 1881-86. NYPL

4997   North American Federation. Minutes of the North American
       Federation of the International Workingmen's Association.
       New York, 1873-76. TIL

4998   Social Democratic Labor Party. Protokoll-Buch der Zweig
       Section der Sozial-demokratischen Arbeiter Partei. York-
       ville, 1878-88. TIL

4999   Social Democratic Worker's Party. Protokoll-Buch für die
       geschäftlichen Sitzungen der Mitgliedschafts New York der
       Social-demokratischen Arbeiter Partei. New York, 1874-78.
       TIL

5000   Socialist Labor Party. Minutes of the Central Committee.
       New York, 1890-94. Text is in German script; includes list
       of all members. TIL

5001   _____. Minutes of the Joint Meetings of the Sections of
       the Socialist Labor Party, New York City, and of the Central
       Committee of the Socialist Labor Party. New York, 1890-
       94. TIL

5002   _____. Minutes of the New York Central Committee.
       New York, 1883-84. TIL

5003   _____. Protokoll-Buch der deutschen Section New York,
       der Socialistischen Arbeiter Partei der Vereinigten Staaten
       von Nord-Amerika. New York, 1878-84. TIL

5004   _____. Protokoll-Buch der Section Hoboken. New York,
       1877-87. TIL

5005   _____. Protokoll-Buch der Sections-Versammlungen und
       Central Committee der Section New York. New York, 1887-
       91. TIL

Radicalism

5006   . Protokoll-Buch des Unterstützungs-Committee der Socialistischen Arbeiter Partei. New York, 1885-90. TIL

5007   . Protokoll-Buch für die Arbeiter-Grauen und Mädchenbund. New York, 1886-89. TIL

5007A   . Protokoll Buch, Section New York. New York, 1886-88. TIL

5008 Sorge, Friedrich. Letters from Engels, Marx and Others: 1867-1906. NYPL

5009   . Socialism and the Worker. London: Twentieth Century Pr., 1910. DLC

5010 Spies, August. Reminiscenzen. Chicago, 1888.

5011 Stiebeling, Georg. Sozialismus und Darwinismus: Eine kritische Studie. New York: Schmidt, 1879. DLC

5012 Struve, Gustaf. Weltgeschichte in neuen Büchern. New York: Struve, 1856-59. DLC

5013 Weitling, Wilhelm. Die Menschheit: Wie sie ist und wie sie sein sollte. München: Dreiländerverlag, 1919. DLC

IX. BIOGRAPHY

Collections

5014   Akademie der Wissenschaften. Oesterreichisches biographisches Lexikon, 1815-1950. Graz-Köln: Böhlhaus, 1954-63.

5015   Allgemeine Deutsche Biographie. Leipzig: Duncker, 1875-
1912.

5016   Apsler, Alfred. Sie kamen aus deutschen Landen. New
York: Appleton-Century Crofts, 1962.

5017   Arnim, Max. Internationale Personalbibliographie, 1800-
1943. Leipzig: Hiersemann, 1944-52.

5018   Biographien hervorragender Deutsch-Amerikaner von Philadelphia, Pennsylvania und Umgegend. Philadelphia: German
Daily Gazette Pub. Co., 1906.

5019   Cincinnati und sein Deutschtum: Ein Geschichte der Gesch-
ichte der Entwicklung Cincinnatis und seines Deutschtums,
Mit biographischen Skizzen und Illustrationen. Cincinnati:
Queen City Pub. Co., 1901.

5020   Cunz, Dieter. They Came from Germany: The Stories of
Famous German-Americans. New York: Dodd, Mead, 1966.

5021   Dargon, Marion. Guide to American Biography. Albuquerque: University of New Mexico Pr., 1949-52.

5022   Eiboeck, Joseph. Die Deutschen von Iowa und deren Errun-
genschaften: Eine Geschichte des Staates, dessen deutscher
Pioniere. Des Moines: Iowa Staats-Anzeiger, 1900. Contains 200 biographical sketches. UM

5023   German-American Biographical Publishing Co. Chicago und
sein Deutschtum. Chicago, 1901-02.

5024   Hamos, Wilson. Mittler Zweier Welten: Friedrich Wilhelm
Steuben, Carl Schurz, Johann Jakob Astor, Friedrich List,
und andere bedeutende deutsch-amerikanische Pioniere. Wiesbaden: Internationale Verlagsgesellschaft, 1956.

Biography   317

5025   Harris, Alex. A Biographical History of Lancaster County.
       Lancaster: Elias Barr, 1872.

5026   Jöcher, Christian. Allgemeines Gelehrten-Lexikon.... Leip-
       zig: Gleditsch, 1750-51.

5027   Kaplan, Louis. A Bibliography of American Autobiographies.
       Madison: University of Wisconsin Pr., 1961.

5028   National Cyclopedia of American Biography. New York:
       White, 1892-1965.

5029   Nead, Daniel. "Index to the Proper Names Mentioned in the
       Proceedings and Addresses of the Pennsylvania German So-
       ciety, Volumes 1-6," PGSP. 4 (1898). 91 pp.

5030   Neue deutsche Biographie. Berlin: Duncker & Humboldt,
       1953-61.

5031   O'Neill, Edward. Biography of Americans, 1658-1936: A
       Subject Bibliography. Philadelphia: University of Pennsyl-
       vania Pr., 1939.

5032   Phillips, Lawrence. Dictionary of Biographical References,
       Containing Over 100,000 Names: Together with a Classed
       Index of the Biographical Literature of Europe and America.
       London: Low, 1889.

5033   Ruedy, August and A. Barthold. Americans of Swiss Origin.
       New York, 1932.

5034   Ruetenik, H. J. Berühmte deutsche Vorkämpfer für Fort-
       schrift, Freiheit und Friede in Nord-Amerika von 1626-1888.
       Cleveland, Ohio: Forest City Bookbinding Co., 1888. A
       valuable reference tool.

5035   Schem, Alexander. Deutsch-Amerikanisches Conversations-
       Lexicon, mit specieller Berücksichtigung auf die Bedürfnisse
       der in Amerika lebenden Deutschen. New York: 1869-74.
       Excellent source of biographical information.

5036   Spengler, Otto. Das deutsche Element der Stadt New York:
       Biographisches Jahrbuch der Deutsch-Amerikaner New York
       und Umgebung. New York: Spengler, 1913.

5037   Tenner, Armin. Cincinnati: Sonst und Jetzt. Cincinnati,
       1878. UK

5038   Wertheimer, Fritz. Von deutschen Parteien und Parteiführer
       im Ausland. Berlin: Zentral-Verlag, 1930. 300 biographies.

5039   Who Was Who. Chicago: Marquis, 1942-60. Covers 1897-
       1960.

5040   Who Was Who in America, 1607-1896:   A Component Volume
        of Who's Who in American History.   Chicago: Marquis, 1963.

5041   Who's Who In World Jewry: A Biographical Dictionary of Out-
        standing Jews.   White Plains: Who's Who in World Jewry,
        1965.

5042   Wisconsin Historical Society.   Dictionary of Wisconsin Biogra-
        phy.   Madison: State Historical Society, 1960.

5043   Wurzbach, Constantin.   Biographisches Lexikon des Kaiser-
        thums Oesterreich....   Wien: Zamarski, 1856-91.

Individual Studies

5044   Adams, Arthur.   "Gaius Marcus Brumbaugh, " NEHGR. 107
        (1953): 81-82.

5045   Almstedt, Hermann.   "In Memoriam, " MO. 46 (1954): 348-
        49.   On Almstedt.

5046   Aubin, Ernest.   "Autobiography of Michael Frank, " WMH. 30
        (1947): 441-81.

5047   Auerheimer, R.   "For Instance Myself, " AGR. 12, v (1949):
        27, 29, 38.

5048   Barry, Colman.   American Nuncio: Cardinal Aloisus Muench.
        Collegeville, Minnesota: St. Johns University Pr., 1969.

5049   Barth, E. H. and J. Klein.   "Henry and Annie M. Pfeiffer:
        Philanthropists Extraordinary, " AGR. 16, iii (1950): 25-
        26.

5050   Bergaust, Erik.   Reaching for the Stars.   Garden City:
        Doubleday, 1960.   On Von Braun.

5051   Berky, Andrew.   The Journals and Papers of David Schultze.
        Pennsburg: Schwenkfelder Library, 1952-53.

5052   _____.   "Practitioner in Physick: A Biography of Abra-
        ham Wagner, 1717-1763, " PGSP. 55 (1954): 175 pp.

5053   Beyreuther, Erich.   Zinzendorf und die sich allhier beisam-
        men finden.   Marburg: Francke, 1959.

5054   Billigmeier, Robert and F. Picard.   The Old Land and the
        New: The Journals of Two Swiss Families in America in
        the 1820's.   Minneapolis, 1965.

5055   Blied, Benjamin.   "Francis X. Weniinger, 1805-88, " AGR.
        15, iv (1949): 25-27.

5056   Boerner, Arthur. "Early Letters of Dr. Theodore E. F.
        Hartwig: Cedarburg's Physician and Surgeon, " WMH. 29
        (1946): 347-56.

5057   Boyd, T. Professional Amateur: The Biography of Charles
        F. Kettering. New York: Dutton, 1957.

5058   [Brach.] "Emil J. Brach, " AGR. 14, iii (1948): 34-35.

5059   Brecht, Arnold. The Political Education of Arnold Brecht:
        An Autobiography, 1884-1970. Princeton: Princeton Univer-
        sity Pr., 1970.

5060   Buranelli, Vincent. "The Myth of Anna Zenger, " WMQ. 13
        (1956): 157-68.

5061   _____. "Peter Zenger's Editor, " AQ. 7 (1955): 174-81.

5062   Burzle, J. "Max Kade: Vermittler zwischen Deutschland und
        Amerika, " GAS. 3 (1971): 3.

5063   Chapman, H. "Bernhard Eduard Fernow, " AGR. 19 (1953):
        13-14.

5064   Charlik, Carl. "Two Early Americans of German Vintage, "
        AGR. 34, iii (1968): 2-6. On F. Grund and E. Reimann.

5065   Clark, Delber. The World of Justus Falckner. Philadelphia:
        Muhlenberg Pr., 1946.

5066   Coenen, F. "In Memoriam Richard Jente, 1888-1952, " MO.
        44 (1952): 420-21.

5067   Cohn, Bernhard. "Lee Merzbacher, " AJA. 6 (1954): 21-24.

5068   Cohn, Emman. "An Honorable Mention for Mrs. Zenger, "
        NYPL. 43 (1959): 260-69.

5069   Cunz, Dieter. "Albert Bernhardt Faust, " RJGAH. 28 (1953):
        86-88.

5070   _____. "John Lederer, Significance and Evaluation, "
        WMCQ. 22 (1942): 175-85.

5071   DeFehr, C. Memories of My Life. Altona, Man.: Friesen,
        1967.

5072   Dielmann, Henry. "Dr. Ferdinand Herff, Pioneer Physician
        and Surgeon, " SwHQ. 57 (1954): 265-84.

5073   Elkinton, H. "George Engelmann: Greatly Interested in
        Plants, " AGR. 12, vi (1946): 16-21.

5074 _____. "Immortal Values, " AGR. 19, v (1953): 20-21.
On Wilbur K. Thomas.

5075 Estill, Julia. "The Hermit of the Palo Alto, " AGR. 13, i
(1946): 29-31.

5076 Finler, Joel. Stroheim. Berkeley: University of California
Pr., 1968.

5077 Fish, Sidney. Aaron Levy: Founder of Aaronsburg. PAJHS,
1951.

5078 Ford, Corey. Where the Sea Breaks Its Back. Boston: Little, Brown & Co., 1966. On Georg Steller.

5079 Ford, Edward. David Rittenhouse: Astronomer-Patriot, 1732-
96. Philadelphia: University of Pennsylvania Pr., 1946.

5080 Frankfurter, Felix. Felix Frankfurter Reminiscences: Recorded in Talks with Dr. H. B. Phillips. New York: Viking,
1960.

5081 Franz, Eckhart. "Ernst Posner und das Archivwesen Amerikas, " JA. 15 (1970): 233-36.

5082 Friedrich, Gerhard. "Johannes Kelpius as Attorney: An Unknown Kelpius Manuscript, " PH. 9 (1942): 267-70.

5083 Friis, Herman. "W. L. G. Joerg, " AAG. 43 (1953): 256-83.

5084 Gates, Paul. "Charles Lewis Fleischmann: German-American Agricultural Authority, " Ag. Hist. 35 (1961): 13-23.

5085 Geiser, Samuel. "Nicholas Mercellus Hentz: Pioneer American Araneologist, " Field & Lab. (Oct. 1956).

5086 Geissler, Ann. Die Spur der Erdentage: Wilhelm Hansens
Lebensweg in Deutschland und Amerika. Stuttgart: Steinkopf,
1955.

5087 Gerhard, Elmer. "What Conrad Weiser Wrote about Count
von Zinzendorf and the Indians, " AGR. 12, iii (1946): 14-16;
iv (1946): 18-20.

5088 Gilbert, Russell. "The Unpublished Autobiography of Ernst
Max Adam, M. D. : Settler in Dunker Blooming Grove, " Susq.
Univ. Studies. 5 (1953): 17-40.

5089 Gillis, Daniel. Furtwängler and America. New York: Many-
land Books, 1970.

5090 Gingerich, Alice. Life and Times of Daniel Kauffman. Scottdale, Pa.: Herald Pr., 1954.

5091   Goldfrank, Esther. "Gladys Amanda Reichard, 1893-1955, "
        JAF. 69 (1956): 53-54.

5092   Grund, Francis. Aristocracy in America: From the Sketch
        Book of a German Nobleman. New York: Harper, 1959.

5093   Gudde, Erwin and Elisabeth. Exploring with Fremont: The
        Private Diaries of Charles Press, Cartographer for John Fre-
        mont on His First, Second and Fourth Expedition to the Far
        West. Norman: University of Oklahoma Pr., 1958.

5094   Hale, Douglas. "Friedrich Adolph Wislizenus: From Rebel
        to Southwestern Explorer, " MHR. 62 (1968): 260-85.

5095   Harley, Herbert. "A Palatine Boor: A Short Comprehensive
        History of the Life of Christopher Laver, " BHS of Montgomery
        Co. 16 (1969): 286-97.

5096   Hawgood, John and J. Stephens. "A Letter from Baron
        Christian von Bunsen to Francis Lieber, " Univ. of Birm.
        HJ. 2 (1949): 97-103.

5097   Heissey, M. L. "The Diary of Harriet Amelia Arndt for
        1865, " LCHP. 50 (1946): 73-76.

5098   Hindle, Brooke and Helen Hindle. "David Rittenhouse and the
        Illusion of Reversible Relief, " Isis. 50 (1959): 135-40.

5099   Hirsch, Felix. "Memories of William Sollmann, " AGR. 19,
        iv (1953): 14-16.

5100   Holinger, Cora. "Charles Follen: A Sketch of His Life in
        New England, " AGR. 14, v (1948): 20-22.

5101   Hollenbach, Raymond. "Heinrich Christof Bleicherodt, In-
        dentured Servant of Jacob and Johannes Clemens, " Eck. (Feb.
        3, 1968).

5102   Holmes, Urban. "Richard Jente: 1888-1952, " SP. 49 (1952):
        551-52.

5103   Hoyt, Edwin. The Guggenheims and the American Dream.
        New York: Funk & Wagnalls, 1967.

5104   Huzel, Dieter. Peenemünde to Canaveral. Englewood Cliffs,
        New Jersey: Prentice-Hall, 1962. On von Braun.

5105   Jenny, Hans. E. W. Hilgard and the Birth of Modern Soil
        Science. Pisa, Italy: Istituto di Chimica Agraria dell' Uni-
        versita, 1961.

5106   Jockers, Ernst. J. Otto Schweizer: The Man and His Work.
        Philadelphia: International Printing Co., 1953.

5107   Johnson, Gerald.   An Honorable Titan: A Biographical Study
        of Adolph S. Ochs.   New York: Harper, 1946.

5108   Jolley, Harley.   "Biltmore Forest Fair 1908, " Forest Hist.
        14 (1970): 6-17.

5109   Jüssen, Antonie.   "Lebenserinnerungen, " AGR. 23, vi (1957):
        22-25.

5110   Kaltenborn, H. V.   Fifty Fabulous Years.   New York: Put-
        nam, 1950.

5111   Kavaler, Lucy.   The Astors: A Family Chronicle of Pomp
        and Power.   New York: Dodd, Mead, 1966.

5112   Kirsch, August.   Franz Lieber: Turner, Freiheitskämpfer
        und Emigrant.   University of Köln: Dissertation, 1953.

5113   Knauth, Theodore.   "Albert Fink, 1829-97:   A Memoir, " AGR.
        15, iii (1949): 12-13, 30.

5114   Kohler, Dayton.   "Conrad Richter: Early American, " Coll.
        Eng. 8 (1947): 221-27.

5115   Krehbiel, Christian.   Prairie Pioneer: The Christian Kreh-
        biel Story.   Newton, Kansas: Faith and Life Pr., 1961.

5116   Kurz, Rudolph.   Journal of Rudolph Friedrich Kurz: An Ac-
        count of His Experiences Among the Fur Traders and Ameri-
        can Indians on the Mississippi and Upper Missouri Rivers,
        During the Years 1846 to 1852.   Lincoln: University of
        Nebraska Pr., 1970.

5117   Lange, Victor.   "In Memory of Albert Bernhardt Faust, "
        AGR. 17, iv (1951): 28.

5118   [Lederer.]   "In Memory of Max Lederer, " BA. 24 (1950):
        316-17.

5119   Leisy, Ernest.   "Dreiser's Mennonite Origin, " ML. 9 (1954):
        179-80.

5120   Lembeck, Fred and W. Giere.   Otto Loewi: Ein Lebensbild
        in Dokumenten.   Berlin: Springer, 1968.

5121   Lewis, Ralph and R. Young.   "The Zenger Memorial, " Amer.
        Her. 5 (1953): 24-25.

5122   Mahr, August.   "A Canoe Journey from the Big Beaver to
        the Tuscarawas in 1773:   A Travel Diary of John Heckewaeld-
        er, " OSAHQ. 41 (1952): 283-98.

5123   Mencken, H. L.   Letters of Mencken.   New York: Knopf,
        1961.

5124   Menzel, Louise. "Louis Albert Fritsche, " AGR. 25, v (1959):
        7-9.

5125   Morris, Richard. "John Peter Zenger: Instrument and Sym-
        bol of the Struggle of a Free Press, " Amer. Her. 5 (1953):
        26-27, 60.

5126   Morton, Frederic. "I Love 83d Street, " AGR. 35, ii (1969):
        25-29.

5127   Mueller, Paul. David Zeisberger's Official Diary, Fairfield,
        1791-95. Columbia University: Dissertation, 1956.

5128   Nolan, J. B. "Dörpfeld on Schliemann, " AGR. 17, v (1951):
        24-27.

5129   Nordsieck, Helen. "Alle guten Gaben: Gerhardt Heinrich
        Wiesehahn of Richmond, Indiana, " AGR. 13, i (1946): 12-13;
        11 (1946): 19-21.

5130   Parsons, Phyllis. "The Life of Daniel Claus, " PH. 29 (1962):
        357-72.

5131   Plaut, Alfred. "Rudolf Virchow and Today's Physicians and
        Scientists, " BHM. 27 (1953): 236-51.

5132   Puknat, Siegfried. "Mencken and the Sudermann Case, " MO.
        51 (1959): 183-89.

5133   Reichard, Harry. "John Baer Stoudt, D. D. : An Apprecia-
        tion, " PGFS. 9 (1946): 221-29.

5134   Reichmann, Felix. The Muehlenberg Family: A Bibliography
        Compiled from the Subject Union Catalog of Americana Ger-
        manica of the Carl Schurz Memorial Foundation. Philadelphia:
        Carl Schurz Memorial Foundation, 1943.

5135   Reinhart, Herman. The Golden Frontier: The Recollection of
        Herman Francis Reinhart, 1851-69. Austin: University of
        Texas Pr. , 1962.

5136   Reynolds, Robert. "A Man of Conscience in an Era When
        Political Morality Had Sunk Low, An Immigrant, Carl Schurz,
        Helped Rally the Republic to its Ancient Ideals, " AH. 14
        (1963): 20-23, 82-91.

5137   _____ . "Theodore F. K. Laetsch--Henry W. Reiman, "
        CTM. 34 (1963): 133-34.

5138   Rieger, Minette S. "Diary of Minette Schemel Rieger, " AGR.
        26, vi (1960): 23-25.

5139   Rosenberger, Francis. "Erasmus Rosenberger of Shenandoah

County and his German Origin, " VMHB. 63 (1955): 84-87.

5140   Royer, B. Franklin. "Willem Stober: A Pioneer of Antitum, " Trans. Kittochtinny HS. 12 (1951): 379-90.

5141   Rupp, William. "Der Huns John: A Unique Character, " PD. (Aug. 1, 1951).

5142   Schirmer, Jacob. "Extracts from the Schirmer Diary, 1860, " SCHM. 61 (1960): 163, 232.

5143   Schneider, Heinrich. "Karl Follen: A Re-Appraisal and Some New Biographical Materials, " RJGAH. 30 (1959): 73-86.

5144   Schroeder, Armin. "Sketch of the Life of Michael Shuck, " KyHS. 44 (1946): 101-118.

5145   Schuchhardt, W. "Georg Karo, der grosse Archäologe, " Auslandswarte. 32 (1953): 32.

5146   Schulz, John. "Some Letters of John Christopher Schulz, 1829-33, " SCHGM. 56 (1955): 1-7.

5147   Seidlin, Oskar. "Frank Wedeking's German-American Parents, " AGR. 12, vi (1946): 24-26.

5148   Shuster, George. In Amerika und Deutschland. Frankfurt: Knecht, 1965.

5149   Simon, Esther and Jessie Bierman. "From Butcher Boy to Buffalo Hunter, " MMH. 11 (1961): 38-55, 56-59. On Henry Bierman.

5150   Spoehr, Florence. "Down Under's First Woman Naturalist, " PS. 6 (1952): 465-75.

5151   Stoudt, John. "Was America's First Autobiography Written in Oley?" HRBC. 26 (1961): 87.

5152   Thomas, Henry. Charles Steinmetz. New York: Putnam, 1959.

5153   Wallace, Paul. "Anna Maria Muhlenberg and Her Children, " HRBC. 15 (1950): 162-65.

5154   [Walz.] "In Memoriam of John Albrecht Walz, " MO. 46 (1954): 390.

5155   Ward, Robert Elmer. "Preston A. Barba in Memoriam, " GAS. 5 (1972): 200-01.

5156   Ward-Leyerle, Robert. "Otto Ruhland, 1886-1968, " W&A. (Jan. 1, 1968).

5157   Weiser, Frederick. "Daniel Schumacher's Baptismal Register," PGS. 1 (1968).

5158   _____. Letters from Mahantongo Valley. Manheim, Pa.: Conrad Weiser Family Assoc., 1968.

5159   Wust, Klaus. "John Thomas Schley Letters Found in Speyer Archives," RJGAH. 30 (1959): 112-14.

5160 American Genealogical-Biographical Index to American Genealogical, Biographical and Local History Materials. Middletown, Conn.: Godfrey Memorial Library, 1952-64.

5161 American Historical Company. Chrysler-Forker and Allied Families: A Genealogical Study With Biographical Notes. Garbisch, New York: Private Pr., 1959.

5162 Arner, George. "The Arner Family," NGSQ. 38 (1950): 101-04.

5163 Ashbaugh Research Guide: An Interim Study of the Family of Johann Heinrich Eschbach, 1706-89. Staten Island: Louis Duermyer, 1963.

5164 Asselstine, Kathryn. A Pioneer Family: The Name Van Ysselsteyn, Esselstein, Asselstine, 1649-1949: Three Hundred Years on the Continent of North America. Windsor, Ont.: Author, 1956.

5165 Baecker, Gertrud and F. Engelmann. Die Nachkommen des Pfarrers und Inspektors Erasmus Theodor Engelmann in Deutschland. Ludwigshafen: Richard Louis, 1958. Contains information on American descendents.

5166 Baker, Robert. The Rosenberger Family: An Addition to the Baker Genealogy. Strasburg, Va.: Private Pr., 1956.

5167 Beckham, William. The Kinslers of South Carolina. Columbia, S.C.: Author, 1964.

5168 Bell, Raymond. The Seibert Family: Wolfersweiler, Saar; Tulpehocken, Pa.; Clear Spring, Md.; Martinsburg, W. Va., Washington, Pa., 1959.

5169 _____. The Sigler Family of Mifflin County, Pennsylvania. Washington, Pa., 1958.

5170 Bender, C. Descendents of Daniel Bender. Berlin, Pa.: Berlin Pub. Co., 1948.

5171 Bennett, Deloris. Descendents of John and Mary Scharnagel in the Families of Willenborg, Eischeid and Testroet. West Covina, Cal., 1960.

5172   Berges, Ruth. "The Damrosch Family, " AGR. 27, iii (1961):
        28-30.

5173   Berk, Imogene. One Line of Descent from Hans Zaug of
        Berne, Switzerland. Manitou Beach, Michigan, 1964.

5174   Billigmeier, Robert and F. Picard. Swiss Families in Amer-
        ica in the 1820's. Minneapolis: University of Minnesota Pr.,
        1965.

5175   Bishop, J. C. The Kitzmiller Family in Pennsylvania Before
        1800. Muscatine, Iowa, 1959.

5176   Blair, Beulah. Some Early Lineages of Berks County, Pa.:
        Clauser (Klauser)--Hicks (Hix) and Associated Lines. Boul-
        der, Colo.: Author, 1961.

5177   Blauvelt, Louis. The Blauvelt Family Genealogy. East
        Orange, New Jersey: Association of Blauvelt Descendents,
        1957.

5178   Bremer, Gladys. Bremer-Muirhead Genealogy of Germany-
        Scotland and the USA. Lawrence, Kansas, 1961.

5179   Carlock, Marion. "The Oldest Known Records of the Tschudi-
        Tschudy-Judy Ancestors of Switzerland and America, " TY. 33
        (1951): 131-40, 208-18, 280-97.

5180   Coddington, John. "Leonard Rupert Record, " NGSQ. 40
        (1952): 142.

5181   DeGraffenried, Thomas. The De Graffenried Family Scrap-
        book, 1191-1956: 765 Years. Charlottesville, Va.: Univer-
        sity of Virginia Pr., 1958.

5182   Diedrich, J. Jost, Conrad, Born in Germany Before 1720
        Died in Limerick Township, Montgomery Co., Pa. in March
        1760. Norfolk, Va.: Author, 1965.

5183   Dierdorff, Lee. Dierdorff Notes: Genealogical Facts and
        Stories of the Dierdorff Family. Greeley, Colo., 1965.

5184   Dunne, John. "The Goshenhoppen Registers: Fifth Series:
        Baptisms: 1807-18, " ACHS. 61 (1950): 57-63, 112-23, 185-
        92, 248-62.

5185   Elling, Edward. The Elling Families from 1660 in Germany
        to 1960 in America. With Some Information on the Baker
        and Beal Families of Illinois and Northeastern Kansas. Kan-
        sas City: Author, 1961.

5186   Evans, Eytive. A Documented History of the Long Family:
        Switzerland to South Carolina, 1758-1956, Including Allied
        Families. n.p., 1956.

5187   Familiengeschichtliche Bibliographie.   Leipzig: Zentralstelle
       für Deutschen Personen u. Familiengeschichte, 1928-62.

5188   Fedorschak, Catharine.   The Foraker Family of Guernsey
       County, Ohio.   Gary, Indiana, 1957-58.

5189   Fetzer, John.   One Man's Family: A History and Genealogy
       of the Fetzer Family.   Ann Arbor: Arbor Pr., 1964.

5190   Francis, Margaret.   "Busch-Kuder Families of Germany,
       Ohio, Illinois and Arkansas, " NGSQ. 53 (1965): 263-70.

5191   Francis, W.   The Harnish Freindschaft.   Gettysburg: F. S.
       Weiser, 1955.

5192   Frank, Helen.   This is The Saga of the Bernd, Bloch and
       Blum Families in the USA.   n. p., 1961.

5193   Frank, Karl.   "Schlegel von Gottleben, " Senftenegger Mon.
       f. G. u. H. 3 (1965): 34-43; 5 (1965): 289-363.

5194   Friedrichs, Heinz.   President Dwight D. Eisenhower's An-
       cestors and Relations.   Neustadt/Aisch: Degener, 1955.

5195   Gaetz, Annie.   Foot Prints of the Gaetz Family: Descendants
       of Martin Gaetz.   Red Deer, Alberta, 1961.

5196   Glick, J.   Across the Years: The Glick Family.   Charlotte,
       N. C.:   The Jos. M. Glick Family Historical Committee,
       1959.

5197   Gnacinski, J.   Marriages Published in Waukesha, Wisconsin
       Newspapers, 1863-81.   West Allis, Wisconsin, Author, 1970.

5198   Goertz, Helene.   Family History of Siebert Goertz and John
       Harms and their Descendants.   North Newton, Kansas, 1965.

5199   Good, Marie.   Puterbaugh-Butterbaugh-Puderbaugh.   Pacific
       Grove, Cal.:   Good, 1961.

5200   Grassel, Gary.   "The German Washingtons, " AGR. 30, i
       (1963): 18-19, 30-31.

5201   [Gugler.]   "The Family Tree: Die Gugler, " AGR. 14, i
       (1947): 32.

5202   Guilnezan, Isabel.   Collection of Letters Written by the
       School Family and Their Kin, 1836-1897.   St. Louis, 1959.

5203   Hall, Helen.   Goetz Genealogy.   Hutchinson, Kansas: Lith-
       O-Crafters, 1963.

5204   Hallman, Kenneth and H. Faulk.   "George Welker, the Miller of New Goshenhoppen: A Genealogy of His Descendants, 1697-1956, " BHSM. 10 (1956): 152-226.

5205   Happoldt, Christopher. The Christopher Happoldt Journal. Charleston, 1960.

5206   Heck, Earl. History of the Heck Family of America; With Special Attention Given to Those Families Who Originated in Indiana, Kentucky, Maryland, Ohio, Pennsylvania and Virginia. Englewood, Ohio, 1959.

5207   Helbig, R. E. "German-American Genealogies, Chiefly Pennsylvania, Found in the New York Public Library, " PG. 8 (1906): 303-07.

5208   Heltzel, Nicholas. Some Descendants of Nicholas and Maria Dorothea Heltzel. Kingston, Pa.: Author, 1948.

5209   Hostetler, John. "Amish Genealogy: A Progress Report, " PFL. 19 (1969): 23-27.

5210   Hug, Bernal. One Hundred Years of Hugs: The Story of the Hug Family in Switzerland and America. Elgin, Oregon: Elgin Recorder, 1960.

5211   Hunsaker, Q. and Gwen Haws. History of Abraham Hunsaker and His Family. Salt Lake City: Hunsaker Family Organization, Desert News Pr., 1957.

5212   Hyskell, Ira. Early Heiskells and Hyskells, With a Genealogical Table of the First Seven Generations in America. New York, 1958.

5213   Index to American Genealogies, and to Genealogical Materials Contained in all Works such as Town Histories, City Histories, Local Histories, Historical Society Publications, Biographies, Historical Periodicals, and Kindred Works, Alphabetically Arranged. Albany, New York: Munsell, 1900. Contains 50, 000 references.

5214   Jewett, Vivian. "Abstracts of Naturalization Records, Circuit Court, District of Columbia, Petitions Received, 1817-50, " NGSQ. (1957): 21-26.

5215   Jung, Hans. Herkunft, Wanderwege und Wirken der südwestdeutschen Familien Anspach. Kaiserslautern, 1958.

5216   Kaufholz, C. F. "American Families Descended from the House of Brabant, " NGSQ. 49 (1961): 201-04.

5217   Keffer, John. The Keffers of the Conewago Valley. Trenton, New Jersey: Author, 1960.

5218   Kennedy, John T.   The Funchess Family: A Brief Record of
the Funchess Family of Orangeburg County, South Carolina.
Columbia, S. C.: Author, 1962.

5219   Kieffer, Elizabeth. "Genealogical Resources of the Historical
Society of the Evangelical and Reformed Church, Fackenthal
Library, Franklin and Marshall College, Lancaster, Pa., "
NGSQ. 48 (1960): 113-26.

5220   Kiehl, Ralph.   Pedigree Charts of the Kiehl/Grinnell and Related Families of Onondaga County, New York. El Cajon,
Cal.: Author, 1959.

5221   Kindig, Bruce and Mrs. Bruce Kindig.   Ancestors, Descendants and Relatives of Charles Daniel Kindig and Ellen Kindig.
Medicine Lodge, Kansas, 1961.

5222   Kistler, John.   Baptismal Records of Jerusalem Lutheran and
Reformed Church, Berks Co., Pa. Washington, D. C.:
NGSQ, 1959.

5223   Klumph, Richard.   Klumph Genealogy and Early Klumph History. Kalamazoo, Michigan: Author, 1960.

5223A   Kniskern, Walter.   Some of the Descendants of Johann Peter
Kniskern of Schoharie County, New York, Born 1685, Died
Nov. 11, 1759. Petersburg, Va.: Plummer Printing, 1960.

5224   Kothe, William.   The Kothe Family. Indianapolis: Herman
W. Kothe, 1961.

5225   Krebs, Friedrich. "What Can the Archives at Speyer Offer
American Genealogy?" NGSQ. 45 (1957): 127-29.

5225A   Lancaster Mennonite Conference Historical Society.   Mennonite Library and Archives. Lancaster: The Society, 1966.
Has 50,000 cards in a genealogical file.

5226   [Lehman.]   A Brief History of the Lehman Family and Genealogical Register of the Descendants of Peter Lehman of
Lancaster County, Pennsylvania With Data for Several Other
Collateral Families. Hagerstown, Md.: Howard Lehman,
1961.

5227   Linenberger, Joseph.   Grandfather's Story. Carthagena,
Ohio, 1962.

5228   Lybarger, Donald.   History of the Lybarger Family. Cleveland: Author, 1959.

5229   Mann, Clair.   From Kansas Dust: A Story of the Sojourn in
Kansas of the Families of Mann, Shedden, and Reser. Rolla,
Missouri, 1962.

5230   Middendorf Family.   Limburg: C. A. Starke, 1963.

5231   Miller Genealogy: Grace Gilbert Robertson and Henry Hollis
        Miller, More Generally Known as Hollis Henry Miller, With
        their Forebears.   Baton Rouge: Ben Robertson Miller, 1961.

5232   Millspaugh, Francis.   Millspaugh-Millspaw.   Swampsot, Mass.:
        Author, 1959.

5233   Mish, Mary.   Jonathan Hager, Founder.   Hagerstown, Md.:
        Stouffer Printing, 1962.

5234   Moore, Lillian and Mildred Steinmeyer.   Steinmeier or Stein-
        meyer, 1857-1957:   One Hundred Years in Kansas and the
        Neighboring States.   n. p. , 1961.

5235   Morton, Nell.   "Abstract of Philip Rupert Bible Record, "
        NGSQ.   40 (1952): 141-42.

5236   Neuenschwander, Albert.   Neuenschwander Family Record:
        Chronology of the Descendants of Christian Neuenschwander,
        1812-1958.   Grabill, Ind. , 1958.

5237   Niepoth, Wilhelm.   "Jakob Gottschalk and His Ancestry, First
        Bishop of the Mennonite Church in America, 1708-63, " MQR.
        23 (1949): 35-47.

5238   _____. "Prerequisite to Research on the Ancestors of the
        Mennonites who Emigrated from the Lower Rhine Country to
        the U. S. in 1863 and Later, " MQR. 28 (1954): 59-61.

5239   Nussbaum, Ben.   Nussbaums: Being an Account of Niklaus
        and Anna Barbara Nussbaum and their Descendants.   Fair-
        bury, Ill. , 1959.

5240   Onthank, Arthur.   The Onthank Family: Its History and Gen-
        ealogy.   Martinsville, Ind.:   Martinsville Reporter Pr. , 1959.

5241   Outlaw, Doris.   The Croom Family.   Kingston, N. C. , 1958.

5242   Overman, William.   Ohio Town Names.   Akron: Atlantic Pr. ,
        1958.

5243   Poellnitz Genealogy: Little Acorns from the Mighty Oak.
        Birmingham, Ala.:   Featon Pr. , 1962.

5244   Pollock, Polly.   Asters at Dusk: The Smelser Family in
        America.   Dayton, Ohio, 1961.

5245   Pringle, Paul.   Progenitors in the Wurttemberg Region, Ger-
        many, of the New York State Wagar, Wager, Weger Families.
        Darien, Conn.:   Author, 1961.

5246   Pritzker Genealogy: The Pritzker Book: Honoring the Past,
        Bringing Togetherness to the Present, Lighting a Path for
        the Future. Baltimore: Lee Pritzker, 1962.

5247   Rahn, Claude. The Yingling Genealogy. Vero Beach, Fla.:
        1958.

5248   Reeser, Nell. "Report on Families of York County, Pennsyl-
        vanis," NGSQ. 38 (1950): 57-58.

5249   Reeser, Nellie. Daniel Knarr and Lucinda Ault. York, Pa.,
        1958.

5250   Reichelderfer, Laura. Ulrey Family of Ohio and Pennsyl-
        vania. St. Louis: Author, 1961.

5251   Reinhart, Herman. The Golden Frontier: Recollections,
        1851-69. Austin, 1962.

5252   Richert Genealogy: The Heinrich Richert Genealogy. N. P.:
        Helene Riesen Goertz, 1963.

5253   [Riegel.] Partial Genealogy and History of the Riegel Family
        in America. Riegelsville, Pa.: B. F. Fackenthal, 1923.

5254   Robinson, Felix. "History of the Garrett County Hinebaughs,"
        Glades Star. 8 (1951): 113-21.

5255   Rogers, Wilmot. Griffey Garten Miller and His Descendants.
        Santa Rosa, Cal., 1958.

5256   Rosenberger, F. Some Notes on the Rosenberger Family in
        Pennsylvania and Virginia, 1729-1950. Richmond, Va., 1950.

5257   Roth, Elfrieda. Your Heritage. Sheboygan, Wisconsin:
        Author, 1963.

5258   Rothrock, Edgar. Some Descendants of Johann George Roth-
        rock, 1721-1806. Vermillion, S.D.: Author, 1962.

5259   Rubincam, M. "American Families of Hessian Descent,"
        NGSQ. 48 (1960): 8-11, 75-80.

5260   _____. Mr. Christian Heinrich and His Mansion. Wash-
        ington: Columbia Hist. Soc., 1963.

5261   _____. "The Noble Ancestry of the Revercomb Family,"
        VMHB. (1961): 448-55.

5262   _____. "Origin of the Belsterling Family," NGSQ. 49
        (1961): 27.

5263   _____. "Origin of the Revercombs of Virginia," VMHB.
        (1955): 76-83.

5264 _____. "The Rubenkam Family of Hessen, Parent Stock of the Rubincam-Revercomb Family of Pennsylvania and Virginia, " PGM. 22 (1961): 85-112.

5265 _____. "A Table of 16th-17th Century German Ancestors, " NGSQ. 44 (1956): 84-85.

5266 _____. The Von Boyneburg genannt Hohenstein Family of Reichensachsen, Hessen-Kassel: Genealogical Problems and Some Solutions. West Hyattsville, Md.: Author, 1963.

5267 Schaller, Grover. The History of the Benedict II and Rosina Haeni Schaller Family, 1759-1957. Daytona Beach, Fla., 1958.

5268 Schultz, Lawrence. Paul Family Record, 1763-1963. Winona Lake, Ind.: Light and Life Pr., 1963.

5269 Schultz, Selina. "Schwenckfelder Genealogical Records, " NGSQ. 39 (1951): 33-37.

5270 Scott, Robert. "What Happened to the Benders?" WI. 9 (1951): 327-37.

5271 Seeley, Ralph. Johannes Kleinjenni of Berks County, Pennsylvania and Some of His Descendants. Candor, New York, 1959.

5272 Seibert, Charles. Memoirs of the Seibert Family. Birmingham: Author, 1965.

5273 Seidner Genealogy: The Story of a Dozen Generations. Tulare, Cal.: Orrin Wade Sidener, 1961.

5274 Sells Chronology: A Chronological Index to Early Records of the Sells, Sills, Zell and von Zellen Family of Pennsylvania. Staten Island: Louis Duermyer, 1962.

5275 Shaver, Frederick. Frederick Shaver, Rhineland, Germany, 1747; Sussex County, New Jersey, 1823, and His Descendants. Mt. Vernon, Iowa: Daphne Shaver Herring, 1952.

5276 Shaw, Aurora. The John Lastinger Family of America: A Record of the Descendants of John Lastinger: Immigrant, 1760-1960. Jacksonville, Fla.: Author, 1960.

5277 Sherfey, William. The Sherfey Family in the U.S., 1751-1948. Greensburg, Ind.: H. E. Sherfey, 1949.

5278 Sides, Roxie. Early American Families: Sides, Sprach, Nading, Rominger, Longworth, Foltz, Rothrock, Shoaf, Vogler. Winston-Salem, N.C.: Author, 1963.

5279   Simmendinger, V. True and Authentic Register of Persons
        who in the Year 1790 Journeyed from Germany to America.
        Baltimore: Genealogical Publications, 1966.

5280   The Smyser Family in America.   York, Pa.: Maple Pr.,
        1947.

5281   Spraker, James. The Spraker Family of the Mohawk Valley.
        Buffalo, New York, 1958.

5282   Stecher, Robert. Cord Stecker and His Descendants in Europe
        and America: A Brief Family History and Genealogy.   Cleve-
        land, 1961.

5283   Stein, Simon. The Steins of Muscatine: A Family Chronicle.
        Muscatine, Iowa: Author, 1962.

5284   Stern, Malcolm. Americans of Jewish Descent.   Washington,
        D. C.: NGSQ. 1958.

5285   _____. Americans of Jewish Descent: A Compendium of
        Genealogy. Cincinnati: Hebrew Union College Pr., 1960.

5286   Stewart, Robert. Index to Printed Virginia Genealogies, In-
        cluding Key and Bibliography. Richmond, Va.: Old Dominion
        Pr., 1930.

5287   Strassburger, R. Pennsylvania German Pioneers: Publications
        of the Original Lists of Arrivals in the Port of Philadelphia,
        1727-1808. Breinigsville, Pa.: Pennsylvania German Society,
        1966.

5288   Stroebe Story: The Descendants in America of Wilhelm Wolf-
        gang Gerhardt Strobe and Anna Catherina Shubelin. n. p.,
        1959.

5289   Tieszen, David. History and Record of the Tieszen Family.
        Marion, S. D., 1954.

5290   Tisdale, Florence. Ancestral Records: Crouie Family of
        Northern Maine. Washington, D. C.: Author, 1965.

5291   Tucker, Eldon. "Records of Salem Evangelical Lutheran
        Church, Aurora, W. Va.," NGSQ. 45 (1957): 16-20.

5292   Vann, Elizabeth and M. Dixon. Brumback-Hotsinspiller Gen-
        ealogy: Some of the Descendants of Melchior Brumback. En-
        glewood, New Jersey: Elizabeth Vann, 1962.

5293   Von Rosenberg-Tomlinson, Alma. The von Rosenberg Family
        of Texas. Boerne, Texas: Toepperwein Publishing Co.,
        1949.

5294   Voth, Maricha. The Heinrich Baltzer Genealogy, 1775-1959.
       North Newton, Kansas, 1961.

5295   Wagschal, George and Louis Wagschal. The Wagschal Fami-
       ly in America. Concord, N. H., 1959.

5296   Warren, Dorothea. The Practical Dreamer: A Story of John
       T. Milner, His Family and Forebears. Birmingham, 1960.

5297   Wayland, John. "John Hoffman of Germanna and some of
       His Descendants, " VMHB. (1955): 454-60.

5298   _____. "Wilbargers in Virginia and Texas, " Rockingham
       Recorder. 2 (1961): 238-39.

5299   Weaver, Esther. Descendants of Henry B. Weaver. Ephrata,
       Pa., 1953.

5300   Wedel, Helmut. Genealogy of the Peter H. Wedel Family,
       1859-64. n. p., 1965.

5301   Weiser, Frederick. "History and the Pennsylvania German
       Genealogist, " IMH. 55 (1959): 59-64.

5302   _____. Parochial Register for Lutheran Congregations in
       Lancaster County, Pennsylvania, 1729-60: A Guide to Genea-
       logical Resources in the Parish Records of Baptisms, Mar-
       riages and Burials as well as to Translations and Copies in
       Print and in Public Institutions. Lancaster: Grace Lutheran
       Church, 1946.

5303   _____. and V. Nelson. "The Registers of Reed's Church
       (Zion and St. John's Lutheran Church), Tulpehocken, " HRBC.
       31 (1965): 14-18, 27.

5304   Wenzlaff, Theodore. The Life of Johann Christian Wenzlaff,
       1827-94. Henderson, Nebraska: Service Pr., 1963.

5305   Wiesenthal, Charles. "Genealogical Notes on Charles Fred-
       erick Wiesenthal, " RJGAH. 28 (1953): 82-85.

5306   Young, Clifford. The Young (Jung) Families of the Mohawk
       Valley, 1710-1946. Albany, New York, 1947.

5307   Zimmerman, David and M. S. Zimmerman. A Twig of the
       Zimmerman Offspring of Glause Zimmerman. Ephrata, Pa.,
       1956.

LIBRARY LOCATIONS

AAAS	American Academy of Arts and Sciences, Boston
AAS	American Antiquarian Society, Worcester
CC	Claremont College, Claremont
CCHS	Carver County Historical Society, Waconia, Minnesota
CLSU	University of Southern California, Los Angeles
CoDB	Bibliographical Center for Research Library, Denver
CoU	University of Colorado, Boulder
CSmH	Henry E. Huntington Library, San Marino
CST	Stanford College Libraries, Stanford
CtHT-W	Trinity College, Watkinson Library, Hartford
CtY	Yale University, New Haven
CU	University of California, Berkeley
DLC	Library of Congress, Washington, D. C.
DU	Duke University, Durham
GSP	German Society of Pennsylvania Library, Philadelphia
HC	Harvard College, Cambridge
HEH	Huntington Library, San Marino
HSP	Historical Society of Pennsylvania, Philadelphia
ICN	Newberry College, Chicago
ICU	University of Chicago, Chicago
IEN	Northwestern University, Evanston
InU	Indiana University, Bloomington
IU	University of Illinois, Urbana
JC	Juniata College, Huntington, Pennsylvania
KMK	Kansas State University, Manhattan
LCP	Library Company of Philadelphia
LOC	Library of Congress, Washington, D. C.
MdBE	Maryland Diocesan Library, Baltimore
MdHi	Maryland Historical Society, Baltimore
MeB	Bowdoin, College, Brunswick
MHS	Minnesota Historical Society, St. Paul
MiU	University of Michigan, Ann Arbor
MKUK	Max Kade German-American Document and Research Center, University of Kansas, Lawrence
MPL	Minneapolis Public Library
MWA	American Antiquarian Society, Worcester
NcD	Duke University, Durham
NcU	University of North Carolina, Chapel Hill
NIC	Cornell University, Ithaca
NUPL	New Ulm Public Library, New Ulm, Minnesota
NYPL	New York Public Library
OCI	Cleveland Public Library

OU	Ohio State University, Columbus
P	Pennsylvania State Library, Harrisburg
PAtM	Muhlenberg College, Allentown
PPCS	Carl Schurz Library, German Society of Pennsylvania, Philadelphia
PPL	Library Company of Philadelphia
PPLT	Kraut Memorial Library, Lutheran Theological Seminary, Mt. Airy, Philadelphia
PPULC	United Lutheran Publishing House, Philadelphia
PST	Pennsylvania State University, University Park
SCC	Charleston Library Society, Charleston
TNJ	Joint University Libraries, Nashville
TXU	University of Texas, Austin
UC	Heinrich Hermann Fick Collection of German-Americana, University of Cincinnati, Cincinnati
UK	University of Kentucky, Lexington
UM	University of Minnesota, Minneapolis
UOP	University of Pennsylvania, Philadelphia
WU	University of Wisconsin, Madison

JOURNALS INDEXED

AA — American Archivist
AAG — Annals of American Geographers
ABC — American Book Collector
ACHS — American Catholic Historical Society
Auslanddeutsche, Der
AGR — American German Review
AH — American Heritage
AHAAR — American Historical Association, Annual Report
AHQ — Arkansas Historical Quarterly
AHR — American Historical Review
AJA — American Jewish Archives
AJHQ — American Jewish Historical Quarterly
ALQ — Abraham Lincoln Quarterly
APSS — American Academy of Political and Social Science
AQ — American Quarterly
AS — American Speech
A-W — Amerika-Woche, Die
Ag. Hist. — Agricultural History
Alberta Hist. Rev. — Alberta Historical Review
Alexandria Gaz. — Alexandria Gazette
Amer. Anthropologist — American Anthropologist
Amer. Antiq. Soc., Proc. — American Antiquarian Society, Proceedings
Amer. Ben. Rev. — American Benedictine Review
Amer. Chora Rev. — American Choral Review
American J. Soc. — American Journal of Sociology
Americana-Austriaca
Annals of Iowa
Arcadia
Archiv des Hist. Vereins Bern — Archiv des Historischen Vereins Bern
Archiv f. Landes-Volksf. — Archiv für Landes-Volksforschung
Archiv f. Sippenforschung u. a. verwandten Geb. — Archiv für Sippenforschung und andere verwandten Gebiete
Archivum Historicum Soc. Jesu — Archivum Historicum Society Jesu
Arizona
Art in Amer. — Art in America
ASch — American Scholar
Aufbau
Auslandswarte

339

BA	Books Abroad
BfddB	Börsenblatt für den deutschen Buchhandel
BFHA	Bulletin of the Friends Historical Association
BHM	Bulletin of the History of Medicine
BHSM	Bulletin of the Historical Society of Montgomery County
BLT	Brethren Life and Thought
BMHS	Bulletin of the Missouri Historical Society
BNYPL	Bulletin of the New York Public Library
B. Post & Z.	Belleviller Post und Zeitung
Beitr. z. Ges. d. deutschen Arbeiterbeweg.	Beiträge zur Geschichte der deutschen Arbeiterbewegung
Beiträge zur Volkskunde	
Bible Soc. Record	Bible Society Record
Bibliog. Soc. America	Bibliographical Society of America
Boston PLQ	Boston Public Library Quarterly
Bronx CHSQ	Bronx County Historical Society Journal
Bul. C. Hist. Soc.	Bulletin of the Cincinnati Historical Society
Bul. J. Rylands L.	Bulletin of the John Rylands Library
Bul. of Bibliogr.	Bulletin of Bibliography
Bul. of the Fort Ticonderoga Museum	Bulletin of the Fort Ticonderoga Museum
Bus. Hist. Rev.	Business History Review
CHSQ	Colorado Historical Society Quarterly
CG	Common Ground
CH	Church History
CHIQ	Concordia Historical Institute Quarterly
CHR	Christian Historical Review
CL	Comparative Literature
CM	Colorado Magazine
COO	Chronicles of Oklahoma
CTM	Concordia Theological Monthly
Can. Geogr. J.	Canadian Geographical Journal
Can. Mod. Lang. Rev.	Canadian Modern Language Review
Canadian Rev. of Soc. Anthrop.	Canadian Review of Sociology and Anthropology
CatHR	Catholic Historical Review
Cedar R. Gaz.	Cedar Rapids Gazette
Chic. H.	Chicago History
Christ Unterwegs	
Christendom	
Cin. K.	Cincinnati Kurier
Coll. Eng.	College English
Commentary	
Comp. Lit. Studies	Comparative Literature Studies
Compar. Ed. Rev.	Comparative Educational Review
Crosscurrents	

DAGB	Deutsch-Amerikanische Geschichtsblätter
DDA	Der Deutsch-Amerikaner
DDP	Der Deutsche Pionier
DIA	Deutschtum im Ausland
DL	Der Lutheraner
DMH	Der Milwaukee Herold
DW	Deutscher Wochenspiegel
D. Rundschau	Deutsche Rundschau
D. Wochenschrift	Deutsche Wochenschrift
D. Z. f. Briefmarkenkunde	Deutsche Zeitschrift für Briefmarkenkunde
D-A Almanach	Deutsch-Amerika Almanach
D-A Kalender	Deutsch-Amerikaner: Kalender
D-A Magazin	Deutsch-Amerikanisches Magazin
Daedalus	
Daily News Record	
Del. H.	Delaware History
Design	
Des Moines Sunday Reg.	Des Moines Sunday Register
Deutsche Kultur im Leben d. Völker	Deutsche Kultur im Leben der Völker
Dichtung & Volkstum	
EJ	English Journal
Eastern Mennonite Col. Bul.	Eastern Mennonite College Bulletin
Echo	
Eck	Allentown Morning Call
Ellis County News	
Elsass Kalender	
emc Bulletin	
Encounter	
Erdkunde	
Euphorion	
Europa und die Niederdte. Welt	Europa und die niederdeutsche Welt
Evang. Rev.	Evangelical Review
FCHQ	Filson Club Historical Quarterly
Family Life	
Field & Lab.	Field and Laboratory
Fontes Artis Musicae	
Forest Hist.	Forest History
Frank. Hefte	Frankfurter Hefte
Friends Intell.	Friends Intelligencer
Fries. Jahrbuch	Friesisches Jahrbuch
Furman Studies	
GaHQ	Georgia Historical Quarterly
G-A Annals	German-American Annals
G-A Studies	German-American Studies
GLL	German Life and Letters
GN	Golden Nugget

G. P. Hist. Bul.	Grand Prairie Historical Bulletin
GQ	German Quarterly
GR	Germanic Review
Genealogie	
Geog. Rev.	Geographical Review
Glades Star	
Gosh. Region	Goshenhoppen Region
Gospel Messenger	
HJ	Historia Judaica
HLQ	Huntington Library Quarterly
HM	Harper's Magazine
HPSO	Historical and Philosophical Society of Ohio, Bulletin
HRBC	Historical Review of Berks County
Hamburg-Amerika-Post	
Hebbel Jahrbuch	
Heimatblätter: Organ f. d. Belange des Heimatbundes L.	Heimatblätter: Organ für die Belange des Heimatbundes Lippstadt
Heimat-Jahrbuch des Kreises Gelnhausen	
Herald Traveler	
Hess. Familienkunde	Hessische Familienkunde
Hietsch	
Hist. Bul	History Bulletin
Hist. Mag. Prot. Episc. Ch.	Historical Magazine of the Protestant Episcopal Church
Hist. Messenger Mil. Co. H. S.	Historical Messenger of the Milwaukee County Historical Society
Hist. of Ed. Q.	History of Education Quarterly
Hist. Wyoming	History of Wyoming
Hist. Zeitschrift	Historische Zeitschrift
Historia	
History	
Humanist	
IJHP	Iowa Journal of History and Politics
Illinois H.	Illinois History
IMH	Indiana Magazine of History
Int. Affairs	International Affairs
Int. Rev. Soc. Hist.	International Review of Social History
Isis	
JA	Jahrbuch für Amerikastudien
JAH	Journal of American History
JEGP	Journal of English and Germanic Philology
JGAH	Journal of German-American History
JHI	Journal of the History of Ideas
JIllHS	Journal of the Illinois Historical Society
JMH	Journal of Modern History
JNI	Jahrbuch des Nordfriesischen Instituts

JPHS	Journal of the Presbyterian Historical Society
JQ	Journalism Quarterly
JR	Journal of Religion
JSH	Journal of Southern History
JSS	Journal of Social Science
J. Alleghenies	Journal of the Alleghenies
J. Amer. Mus. Soc.	Journal of the American Music Society
J. Amer. Vet. Med. Assoc.	Journal of the American Veterinary Medicine Association
J. Beh. Sci.	Journal of Behavioral Science
J. Hist. Beh. Sci.	Journal of the History of Behavioral Science
J. Int. Folk Music Council	Journal of the International Folk Music Council
J. Lanc. Co. Hist. So.	Journal of the Lancaster County Historical Society
J. of Ch. & State	Journal of Church and State
J. of Psych.	Journal of Psychology
J. of the West	Journal of the West
J. Presb. Hist.	Journal of Presbyterian History
J. Res. in Mus. Ed.	Journal of Research in Music Education
KHQ	Kansas Historical Quarterly
KHSR	Kentucky Historical Society Register
Keystone FQ	Keystone Folklore Quarterly
Kirch. Monatsblatt	Kirchliches Monatsblatt
Kurtrierisches Jahrbuch	
LCHP	Lancaster County Historical Publications
LCQ	Library of Congress Quarterly
LHQ	Lutheran Historical Quarterly
LQ	Lutheran Quarterly
Landscape	
Le Maitre Phonetique	
LibB	Library Bulletin
Libri	
Litterarische Echo, Das	
Luth. Standard	Lutheran Standard
Lyons Republican	
M-A	Mid-America
MH	Minnesota History
MHR	Missouri Historical Review
MHSB	Missouri Historical Society Bulletin
ML	Mennonite Life
MLA Report	
MLF	Modern Language Forum
MLJ	Modern Language Journal
MLN	Modern Language Notes
MMH	Montana Magazine of History
MQR	Mennonite Quarterly Review
MRJ	Mennonite Research Journal
MVHR	Mississippi Valley Historical Review

Maske und Kothurn	
Meth. Hist.	Methodist History
MdMH	Maryland Magazine of History
Menn. Gemeinde-Kalender	Mennonitischer Gemeinde-Kalender
Mich. Heritage	Michigan Heritage
MichH	Michigan History
Mid-America: American Historical Review	
Mitt. z. Wanderungsges. d.	Mitteilungen zur Wanderungsgeschichte
Pfälzer	der Pfälzer
Mitteilungen des Deutschen	Mitteilungen des Deutschen Pionier-
Pionier-Verein von Phil.	Verein von Philadelphia
Mitteilungen d. oberös.	Mitteilungen des oberösterreichischen
Landesarchivs	Landesarchivs
Mo.	Monatshefte
Montana: Mag. West. Hist.	Montana: Magazine of Western History
Monthly Labor Rev.	Monthly Labor Review
Mpls. Star	Minneapolis Star
Mühlenberg Monthly	
Mus. J.	Music Journal
Mus. Q.	Music Quarterly
Museum Echo	
Mutt.	Muttersprache
NCoHSP	Northumberland County Historical So-
	ciety Proceedings
NDH	North Dakota History
NDQ	North Dakota Quarterly
NEHGR	New England Historical and Genealogical
	Review
NEQ	New England Quarterly
NGM	National Geographic Magazine
NGSQ	National Genealogical Society Quarterly
NH	Nebraska History
NJHS	New Jersey Historical Society
NMHR	New Mexico Historical Review
NPfG	Nordpfalzer Geschichtsverein
NwOQ	Northwest Ohio Quarterly
NY Gen. & Biog. Record	New York Genealogical & Biographical
	Record
NYFQ	New York Folklore Quarterly
NYH	New York History
NYHSQ	New York Historical Society Quarterly
NYSZH	New York Staatszeitung und Herold
NYTBR	New York Times Book Review
N. Rundschau	Neue Rundschau
NY Times	New York Times
Names	
Nation und Staat	
National Observer	
Neue Zeit	
New England Q.	New England Quarterly
New Yorker	
News Letter	
Norddeutsche Familienkunde	

OFL	Ohio Folk Lore
OH	Ohio History
OSAHQ	Ohio Sciences, Arts and Historical Quarterly
OHQ	Ohio Historical Quarterly
OVZT	Omaha Volkszeitung-Tribüne
O. Hochschulzeitung	Oesterreichische Hochschulzeitung
Ohio State Med. J.	Ohio State Medical Journal
Opera News	
Orbis	
PAAS	Proceedings of the American Academy of Science
PAJHS	Publications of the American Jewish Historical Society
PBSA	Publications of the Bibliographical Society of America
PD	Pennsylvania Dutchman
PFL	Pennsylvania Folk Lore
PG	Penn German
PGM	Petermanns Geographische Mitteilungen
PGSP	Pennsylvania German Society Proceedings
PH	Pennsylvania History
PMHB	Pennsylvania Magazine of History and Biography
PNQ	Pacific Northwest Quarterly
Palimpsest	
Panorama	
Password	
Penn. Gen. Mag.	Pennsylvania Genealogical Magazine
Penn Germania	
Penn. Traveler	Pennsylvania Traveler
Perkiomen Region	
Pfälz. Familien u. Wappenkunde	Pfälzische Familien und Wappenkunde
Pfälzer Heimat	
Phylon	
Poet Lore	
Pol. Sci. Q.	Political Science Quarterly
Proc. Amer. Antiq. Soc.	Proceedings, American Antiquarian Society
Proc. Amer. Phil. Soc.	Proceedings of the American Philosophical Society
Pub. Hist. Soc. of S. C.	Publications of the Historical Society of South Carolina
Proc. Lehigh Co. Hist. Soc.	Proceedings of the Lehigh County Historical Society
Pub. Oswego Co. Hist. Soc.	Publications of the Oswego County Historical Society
Pubs. Am. Dialect Soc.	Publications of the American Dialect Society

Quellen & Forsch zur ostfr.   Quellen und Forschungen zur ostfriesi-
  FWK   schen Familien und Wappenkunde

RH   Rochester History
RJGAH   Report: Journal of German-American
                                    History
R. Heimathefte   Rudolstadter Heimathefte
Recs. Amer. Cath. Hist.   Records of the American Catholic His-
  Soc. of Phil.   torical Society of Philadelphia
Reggeboge, Der
Relig. Telescope   Religious Telescope
Reportage
Reserve Tribune
Rev. of Politics   Review of Politics
Rev. of Relig. Res.   Review of Religious Research
Rice Inst. Pamphlet   Rice Institute Pamphlet
Richmond Cty. Hist.   Richmond County History
Richmond Times Dispatch
Rock. Mt. SSJ   Rockie Mountain Social Science Journal
Rockingham Recorder
Rural Sociology
Rushlight

SAB   South Atlantic Bulletin
SAHS   Swiss American Historical Society
SAQ   South Atlantic Quarterly
SCHGM   South Carolina Historical and Genea-
                                    logical Magazine
SFQ   Southern Folklore Quarterly
SJR   Social Justice Review
S. L. Cath. Hist. Rev.   St. Louis Catholic Historical Review
SP   Studies in Philosophy
SwHQ   Southwest Historical Quarterly
Sy   Symposium
Salesianum
Saskatchewan Hist.   Saskatchewan History
Schoharie Co. H. R.   Schoharie County Historical Review
School & Society
Schwarzenau
Die Schaumbirg-Lippische Heimat
Schweizer B. z. allg. Ges.   Schweizer Beiträge zur allgemeinen
  allgemeinen Geschichte   Geschichte
Schwenck.   Schwenckfelder
Sci. Monthly   Scientific Monthly
Senftenegger Mon. f. G.   Senftenegger Monatsblatt für Geschichte
  u. für Geschichte und   und Historie
  Historie
Serapeum
Siebenbürger Sachsen heute: Die Wegweiser
Sierra Club B.   Sierra Club Bulletin
Singers & Storyteller
Sociologus
Southwestern Studies

Sprachspiegel
Steugen News
Studies in German Literature
Sudeten Bulletin
Süddeutsche Blätter f. F. u.   Süddeutsche Blätter für Familien und
  W.   Wappenkunde
Susquehanna Univ. Studies   Susquehanna University Studies

THQ	Tennessee Historical Quarterly
Ty	Tyler's Quarterly Historical and Genealogical Magazine
Tenn. FSQ	Tennessee Folklore Society Quarterly
Texana	
Th. Arts	Theatre Arts
Trade World	
Trans. C. S. Peirce Soc.	Transactions, C. S. Peirce Society
Trans. Morav. Hist. Soc.	Transactions of the Moravian Historical Society
Trans. Wisc. Acad. Sci., & Letters	Transactions of the Wisconsin Academy of Science, Art and Letters
UHQ	Utah Historical Quarterly
Univ. of Birm. H. J.	University of Birmingham Historical Journal
Unterrichtspraxis	
U. S. Cath. Hist. Soc. Recs. & Stud.	U. S. Catholic Historical Society Records and Studies
VF	Volksforschung
VMHB	Virginia Magazine of History and Biography
V. Cavalcade	Virginia Cavalcade
V. Hist.	Vermont History
Va. Geogr.	Virginia Geography
Va. Q. Rev.	Virginia Quarterly Review
Valleys of Hist.	Valleys of History
Volk und Reich	
Vorträge anlässlich der Hess. Hochschulwochen für staatswissen. Fortbildung	Vorträge anlässlich der Hessischen Hochschulwochen für staatswissenschaftlichen Fortbildung
WA	Wissenschaftliche Annalen
W & A	Wächter und Anzeiger
W-J	Washington Journal
WMCQ	William and Mary College Quarterly
WMH	Wisconsin Magazine of History
WPHM	Western Pennsylvania Historical Magazine
Wash. Missourian	Washington Missourian
Wash. Post	Washington Post
Waterloo HS	Waterloo Historical Society
Welt als Gesch.	Welt als Geschichte

Westport HQ	Westport Historical Quarterly
Western Hum. Rev.	Western Humanities Review
Wirkendes Wort	
Wisc. Tales & Trails	Wisconsin Tales & Trails
YIVO Annual of J. Soc. Sci.	YIVO Annual of Jewish Social Science
Yale Rev.	Yale Review
Yearbook LBI	Yearbook of the Leo Baeck Institute
ZAA	Zeitschrift für Anglistik und Amerikanistik
ZRG	Zeitschrift für Reformationsgeschichte
Z. f. ärztliche Fortbildung	Zeitschrift für ärztliche Fortbildung
Z. f. bayer. Landesges.	Zeitschrift für bayerische Landesgeschichte
Z. f. d. Ges. d. Oberrheins	Zeitschrift für die Geschichte des Oberrheins
Z. f. Mundartforschung	Zeitschrift für Mundartforschung
Z. f. phil. Forsch.	Zeitschrift für philosophische Forschung
Z. f. Politik	Zeitschrift für Politik
Zeitwende	

AUTHOR INDEX

(Title or key-word is listed for anonymous works)

Abeles, J. 461
Abendpost 2474
Aberbach, M. 3545
Abgeforderte Relation 2062
Ackermann, A. 3344
Adams, A. 5044
Adams, H. 265
Adams, K. 3966
Adler, C. 4709
Adler, J. 4710
Adler, S. 3546, 4229
Adler's Foreign Books 2839
Adornes, T. 4419
Adressbuch 2820
Akademie der Wissenschaften 5014
Akselrod, R-M. 1800
Alander, U. 1061
Albrecht, E. 73, 303, 1569, 1742, 1801
Albrecht, G. 1743
Alden, J. 74
Alderfer, E. 781-82
Alderfer, E. G. 4929
Alderfer, G. 4492
Alderfer, H. 4493
Alderfer, O. 3264
Alderfer, W. 3967
Alemann, T. 266
Alexander, J. 1466
Alfonte, J. 417
Alfredo, W. 2409
Allard, A. 2995
Allbeck, W. 3345-49
Allen, G. 3968
Allen, H. 1467
Allen, O. 1322
Allgemeine deutsche Biographie 5015
Allgemeiner Schulverein 3851

Allman, C. B. 1323
Almstedt, H. 5045
Alstetter, M. F. 203
Altgeld, J. P. 1468
Altgelt, E. 928
Ambler, C. 970
Amelung, J. 4711
America: History and Life 204
American Antiquarian Society 1
American Association for State and Local History 75
American Austrian Society 187
American Catalog of Books 2747
American Church History Series 2932
American Council for Nationalities Service 2
American Federation of Jews from Central Europe 3547
American Genealogical and Biographical Index 5160
American-German Review 1032
American Historical Association 76, 205-06
American Historical Company 6161
American Historical Society of the Germans from Russia 198, 1033, 1130
American Lutheran Church 3343
American Secular Union 3771
American Turnerbund 188
American Turner Topics 2475
American Turners 567
Americana-Germanica 207
Amerika-Herold-Lincoln-Freie-Presse 2476
Amerika-Institut 267
Amerika-Schweizer Zeitung 2477
Amish Conference 3059

349